GOLDEN GLORY

THE FIRST 50 YEARS OF THE ACC

BARRY JACOBS

SIDEBAR AUTHORS

Tony Barnhart is a national sports reporter for *The Atlanta Journal-Constitution* and ESPN. He has covered Atlantic Coast Conference athletics since 1977.

Dan Collins was born and raised in Franklin, N.C., and educated at the University of North Carolina (class of 1974). Collins is a 30-year veteran of the ACC football and basketball wars. He worked at the *The Chapel Hill Newspaper* from 1972-1978 and has been with the *Winston-Salem Journal* since.

Tim Crothers, a freelance writer, has worked as a volunteer assistant coach for UNC women's soccer and as a senior writer at *Sports Illustrated.* He lives in Chapel Hill, N.C.

Rob Daniels has been a reporter for the *News & Record* of Greensboro since 1997. He wrote *Arena Ball: The Building of Virginia's Soccer Dynasty* while at the *Daily Progress* of Charlottesville, Va., in 1994.

John Evans lives in Easton, Maryland with his wife, Linda. He works for the *Annapolis Capital* newspaper in Annapolis, Md. John has worked for the *Durham* (N.C.) *Herald* and as sports editor of the *Rocky Mount* (N.C.) *Telegram,* the *Gazette* Newspapers in Maryland and the Salisbury (Md.) *Daily Times.* He is also a TV sports analyst for a cable station in Easton.

Sarah Sue Ingram is author of the book *Pack Attack: The 1983 Championship Season.* The native of Thomasville, N.C., and University of Georgia graduate is a senior reporter at *The Daily Press* in Newport News and lives in Hampton, Va.

Ron Morris is the deputy sports editor of *The State* newspaper in Columbia, S.C. He previously covered the ACC as sports editor of *The Chapel Hill Newspaper* and the *Durham Herald-Sun* and as executive sports editor of the *Tallahassee Democrat.* He is the author of *ACC Basketball: An Illustrated History*, published in 1988.

Patrick O'Neill is a freelance journalist who has been reporting on ACC cross country and track and field for 15 years. Patrick and his wife, Mary Rider, are co-directors of the Father Charlie Mulholland Catholic Worker House, a Christian community in Garner, N.C., that provides hospitality for women and children in crisis. They have seven children.

Tim Peeler is a proud native of Cat Square, N.C. He received his B.A. in English from North Carolina State University in 1987. During an 18-year newspaper career that began during his sophomore year in college, Peeler has written for papers in North Carolina and South Carolina. He now covers college sports for the Greensboro *News & Record,* and lives with his wife, Elizabeth, and son, Michael, in Cary, N.C.

Bryan Strickland is the Duke beat writer for the *Durham* (N.C.) *Herald-Sun.* He has worked for the *Salisbury Post* and the *Lexington Dispatch.* He's a 1993 graduate of UNC at Chapel Hill. He lives in Durham with his wife, Leigh, and loves sunsets, long walks on the beach and corn dogs.

David Teel is the sports columnist at the *Daily Press* in Newport News, Va. He twice won the free throw shooting tournament at Lefty Driesell's University of Maryland basketball camp.

Bill Vilona joined the *Pensacola* (Fla.) *News Journal* in 1987 and has covered the Florida State athletic program since 1988. A 1981 graduate of the University of Tennessee, Vilona slowly migrated south from Pittsburgh, where he was born and graduated from high school.

CREDITS

Copyright (c) 2002 by Mann Media, Inc.
All rights reserved.
Published by Mann Media, Inc.
Post Office Box 4552, Greensboro, North Carolina 27404
(800) 948-1409

Printed in the United States of America by R.R. Donnelley & Sons

PUBLISHER Bernie Mann
EDITOR/PROJECT MANAGER Eddy Landreth
ART DIRECTOR Larry Williams
PRODUCTION DIRECTOR Cheryl Bissett
DISTRIBUTION MANAGER Erica Derr
COVER PHOTOGRAPHY Mark Wagoner

The paper in this book meets the guidelines for permanence and durability of the Committee on Production Guidelines for Book Longevity of the Council on Library Resources.

Library of Congress Cataloging-in-Publication Data

Jacobs, Barry.
Golden glory : the first 50 years of the ACC / Barry Jacobs.
p. cm.
Includes index.
ISBN 0-9723396-0-4 (hardcover : alk. paper)
1. Atlantic Coast Conference—History. 2. College sports—Southern States—History. I. Title.
GV351.3.S684 J33 2002
796.04'3'0975—dc21

2002154571

IDENTIFICATION OF PICTURES ON OPENING CHAPTER PAGES

1950s: Triumphant North Carolina basketball player Lennie Rosenbluth walks off the court at the Dixie Classic.

1960s: Left-to-right, basketball coaches Dean Smith, Vic Bubas, Everett Case and Horace "Bones" McKinney.

1970s: Left-to-right, Maryland football coach Jerry Claiborne, Mildred The Bear lookalike, N.C. State football coach Lou Holtz, Duke football coach Mike McGee, ACC Commissioner Bob James, Virginia football coach Don Lawrence, Clemson football coach Hootie Ingram.

1980s: N.C. State basketball coach Jim Valvano runs across the court after the Wolfpack captures the 1983 national championship.

1990s: Virginia students spell "Miracle Groh" in honor of quarterback Mike Groh during the Cavaliers' 1995 upset of Florida State.

2000s: Maryland basketball coach Gary Williams and his team celebrate after winning the 2002 national championship.

WE WOULD LIKE TO THANK THE OFFICIAL CORPORATE PARTNERS OF THE ACC.

DEDICATION:

To the people of the Atlantic Coast Conference, living and gone, acclaimed and unsung.

ACKNOWLEDGEMENTS

The act of writing a book is ultimately a lone occupation, but the preparatory work and the conversion to a printed product are very much collaborative efforts.

This book would not be possible without the generous support of many people, particularly those participants in shaping ACC history who willingly shared their experiences — Vic Bubas, John Bunting, Bruce Corrie, Gene Corrigan, Nora Lynn Finch, Marvin Francis, William Friday, Thomas Hearn, Terry Holland, Gene Hooks, Ernie Jackson, Carl James, Banks McFadden, Bernadette McGlade, Bill McLellan, Johnny Moore, Bill Overton, Dan Pollitt, Tom Price, Homer Rice, Irwin Smallwood, John Swofford, Bill Tate, Nancy Thompson, Frank Weedon, Chris Weller, George Welsh and Gary Williams.

Thanks go to the many photographers for their brilliant art that enriched the book, and in particular to Hugh Morton, who generously donated his photographs.

Invaluable assistance was provided by archivists at Duke University, the University of North Carolina, the University of Virginia and Wake Forest University, and by the sports information staffs at all nine ACC schools. Those at the ACC office were especially helpful, notably Fred Barakat, Barbara Dery, Jeff Elliott, Mike Finn, Stephen Herbster, Kathy Hunt, Brian Morrison and Brian Psota.

The following books also proved to be valuable resources: *Red, White, and Amen* by Kent Baker (Strode Publishers, 1979); *Southern Fried Football* by Tony Barnhart (Triumph Books, 2000); *On Tobacco Road, Basketball in North Carolina* by Smith Barrier (Leisure Press, 1983); *Kings of American Football* by Morris A. Bealle (Columbia Publishing, 1952); *The Wolfpack...* by Bill Beezley (University Graphics, N.C. State, 1976); *The Philosophy of Athletics* by Elmer Berry (A.S. Barnes and Co., 1927); *Clemson: Where the Tigers Play* by Sam Blackman and Bob Bradley (Sports Publishing Inc., 1999); *Saint Bobby and the Barbarians* by Ben Brown (Doubleday, 1992); *Cavaliers! A Pictorial History of UVA Basketball* by Gary Cramer (Spring House Publishing, 1983); *The Atlantic Coast Conference, 1953-1978* by Bruce A. Corrie (Carolina Academic Press, 1978); *Battle of the Blue* by Bill Cromartie (Gridiron Publishers, 1992); *Encyclopedia of College Basketball* by Mike Douchant (Visible Ink Press, 1995); *Carolina vs. Clemson* by John Chandler Griffin (Summerhouse Press, 1998); *The First Hundred Years, A History of South Carolina Football* by John Chandler Griffin (Longstreet Press, 1992); *Georgia vs. Georgia Tech, Gridiron Grudge Since 1893* by John Chandler Griffin (Hill Street Press, 2000); *Learning to Win* by Pamela Grundy (The University of North Carolina Press, 2001); *A Whole New Ball Game* by Allen Guttman (The University of North Carolina Press, 1988); *The Fifties* by David Halberstam (Villard Books, 1993); *Pack Pride* by Douglas Herakovich (Yesterday's Future, 1994); *Touchdown Wolfpack!* by Douglas Herakovich (Yesterday's Future, 1995); *Three Paths to Glory* by Barry Jacobs (MacMillan, 1993); *The World According to Dean* by Barry Jacobs (Total Sports, 1998); *Coach K's Little Blue Book* by Barry Jacobs (Total Sports, 2000); *Home Court: Fifty Years of Cameron Indoor Stadium* by Hazel Landwehr (Phoenix Communications,1989); *Demon Deacon Hoops* by Barry Alan Lawing (Barry A. Lawing Publishing, 2000); *Winning A Day at a Time* by John Lucas and Joseph Moriarty (Hazelden Foundation, 1994); *ACC Basketball, An Illustrated History* by Ron Morris (Four Corners Press, 1988); *Go Wolfpack! North Carolina State Football* by Thad Mumau (Strode Publishers, 1981); *North Carolina Through Four Centuries* by William Powell (University of North Carolina Press, 1989); *Lessons for Leaders* by Homer Rice (Longstreet Press, 2000); *The Rose Bowl Game* by Rube Samuelsen (Doubleday and Co., 1951); *The History of Wake Forest College* by Bynum Shaw (Wake Forest University, 1988); *A History of Sports in North Carolina* by Jim L. Sumner (North Carolina Division of Archives And History, 1990); *Focused on the Top* by Jack Wilkinson (Longstreet Press, 1991).

Thanks to Bernie Mann for supplying the vision, resources and commitment to make this project possible, Larry Williams for turning that vision into a lovely reality, and to Cheryl Bissett for keeping the vision on track and within budget. Also thanks to Betty Work for her thorough and accurate attention to detail.

I deeply appreciate the personal support lent in various ways by Ford, Grant, Sharn Jeffries, Sharon and Jim Kirkman, Madonna, Mary Moore, Ron Morris, Michael Palmer, Teresa Snipes, Truman and Steve Winwood.

This project could not have proceeded, let alone prospered, without the determined and gifted efforts of Eddy Landreth, a fine editor and a finer friend.

And every task is graced by my wife Robin's presence in my life, a gift no words can do justice.

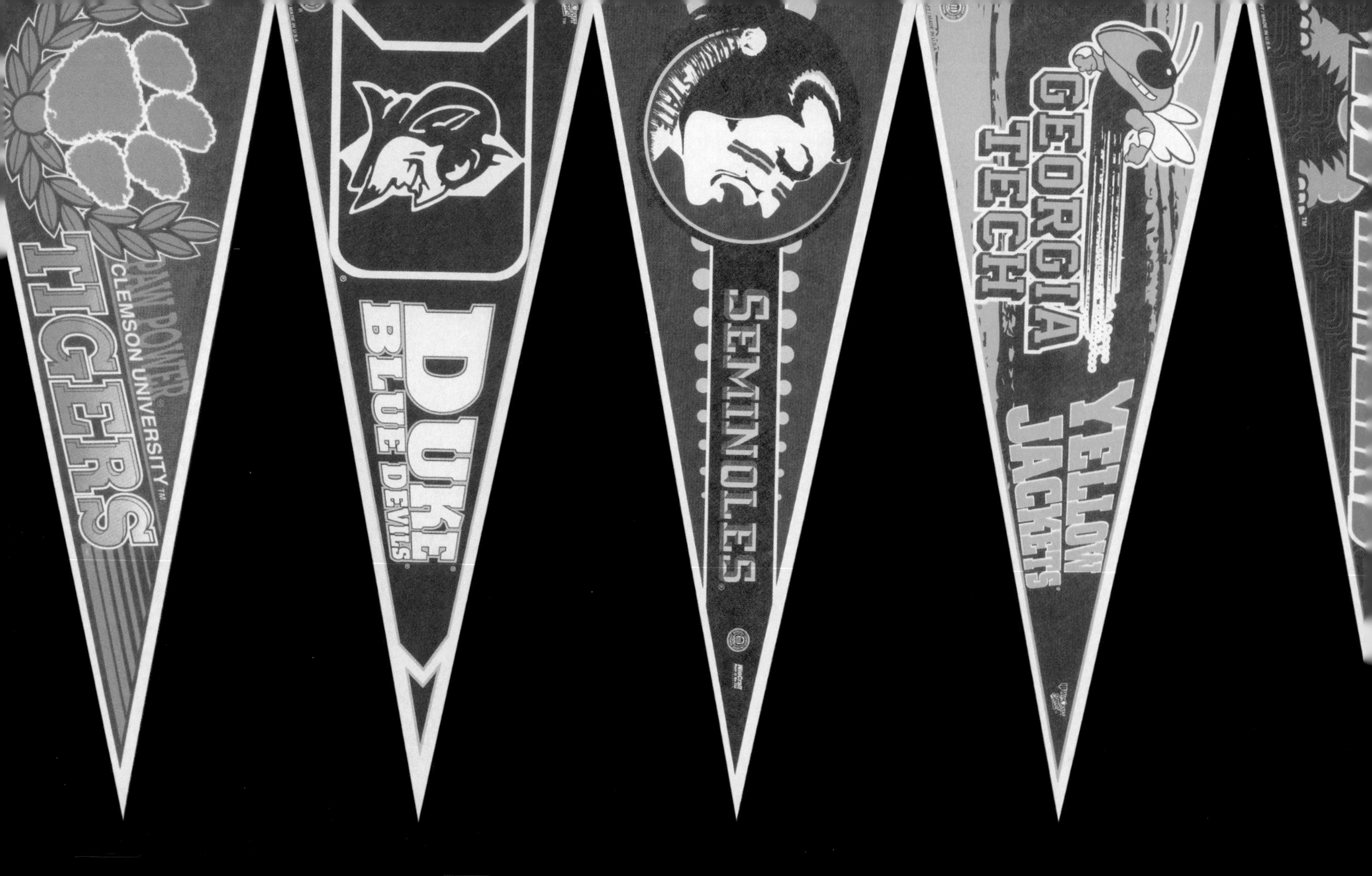
PAW POWER
CLEMSON UNIVERSITY
TIGERS
DUKE
BLUE DEVILS
SEMINOLES
GEORGIA TECH
GEORGIA
YELLOW JACKETS

N.C. STATE
Wolfpack
CAROLINA
TAR HEELS
NORTH CAROLINA
TAR HEELS
VIRGINIA
VIRGINIA
VIRGINIA
CAVALIERS
WAKE FOREST

FOREWORD

BY JOHN D. SWOFFORD

By the time I was 5 years old, the ACC had started its journey to become one of the premier intercollegiate athletic conferences in this great country of ours. It was also on its way to becoming a significant part of the very culture of the geographic footprint that now covers six states.

When I was old enough to follow sports, the ACC and its member schools were always my focus: attending the Everett Case Basketball School at N.C. State and following my older brother Jim's football career at Duke, traveling to Wake Forest from nearby North Wilkesboro to see ACC football and basketball games, being recruited by ACC member schools, enrolling as a student-athlete at the University of North Carolina, holding my first job in athletics at the University of Virginia, being an AD in the conference for 17 years, and now having the privilege of serving the best group of schools I could imagine as the league's fourth commissioner.

I am fortunate to have grown up with this league, to have witnessed so much of its history and to have known so many of its superb leaders, to have seen so many of its extraordinary number of great athletes compete and to have admired firsthand the accomplishments of so many of the legendary and charismatic coaches who have graced our conference.

It all started with a courageous and visionary step — leaving the Southern Conference to form a new league. From that point forward, the Atlantic Coast Conference has always been about more than just its impressive accomplishments. From its inception, the ACC has held sacred the principles of integrity and academics as well as athletics while seeking to conduct its business in an environment of respect and collegiality. The end result has been a closely knit collection of academically prominent schools that have been successful in the athletic arena, but even more important, that are also respected for the way they have achieved this success.

This road, though, has never been easy. At many junctures and turns in the ACC's history, its leaders have faced difficult decisions on a variety of challenges — from academic integrity, to honesty in competition, to the importance of sportsmanship on and off the playing field and, finally, to the difficult task associated with dramatic social change.

Fortunately for all of us, each time the ACC has been blessed with enlightened leadership that pointed it in the right direction. Much of that leadership emanated from the ACC's previous commissioners. Jim Weaver, our first commissioner, helped form the ACC and guided it throughout the early years to maturity. The former Wake Forest athletics director led the conference for 16 years until his untimely death in 1970. He set the tone for the conference as it developed into a power in intercollegiate athletics and presided gracefully over the ACC during some of its acrimonious years.

Bob James, who succeeded Weaver in 1970, served 17 years during a period of prosperity and growth. The former Maryland student and faculty member oversaw the ACC during a time when it achieved national prominence in a variety of sports, including the establishment of women's intercollegiate athletics. The James era also saw the addition of Georgia Tech to the league and the ACC basketball television packages become the nation's best.

After Bob died in 1987, Gene Corrigan returned home to become the ACC's third commissioner, after serving as the athletics director at Notre Dame. Gene was a former student-athlete at Duke, an assistant commissioner of the conference and athletics director at Virginia. Corrigan guided the ACC to much of the national prestige that it enjoys today. During his tenure, Florida State joined the league. Our broad-based athletic programs enjoyed national success in a variety of sports, and the league continued its unprecedented growth until his retirement in 1997.

While all of us owe a deep debt of gratitude to these three men, there are also countless others — presidents, athletics directors, coaches, faculty representatives, senior women administrators and fans — who have given of their leadership, enthusiasm and dedication to the conference through the years. I have had the honor to work with many of them. Their legacy is our league's heritage.

This book, *Golden Glory: The First 50 Years of the ACC* is a detailed story of this journey. The author, Barry Jacobs, has put together the history of our conference, virtually uncut and uncensored. It details the dilemmas the conference has faced and documents the efforts that led to our present success. Always, the ACC has had as its primary goal the overall welfare of the student-athletes while seeking to preserve the integrity of intercollegiate athletics and the educational process. As we head into the second half-century of our league's existence, I would like to end with the ACC's mission statement because this sums up not only who we are but also whom we aspire to be, both now and in the years to come:

"The Atlantic Coast Conference, through its member institutions, seeks to maximize the educational and athletic opportunities of its student-athletes while enriching their quality of life. It strives to do so by affording individuals equitable opportunity to pursue academic excellence and compete successfully at the highest level of intercollegiate athletics competition in a broad spectrum of sports and championships. The conference will provide leadership in attaining these goals, by promoting diversity and mutual trust among its member institutions, in a spirit of fairness for all. It strongly adheres to the principles of integrity and sportsmanship, and supports the total development of the student-athlete and each member institution's athletics department staff, with the intent of producing enlightened leadership for tomorrow."

Thank you for your interest in the ACC. May the next 50 years be as exciting, eventful and productive for our schools, our student-athletes, our coaches and our fans as the first 50.

John D. Swofford
Commissioner

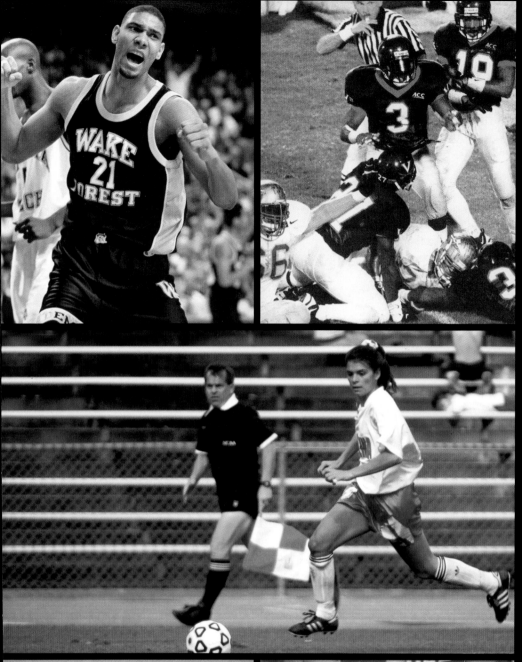

If you're going to do it, if you're going to be in big-time sports, **the ACC does it about as well as you can expect anybody to do it.**

— William Friday

INTRODUCTION

TRUE VISION

The Atlantic Coast Conference, as the country itself, overcame forces that threatened to tear it apart as the 1970s unfolded.

The United States was at war in Southeast Asia, a conflict that intensified divisions among Americans. Changes in attitudes toward race, sex and social norms swirled through society. College campuses became heated centers of activism. Wake Forest President James Scales entered the 1969-70 academic year with a temporary restraining order in hand, particulars to be filled in as necessary to thwart unruly students.

Sure enough, the following spring a widening of the Indochina war sparked protests on more than 200 campuses. The unrest affected most ACC schools, Wake among them. National Guard troops shot and killed four students at Kent State in Ohio. Scales soon called 1970 "the most violent year in the history of American higher education."

Amid the turmoil, the eight members of the ACC — Clemson, Duke, Maryland, North Carolina, North Carolina State, South Carolina, Virginia and Wake Forest — struggled to maintain the course they undertook in 1953, when they forged an uncommon, evolving balance between academic integrity and big-time athletic success.

"The presidents thought that bringing these institutions together, being the schools they were, it would create a group that had very common interests," said William Friday, then an assistant to Gordon Gray, president of the consolidated University of North Carolina. "And it's been true. The conference has been one of the best."

The path has been far from smooth, however, and it was never rougher than in the early 1970s. Most ACC schools have reappraised athletics' place among their institutional goals at one time or another, so it wasn't unique to find Duke faculty publicly toying with leaving the league and de-emphasizing sports, arguing intercollegiate athletics had become "the tail that wags the university dog."

Unfortunately, at about the same time the conference was hit from another direction as three ACC members challenged a self-imposed academic standard, the so-called "800 rule."

The ACC instituted a 750 Scholastic Aptitude Test minimum score for athletic participation (400 points were automatic) in May 1960. The standard was raised to 800 for the 1965-66 academic year. By then the NCAA had adopted a more flexible standard, requiring a high-school performance that projected a 1.600 grade-point average in college. The ACC's willingness to surpass national requirements, to attempt a leadership role in merging athletics and academics, set it apart for more than a decade.

Carl James, then the associate athletics director at Duke and later AD there and at Maryland, recalled the 800 rule was "a comfortable compromise for most people." Gene Corrigan, in a letter written prior to his assumption of the athletics director's duties at Virginia in 1971, insisted: "While the score is extremely low, it does at least put a cutoff on some of our conference members. It keeps us closer together than we otherwise would be."

Maintaining a level playing field in a diverse conference was a central concern, reflected in early agreements to equitably share revenues from postseason competition and league television packages. But internal differences endured. Wake Forest and Duke, comprising a quarter of the ACC's membership, were private schools with modest-sized student bodies, a unique divergence from other major conferences until formation of the Big East in 1979-80. ACC members also infused their athletic programs with vastly differing amounts of resources, a fact often reflected competitively.

Compounding the difficulties, the NCAA national football television package largely excluded the ACC. Unlike basketball, football had no compensatory regional exposure to combat higher-profile neighbors.

"Taking the opposite tack, it would seem that the 800 is quite restrictive to some of our ACC schools that play and lose — consistently — to other major conference schools," wrote Corrigan, a Duke graduate who served as the ACC's third commissioner from 1987 to 1997. "This gives the ACC a reputation, among the press in particular, of being a second-rate football conference. Our proximity to the [Southeastern Conference] magnifies this situation."

Decrying a competitive disadvantage in football recruiting, Maryland, at the league's northern terminus, and Clemson and South Carolina, the southernmost members, challenged the ACC's heightened academic standard. Bill McLellan, a former Clemson player and athletics director, noted his school played Georgia almost every year between 1962 and 1971, and the Bulldogs had the advantage of utilizing many players who did not score 800 on the SAT. Paul Dietzel, the Gamecocks' football coach and athletics director, insisted only two in 10 top football prospects in South Carolina could surpass the ACC's academic bar.

"I felt at the time that we had to get the bulk of our players from the state of South Carolina, and the ACC rules were going to make that impossible," he said.

Clemson President R.C. Edwards, speaking late in 1970, said his school found it "... increasingly difficult to establish and maintain a sound and financially solvent intercollegiate athletic program under the existing Atlantic Coast Conference regulations. To be successful, we must be able to compete on equal terms with the teams we play."

Rumors had Clemson and South Carolina serving as "the keystone of a new conference," according to Whitey Kelley of the *Charlotte* (N.C.) *Observer*. But Edwards insisted to Dan Foster of the *Greenville* (S.C.) *News*: "The best thing for us would be to solve our problems within the Atlantic Coast Conference by changing some of the conference policies. I hope we can do it within the conference, and we will do everything we possibly can to accomplish that."

South Carolina was less conciliatory. Defying league rules, on Oct. 23, 1970, USC trustees approved the admission of athletes who qualified simply under the NCAA's lesser standard. Leading the charge was Dietzel, who had won a national football title at Louisiana State in 1958 and insisted he could make South Carolina "the Notre Dame of the South."

That apparently meant leaving the ACC. McLellan, who became Clemson's athletics director in 1971, recalled Dietzel "wanted Clemson to go with them." Most observers thought Dietzel would get his way. Writing in the *Washington* (D.C.) *Star* late in 1970, Steve Hershey characterized the ACC as "strife-ridden" and said "break-up ... appears inevitable."

Surveying the situation in November 1970, the *Greensboro* (N.C.) *Daily News* essentially welcomed South Carolina's departure from the ACC. "The trustee decision climaxes a half-decade in which USC has moved determinedly into 'big-time' intercollegiate sports," editorialized the newspaper in the city that for 50 years has been the ACC's headquarters. "In that period it has hired two big-time coaches, Paul Dietzel and Frank McGuire, built a lavish new basketball arena and added thousands of seats to the football stadium. ... The ACC, though it has been 'big-time' in many ways, has always recognized this essential truth: academics first, athletics second. The trustees of the University of South Carolina obviously have reversed the order of priorities."

Complicating matters for all concerned, even as these fundamental issues came to a head, other profound changes reshaped the face and character of the Atlantic Coast Conference.

Enrollments expanded during the decade of the 1960s at every state university within the conference. The student population more than doubled at North Carolina State and Virginia from 1960 to 1970, doubled at South Carolina and almost doubled at Maryland and North Carolina. Clemson's enrollment increased nearly 75 percent.

These burgeoning campuses saw key elements of the conference's old guard pass from the scene.

James "Big Jim" Weaver, the first and only full-time commissioner the league had known, died of a heart attack at age 67 while attending a July 1970 conference in Colorado. (Wallace Wade served as dual head of the Southern Conference and its offshoot branch through the ACC's first year.)

Tough, fair and conscientious, Weaver, a former athletics director at Wake Forest, was replaced late in the year by 49-year-old Bob James, a Maryland graduate. James took office March 1, 1971, on the eve of what would prove South Carolina's valedictory Atlantic Coast Conference men's basketball tournament.

Clemson's Frank Howard, who doubled as athletics director, finished 30 years as football coach there in 1969. Vic Bubas, an ex-N.C. State player and assistant coach, retired in '69 after upgrading Duke basketball and earning three trips to the Final Four between 1963 and 1966.

Longtime athletics directors at Maryland, North Carolina and N.C. State stepped aside that year.

The long-delayed but inescapable rise to prominence of the African-American athlete also occurred as the 1970s dawned.

Virginia became the last ACC school to add an African-American basketball player, Al Drummond, in 1970. That same year Charles Scott, the league's first great, accomplished African-American athlete, graduated from North Carolina, which had reached new heights with consecutive Final Four appearances from 1967-69 under Dean Smith.

"Of all the forces of change that have affected college basketball during the past half-century," Norman Sloan, head basketball coach at N.C. State from 1966-80, wrote in his book *Confessions of a Coach*, "easily the most dramatic and far-reaching has been the advent of racial integration."

By 1971 the ACC celebrated its first African-American players of the year in basketball, Wake's Charlie Davis, and in football, Duke's Ernie Jackson.

Jackson, from just outside Columbia, S.C., earned All-America honors after being ignored by the Gamecocks, who claimed to be starved for local talent. Life still was not easy at Duke, which along with Wake Forest was among the last schools in the league to integrate its undergraduate student body.

"I had a lot of honors there from an athletic standpoint," Jackson said recently of the Durham, N.C., school, "but the thing I recall more than anything else was when I'd walk through the dorms on the way to practice every day. Most of the football players were [fraternity] members, I believe. And when you saw the Confederate flag hoisted out of their dorm all the time, it was extremely difficult to have to go to war with those guys and play with them from a teammate perspective to see them display that."

Even as the complexion of sports changed — dissolving old barriers and opening minds to new possibilities — women joined the chorus arguing for equal access, an equal chance to compete. This came in an era when women were still off-handedly called girls and locked away in their college dorms at night.

"We didn't think of equal opportunity; you didn't think that way then," acknowledged Homer Rice, athletics director at the University of North Carolina from 1969-75 and later at Georgia Tech, which joined the ACC in 1978.

After all, it wasn't until 1969 that the state of South Carolina allowed women to sit on juries. Not until 1970 did the University of Virginia fall in line with the rest of the ACC and admit female undergraduates.

"Athletics wasn't even for women," recalled Chris Weller, who retired in 2002 after 25 years as Maryland's women's basketball coach. "We were considered almost deviant in our desire just to enjoy competing. That was back in the days when they used to joke about women drivers. I used to say constantly, 'That's because you keep women from learning how to be competitive, because you have to be somewhat competitive in driving.'"

Student assertiveness and resistance to authority filtered to the ranks of athletes. Maryland head football coach Bob Ward, faced with avowed displeasure from most of his players, resigned in 1969. Barely a week later, Virginia head basketball coach Bill "Hoot" Gibson faced, and survived, a campaign to "Boot the Hoot," led by several of his players. Transfers beset Duke's Raymond "Bucky" Waters, a crew-cut disciplinarian who denounced locker-room use of hair dryers before even arriving on campus. He failed to sustain Bubas' success.

Florida State football coach Bobby Bowden, recalling the head coaching job he took in 1970, told Ben Brown, author of *Saint Bobby and the Barbarians*: "I think when I went to West Virginia is when I began to see the change starting, the players demanding more input. It was more 'Why are we doing this?' and 'We've got our rights, too.' That movement started in the late '60s, and I learned to adapt with it."

Challenging the status quo wasn't restricted to students. McGuire, who won an NCAA basketball title at North Carolina in 1957, returned to the ACC in 1964 as head coach at South Carolina and soon struck a combative note.

"Frank enjoyed controversy," said Tom Price, a sports historian and retired sports information director at South Carolina. "He was never happy unless he was involved in controversy." Embroiled in a tussle over a prized recruit's failure to achieve an 800 SAT score, McGuire denounced the "skunks" in the ACC, including several athletics directors, and so inflamed sentiments that the South Carolina-Duke basketball series was canceled in 1967.

"We're fighting for respect," McGuire declared in 1969. "I was on the other side of the fence at North Carolina and know what those people think of South Carolina. But we're making progress, and we will not be patsies anymore."

Scuffles and outright fights increasingly accompanied Gamecock basketball games. "Things got bitter at the end," Dietzel said years later.

When Maryland hired a new men's basketball coach in March 1969, McGuire made it sound as if a pincers movement had been launched against the league's North Carolina schools, which comprised half the ACC's membership. "It's going to be a two-pronged attack," he said. "There's going to be competition from the north and south now that Lefty Driesell is at Maryland. There will be no more honeymoon around here."

Forget the honeymoon. Soon the end was in sight for the marriage of athletics and academic integrity that had included South Carolina as a partner. Compromises were proposed to soften the ACC's eligibility requirements but failed to achieve the necessary three-fourths approval by league members.

"We still feel that the ACC should lead, rather than follow, NCAA practices in these matters," Duke replied to a survey of institutional heads in 1970. Others agreed, and refused to budge. "Of course people dug their heels in and drew a line, and there was no compromise," Carl James said.

Matters came to a head in March 1971.

On the same Saturday that South Carolina captured its only ACC basketball title — besting North Carolina 52-51 after 6-foot-3 Kevin Joyce out-jumped 6-10 Lee Dedmon on a jump ball leading to the decisive layup — Clemson's Edwards released a statement reaffirming his school's commitment to the ACC. But barely two weeks later, reprising a role filled by the Palmetto State on a far grander scale 110 years earlier at the outset of the Civil War, South Carolina's trustees officially moved to secede from the ACC. The "resignation," as the university called it, became effective May 6.

Hard times followed for South Carolina athletics, which operated on an independent basis until joining the Southeastern Conference, another Southern Conference offshoot, for the 1992 season.

Barely a year after South Carolina withdrew, the ACC succumbed to an adverse court ruling and rescinded the 800 rule. The league has operated in virtual tandem with NCAA standards since.

Yet the defection of South Carolina proved a defining moment for the ACC. Rarely has an intercollegiate conference stood its academic ground at the price of losing a member. Although buffeted and bent by shifting and sometimes conflicting imperatives, the ACC has stuck to its founders' vision with uncommon diligence, emerging in the process with premier teams in a full range of sports and an enduring position of leadership in intercollegiate athletics.

Georgia Tech and Florida State joined the ACC's ranks over the years, to great effect. With their participation, ACC teams have won nine men's basketball titles, five national football championships, a women's basketball crown and dozens of individual and team titles in the 22 other sports in which the league competes.

The record impresses even Friday, president-emeritus of the consolidated University of North Carolina and a persistent critic of excess in college athletics. "If you're going to do it, if you're going to be in big-time sports," said the one-time sports editor of N.C. State's student newspaper, "the ACC does it about as well as you can expect anybody to do it." ✶

THE COMMISSIONERS

JAMES H. WEAVER

Jim Weaver, a North Carolina native born on March 29, 1903, served as ACC commissioner for 17 years.

Weaver began his athletic career at Virginia's Emory and Henry College, where he played football, basketball and baseball. Later he briefly attended Duke University before graduating from Centenary College in Louisiana in 1924.

Weaver became head football coach at Wake Forest in 1933, posting a 10-23-1 record over four seasons. He was named Wake's athletics director in 1937 and held the position through 1954, except for three years in the U.S. Navy during World War II. Weaver also was the golf coach who brought Hall of Famer Arnold Palmer to Wake Forest in 1948.

Weaver took office as the ACC's first full-time commissioner on July 1, 1954. He served in that capacity until his death of a heart attack on July 11, 1970.

ROBERT C. JAMES

Bob James, a native Pennsylvanian born on Jan. 28, 1921, was ACC commissioner for 16 years.

James attended the University of Maryland before and after serving in the U.S. Army during World War II. James won letters in football, basketball and track as a Terrapin, graduating in 1947.

James remained at Maryland as assistant dean of men and in 1956 was voted the school's outstanding faculty member. Two years later James was appointed associate dean for student life. In February 1960 he moved to athletic administration as civilian director of athletics at the Air Force Academy. James was named commissioner of the Mid-American Conference in 1965, a position he held until taking office as ACC commissioner on March 1, 1971.

James served as commissioner until his death of stomach cancer on May 12, 1987.

EUGENE F. CORRIGAN

Gene Corrigan, a native of Baltimore, Md., born on April 14, 1928, served as ACC commissioner for 11 years.

Corrigan served in the U.S. Army after finishing high school in Maryland, then enrolled at Duke University. Corrigan was a four-year starter in lacrosse for the Blue Devils, graduating in 1952.

Corrigan coached basketball, soccer and lacrosse at Washington and Lee and at the University of Virginia. He later was UVa's sports information director.

Corrigan became the ACC's first full-time Service Bureau director in 1967, also serving as assistant to Commissioner Jim Weaver. Two years later Corrigan returned to Washington and Lee as athletics director and head of the physical education department. He served as AD at Virginia from 1971 though 1981, then occupied the same position at Notre Dame for six years.

Corrigan officially took office as the ACC's third commissioner on Sept. 1, 1987. He served until his retirement in 1997.

JOHN D. SWOFFORD

John Swofford, a North Carolina native born on Dec. 6, 1948, has served as ACC commissioner since 1997.

Swofford attended the University of North Carolina on a Morehead academic scholarship. He played quarterback and defensive back in football, graduating in 1971.

Swofford earned a master's degree in athletic administration in 1973 at Ohio University. From 1973 through 1976 Swofford served under Gene Corrigan at Virginia as a ticket manager and assistant to the athletics director. Swofford returned to his alma mater in 1976 as assistant athletics director and business manager. Three years later Swofford became assistant executive vice president of the Educational Foundation, which raises funds for athletics. In 1980 Swofford became UNC's director of athletics, a job he held for 17 years.

Swofford officially took office as the ACC's fourth commissioner on July 1, 1997, and remains in that position.

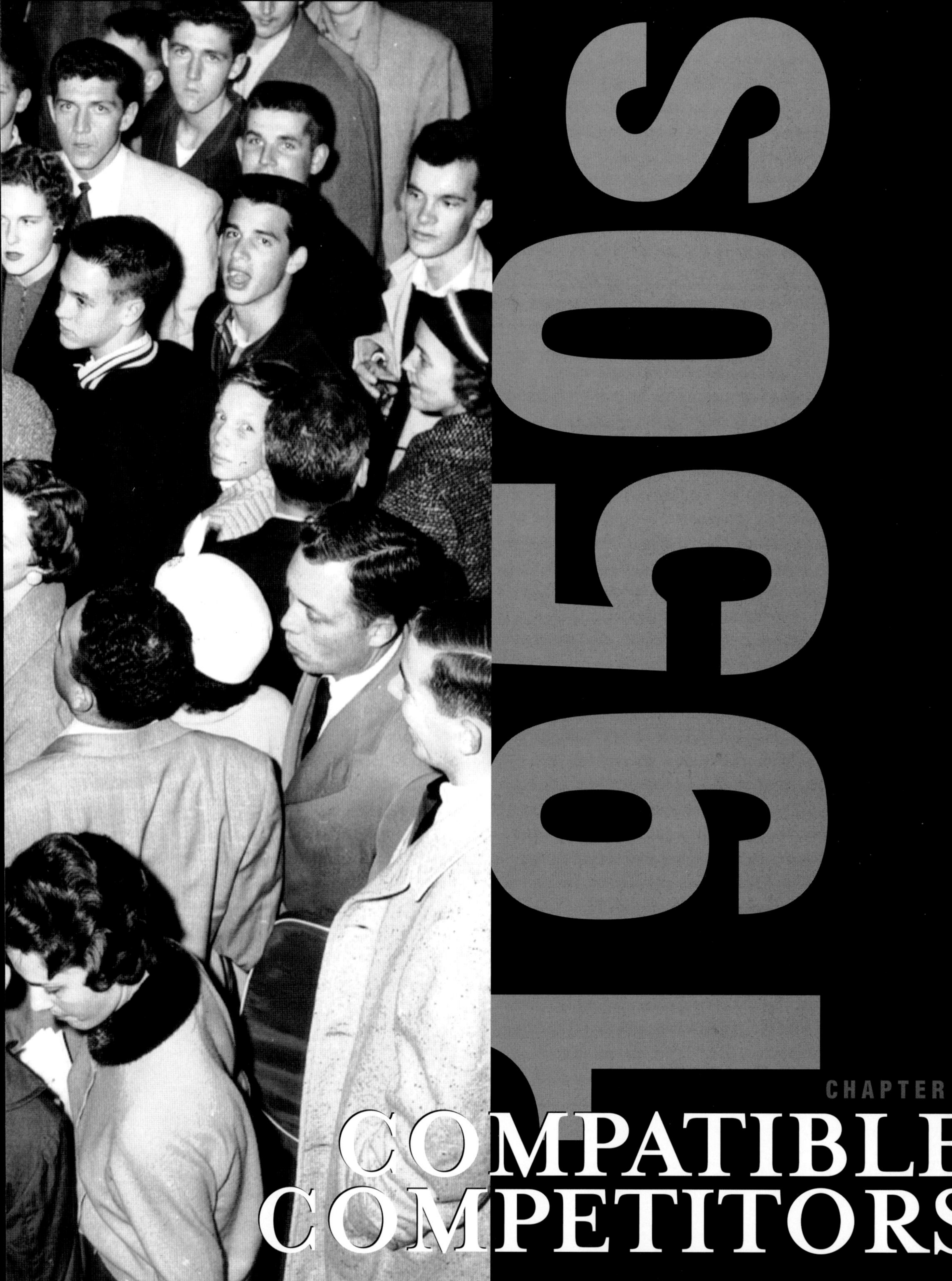

1950s

CHAPTER 1

COMPATIBLE COMPETITORS

The transforming moment for the Atlantic Coast Conference came in improbable fashion as the league finished its fourth year of existence.

There had been earlier successes, to be sure. Maryland, a national football power under coach Jim Tatum, finished atop the 1953 polls before losing to Oklahoma in the Orange Bowl. Maryland won the national championship anyway because the final vote was taken before the bowls were played.

Tatum, among a trio of Hall of Fame coaches roaming the sidelines of the eight-school conference, had built a well-rounded program as Maryland's athletics director, reflected in national lacrosse titles in 1955 and 1956. Wake Forest, the smallest school in the league, won the 1955 College World Series, still the only baseball title earned by an ACC club.

But it was the 1957 North Carolina basketball team — undefeated at 32-0 and survivor of consecutive triple-overtime games in the Final Four at Kansas City and conqueror of giant center Wilt Chamberlain and Kansas, 54-53 — that brought the upstart ACC quick prominence, a measure of competitive legitimacy and a lasting link with the comparably youthful medium of television, the single most powerful force in post-World War II American sports.

Basketball figured far less than football in the birth of the ACC on May 9, 1953, despite basketball's later emergence as the league's signature sport and its post-season tournament as the conference's trademark event.

"King Football" was the subject of great debate as the 1950s dawned, denounced from Honolulu to Chapel Hill for its corrupting influence on college life. A 1951 article in *Town and Country* magazine written by a former Dartmouth football All-American said colleges found the sport to be a "sick and gasping creature that is odiously reposing on their collective doorstep."

A Virginia group headed by Robert K. Gooch, a political science professor and former star Cavalier football player, called for "less professional football teams" and suggested de-emphasizing athletics if necessary.

"We have never felt it to be the function of a university to provide a moneymaking spectacle of athletic virtuosity for Saturday afternoon entertainment," the 1951

RIGHT
The 1955 Wake Forest baseball team won the College World Series, the only Atlantic Coast Conference school to capture that title.

report stated. "Big-time football is not in line with the essential educational function of the University."

The *Richmond News Leader* took much the same tack in a Sept. 27, 1951, editorial after examining the football program at Virginia, which left the Southern Conference in 1936. "Looking over all of this — the analgesic balm, the rolls of tape, the $14 football shoes, the movie projectors, the occasional luncheon checks for 'Mr. [head football coach Art] Guepe and Two,' the megaphones, stop watches, gauze bandage, the crutch tips — one is constrained to ask two simple questions: Proper function of higher education? And how much represents an expensive, unnecessary, undesirable floating along on the tide of lavish spectator sports?"

While Virginia, founded and designed by Thomas Jefferson in the early 1800s, navigated an independent course, disputes over bowl participation became a source of contention among the 17 members of the surrounding Southern Conference. Many in the league objected to the emphasis created by such ballyhooed, moneymaking distractions. The issue came to a boil in 1951, when members voted 14-3 to deny Maryland and Clemson permission to accept bowl bids. (South Carolina voted with the bowl aspirants.)

Point-shaving scandals in basketball, and a cheating scandal at West Point that heavily involved football players, also caused consternation and led in part to the bowl ban. "Any practice which tends to commercialize athletics or cheapen the academic offerings of an educational institution," Duke President A. Hollis Edens wrote in defense of his school's stance, "thwarts the purpose of an athletic program and destroys its values."

Denied approval, Clemson and Maryland went to bowls anyway, with the Terrapins beating top-ranked Tennessee 28-13 in the 1951 Sugar Bowl to finish 10-0. As punishment, both the Tigers and Terps were suspended from Southern Conference play during the 1952 season. President Colgate Darden similarly blocked an 8-1 Virginia football squad from participating in postseason play in 1951.

"The team cannot take the time to go on through December in a strenuous period of practice for a game on New Year's Day and stand a reasonable chance of surviving the mid-year examinations," Darden said. The Cavaliers would not attend a bowl until December 1984.

"How have bowl games become such evils overnight?" asked Jack Horner of the *Durham Morning Herald*. "I haven't heard of any bowl games being thrown, or the points being shaved. No other conference bans participation in postseason games. Since when did the Southern Conference become a crusader?"

To say such confusion was nothing new is to understate the issue. Football elicited calls for control or elimination almost since its inception at the college level in the latter 19th century. Decried for its violence and effect on morality, the sport was banned for a time at schools from Harvard

J
80

to Trinity College, a Methodist school in North Carolina that dropped football from 1893 through 1921, or almost until it became Duke University.

Methodist leaders told Trinity trustees football was "a source of evil, and of no little evil, and ought to be stopped." President John Franklin Crowell doubled as the school's head football coach. He refused to disband the team and resigned, becoming an early casualty of a campus football dispute.

The very roots of the National Collegiate Athletic Association trace to attempts to address corruption related primarily to football. So did periodic efforts to restrict recruiting and to limit athletic grants-in-aid to a need basis, notably the short-lived "Graham Plan" attempted in the Southern Conference during the 1930s under the leadership of University of North Carolina system President Frank Porter Graham and the "Sanity Code" adopted by the NCAA in 1947 and abandoned by 1951.

"The problem of subsidization is a vexing and troublesome one," Virginia's Darden wrote in 1954. "One of the things that gives me great difficulty is how a boy who is not a particularly good student but who is ambitious for an education can be helped. That he is interested in athletics is to his credit, and this should not stand in the way of his being assisted, but I have never been able to devise a plan in my own mind that would make this possible without the machinery being used for the promotion of boys who are primarily interested in athletics and not concerned particularly with an education."

The ability and willingness to support big-time football increasingly divided the sprawling and diverse Southern Conference following World War II.

Typical of the divisions, larger schools wanted to maintain freshman teams while smaller schools were eager to impose a complete ban on first-year participation at a time when freshmen were ineligible for varsity competition.

"There was just too much difference," said Carl James, who played football at Duke under Wallace Wade. The gap within the Southern Conference grew so wide that a writer at Washington and Lee asked plaintively in 1954: "Breathes there an alumnus with soul so dead who, glancing at Sunday's paper, never to himself has said: 'What are we doing playing Maryland?'"

By then, "Sunny Jim" Tatum's Maryland teams were among the nation's best. The

FACING PAGE
"Sunny Jim" Tatum coached Maryland to a national championship in 1953, the ACC's first year of existence. He also served as director of athletics for the Terrapins. Tatum, a UNC alumnus, later returned to Chapel Hill to coach the Tar Heels. Tatum died an untimely death of Rocky Mountain spotted fever at age 46 in 1959.

BELOW
The 1953 national championship Maryland football team poses together before embarking on a 10-0 regular season. The Terrapins lost 7-0 to Oklahoma in the Orange Bowl, but the final vote in the national polls was taken before the bowl games.

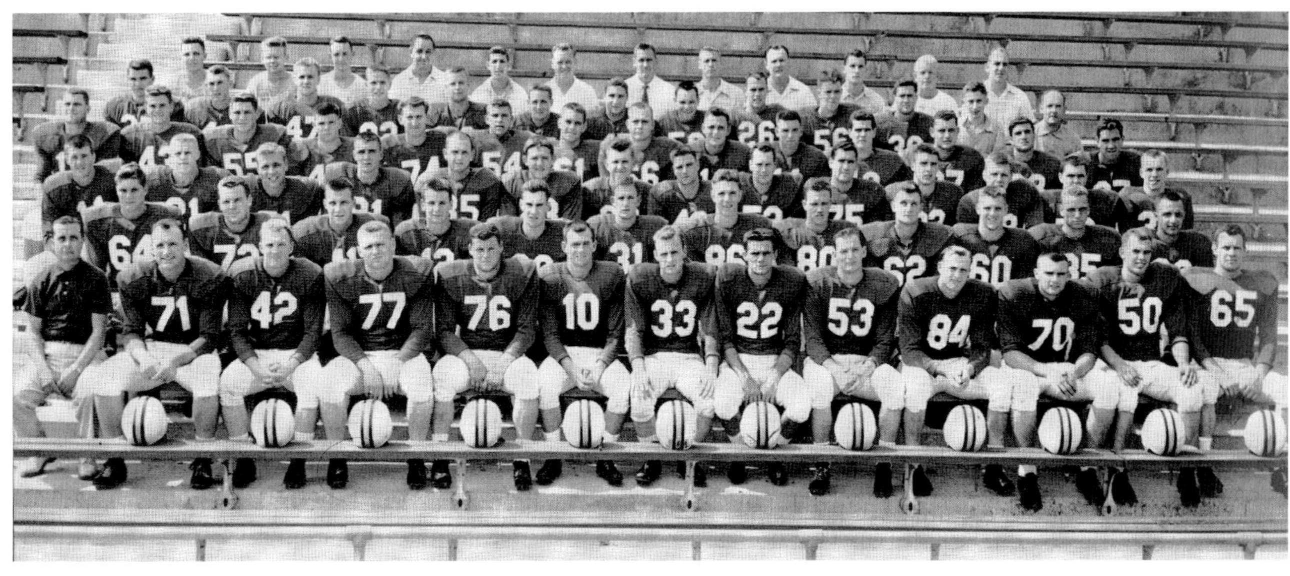

Terrapins were undefeated during the 1951, 1953 and 1955 regular seasons. The last two times they played little Washington and Lee, the Terps won by scores of 54-14 and 52-0.

Maryland's ascendance gave the Southern Conference a pair of powerhouse football programs. Duke was the other. Renamed after a tobacco magnate in 1924, the school had so completely shed its earlier distaste for football, it lured away Wade, an eventual Hall of Famer, from Alabama. Wade elevated Duke's institutional visibility and football prowess, just as he had done for the Crimson Tide, with which he won national championships in 1926 and 1930 and appeared in three Rose Bowls.

The 1930 squad was Wade's last at Tuscaloosa and counted among its starters 180-pound guard Frank Howard.

Thanks to Howard, the Clemson head coach from 1940-69, the Tigers were also an emerging football power as the 1950s dawned. Howard led teams to bowls in 1949, '51 and '52. An honors student in college, Howard was noted for a tough demeanor and a down-home style.

"He'd tell you what he thought about you right quick," said Banks McFadden, a former player and assistant coach. "But if you did something right, he would say something nice to you." Bill McLellan, another former player and later the school's AD, said Howard was fair but "you could be scared to death of him."

Howard, Tatum and Duke's Bill Murray, who succeeded Wade in 1951, eventually were voted to college football's Hall of Fame.

Facing uncertainties and uneven competition, many schools searched for compatible realignments. The president of Vanderbilt, an SEC member, discussed with Virginia's Darden an Ivy League-type association to include their schools along with Duke, Washington University in St. Louis and other "institutions recognized as first-rate." President Milton Eisenhower of Penn State proposed forming a football conference with North Carolina, which in 1795 was the first state university in the nation to open its doors, and other schools sharing "like ideals and like traditions" in intercollegiate athletics.

Duke considered joining a group with North Carolina, Notre Dame, Penn State, Pittsburgh, the U.S. Military Academy and the U.S. Naval Academy, with Syracuse, Pennsylvania, Georgia Tech and Virginia as possibilities.

The ACC emerged from this period of reappraisal, engineered by schools whose athletics directors without exception either had been or remained head football coaches. Such dual roles were peculiarly Southern. "The ACC to me, and in the world of people's thoughts, was originally formed as a football league," said Herman "Bud" Millikan, Maryland's basketball coach from 1950 through 1967.

The surprise announcement of the league's birth came on May 8, 1953, at

1953

5.7.53
First meeting of ACC founders at Sedgefield Inn at Greensboro

5.8.53
ACC officially formed at Sedgefield Inn

5.14.53
New league adopts by-laws and the name **Atlantic Coast Conference** at meeting at Raleigh's Sir Walter Hotel

11.30.53
Maryland finishes first in the final Associated Press and United Press International football polls, earning the national championship

Greensboro's Sedgefield Inn, located on a golf course where the Southern Conference convened to discuss, among other matters, bowl participation and freshman eligibility. Late the previous night, 15 faculty and athletics representatives from Clemson, Duke, Maryland, North Carolina, N.C. State, South Carolina and Wake Forest, along with UNC Chancellor R.B. House and Wake President Harold Tribble, met for an hour in Room 230 to ratify formation of a smaller conference.

This culminated more than a year of private discussion, most prominently among athletics directors Eddie Cameron of Duke, North Carolina's Charles "Chuck" Erickson, Maryland's Tatum and South Carolina's Rex Enright, who had played for Knute Rockne at Notre Dame.

"The athletics directors were probably as strong as anybody in the country," Carl James said. Others were Clemson's Howard, N.C. State's Roy Clogston and Wake's Jim Weaver, who would be elected the ACC's first commissioner the following spring.

The presidents of the various schools — brought together in the Morehead Building at UNC by invitation of Duke's Edens and Gordon Gray, president of the University of North Carolina system — had previously given the new league their blessing. Several ideas were central to formation of the as-yet-unnamed conference. President Gray, whose bailiwick encompassed UNC and N.C. State, articulated interest in freshman ineligibility in varsity sports, adequate admissions standards and requirements for progress toward degrees, competition in a full range of sports, shared revenues to remove "the commercial aspects of postseason games" and a "round-robin" playing schedule.

"Mr. Gray's ambition then was to do exactly what was done, which was to form the ACC," recalled William Friday, Gray's assistant at the time. "That was Mr. Gray's coming behind the Graham Plan."

Also instrumental was Maryland President Harry "Curly" Byrd, the Terrapin football coach from 1911 through 1934. Byrd previously had starred at College Park in football, baseball and track, cutting so impressive a swath that the school paper wrote: "His paths are strewn with the broken hearts of guileless maidens whom he has 'loved to death,' he-siren that he is."

When the Southern Conference convened its annual meeting a little after 10 a.m. on May 8, it immediately moved into closed session. There, James T. Penney, South Carolina's faculty chairman and the ACC's first president, announced the breakaway movement. "This action was taken with mixed feeling, as all of us have formed many personal and institutional friendships through the years," Penney read from a prepared statement. "It is our belief that this action will be the best for all concerned."

A fundamental shift from Southern Conference participation was the notion

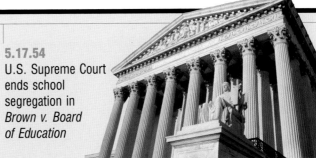

2.4.53
irginia joins ACC as
ne eighth member

1954

2.25.54
N.C. State wins first ACC championship ever contested, in men's swimming

3.6.54
N.C. State wins first ACC Tournament at Raleigh's Reynolds Coliseum

5.17.54
U.S. Supreme Court ends school segregation in *Brown v. Board of Education*

the ACC was to be a "playing league," in which members faced one another on a regular basis. The size of the old league allowed teams to schedule weaker basketball members and avoid stronger ones, in order to qualify for the eight-team postseason tournament that decided a conference champion.

Schools with large football facilities also were hesitant to play at the league's smaller venues, among them N.C. State. Minimal gate receipts at 19,000-seat Riddick Stadium, along with shaky athletic finances, brought N.C. State's initial ACC membership into question.

Those handicaps caused the school to play all but two games with archrival North Carolina at Chapel Hill between 1943 and 1964. For years after football coach Earle Edwards was hired in 1954, he carefully orchestrated recruits' campus visits to avoid the school's football facilities. "When we did get them to visit, we didn't show them the stadium," Edwards said. "We made sure they stayed around Reynolds Coliseum."

The Citadel, Davidson, Furman, George Washington, Richmond, Virginia Military Institute, Virginia Tech, Washington and Lee, and West Virginia were left behind by the ACC split. The Southern Conference, formed in 1921 in Atlanta, had previously subdivided in 1932, when 10 members withdrew to form the Southeastern Conference (SEC).

Now the conference had divided again. In a meeting at Raleigh's Sir Walter Hotel one month after the second split, the new league took the name Atlantic Coast Conference upon motion of Duke's Cameron. Other names in the mix included the Big Eight, Blue-Gray, Colonial, Confederate, Cotton, Dixie, East Coast, Mid-Atlantic, Mid-South, Piedmont, Rebel, Seaboard, Shoreline, Southern Seven and Tobacco.

By the end of 1953, the ACC had added Virginia as an eighth member, agreed to a tie-in with the Orange Bowl, established that it would share revenues from bowls, and fended off several suitors eager to join. Initiatives on behalf of West Virginia and Virginia Tech were voted on and rejected, in part because they were difficult travel destinations. Mississippi Southern, Florida State and Miami (Fla.) also expressed early interest but never came up for a vote.

While quickly offered, Virginia's place in the ACC was not readily accepted. Darden, a former governor, was reluctant to abandon the other state schools against which the Cavaliers regularly competed. An athletic council analysis further warned that the "tempo" set by powers such as Maryland, Wake Forest and Duke could force the school to make "out of character" changes that, unmet, "would relegate Virginia to a door-mat role."

But the council unanimously agreed that public and player preference, as well as scheduling and economic considerations, clearly favored joining the ACC. Otherwise Virginia "could be left on the platform with a ticket in our pocket, baggage in our hand, but no train to ride." Carrying this message, athletics director

Gus Tebell — who had coached and won in football and basketball at N.C. State during the 1920s and later at Virginia — convinced a sharply divided university Board of Visitors to approve ACC membership.

The deal with the Orange Bowl, which pitted an ACC member against a team from the Big Seven (later Big Eight and then Big 12), was similarly crucial to a successful start for the fledgling league. Unlike today, in which there are more bowls than letters in the alphabet, there were few tie-ins and only eight bowls: the Orange, Cotton, Sugar, Rose, Gator, Sun, Tangerine and Refrigerator.

"That was huge," Carl James said of the Orange Bowl pact, which added instant credibility and cash, with each participant guaranteed $110,600, big money at the time. "You've heard the old cliché, 'They hit the floor running.' Well, they hit the floor running."

Maryland, atop all three national polls and at the height of its prowess, was chosen as the ACC's first Orange Bowl representative, even though Duke matched the Terps by finishing undefeated against a partial schedule of league foes.

Paced by All-America right tackle Stan Jones, Maryland led the nation in 1953 in rushing defense (83.9 yards) and scoring defense (3.1 points per game), recording six shutouts. No ACC squad since has been more sparing in yielding points. Jones had a long career in the National Football League, and was inducted into the Pro Football and College Football halls of fame.

Tatum's split-T offense was comparably impressive in 1953, scoring 298 points in 10 regular-season games (an ACC mark until 1968) behind guard Bob Pellegrini, halfback Chester Hanulak and quarterback Bernie Faloney, the 1953 ACC player of the year. Faloney's injury doomed the attack in

LEFT TO RIGHT
Stan Jones (77) was the starting right tackle on a Terrapin defense that allowed just 31 points in 10 regular-season games in 1953. Bob Pellegrini (50) was recruited to play quarterback but switched to the line and eventually became the ACC player of the year in 1955. Terrapin quarterback Bernie Faloney was the first ACC player of the year in football, earning the honor for the 1953 season.

By Sarah Sue Ingram

ACC EXCELLENCE

YOW SISTERS MAKE LASTING IMPACT ON ACC SPORTS

No single family has had a greater impact on Atlantic Coast Conference sports than the Yows of Gibsonville, N.C.

Of the three sisters, one rebuilt a financially strapped athletic program at the University of Maryland, another became a Hall of Fame basketball coach at North Carolina State and yet another became the first Kodak All-American for the Wolfpack women.

Debbie Yow is the only female athletics director in the history of the ACC and one of only two in the nation's six "power" conferences. Kay Yow is the 1988 U.S. Olympic women's basketball coach who guided the team to a gold medal. She was also a 2002 inductee into the Naismith Basketball Hall of Fame. Their younger sister, Susan, played for Kay at N.C. State and is now a collegiate head coach.

Having three members of one family make such an imprint on the ACC is remarkable. Their separate, pioneering paths are even more impressive.

Kay, eight years older than Debbie, was an English teacher and librarian at Allen Jay High School in High Point, N.C. She coached the girls' basketball team to four consecutive conference championships. Debbie was a free spirit who wore halter-tops and bell-bottom jeans and dropped out of college to embrace the counterculture.

Debbie Yow is the ACC's only female athletics director. She has overcome a huge budget deficit and led Terrapin athletics to new heights during her tenure at the school.

Debbie was an aggressor. Kay has been an ambassador of goodwill. Debbie is married. Kay is single.

Kay has willingly been cemented for 27 years, and counting, in N.C. State's Reynolds Coliseum, the site where her dad, Hilton, took her to Dixie Classic basketball games. Debbie soared without a tether — first as a women's basketball coach who turned Kentucky, Oral Roberts and the University of Florida into top-20 teams and then as an administrator at Florida, the University of North Carolina at Greensboro, Saint Louis University and Maryland.

Kay is more serious. Debbie has a superb sense of humor.

When Debbie interviewed for the athletics directors job at Saint Louis in 1990, she walked into a room with 10 men sitting in the only chairs available. "Where's the hot seat?" she quipped. One sullen man replied, "Anywhere you choose to sit."

Debbie needed more than a sense of humor when she came to College Park. She inherited the athletic department's multimillion dollar deficit. In eight years, she balanced the budget while at the same time building the $125 million Comcast Center for basketball.

Finances are not the sole gauge of her success, however. In 2001, Yow approved an order for 180 rings inscribed "ACC Champion" for the Maryland football team and staff. A few months later, Maryland ordered 26 more rings. This time, the inscription read "2002 NCAA Men's Basketball Champion."

"I have friends in the industry who are excellent athletic directors who never coached, but I don't understand how they do it," Debbie said. "Whether it's financing or recruiting or traveling decisions, I always revert back to my coaching experiences."

Debbie's finest Maryland moments begin with every graduation day. After that comes the football team's come-from-behind win at N.C. State to clinch an Orange Bowl berth, seven straight women's lacrosse national

Kay Yow, far right, is a Hall of Fame women's basketball coach at N.C. State. Her sister, Susan (far left), was the first Kodak All-America women's basketball player for the Wolfpack. Nora Lynn Finch (center) is a former assistant coach to Kay Yow and is an administrator at N.C. State.

championships, a field hockey national title and the men's basketball national championship.

The ACC is no stranger to NCAA basketball championships. Yet in its storied history, only six people had been selected to the Naismith Basketball Hall of Fame: Everett Case, Billy Cunningham, Frank McGuire, Dean Smith, David Thompson and Mike Krzyzewski. Kay Yow joined them in September 2002. (Dave Cowens, also in the Hall, played at Florida State before FSU joined the ACC.)

The 625 collegiate wins Kay had entering the 2002-03 season were fifth best in women's basketball history. Her record at N.C. State was 568-249, with five regular-season and four ACC Tournament titles and a Final Four appearance in 1998.

"Kay and Debbie both have drive, passion and focus," Susan said. "They just have different styles."

Kay, Debbie and Susan each, in turn, wore No. 14 at Gibsonville High School. Kay once scored 52 points in a single game while wearing her white Chuck Taylor Converse high-top sneakers. Kay later worked with Duke's Steve Vacendak and Wake Forest's Eddie Payne at Carl James' basketball camp when Taylor came to lecture.

"Chuck Taylor was in his 80s, but he was still like a magician with the ball," Kay said. "That's where I first found out about passing lanes."

Susan, now head coach at Providence College, was an inaugural Kodak All-American while playing for Kay at Elon. She transferred to N.C. State in 1975 when Kay became the Wolfpack's head coach. There she earned her second Kodak All-America honor as a senior. She later transferred back to Elon and earned her degree.

"Susan was a finesse-moves type player, and Debbie was a very aggressive competitor," Kay said. "Debbie's strengths were boxing out and rebounding and defense — the hustle parts of the game."

The Yow family has always embraced athletics. Brother Ronnie attended Clemson on a football scholarship as a running back. Their mother, Lib, finally quit playing backyard basketball after breaking both her wrists at age 48.

"A great love for sports was certainly implanted," Kay said. "I always wanted to do well so my parents wouldn't be disappointed. So I've always been motivated to a certain extent by other people believing in me. And once my faith was developed, I wanted to be the best I could because of the talents that God has given me."

The Yow family lineage can be traced back almost to the beginning of women's basketball. During the '60s, Kay and then Debbie worked at Camp PlaMor, which was run by their older second cousin, Virgil Yow. He coached the High Point College men and the Hanes Hosiery women's team, which won a world championship in the same industrial leagues where Babe Didrikson had played.

Kay recalls listening intently to camp lectures by Hazel Phillips, a Hanes Hosiery player and the world free-throw shooting champion, and by Frank McGuire, former coach at the University of North Carolina and the University of South Carolina.

McGuire coached the first basketball game Kay ever saw on television. The Yow family, sitting in front of its original television set in 1957, watched McGuire direct North Carolina's 54-53 triple overtime win over Kansas for the NCAA national championship.

Kay didn't realize that 15 years later all the Yow sisters' destinies would change, thanks to Title IX, a section of federal law that mandates equal access to athletic opportunity. *

a 7-0 Orange Bowl loss to Oklahoma.

As good a start as the ACC had in football, in basketball it confronted an unwelcome challenge right from the opening tap.

Good talent, coaching and competitiveness abounded, to be sure. Two of the eight coaches, N.C. State's Everett Case and UNC's Frank McGuire, wound up in basketball's Hall of Fame. "They had some outstanding people in the conference during that time," said McFadden, Clemson's coach from 1947-56. Ray Reeve and radio's Tobacco Sports Network made sure folks far and wide knew all about it.

Hal Bradley's Duke squad finished first during the inaugural 1953-54 regular season, among its players Charles "Lefty" Driesell, eventually Maryland's head coach. Millikan, a disciple of Henry Iba of Oklahoma A&I, did well on a relative shoestring with a Terrapin squad led by Gene Shue, an all-conference pick in 1954.

"I didn't receive any money until the last year I was there," Shue, the player nicknamed "Little Mouse," said of his work-study status. "Maryland was a football school, one of the top-rated ones in the country. Basketball was in its infancy and considered minor."

Murray Greason's Wake Forest Demon Deacons were fresh from winning the 1953 Southern Conference tournament, and center Dickie Hemric was 1954 ACC player of the year. Richard "Buzz" Wilkinson led the league by averaging 30.1 points as Virginia posted its last winning season until 1971. North Carolina enjoyed a second straight winning record under McGuire, who had ended the Tar Heels' 15-game losing streak against N.C. State in his first try in 1953.

South Carolina lagged behind, with Clemson, an all-male military and agricultural school, bringing up the rear. The Tigers lost their first 26 conference games over three seasons before beating Virginia at home on Dec. 16, 1956.

"We were not competitive in anything except football, but we were pretty competitive in football," said McFadden, a 1939 All-American in both football and basketball at Clemson. "In the other sports, where other people could give scholarships, we just didn't have the money to give them." Other teams faced similar limitations.

Just prior to the ACC's start, at least one school spent more on boxing than basketball. Virginia coach Evan J. "Bus" Male, who shared practice time at 5,000-seat Memorial Gym with the wrestling, gymnastics and freshman basketball squads, said trying to compete in the new league was like "bear hunting with a switch."

North Carolina's Dean Smith, who arrived as an assistant coach under McGuire in 1958-59, recalled the imbalance was pronounced. "It was easier to be a dominant team in the ACC in the '50s and early '60s because there were three teams that didn't really care about basketball since there wasn't any money involved," the major-college leader in career wins (879) said in 1984. "When I came with Frank, he said he got six sure wins in the conference: two South Carolina, two Clemson and two Virginia."

The team to beat in those early years, the power McGuire was hired to counter, was N.C. State. Case, a coach since his high-school days in Indiana, directed the Wolfpack. "Even then, the Carolina schools were out of their minds for basketball," Maryland's John Sandbower (1953-56) told author Kent Baker.

Case brought an up-tempo style to the Southern Conference for the 1946-47 season, along with an infusion of talented World War II veterans. "He loved the fast-break style of play," said Vic Bubas, who played for and later assisted Case. "I thought that he was probably the best teacher of the fastbreak that I ever saw."

Equally important, Case's exciting on-court approach was matched by a showman's flair. "There is one thing I say about Everett Case that other people don't realize," Bubas said. "Surely he was a great coach. He was awarded many honors and he did a great job, but he was an even better seller and promoter of basketball." Bubas proudly noted Case was named Raleigh's best salesman in 1959, at the height of his influence.

Case arrived at N.C. State when the largest arena south of Philadelphia was Duke Indoor Stadium, built for $400,000 and opened in 1940. Still, the Southern Conference basketball tournament was held at the Raleigh Auditorium until 1947, when ticket demand forced a move to Duke's larger, 9,000-seat arena.

The next year Case instigated the expansion and completion of Reynolds Coliseum, a steel skeleton frozen in place since 1942. The $2.5 million building, which also served as a military training facility and Cold War bomb shelter for federal employees, opened Dec. 2, 1949, with an N.C. State victory over Southern rival Washington and Lee.

Reynolds, which seated 12,400, 10 times more than the team's previous gymnasium, easily surpassed the capacity of the Duke arena on which it was modeled. The Wolfpack proceeded to lead the nation in attendance for the next decade. By 1951

LEFT
Reynolds Coliseum would become the largest basketball arena in the South eventually, but it sat as a skeleton for several years before coach Everett Case had it enlarged and completed. The Wolfpack led the nation in attendance for 10 years after the building was finished. Reynolds was the site for the ACC Tournament from 1954 through 1966.

80
84
76

Reynolds also recaptured the league tournament, remaining the sole venue for the Southern Conference and later the ACC events through 1966.

Case livened every aspect of the game experience at his new arena, from providing an organist and a subtly manipulated noise meter to spotlighting pregame player introductions. "I don't even know if they played the national anthem back then," said Marvin "Skeeter" Francis, an early Wake Forest sports information director and later the ACC's publicity chief. "They'd just toss it up and play."

The same year Reynolds opened, Case inaugurated the post-Christmas Dixie Classic, a three-day tournament in which Duke, North Carolina, N.C. State and Wake Forest hosted four prominent non-conference teams. Soon, in an era before television provided glimpses of diverse national powers, the Dixie grew into one of the premier sporting events in the South.

"It was a classic in deed as well as in name," veteran Greensboro journalist Irwin Smallwood said. Added UNC's William Friday, "It was the Sugar Bowl and the Rose Bowl rolled into one."

Case engineered all this, and found time to win with crushing regularity. Basketball then, as now, required less of an investment to return positive results, and the struggling N.C. State athletic program relied heavily on Case's clubs. A devout tournament coach, he won the Southern Conference title every year

LEFT

A jubilant N.C. State basketball team carries coach Everett Case off the court after another victory. Case is known as the "Father of ACC basketball." His teams won the first three ACC championships, four of the first six. Case also created the highly successful Dixie Classic, which brought some of the top teams in the nation to Raleigh each year.

from 1947 through 1952 and then won the first three ACC championships behind players such as forward Ronnie Shavlik and guard Vic Molodet.

From 1947-56, Case's teams never won fewer than 24 games and averaged a 26-6 record. His 1950 team reached the Final Four, finishing third. "Everett Case is the one that started all the hullabaloo, maybe you would say," McFadden said.

Case's influence was felt in more subtle ways, according to McFadden. Visiting squads routinely reduced expenses by taking advantage of what was called "local entertainment." That meant staying in the host school's dormitories or in bunk beds in the gym itself, and eating meals at the home team's training table.

But, in an early harbinger of the athletic arms race that continues today, Case promised recruits more. "He got everything set so they could have them a budget," McFadden said. "So, when they went to play, they stayed in motels. They fed themselves, had their own transportation, everything. But nobody else did that for two or three years until they found out that Case meant what he was saying about it.

"When he started winning all the games, they took a big look at it and found out he said that was the only way he would take the job at N.C. State and stay there. Therefore, Duke and North Carolina began to pick it up and, before it was all over with, all of them do it now. They do a first-class job."

Unfortunately, even as the ACC coalesced, Case also got caught bending the rules. McFadden said this was easy to do. "No one knew about the rules in the NCAA," he said. "You were lucky to talk about what happened in your state."

The ACC's leadership knew the rules. The league was barely three months old when Wade, serving as interim commissioner, informed members at an Aug. 7, 1953, meeting of NCAA claims that N.C. State illegally held tryouts for 17 players and used school funds to improperly transport prospects to campus. Provision of excess benefits for scholarship athletes was also alleged.

Upon review of the evidence, and with the support of N.C. State, including its chancellor, the ACC sustained the first two charges and voted to place Case's program on one year of probation, to be effective in 1954-55.

Bruce Corrie, in a highly respected 1978 history of the conference, said Wade cited the incident as "the key to the future success of the ACC." The action proved, Corrie wrote, that "the founders of the Atlantic Coast Conference were so intent on developing the ACC as a leading athletic conference that they were able to put the welfare of the conference ahead of their own institutional advantage."

Current ACC leaders, from Commissioner John Swofford to Duke basketball's Mike Krzyzewski, chief in seniority among league coaches, argue for

1954

7.1.54
Jim Weaver starts job as ACC's first full-time commissioner

7.5.54
Elvis Presley cuts first record

12.31.54
ACC signs contract with Orange Bowl for three years, facing Big Seven

preservation of that ethic. But as impressive as the ACC's self-policing may have been, it was difficult to sustain.

The following spring, at the same May 28, 1954, meeting at which Wake's Jim Weaver was chosen over Virginia's Gus Tebell to serve as the ACC's first commissioner, a surprise vote was taken. Those present passed a resolution "to appeal the NCAA decision on N.C. State relative to basketball if this action is approved by the officials (Chancellor, President and others) of the Consolidated University of North Carolina."

This was decidedly unacceptable to Gray, head of the university system. Noting that no school's president was in attendance when the vote was cast, he wrote five days later: "I see no justification whatsoever for appealing the NCAA decisions. In deed, it is my conviction that we were dealt with very generously in this matter." To appeal, Gray said, "would be in effect a statement by the conference that there should be no penalties for infractions."

Gray soon received a report from a participant explaining that, given the heavy representation of coaches and former coaches at the meeting, "much confessing of sins was made and all agreed that the others were guilty of the same offenses and they in good conscience did not want to see State punished."

Gray, soon to join President Dwight Eisenhower's administration, rising to special assistant for national security affairs in 1958, later wrote to other ACC administrative heads urging their attendance at league meetings, "assuming and exercising their unrelinquishable responsibilities."

He drew a lukewarm response, at best.

Nancy Thompson, secretary to ACC commissioners for the league's first 43 years, didn't recall a university head at a subsequent meeting until Wake's Thomas Hearn in the mid-1980s. One president who expressed immediate enthusiasm for Gray's proposal to improve oversight of athletics was Wake's Harold Tribble, who fought a constant and somewhat public battle to balance containment of costs with pleasing alumni and fielding competitive teams.

Tribble, a Charlottesville, Va., native, served as Wake's president from 1950 through 1967. His key task was overseeing one of the rarest physical and cultural transformations in American higher education in the last half-century — the long-planned move of an entire school from an old, established campus to a new one 110 miles away.

"President Tribble was hired to bring Wake Forest to Winston-Salem, despite all odds," said Hearn, Wake's current president. "The decision divided every constituency of the institution — students, faculty, alumni, trustees. And the only way it could have been accomplished was by his unswerving determination. There were a lot of people made angry by a lot of things that he did."

1955

5.31.55
U.S. Supreme Court orders integration with "all deliberate speed"

6.12.55
Wake baseball plays in College World Series on Sunday, beats Colorado State College, 12-0

12.2.55
Cole Field House opens. Maryland beats Virginia, 67-55

By Ron Morris

ACC EXCELLENCE

WILHELM CARVES STRONG TRADITION FOR ACC BASEBALL

The rich green baseball field at Doug Kingsmore Stadium seems larger than most. Maybe it's because there is no warning track in the outfield. Or maybe it's because the hedges that encircle the outfield fence serve as foreground to a greater field that rolls into a valley and beyond.

Almost as striking is the lack of recognition at the stadium for the man who designed the ballpark, and assembled and guided teams that for nearly four decades made Clemson known from coast to coast for its outstanding baseball.

When the school hung a replica jersey No. 38 sign on the outfield fence to honor Coach Bill Wilhelm, he had it removed. No player or coach has worn that jersey number since he retired from coaching following the 1993 season, and the school will never again permit a player or coach to wear it.

When athletic officials approached Wilhelm about naming the ballpark after him, he simply said, "Thanks ... but no thanks."

"That's just not me," Wilhelm said. "I don't want that."

Likewise, Wilhelm refuses admission to the school's athletics Hall of Fame or its heralded Ring of Honor. But there is one bit of recognition that Wilhelm simply can't escape. Through his undying love for the game of baseball and his dedication to making it a major sport in the Atlantic Coast Conference, Wilhelm is — at once — the grandfather, father and godfather of baseball in the conference.

"He's the daddy rabbit of baseball in the Atlantic Coast Conference," said Harold Stowe, the ace pitcher on Wilhelm's first Clemson team, the 1958 squad that advanced to the College World Series. "There's no doubt about it."

To comprehend the scope of Bill Wilhelm's tenure at Clemson, digest a few numbers. His teams won 1,161 games and six times played in the College World Series. He won 19 ACC regular-season titles and seven tournament championships, and his team made 17 NCAA tournament appearances. He also never had a losing season.

There is more to the Wilhelm story than victories and championships, however. He so deeply loved and respected baseball that he demanded the same devotion from players, opposing coaches and administrators. Along the way, he feuded with them all. At the core of each scrap was a belief someone didn't share his conviction that baseball should command the same reverence as football and basketball.

Wilhelm's dogged fight resulted in what often was a one-man crusade to establish an ACC baseball tournament, an event that flourished over the years and has forced other conferences to keep pace by staging their own tournaments. The establishment of the league tournament in 1973 was easily Wilhelm's biggest gift to the conference.

It did not come easily.

With Wilhelm and longtime North Carolina coach Walter Rabb pushing the issue, league officials first approved of the tournament for the 1973 season. In his letter to the league as chairman of the baseball committee, Wilhelm insisted that a conference tournament would give baseball unprecedented media attention, even if it did have to be played in April to avoid interfering with final exams.

Not satisfied, Wilhelm clamored for more. He got the tournament date moved to

Bill Wilhelm Career Record 1161-536-10 1958-1993

Clemson coach Bill Wilhelm and his love for the game helped to make ACC baseball what it is today. He worked to expand and strengthen regular-season schedules and create a postseason tournament, which is still going strong. His teams always stressed fundamentals and won with regularity. He retired in 1993.

May, although Duke protested at first and did not participate. Then he pleaded with other coaches and athletic officials to elevate the overall play of the league, which by the early 1980s was considered among the poorest in the country by noted publication *Baseball America*.

Once a postseason tournament had been secured, Wilhelm pushed for it to be played at a neutral site. He also convinced other schools to follow his lead and play more regular-season games, and in particular to play a more demanding non-conference schedule.

The 21 regular-season games Clemson played in Wilhelm's first year, 1958, were simply not enough, although it was a comparable number to every other school in the league. By 2002, all nine ACC schools played the maximum 56 games allowed by the NCAA, and each league member took a spring trip to play some of the top non-conference teams in the country.

Wilhelm also demanded a financial commitment to baseball. His early requests were often denied, but Wilhelm persisted.

"I want 24 dozen baseballs," Wilhelm told Clemson athletics director Frank Howard when the young coach was first hired after serving as an assistant at UNC.

"Wilhelm," Howard replied, "what are you going to do with 24 dozen baseballs?" To preserve what few new baseballs Wilhelm did get from Howard, he had the team warm up by throwing footballs.

His first budget in 1958 was an estimated $15,000. Wilhelm's early teams played on a pasture with wooden benches that served as dugouts and had no locker-room facilities. Much as the rest of the ACC, Clemson offered few if any athletic scholarships for baseball when Wilhelm arrived. Stowe, the All-America pitcher, was the lone scholarship player in 1958.

Otherwise, Wilhelm had a collection of basketball and football players who wanted to stay in shape during the off-season.

On road trips, Wilhelm at first conformed to a league policy that had teams stay in dormitories of fellow conference schools and eat on campus. At N.C. State, Duke and North Carolina, visiting teams often bunked in the basement of Reynolds Coliseum in Raleigh. That wasn't to Wilhelm's liking, and he was one of the first to book hotel rooms for his players and provide them with a per diem for meals at local cafeterias.

Wilhelm knew a thing or two about handling money. As the son of a tenant farmer in the Landis/China Grove area of North Carolina north of Charlotte, Wilhelm learned to live without. His father died when Wilhelm was 2, and his mother worked most of his childhood on 10-hour shifts for one dollar a day at a nearby textile mill. It was a big deal to young Wilhelm when the Landis professional baseball team raised the price of ice cream from a nickel a scoop to two for 15 cents.

His salary didn't reach $10,000 until his 11th season at Clemson. So it's little wonder Wilhelm shakes his head in disbelief when told Clemson recently built a centerfield backdrop for hitters at a cost of $80,000. By 2003, Clemson's $560,000 budget for baseball was representative of all those in the ACC. By 2003, Clemson coach Jack Leggett was earning $100,000, and every coach was indebted to Wilhelm.

He fought early for athletics directors to hire full-time baseball coaches and not to simply shuffle a football assistant to coach baseball in the "off-season."

The man had foresight, always seeming to view the game as if he were not only looking down the road but around the next corner. Wilhelm's teams in the late 1960s were among the first in the country to abandon wool uniforms in favor of the nylon stretch material still worn at all levels of the game today. In the early 1970s, Wilhelm changed from the common stirrup socks to pants with stripes down the side that were worn to the tops of the shoes.

By the turn of the century, the sans-stirrup look was all the rage in baseball.

"He loves the game of baseball and thought it should be played a certain way," said Neil Simons, an outfielder who played on the 1977 and 1980 Clemson teams that advanced to the College World Series. "He was interested in getting the best players he could and getting us to play our best. He always said, 'Let's play hard and play it right, and we'll come away winners.'"

For 36 years Wilhelm did it his way. His teams won 50 or more games five times. He produced 20 All-Americans and 100 players who signed professional baseball contracts. He elevated Clemson to national prominence and later was the guiding force in the ACC's being considered one of the nation's top baseball leagues.

"The game deserves our utmost respect," Wilhelm said. "It had my respect. I don't like to see people do things that seem to tarnish the image of baseball. I think it's because baseball is really the greatest game."

Tribble came across as "a dictator" according to Gene Hooks, who served under him as athletics director. The president hadn't been in place long when popular, successful football coach Douglas "Peahead" Walker, who took Wake to the 1949 Dixie Bowl, left for another job. In what's possibly an apocryphal story, Walker is credited with once convincing a prospect to come to Wake by taking him to Duke and calling it the Baptist school's "west campus."

According to one report, Tribble also wanted to fire basketball coach Murray Greason in 1955 for failure to properly teach free-throw shooting. This a mere two years after Wake, in its Southern Conference farewell, won the league tournament and title, breaking N.C. State's stranglehold.

Greason, a star forward on Wake's 1924 team, was the school's 11th basketball coach in 16 years when hired in 1934. He lived a block from Gore Gym, Wake's cozy, 2,200-seat brick arena, and is often remembered for a photo taken on Gore's steps surrounded by his dogs.

BELOW
Wake Forest men's basketball coach Murray Greason, shown here with his hunting dogs, was an avid outdoorsman. He often wore his hunting clothes to work because "I'm going hunting one of these days and [the athletics director] won't know what day it is."

The low-key Greason once sat through a game in a chair at mid-court beside a friend who coached the opposing team. He typically showed up for work dressed in hunting clothes. "Coach, why are you wearing your hunting clothes?" Francis, the sports information director, once asked. "I'm going hunting one of these days," came the reply, "and [athletics director] Weaver won't know what day it is."

Tribble's troubles intensified during the spring of 1955, when the baseball team reached the College World Series. Wake was the oldest Baptist college in the country and a showcase of social conservatism. When trustees voted in 1957 to allow dancing on campus, the issue became a statewide cause célébre and the decision was reversed. So of course Demon Deacon teams were forbidden to play on Sundays, a prohibition readily accommodated during the regular season.

Scheduling in the NCAA baseball tournament was less flexible. On the night of June 12, 1955, a Sunday, the Deacons played and beat Colorado State College, unleashing a furor back home. "Forfeit of the game is preferable to forfeit of the principles of Christianity," declared a Durham minister. Tribble rushed to offer assurance that "if I had known about this Sunday game, I would never have given my permission for it to be played."

Wake lost its next game, then rallied to win three straight and the 1955 baseball title, defeating Western Michigan in the final, 7-6. The team was greeted by 500 fans upon arrival at Raleigh-Durham airport and feted with a dinner at a Raleigh cafeteria. A year later, though, coach Taylor Sanford was forced to resign, pronouncing himself "disillusioned and deeply hurt by my situation here."

By November 1955, as tensions mounted over the move scheduled for June 1956 — an event ultimately chronicled in a four-page spread in *Life* magazine — Wake Forest trustees launched an investigation into the "overall situation" at the school. Wake historian Bynum Shaw wrote that "it was Tribble's relationship with the athletic program that brought all the resentments to a head."

An embittered Wake alumnus from Charlotte sent Tribble the following telegram during this period: "Once upon a time [President Harry] Truman flew over North Carolina with his family. His wife, Bess, said, 'I will make someone happy by dropping a dollar bill.' Margaret [his daughter] said, 'I will make two people happy by dropping two dollar bills.' The pilot and the entire crew said, 'Mr. Tribble, you drop out and make everybody happy.'"

Ill will spilled over on the night of Dec. 5, 1955. Wake football coach Tom Rogers had been fired and AD Pat Preston resigned. This sparked rumors athletics were being de-emphasized, prompting several hundred torch-carrying students to rally in protest.

Hanging someone in effigy was a fairly common occurrence.

Complete with signs such as "We want big-time athletics" and "Preston Gone, Rogers Gone, Tribble Next," they gathered on the president's lawn and burned him in effigy. Before moving to Rogers' home, then to a women's dorm — their focus dissolving into chants of "Beat State!" and "Panties!" — the students heard reassurance from Tribble, dressed in his bathrobe.

"The rumors about a de-emphasis plan at Wake Forest are entirely erroneous," he said. "There isn't anything in the world to that."

Hanging someone in effigy was a fairly common occurrence. Days before Wake students hoisted Tribble, Georgia Tech students gave Georgia Gov. Marvin Griffin the same treatment. They were angered that the Yellow Jackets might be kept from playing in a bowl game because the opponent had a black player. N.C. State fans hanged an effigy of Commissioner Weaver in 1957. Wake students did the same in 1959 and two years later hanged their own players in effigy. Maryland's Millikan was hanged by students in 1963, an action denounced by a school official as "strictly the work of a small group of campus beatniks."

Virginia students hanged their president in effigy during the 1970s for raising athletic fees; and, of course, in 1965 North Carolina students twice extended

87
24

similar treatment to Dean Smith, their young basketball coach.

Tribble became accustomed to being hanged in effigy. After Hooks chose not to retain interim basketball coach Jackie Murdock in 1966, word came that students planned to hang the AD in effigy, then repeat the treatment for the president.

"So I called Dr. Tribble and told him what was taking place," Hooks said. "About nine o'clock he called and said, 'Gene, have they come to your house yet?' I said, 'No, but I think I hear them coming down the street.' They were yelling, 'We want Jack back!' He said, 'How about telling them that if they don't come to my house by 9:30, I'm going to bed?'"

Murdock's presence recalled more glorious times. He had twice been an all-conference selection after playing a season alongside Dickie Hemric, the first Demon Deacon to have his jersey number retired.

Hemric repeated in 1955 as ACC player of the year. Only nine players have won the award at least twice, a third of them from Wake Forest. Hemric, the powerful, sure-handed center, finished with 2,587 points and 1,802 rebounds. Neither of his career totals has been matched by another ACC performer.

The 1955 season also saw Virginia's Buzz Wilkinson, a 6-2 guard, become the first college player to post consecutive 30-point seasons. Wilkinson's 32.1 average in 1955 remains the standard in ACC play. Duke, with Ronnie Mayer and Joe Belmont, went to the 1955 NCAA Tournament, replacing fourth-ranked N.C. State, the ACC's first-place finisher, tournament winner and automatic qualifier. The Wolfpack was on probation.

Duke tied for first in football with Maryland in 1955, a year after winning the ACC title outright. The Blue Devils had gone to the 1954 Orange Bowl and beaten Nebraska, 34-7. In 1955, third-ranked Maryland, 10-0 and the nation's leader in rushing defense, got the Orange Bowl bid to face Oklahoma. The Terps suffered a 20-6 loss, Tatum's second defeat at the hands of Bud Wilkinson, a protégé who took the reins when his boss moved to College Park following the 1946 season.

Maryland did win the first of its seven national men's lacrosse titles in 1955. ACC teams have won more championships in lacrosse, 14, than in any other men's sport: Maryland with seven (1955, 1956, 1960,

FACING PAGE
Wake Forest star Dickie Hemric (24) was the first Demon Deacon to have his jersey retired. He won the first two player of the year awards in the ACC. Hemric set the career ACC scoring (2,587 points) and rebounding (1,802 boards) records. He was named to the league's 50th anniversary team.

BELOW
Virginia guard Buzz Wilkinson's scoring average of 32.1 points per game in 1955 set a conference record. His 28.63-point scoring average is tops in ACC history.

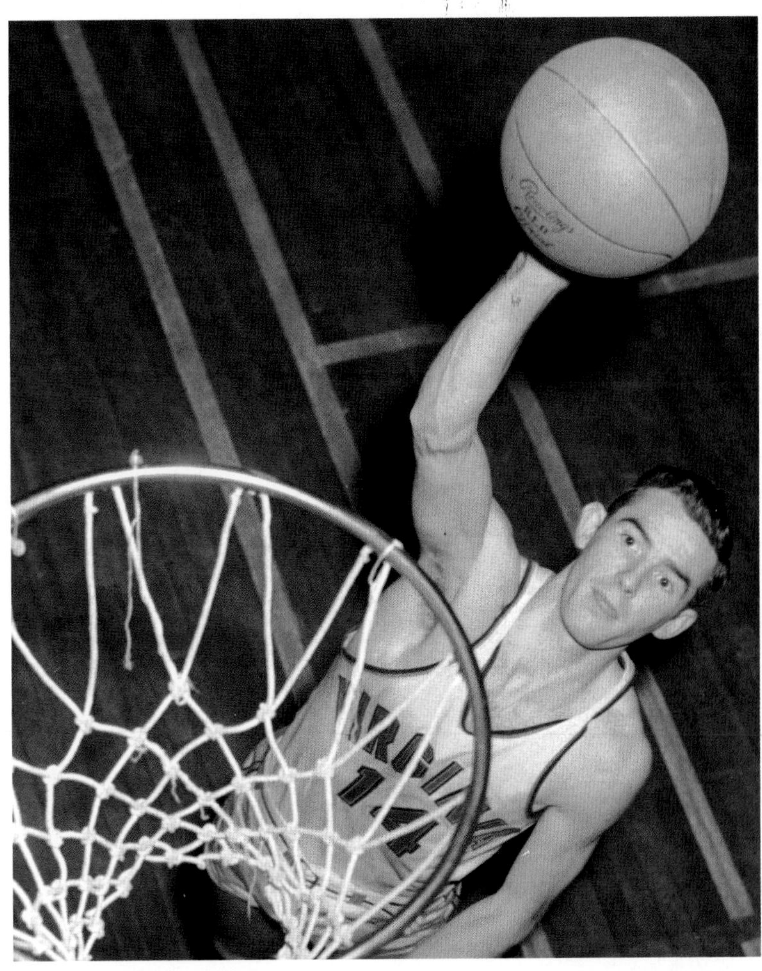

1967, 1968, 1973, 1975); North Carolina, four (1981, 1982, 1986, 1991), and Virginia, three (1970, 1972, 1999). The most pronounced ACC dominance is in women's soccer. North Carolina had won 17 of the 22 women's national championships contested through 2002, including 16 under NCAA sponsorship.

The athletic picture seemed even brighter at Maryland when the school opened its 14,500-seat Student Activities Center, better known as Cole Field House, on Dec. 2, 1955. The glow quickly faded. The following month Tatum announced that he had signed to coach at North Carolina, his alma mater.

Tatum, UNC Class of 1935, was recognized as one of the premier coaches at the time, particularly on the defensive side. His nine-year Maryland record was 73-15-4, with five bowl appearances, three undefeated regular seasons, three top-10 finishes in the polls and a national title.

The decision to return Tatum to Chapel Hill occasioned fierce internal debate at the university, Friday recalled. "There were lots of people that just didn't want him," Friday said. "He symbolized big-time college football, but he was an alumnus, and he came."

N.C. State had tried to sign Tatum several years earlier, but failed. Instead, in 1954 the Wolfpack turned to Earle Edwards, a Michigan State assistant and Penn State grad who proved one of the great program-builders in ACC football history.

At UNC, Tatum replaced George Barclay, a former teammate and the school's first football All-American in 1934. Dick Herbert, writing in Raleigh's *News & Observer*, called Tatum's Maryland success "phenomenal" and offered "that the Tar Heels will be a more formidable foe on the football field is almost certain."

Smallwood said that Tatum, who took a pay cut to go to UNC, was among the first modern coaches so organized that he would attend a game with a winner's speech in one pocket and a loser's remarks in the other. "Tatum was larger than life," Smallwood said. "Nice guy. I loved him. Tatum was probably dominant because he was years ahead of his peers in organization."

Duke's Carl James still speaks glowingly of Tatum's charisma. "I always felt, had Jim Tatum lived, North Carolina football would have been almost untouchable," he said. But Tatum would be dead before the decade ended, a victim of Rocky Mountain spotted fever in July 1959 at age 46. The North Carolina football program received no immediate bump from Tatum's presence, and Maryland went into a prolonged funk without him, failing to finish higher than third in the league for the next 17 seasons.

Clemson filled the breach, winning three of four ACC titles starting in 1956. The Tigers own part or all of 13 ACC football championships, most in history. The 1956 Tigers (7-2-2) lost to Colorado in the

12.5.55
Wake Forest students burn President Harold Tribble in effigy, protesting personnel changes and a reputed de-emphasis of athletics

1956

1.8.56
Jim Tatum signs as head football coach at UNC, leaving Maryland

5.5.56
Duke's Dave Sime sets a world's record in the 220-yard low hurdles with a time of 22.2 seconds

6.3.56
Duke's Dave Sime ties a world record in the 100-yard dash with a time of 9.3 seconds

Orange Bowl 27-21, rallying from a 20-point halftime deficit only to fall short after an onside kick backfired.

Two years later, again the ACC champion, Clemson finished 8-3, dropping a 7-0 decision in the Sugar Bowl that gave Louisiana State coach Paul Dietzel a national title. Then the 1959 Clemson squad beat Texas Christian in the Bluebonnet Bowl 23-7 to conclude a 9-2 season.

Now in Winston-Salem, Wake's Demon Deacons entered the 1956 season without a nearby football stadium, as would remain the case for the next dozen years. Bowman Gray Stadium served as the interim facility. It was located across town and notable for an asphalt track that surrounded the playing field. The track was used for stock-car racing.

The unfamiliar setting didn't bother the Deacons' Billy Barnes, who in 1956 became the first ACC back to rush for more than 1,000 yards (1,010 on 168 carries). Barnes was chosen the league's player of the year; the only other Wake players so honored were Brian Piccolo (1964) and Jay Venuto (1979).

The most intriguing development of the 1956 football season was the appearance of a four-game ACC regional television package put together by an entrepreneur named Castleman D. Chesley.

Television, as rock 'n' roll, had recently asserted its grip on American consciousness. As recently as 1949, the United States contained little more than a million television sets, almost half in New York City. There were 19 million sets three years later. A revolution in communication was in progress.

"People now expected to see events, not merely read about or hear them," David Halberstam wrote in *The Fifties*. "At the same time, the line between what happened in real life and what people saw on television began to merge; many Americans were now living far from their families, in brand-new suburbs where they barely knew their neighbors. Sometimes they felt closer to the people they watched on television than they did to their neighbors and distant families."

Soon, despite misgivings about compromising gate receipts and the electric thrill of a full house, the ACC would be among the first sports entities elevated by the new medium, its coaches, players and sponsors

BELOW
N.C. State's John Richter (left) and Lou Pucillo are two of the finest players in league history. Richter was a first-team All-ACC selection in 1959 and a first-round National Basketball Association draft choice. Pucillo won the awards as the 1959 ACC player of the year and athlete of the year.

“Nobody ever dreamed it,
WERE CLOSE FRIENDS unti

ABOVE
Vic Bubas, a former N.C. State player and future Duke head coach, sits next to Everett Case during Bubas' time as an assistant for the Wolfpack. Bubas, Case and Frank McGuire (right) are three of the most successful coaches in the history of Atlantic Coast Conference men's basketball.

but **EVERETT CASE AND I** the night we played."

— Frank McGuire

ABOVE

Frank McGuire was hired as the coach at North Carolina to counter Case's great success at N.C. State. The two coaches helped to make ACC basketball popular across the country as well as the region. McGuire's 1957 Tar Heels won the league's first national title in the sport. He left UNC in 1961, but later returned to the ACC to coach South Carolina.

transformed into familiar visitors to a region's living rooms. "Sail with the Pilot," theme music for Pilot Life Insurance commercials, still comes readily to the lips of many longtime viewers.

Although television found ACC football first, it would be through basketball telecasts that the league developed its cache. Perhaps had N.C. State, the nation's second-ranked team and the ACC's automatic qualifier, advanced to face No. 1 San Francisco with Bill Russell and K.C. Jones in the 1956 NCAA Tournament, the marriage might have happened sooner. But in one of the great upsets of the era, Canisius ousted the Wolfpack and the injured Shavlik, the league's player of the year, in four overtimes in their NCAA opener.

N.C. State would not make another visit to the NCAA Tournament until 1965.

Even when the Wolfpack won the ACC Tournament in 1959 behind Lou Pucillo's play, it was North Carolina that carried the conference banner in postseason. Case and staff had again run afoul of NCAA regulations. This time, illegal inducements in the 1956 recruitment of Jackie Moreland, a top prospect from Louisiana, had landed N.C. State a four-year, program-wide probation, a penalty virtually unmatched for the next three decades.

"We were sort of stunned by the fact that it resulted in that kind of action," said Vic Bubas, then Case's top assistant.

The Moreland case was an early test for Weaver, the second-year commissioner. After making his own investigation, he upheld the NCAA verdict and added sanctions, including that Moreland not play for the Wolfpack. The 6-7 center went on to Louisiana Tech and made his home state's basketball Hall of Fame.

"Jim Weaver wanted this conference to be admired for its integrity," said Gene Corrigan, who worked for Weaver as a young man and returned to serve as commissioner in 1987. "The NCAA wasn't a factor then. Conferences took care of all penalties. He had a very, very difficult job."

Today the ACC is a multimillion-dollar entity with almost two dozen employees and its own office building. In the early years, the league was staffed by Weaver and Thompson, his secretary, and headquartered in a two-room mezzanine suite in Greensboro's King Cotton Hotel.

The hotel was a favorite downtown eating spot, the dining ambience enhanced by a pianist stationed on the mezzanine. The pianist soon learned the fight songs for all the ACC schools, and at a sign from Thompson the appropriate melody would be offered to make guests feel welcome as Weaver escorted them downstairs for lunch.

But the commissioner also was required to set a different sort of tone, a fact that weighed heavily on Weaver, a big, outwardly gruff man with a long drawl and a dry wit. "Nobody in the whole world would know

11.30.56
Georgia Tech opens Alexander Memorial Coliseum with a 71-61 loss to Duke

2.9.57
Irwin Holmes and Manuel Crockett, the ACC's first African-American athletes, compete for N.C. State in a track meet against UNC

3.23.57
UNC beats Kansas 54-53 in three overtimes to win NCAA men's basketball title

10.19.57
Queen Elizabeth II and Prince Philip attend Maryland's 21-7 home football victory over North Carolina

how much Mr. Weaver agonized over a decision," Thompson said. "He agonized over being fair and doing what was right, not only for the conference but doing what was right for the kid."

The Moreland case, she said, proved especially painful. Weaver's verdict, while contested by N.C. State, was ultimately upheld. "I don't think you meet many people in your life that you can honestly say are wise," Smallwood said. "He was the wisest man I ever met."

Corrigan was similarly impressed. "He was really, truly my mentor, the best person I ever knew," Corrigan said. "He worried about the conference. He didn't trust the coaches. He knew some people couldn't count to 120 football scholarships (the limit at the time), and some people were walking around with a lot of money in their pockets for basketball players."

Fortunately for the ACC, while its premier basketball program was reeling, McGuire, Case's chief rival and public adversary, stepped to the fore. "Nobody ever dreamed it, but Everett Case and I were close friends until the night we played," McGuire said, "and then we were mad at each other."

Football was the dominant schoolboy sport in the Carolinas and points south, so McGuire, a native of Manhattan's East Side, imported players from his old haunts. The pipeline was dubbed the "Underground Railroad," reversing the direction of the clandestine network that led Southern slaves to freedom in pre-Civil War days.

Soon the Tar Heel starters hailed from the New York area — Joe Quigg and Pete Brennan from Brooklyn, Bob Cunningham and Lennie Rosenbluth from New York, Tommy Kearns from New Jersey. All but Rosenbluth were Catholics in a predominantly Baptist state. As McGuire's team became more successful, children in Chapel Hill and beyond began emulating their heroes by crossing themselves before shooting.

Led by Rosenbluth, a 6-5 senior, the 1956-57 Tar Heels made it through the regular season undefeated, their closest call coming at Maryland before 14,000 fans, then the largest crowd to watch an ACC game. Millikan was building a team that would win the next year's ACC Tournament, the only non-North Carolina squad to achieve that feat in the conference's first 17 years.

"The more you saw of McGuire's team that season, the more you caught the feeling it was a team of destiny," Add Penfield, an early radio announcer at Duke and Wake, recalled of the 1957 Tar Heels. "It was a team to capture the imagination, the product of the coaching genius that was McGuire."

The Tar Heels easily handled Clemson to open the ACC Tournament as Rosenbluth scored 45 points, a one-game record in the event that still stands. But, with a single team advancing from each league to the

1958

5.2.58
Open bowl policy adopted by ACC

1.1.59
Clemson loses Sugar Bowl 7-0 as Louisiana State and coach Paul Dietzel win national championship

1959

2.12.59
Fight erupts during Wake Forest basketball game versus North Carolina

5.6.59
Vic Bubas hired as Duke head coach, replacing Hal Bradley

7.23.59
North Carolina football coach Jim Tatum dies of Rocky Mountain spotted fever

NCAA Tournament, the season labeled "McGuire's Miracle" nearly ended in the semifinals against Greason's last Wake Forest club.

Wake held a two-point lead with less than a minute left. Rosenbluth, the 1957 ACC and national player of the year, drove down the lane. As he launched a hook shot, the Tar Heel center collided with Deacon defender Wendell Carr. The shot went in. Referee Jim Mills blew his whistle. In one of the most controversial calls in conference history, the basket counted and Rosenbluth was awarded a free throw. He made that too, and UNC hung on for a 61-59 victory.

The next night North Carolina earned the automatic bid, easily besting South Carolina and Grady Wallace, whose 31.2-point average made him the first and only ACC player to lead the NCAA in scoring.

By now Chesley, a former UNC football player who had had experience with the ABC, NBC and Dumont TV sports divisions, had taken acute notice. When the Tar Heels reached the Final Four, he began telecasting the games back to North Carolina on a five-station network.

The Tar Heels put on an excellent show. First they beat Michigan State in triple overtime. The next day they faced Kansas and 7-foot center Wilt Chamberlain, a sophomore who averaged nearly 30 points per game. "Nobody thought they had a chance in this world," Smallwood said.

In a breathtaking act of daring, McGuire sent the 5-11 Kearns to contest the opening tap against Chamberlain. "When he jauntily stepped in against Chamberlain, Wilt was as thunderstruck as the spectators and the Kansas bench were," announcer Penfield wrote in his memoirs. "Kearns' appearance in this outwardly ridiculous role was, of course, a carefully-thought-out piece of strategy concocted by McGuire, the crafty New York Irishman, and his sidekick, Buck Freeman. They felt they had to do something to psychologically throw Chamberlain off stride.

"They succeeded."

Despite losing Rosenbluth to fouls during regulation play, UNC emerged victorious by a point, the difference a pair of free throws by Quigg with six seconds remaining in the third overtime.

The response among North Carolinians was tremendous. "As a single event, probably nothing so mesmerized the state as that did," Smallwood said.

"They were renting TV sets for hospitals," Chesley told the *Greensboro Daily News*. "It was the damnedest thing you ever heard of. I knew right then and there that ACC basketball could be as popular as any TV show that was shown in North Carolina."

The next season, Chesley presented a

FACING PAGE
South Carolina's Grady Wallace led the nation in scoring in 1957 by averaging 31.2 points per game. He remains the only ACC player to lead the nation in scoring.

BELOW
North Carolina's 1957 team won the ACC's first national championship in men's basketball, going 32-0 and defeating heavy favorite Kansas and center Wilt Chamberlain in the title game. ACC basketball exploded onto the scene after that, thanks in part to the television broadcast of the game.

CAROLINA
42

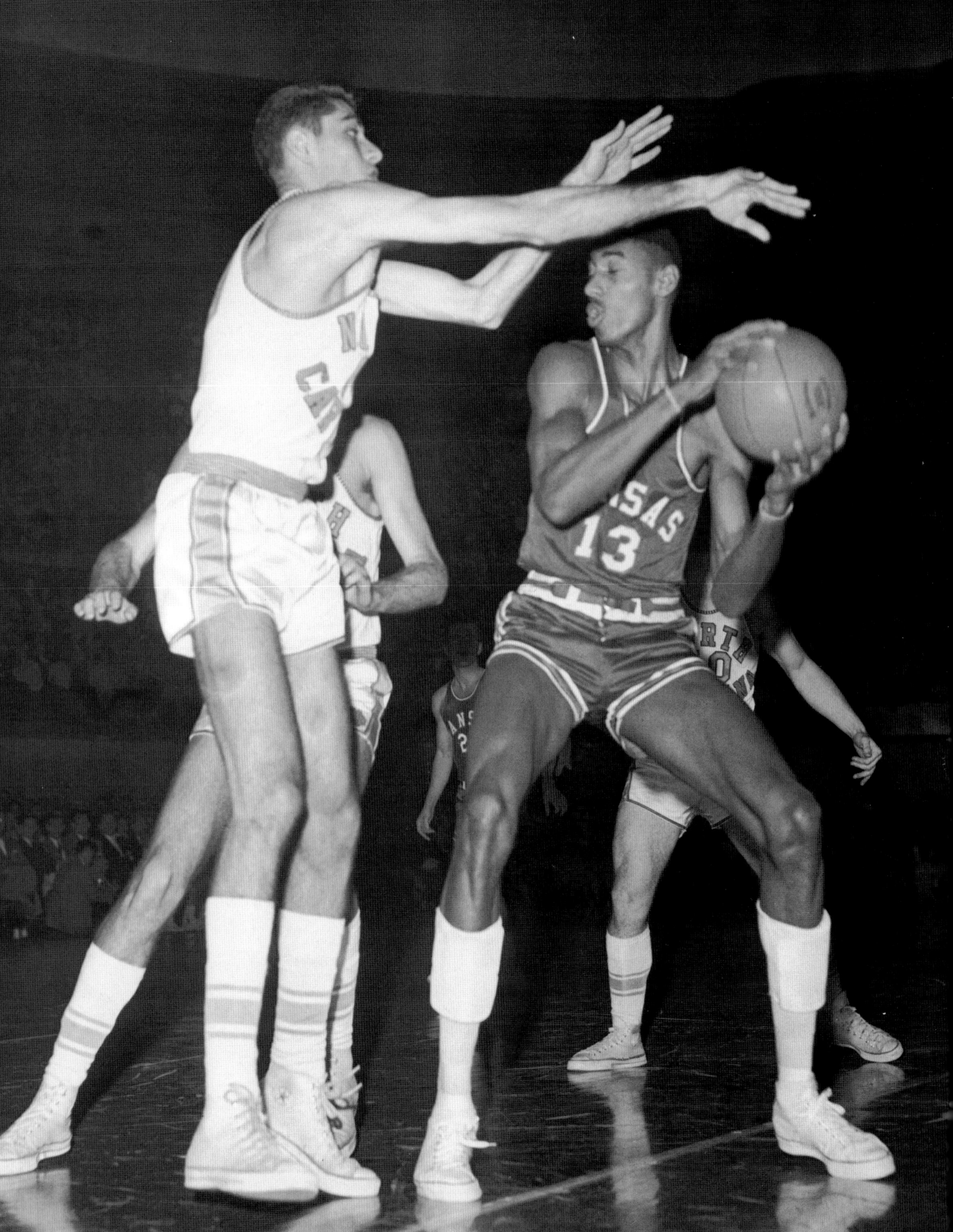
13

regular schedule of ACC telecasts and the landscape of regional and national sports began to change. "His was strictly a business scheme, but what he meant to the conference can never be calculated in dollars and exposure," Bob Quincy of the *Charlotte Observer* wrote of Chesley.

"To me, the thing that probably made the ACC a household name was C.D. Chesley," Corrigan said. "And even today, nobody makes the money off basketball that the ACC does."

While UNC basked in its basketball supremacy, the first of nine men's titles won by league members, virtually no fanfare greeted another ACC milestone that winter semester of 1957. Irwin Holmes and Manuel Crockett, a pair of N.C. State runners, competed in a February track meet against North Carolina. It was the first time African-American athletes appeared in ACC competition.

Later that same year the ACC football season proved nearly as memorable as its winter counterparts. Queen Elizabeth II and Prince Philip of England, featured on the cover of the Maryland football media guide, attended the Terrapins' Oct. 19 home game. Maryland beat North Carolina and Tatum, 21-7.

More important, the league race came down to the last weekend and the deciding contest came down to the final play, a moment that capped the greatest individual performance in ACC football history.

Edwards' first N.C. State recruiting class had matured into seniors. Led by the "Pony Backfield" of Dick Hunter and Dick Christy, the 1957 ACC player of the year — "We're Bettin' on the Ponies!" proclaimed the cover of the school's football media guide — the Wolfpack journeyed to South Carolina battling Duke for the conference football title. Since the school's basketball-spawned probation barred postseason play, in essence this was the Wolfpack's bowl game.

Rain fell on the morning of Nov. 23, and gray clouds overhung Carolina Stadium as halfback Alex Hawkins and the Gamecocks jumped to a 19-6 lead late in the second quarter. No other team all year scored more than two touchdowns against N.C. State.

MEET THE 1957
WOLFPACK
WE'RE BETTIN' ON THE PONIES!
DICK CHRISTY
DICK HUNTER
NORTH CAROLINA STATE COLLEGE
RALEIGH, N. C.

FACING PAGE
North Carolina All-American Lennie Rosenbluth leans over Kansas center Wilt Chamberlain in the 1957 national championship game. The Tar Heels upset Kansas to win the title, the first national championship for the ACC in men's basketball. The Helms Foundation named Rosenbluth the national player of year. Rosenbluth still ranks among the leaders at UNC in many statistical categories.

LEFT
The 1957 N.C. State media guide featured the "Pony Backfield" of Dick Hunter and Dick Christy. Christy was the ACC player of the year that season and the athlete of the year in the league. A first-team All-American in 1957, Christy held 14 school and four conference records when his career ended. He went on to play five seasons in professional football and was selected team MVP in 1962 for the New York Titans (later Jets), when he led the team in rushing, punt returns and kickoff returns.

FACING PAGE
Teammates and fans carry Dick Christy off the field after he scored all of the Wolfpack's 29 points in a stirring victory at South Carolina in the final regular-season game of 1957. The winning score came on the only field goal of his career. He also scored four touchdowns and kicked two extra points.

BELOW
Alex Hawkins of South Carolina was the 1958 ACC player of the year. Hawkins played both offense and defense. He played pro football and has written two best-selling books on his experiences in football and life. He is a member of the league's 50th anniversary team.

Christy, who ran for the Wolfpack's first touchdown, scored again to cut the lead just before halftime. Then he capped a drive to open the second half with a touchdown run that tied the score at 19. "He was a super athlete," recalled Bill McLellan, a former Clemson player, coach and athletics director. "Given an opportunity, he could go the distance any time."

N.C. State went ahead late in the game 26-19 as again Christy ran it in and again kicked the extra point, his second of the game and his career. Hunter was missing extra points, so he and Christy, the holder, had traded places.

USC rallied to tie the score at 26-26 with 1:19 to go. Edwards believed in passing sparingly — 87 times all year — but as time ran down, his quarterback threw and Hawkins made what seemed a game-saving interception. Hawkins, who would be the 1958 ACC player of the year, ran the ball back 68 yards to the N.C. State 17-yard line. The game clock expired, and fans swarmed the field in celebration.

Unfortunately for the home crowd, as in the 1957 ACC Tournament, a penalty swung the balance. Defensive interference was called on South Carolina. The ball was placed on the USC 30 with no time showing on the clock.

Christy, who had occasionally made field goals in practice, now asked Edwards to let him try a 46-yarder. With little to lose, the coach consented. "The ball was low, and it seemed to hang in the heavy air," Jack Briebart wrote in Raleigh's *The News & Observer*. "But it reached its mark, and it was accurate."

Christy never raised his gaze until the ball went through the uprights. "Man, I was stunned," he said. "But, oh, it felt good."

Then word came North Carolina had rallied from 13 points down to upset Duke after seven straight losses in the series, clinching the Wolfpack's first undisputed league title, Southern Conference included. UNC's Tatum called the Tar Heels' win "my greatest thrill in football" and "the happiest day I've ever known," his grin "as wide as his five-gallon hat," according to an observer.

Duke had the last laugh. N.C. State was on probation, so the Blue Devils were picked to go to the 1957 Orange Bowl. They lost to Oklahoma 48-21. N.C. State folks celebrated, too. Players tossed Edwards and his assistants in the shower.

Christy, killed nine years later in an auto accident, took off his uniform for the last time. He had unknowingly achieved ACC immortality, accounting for every one of his team's 29 points. The winning score to clinch the title came on the only field goal of his career. ✯

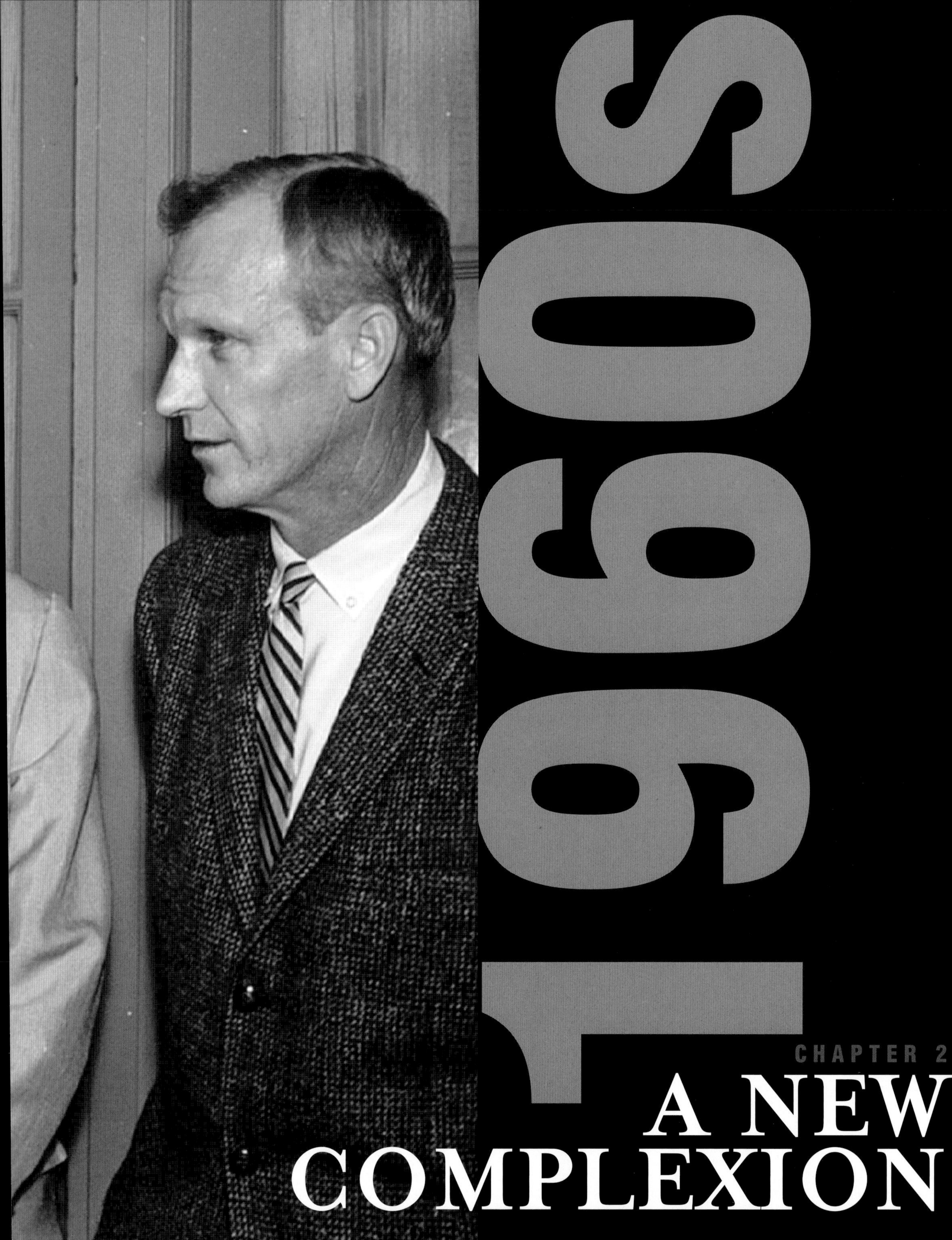

1960s

CHAPTER 2

A NEW COMPLEXION

FACING PAGE
Wake Forest sophomore Billy Packer (right) stands next to teammate Dave Budd. Packer played for the Deacons from 1960-62 and was a member of the school's only Final Four team. He went on to become a renowned television analyst for college basketball.

BELOW
The Dixie Classic, started by N.C. State coach Everett Case and played at Reynolds Coliseum, was one of the most popular holiday tournaments in the United States. Top collegiate teams from around the nation came to Raleigh to play the Wolfpack, Duke, North Carolina and Wake Forest.

The dawn of the 1960s was neither kind nor gentle, in keeping with the tumult and challenges to come. Driving home from Raleigh on New Year's Day in 1960, Murray Greason, the retired and retiring Wake Forest basketball coach, apparently fell asleep at the wheel of his Buick sedan, hit a Greensboro bridge abutment and was killed on impact.

Greason, then a Wake Forest assistant athletics director for public relations, had interrupted an outdoorsman's vacation to attend the 1959 Dixie Classic. The 58-year-old saw quite a show: Wake's first title of any kind in seven seasons.

The Deacons, led by sophomore guard Billy Packer, dispatched ranked teams from Holy Cross and Dayton before beating North Carolina 53-50 for the Dixie championship. The Deacons had never previously won the prestigious event. When the game ended, a happy Greason ran onto the court shouting "We did it! We did it!" and danced a jig with Horace "Bones" McKinney, his former assistant, 1957 co-coach and successor on the bench.

Barely a year later, the Dixie Classic, too, was gone, victim of the second national point-shaving scandal in little more than a decade.

Unhappy endings weren't confined to ACC basketball. The '60s dawned without "Big Thursday," South Carolina's hoariest football tradition, the annual match-up between the Clemson Tigers and South Carolina Gamecocks during the state fair.

The teams met in late October or early November all but seven years starting in 1896, giving athletic form to a rivalry sparked by Gov. Ben "Pitchfork" Tillman. Disdainful of the supposedly elitist university in Columbia, he helped start an agricultural college at Clemson. "It's time the citizens of South Carolina had a state college they can be proud of," he said. To which one state legislator replied, "The farmers of this state need a college education like they need a telegraph line to the moon."

The well-attended Tiger-Gamecock games were always played in Columbia, site of the state fair, because USC's stadium held far more spectators than Memorial Coliseum, Clemson's 20,500-seat home field. Clemson was a military school until 1955, and its students arrived by the trainload to bivouac on the state fairgrounds, where their rifles, bayonets fixed, were ceremoniously stacked outside their tents.

Big Thursday reached a popular crescendo in 1946. Thousands of counterfeit tickets were printed to the sold-out game, causing would-be spectators to angrily storm the gates. With no seats available, fans lined the field to watch the Gamecocks win, 26-14. Afterward Clemson's Frank

AKE FOR
REST
34
EAST BILT

Howard claimed he spent the entire contest standing behind a woman with a big hat. "Every few minutes I'd tap her on the shoulder and ask how Clemson was doing," the coach said. "She'd just turn around and glare at me, so I figured Clemson must not be doing too good."

Clemson's Memorial Coliseum, constructed in 1941 with the help of Howard and some of his tree-clearing players, was expanded to outstrip South Carolina's capacity. By 1960, Big Thursday was history, the game rotating annually between the schools.

Meanwhile, there was rich symbolism in a death in Texas on the eve of the 1960s. Walter Williams, the last surviving veteran of the Civil War, died at age 117 on Dec. 20, 1959. The war he had fought had finally passed beyond living memory.

Yet fundamental differences involved in that struggle endured, and during the '60s agitation to end racial discrimination peaked.

A key chapter in the fight to achieve full citizenship for African-Americans opened just down the street from the ACC's Greensboro office, as black students began a galvanizing lunch counter sit-in at Woolworth's on February 1, 1960. Soon civil rights demonstrations became an uncomfortable part of American life in communities around the country.

Segregation was common in much of the United States, although observed more by custom than law outside the South. Racial separation and a code of conduct and thought that stressed the superiority of whites were painstakingly legislated and strictly enforced in the South and many adjoining states, beginning in the late 19th century. Las Vegas even banned blacks as gamblers at its casinos until 1960.

For many years an unwritten rule kept Northern teams from using African-American players against a Southern opponent, regardless of where the game took place. Finally in early 1941, Maryland permitted a black lacrosse player from Harvard to compete in a match at College Park, a first for a school south of the Mason-Dixon line. Virginia broke another barrier in October 1947 when it played a Harvard football squad that included an African-American. (On that Crimson roster was Robert F. Kennedy, the future U.S. attorney general and senator who attended law school at Virginia.)

Integrated teams soon played on ACC basketball courts, particularly in the Dixie Classic. Black spectators sat in Reynolds Coliseum's Section 48 and saw the likes of Cincinnati's Oscar Robertson and Michigan State's Johnny Green compete against the ACC's all-white squads.

Typical of the times, some white spectators recall no catcalls or boos directed at Robertson during a 1958 appearance marred by a tussle with Wake's combative Dave Budd. African-Americans in attendance, and others such as Packer, a Wake freshman from Pennsylvania, heard plenty.

1960

1.1.60
Former Wake Forest basketball coach Murray Greason killed in auto accident

1961

7.1.61
ACC minimum SAT score of 750 goes into effect for athletic eligibility

750

11.11.61
South Carolina students impersonate Clemson football players prior to game, nearly sparking melee

William Friday, longtime president of the consolidated University of North Carolina system, recalled a positive reception for Robertson, Green and others at the Dixie Classic and found affirmation in what he witnessed.

"I knew that sport was going to be the way that people would get to understand what integration really means," Friday said. "You see, everybody identifies with sports. ... It became the vehicle of integration in the South. No question about it."

Integration came gradually to ACC student bodies and teams, even in the wake of the U.S. Supreme Court's 1954 ruling in *Brown v. Board of Education,* which found that "separate education facilities are inherently unequal." Responding proactively to a ruling many Southern political leaders vowed to resist, ACC members Maryland, North Carolina and N.C. State quickly opened their doors to undergraduate students regardless of race.

The majority of league schools waited until the early '60s. "Men of good will who are most dedicated to the interests of the University honestly differ about the issue," wrote Duke President A. Hollis Edens. A majority of Wake Forest students voted in chapel just two months after lunch counter sit-ins started in nearby Greensboro that they preferred to "never integrate."

Three years later, Wake had integrated and announced boldly it was "actively recruiting" black athletes.

By decade's end, many predominantly white Southern schools had only a smattering of African-American undergraduates. Ernie Jackson, among Duke's first black football players in 1967, recalled few African-Americans on campus during his career. Virginia, still all male, had 22 African-American undergrads out of 4,500 in 1968. "Trying to convince prospective black student-athletes that Virginia was the place for them was like trying to persuade [actress] Zsa Zsa Gabor that a fortnight at a cloistered nunnery would be fun," author Gary Cramer wrote of that period.

Complicating the issue, African-American students emerged from historically underfunded educational institutions, as well as from a distinctly separate culture.

The first ACC squad to integrate was N.C. State's track team with sprinters Manuel Crockett and Irwin Holmes. The two competed in a meet against UNC in February 1957. Later that semester Holmes switched to tennis, advancing to co-captain by 1960, his senior year. That, too, was a first for an African-American in the ACC, according to Charles H. Martin's excellent 1999 study, *The Rise and Fall of Jim Crow in Southern College Sports: The Case of the Atlantic Coast Conference.*

As integration advanced some ACC football and basketball coaches entertained the possibility of recruiting top African-American athletes who previously attended all-black schools or fled the region entirely. "[Leaving] was a route that a lot of kids had to take," Duke's Jackson said. "There

1962

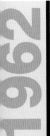

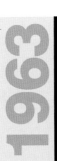

3.23.62
Wake Forest loses 84-68 against Ohio State in its only Final Four appearance

1963

8.28.63
Martin Luther King Jr. leads March on Washington for equal rights

11.22.63
President John Kennedy assassinated

ABOVE
Wake Forest's Charlie Davis (12) became the first African-American to be named ACC player of the year in basketball. Davis was a three-time All-ACC selection from 1969-71. His career scoring average of 24.9 is among the best in the league and set a school record.

was no room for you in Southern schools."

Years later, when Michigan State finished second in the football polls, its only blemish a tie against Notre Dame, the Spartan quarterback was Jimmy Raye from Fayetteville, N.C. He had been interested in UNC, N.C. State or Wake Forest, he told Robert C. Hunter of *Ebony* magazine in 1966. "Any one of those three schools would have been all right with me, but I didn't get the opportunity to go."

Maryland, farthest north in the ACC, finally broke the league's color barrier in football when Darryl Hill, a transfer from Navy, played for coach Tom Nugent in 1963 and '64. Hill, a 6-foot wingback who also kicked extra points and returned kickoffs and punts, finished third in the league in 1963 with 43 pass receptions, averaging 12 yards per catch. Hill was second in scoring behind Duke running back Jay Wilkinson and caught seven touchdown passes, an ACC record at the time. (The current record for single-season touchdown receptions is 17, set by Duke's Clarkston Hines in 1989.) Among Hill's TD catches was a game-winner with three seconds remaining against Air Force.

Maryland likewise had the ACC's first African-American basketball players, local products Julius "Pete" Johnson and Billy Jones.

The pair played freshman ball in 1964-65. The next season Jones moved to the

ABOVE
Charles Scott of North Carolina was the first nationally prominent African-American bask ball player in the ACC. His success helped pa the way for minorities for years to come. He averaged 22.1 points p game and still ranks among the most prolifi scorers in UNC history. He was a two-time All-American and an academic All-American

WARMER CLIMES

Notable African-American Players From ACC Region
Forced To Go North And West To Play Major-College Basketball

Player	College Attended (Years)	Departed From
Elgin Baylor	Seattle (1956-58)	Washington, D.C.
Walt Bellamy	Indiana (1959-61)	New Bern, N.C.
Walt Frazier	Southern Illinois (1964-67)	Atlanta, Ga.
Lou Hudson	Minnesota (1964-66)	Greensboro, N.C.
Dave Bing	Syracuse (1964-66)	Washington, D.C.

varsity while Johnson was redshirted. Each played three varsity seasons under Bud Millikan. By the time Johnson completed his career in 1969, all four ACC schools in North Carolina had black players. Two were destined for stardom, North Carolina's Charles Scott and Wake's Charlie Davis.

More mundane considerations, particularly commitment of resources, quickly distanced the North Carolina schools from the rest of the ACC in basketball.

While Duke, UNC, N.C. State and Wake each had two full-time assistants at the start of the '60s, Virginia's Billy McCann had none, and the South Carolina schools and Maryland had one each. Millikan didn't have a full-time assistant at College Park until the 1961-62 season. McCann got one at Charlottesville the following year.

"Frank Fellows was [Bud's] main assistant when I was there," said Gary Williams, a Terrapin guard from 1964-67 and now the Maryland head coach. "Frank Fellows taught three PE (physical education) courses a day. He was supposed to be his recruiter, scout. That's when you could go scout games, and Frank couldn't leave all the time because of his class schedule. It was a joke."

Imbalances in resources and competitive success were not limited to basketball. Gene Corrigan took over as Virginia's director of athletics in 1971, and in 1979 issued an internal report outlining numerous steps needed to bring the Cavaliers up to speed with the rest of the ACC. "It took them 20 years to make a commitment to be in the ACC," Corrigan said. "That's why they were so bad."

Virginia had a single winning record in football during the '60s and none in basketball, in which it finished last in the ACC from 1960 through 1964. Only once during the decade (1969) did Virginia reach double-digits in basketball wins. The football Cavaliers started the decade on an ACC-record 28-game losing streak, which began in 1958 and didn't end until the '61 opener against William & Mary.

Wake, at which salaries and other spending long trailed the rest of the league, didn't have a winning football season during the 1960s, either. "I think we had $10,000 to recruit with, and our scholarships were limited," said Bill Tate, Wake coach from 1964-68. "I think we had in the neighborhood of 60 scholarships." The ACC allowed twice that many.

North Carolina enjoyed a single winning season during the decade, going 9-2 in 1963 under coach Jim Hickey. South Carolina didn't post a winning football record until the final year of the decade, when it captured its first and only ACC title.

Maybe the best football team of the period was Duke's 1960 squad. Bill Murray's 8-3 Blue Devils finished 10th in the polls and beat No. 7 Arkansas 7-6 before 74,000 fans at the Cotton Bowl. A 9-yard pass from quarterback Don Altman to end Tee Moorman in the final three minutes, followed by Art Browning's extra point, secured the victory. That proved the ACC's last berth in the major New Year's Day bowls (Rose, Cotton, Orange, Sugar) until Maryland made the top 10 in 1976.

Duke won its fourth ACC title in 1960, and by 1965 had six first-place finishes in the league's 13 seasons. Yet Murray had to lobby athletics director Eddie Cameron to increase his full-time assistants to seven, the number serving Jim Tatum when Maryland football reached prominence a decade earlier.

Television served as a major handicap for ACC football, while the regional basketball network was a league bulwark.

The NCAA had a national television football package that guaranteed each major conference three regional or national appearances over a two-year span. Surveying 1966 and '67, ACC administrators found the league had gotten the minimal three exposures. That trailed 10 other conferences. Teams such as Southern California, Michigan, Texas, Nebraska, Alabama and Notre Dame showed up regularly in the top 10 and seemed omnipresent on the airwaves.

"I can remember wondering," said John Swofford, a UNC football player who graduated in 1971 and is now ACC commissioner, "because we didn't have many games on television ... and it seemed like a few conferences, very few conferences, had a real monopoly on that and consequently that was what people perceived to be better than the programs that weren't on television."

Nor was opportunity shared evenly within the ACC. Most games involving league teams showed Duke, North Carolina, Maryland and Clemson, in that order, and were regional, not national, telecasts.

A document prepared at one have-not school arguing for a more inclusive policy was revealingly titled "Wake Forest University Should Be on NCAA Football Television in 1968!" Among the arguments marshaled was that "our neighboring conference, the Southeast (sic), has developed

Perhaps the **BEST FOOTBALL TEAM** of the period was **DUKE'S 1960 SQUAD.**

ABOVE
Coach Bill Murray is carried off the field by a jubilant Duke football team after a victory over rival North Carolina. Murray was a former Blue Devil player who returned to coach Duke from 1951-65. A member of the college football Hall of Fame, Murray's teams at Duke and Delaware went 144-68-12. His 1960 Blue Devils won the school's fourth league championship and then defeated Arkansas 7-6 in the Cotton Bowl. His Duke teams were in the Orange Bowl in 1955 and '58.

a tremendous program, largely through television and has grown so wealthy through the process that many schools in that conference keep full-time recruiters in the ACC and other conference areas."

There was much discussion of another perceived recruiting disadvantage in relation to the SEC, talk that would ultimately lead to South Carolina's withdrawal from the ACC.

Commissioner Weaver argued in a November 1959 ACC bulletin that "we would be making a lasting contribution to the betterment of intercollegiate athletics should we adopt legislation assuring a uniform academic standard which must be met by the recipients of aid." The ACC's leadership agreed, and in May 1960 the league unilaterally adopted a minimum SAT score of 750 for incoming students to compete in intercollegiate athletics. This came at a time when some powerful national programs were revealed to be using players who lacked high-school diplomas.

By 1964 the ACC had raised the SAT bar to a score of 800. Soon thereafter, the NCAA adopted a uniform standard, one lower than the ACC's. The SEC went with the NCAA rule.

"The football coaches from back then would tell you, if they were alive, that the 800 rule killed them," Corrigan said. "It didn't hurt basketball."

ACC basketball did flourish, but not before suffering serious setbacks during the early '60s. The blows landed in a hurry — in some cases quite literally as serious fights erupted during games. Frank McGuire's Tar Heels were usually involved.

Late in a contest at Winston-Salem on Feb. 12, 1959, a fight started after UNC's Lee Shaffer and Wake's Budd and Charlie Forte struggled for a rebound. Punches were thrown, reserves rushed into the fray from team benches under the baskets, and fans came out of the stands.

Police and others moved to restore order while the pep band played the Wake fight song and the national anthem. Commissioner Jim Weaver reprimanded Budd and censured the coaches. The commissioner had earlier confided a warning to Wake President Harold Tribble that "the antics of Bones McKinney" were "not taken seriously by anyone" but at home "might tend to incite the students."

Two years after the dustup in Winston-Salem, another fight resulted in the suspension of three players for the remainder of the 1961 regular season. This time the scuffle was ignited by Art Heyman's hard foul in the final seconds of Duke's 81-77 win over North Carolina at Durham. Again players, students and other spectators participated in the brawl.

Weaver tabbed Heyman, UNC's Larry Brown and Don Walsh as the primary culprits, although he had words of rebuke for argumentative coaches, rude fans and "juvenile delinquents" among students. "Basketball in this area has developed

1964

3.64
Frank McGuire returns to college and ACC as head coach at South Carolina

7.1.64
800 SAT minimum adopted by ACC

1965

1.6.65
Dean Smith hanged in effigy after a 107-85 loss to Wake

1.13.65
Dean Smith hanged in effigy after a 65-62 loss to N.C. State

tremendously during the past decade; player technique is at times phenomenal," Weaver said. "It is regrettable that spectator conduct has not kept pace."

Heyman sat out six games but was allowed to compete in the ACC Tournament. The issue of postseason play did not arise for the Tar Heels. McGuire decided to hold his fifth-ranked team out of the tournament because it was on a year's probation and couldn't compete in the NCAAs, anyway. The punishment resulted from excessive entertainment expenses in recruiting and lack of adequate accounting procedures.

The only other time a team did not compete in the ACC Tournament was 1991, when Maryland was on probation.

These blemishes were nothing compared with the national point-shaving scandal that engulfed North Carolina, N.C. State and 23 other schools in 1961.

An investigation by New York district attorney Frank Hogan led to accusations that more than 50 players fixed some 54 games between 1956 and 1961. Four N.C. State players — Don Gallagher, Terry Litchfield, Anton Muehlbauer and Stan Niewierowski — and North Carolina's Lou Brown shaved points for pay. Two other UNC players, Ray Stanley and Doug Moe, were suspended from school for not reporting bribery attempts. Only Brown was ever convicted of a crime, although the N.C. State players admitted their complicity and cooperated with investigators.

Memories of a similarly far-reaching betting scandal a decade earlier were still fresh in many minds. The revelations devastated previously powerful programs at Long Island University and City College of New York and made Madison Square Garden a pariah in college sports. To prevent similar fallout, North Carolina university leaders took decisive action. Schedules and scholarships were reduced at N.C. State and North Carolina. Organized summer basketball participation was banned.

Most notably, an end was ordered to the 12-year-old Dixie Classic, which President Friday said exemplified "the exploitation for public entertainment or for budgetary or commercial purpose of a sports program which properly exists as an adjunct to collegiate education." Despite the fact the Dixie Classic was not directly tainted by game-fixing, drew 70,000 fans in 1960 and had an estimated economic impact of seven to nine million dollars in the Raleigh area, Friday said he never regretted his decision.

"It was hard because I knew what I was getting into — the harshest public criticism of anything you could do," Friday said. "I was actually told by the district attorney that these gamblers had taken these athletes outside Reynolds Coliseum, stuck a gun in their stomach, and said, 'Give me back the money.' You have something like that on your hands, you have to get rid of it."

Reynolds remained the region's prime

.13.65
.C. State defeats
orida State 3-0 in
e Wolfpack's last
ame at 59-year-old
ddick Stadium

12.5.65
Virginia opens University Hall with a 99-73 loss to Kentucky

1966

4.30.66
Everett Case dies. Press Maravich announced as LSU head coach

9.24.66
Howard's Rock installed at Death Valley

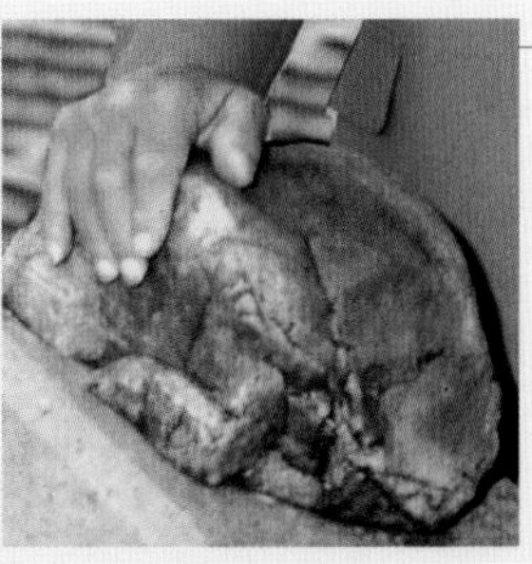

By Bryan Strickland

ACC EXCELLENCE

BLUE DEVILS SET STANDARD IN WOMEN'S TENNIS

Women's tennis at Duke looked a lot like the other ACC programs in the mid-1980s. The Blue Devils had enjoyed their share of success, posting a winning record in 12 of their first 14 years of existence, but the program hadn't really done anything to set it apart.

But the Blue Devils soon took on a much different image — the unmistakable look of an ACC dynasty. They began to separate themselves when three players who couldn't be distinguished from one another took the courts at Duke Tennis Stadium.

The O'Reilly sisters, a set of identical triplets from New Jersey, posted a true triple threat that helped put Duke women's tennis atop the ACC to stay.

"That was sort of the beginning of the dynasty," said Jacki Silar, an associate director of athletics at Duke. "It's kind of like what they talk about when Coach (Mike Krzyzewski) got Johnny Dawkins — it was just kind of the snowball effect."

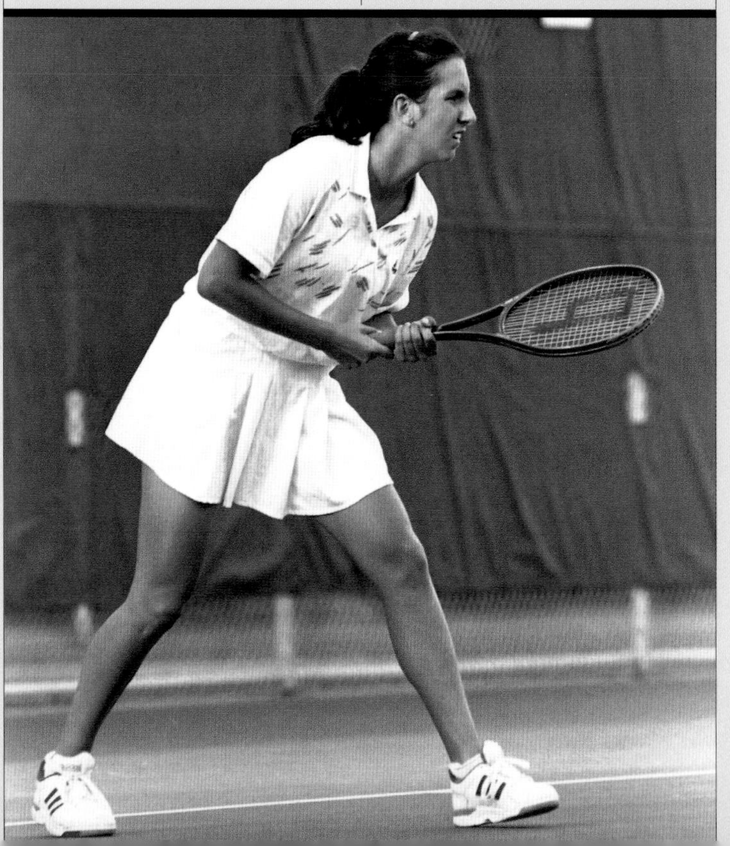

From 1987-90, the O'Reilly sisters — Patti, Christine and Theresa — launched an all-out assault on the ACC. Patti was twice named an All-American. She and Christine won ACC individual titles, but the triplets' cumulative contributions went well beyond their trophies.

The O'Reillys' decision to attend Duke instead of national power Stanford — and Duke's decision to spend the money on scholarships for them — led other top tennis players to consider Duke. By their sophomore season, the O'Reillys had helped Duke rise to the top of the ACC. During their junior season in 1989, the O'Reillys helped Duke start a winning streak in ACC matches that didn't end until the turn of the new century.

"They were certainly a boost," said Jane Preyer, the former Duke coach who recruited the O'Reillys. "First of all, they were excellent players. Second, they were very team-oriented. They had been their own little team all their lives, and they brought that to the rest of the team. And third, it was a unique situation that brought a lot of visibility to the program."

Duke's tennis program actually began when the O'Reillys were toddlers, and it started with great promise. Duke's first coach, Calla Raynor, guided the Blue Devils to a 100-25 record from 1973-81.

But in the early days of ACC women's tennis, it was UNC and Clemson — not Duke — that dominated play. The Tar Heels, behind longtime coach Kitty Harrison, won the first four ACC championships from 1977-80. The Tigers, led by four-time ACC player of the year Susan Hill and future pro star Gigi Fernandez, won the next six titles from 1981-87.

But in 1988, the O'Reillys' sophomore year, Duke won the first of 14 consecutive ACC tournament titles, a conference record.

The remarkable run began to take shape in 1986 when Preyer took over as head coach. A North Carolina graduate, Preyer played professional tennis in the late 1970s and early 1980s, climbing to a No. 42 world ranking before an elbow injury ended her career.

Preyer turned to coaching, accepting the head job at Duke before the 1986 season. Her presence made an immediate difference. Duke went 11-14 in 1985, but the Blue Devils finished 21-7 during Preyer's first season.

When Preyer wasn't

coaching, she was recruiting. She hit the road in the summer — something previous Duke coaches hadn't done — and the investment paid off in 1986 when the O'Reillys picked Duke over Stanford, a program that won eight national titles from 1982-91.

"I think they were excited about the chance to come in and help build a program," Preyer said. "I'm sure it was a tough decision for them. They had a chance to go to the top program in the country. But they really liked the idea of building a program to that point."

Once Preyer sold the triplets, her job was only half done. Next she had to win over Duke athletics director Tom Butters, convincing him to add another scholarship to the two she had to offer that year.

"He thought about it, and then he decided to take the plunge," Preyer said. "He decided it was a chance worth taking. He saw it as an opportunity. He was really making some commitments to women's teams during that time. The athletic department was beginning to recognize women's sports more strongly and began rewarding them."

The triplets served as a significant start, but Preyer knew they weren't the end-all. She recruited at least as hard in the years that followed, landing Susan Sabo and Katrina Greenman the next year, getting Susan Sommerville and Julie Exum two years later.

Those four recruits — along with Patti O'Reilly — became the first five players to post 100 victories at Duke. O'Reilly, followed by Sabo, Exum and then Sommerville, became Duke's first four All-Americans.

Preyer left after the 1991 season, but the success she created remains. Geoff Macdonald directed the program for three years, followed by Jody Hyden for three and now Jamie Ashworth, who has been head coach since 1997.

Ashworth is the ACC leader in career winning percentage, followed by Macdonald, Hyden and Raynor.

From 1988, when Patti O'Reilly was named Duke's first All-American, to 2002, 20 Blue Devils earned All-America status. Individually, Vanessa Webb won the NCAA singles championship in 1998. As a team, the Blue Devils won 116 consecutive ACC matches from 1991-99 and reached the semifinals of the NCAA Tournament each year from 1996-99.

"I think the tradition feeds off itself," Ashworth said. "The girls coming into our program are aware of the wins this program has had, and there's a really strong bond between present players and past players. Our past players talk to our present players a lot, and it creates a pretty good family atmosphere.

"The present players know that the foundation was built before they got here, and they don't want to be the ones responsible for the downfall of Duke tennis. I think that drives them a lot and motivates them a lot." ✶

ABOVE: Terri, Patti and Christine O'Reilly helped to make Duke the most powerful women's tennis program in the ACC. Christine suffered an untimely death at age 25 in an automobile accident.

FACING PAGE: Susan Sommerville was one of the Blue Devils' first four All-Americans in women's tennis.

basketball venue even without the Dixie Classic because it continued to host the ACC Tournament, the conference's signature event. The founders of the league, starting from scratch financially, regarded a postseason basketball tournament as key to revenue production. The ACC Tournament long served as the conference's financial mainstay.

At a time when a single entrant from each league went to the NCAA Tournament, the event was not without its critics, including most ACC basketball coaches. They preferred crowning the regular season's first-place finisher as the league champion. "The tournament is like a plane crash," Wake's Greason said in 1957. "You go down once, and you're a goner."

Everett Case, founder of the Dixie Classic, felt differently about the value of tournament testing. Appropriately, then, it was the first of Case's protégés to become an ACC head coach who quickly established himself by winning the 1960 ACC Tournament.

Vic Bubas had been sought by Clemson but waited until the Duke job opened. "Everett Case said the greatest compliment ever paid his basketball program was the day Eddie Cameron asked to hire his assistant," Greensboro journalist Irwin Smallwood said.

Cameron, a former basketball and football head coach at Duke, chose wisely. Borrowing liberally from his mentor, Bubas modernized the Duke program in style, structure and marketing. He also quickly secured the services of a star New York-area player, Art Heyman, who had already committed to McGuire's North Carolina program when Bubas was hired on May 6, 1959.

"Art, I always liked to say, he was our pioneer," Bubas said. "I appealed to him in that way." Bubas employed unusually systematic recruiting to spread Duke's appeal, assisted by a staff that during his 10-year tenure included future head coaches Chuck Daly, Hubie Brown, Raymond "Bucky" Waters and Fred Shabel.

Seeking greater efficiency in winnowing the field of prospects, and hoping to get a head start on the competition in an era

FACING PAGE
Duke All-American Art Heyman helped to solidify Vic Bubas' program. Heyman, a member of the ACC's 50th anniversary team, averaged 25.1 points during his career. He led Duke to its first Final Four appearance in 1963. Heyman was the national player of the year as well as the most outstanding player at the Final Four. His senior year, the Blue Devils went 27-3 overall, 14-0 in the ACC.

RIGHT
Duke head coach Vic Bubas (right) put together a strong coaching staff. Assistants Hubie Brown (left) and Chuck Daly (center) later became head coaches in the National Basketball Association.

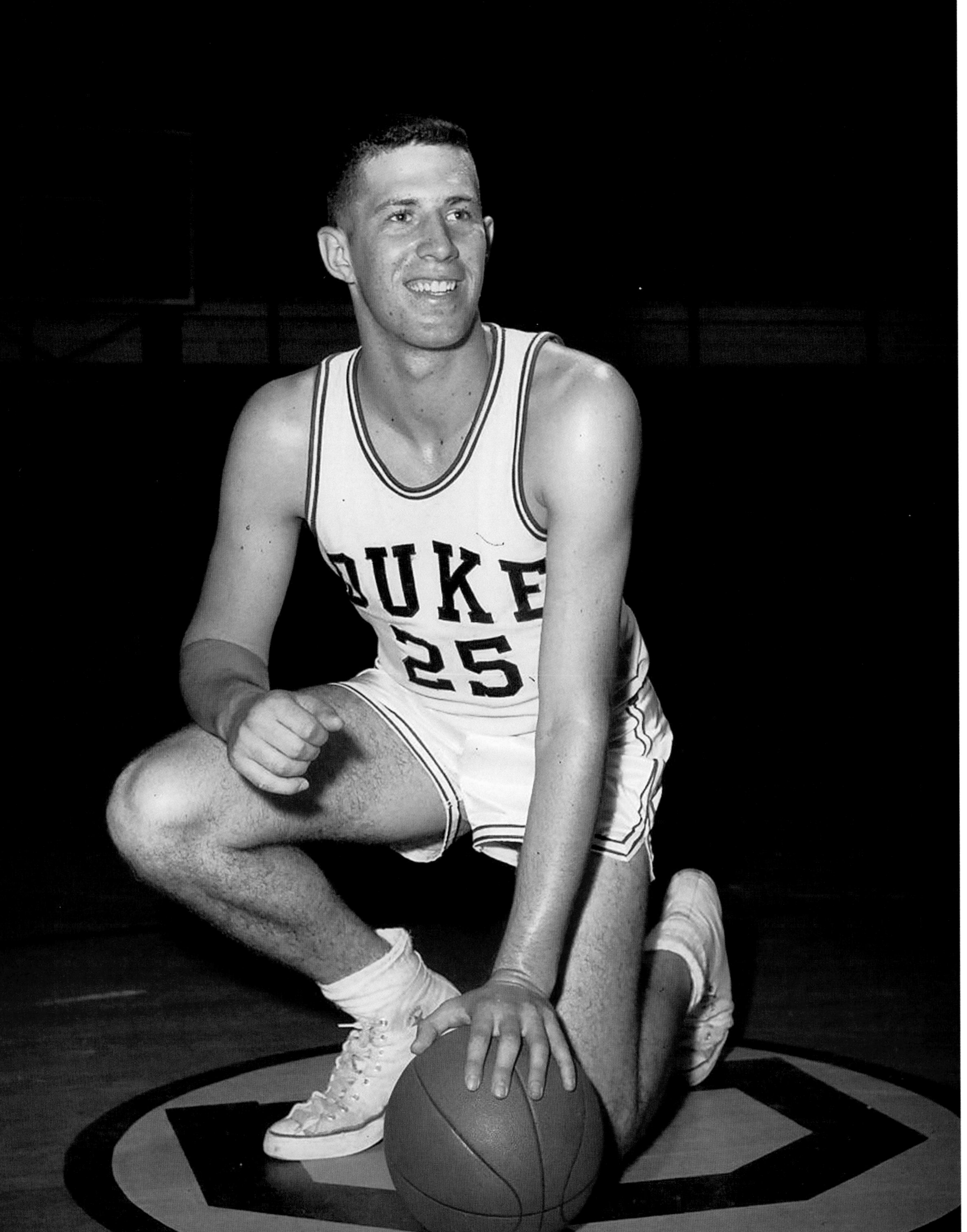
DUKE
25

prior to the advent of recruiting services, Bubas and staff flooded the country with letters. Queries about players' academic credentials went to guidance counselors and coaches everywhere. "As a result, we sent out so many letters and got so many responses, it led people to believe that we were recruiting everybody in the United States," Bubas said. "I think we did a good job of covering the country. But I think once we identified them, I'm not sure we were better recruiters than anyone else."

Bubas did have a smooth approach, however. "He was a refined, gentlemanly man; he was not rough-hewn," Smallwood said. "He wasn't salty-tongued. He was the kind of guy you'd want your kid to play for."

The parents of talented players apparently shared that view. Three of Bubas' recruits earned ACC player of the year honors within a four-year span at mid-decade — Long Island's Heyman in 1963; Jeff Mullins from Lexington, Ky., in 1964; and Pennsylvanian Steve Vacendak in 1966. Between 1961 and 1967 Heyman, Mullins, Jack Marin and Bob Verga were voted consensus All-Americans and earned 11 berths on the all-conference first team.

Bubas also attracted players by employing an up-tempo style. "He got it up and down; he'd press and do all of those things," said Maryland's Williams, who by 1965 was studying ACC coaches in preparation for an expected post-graduate career as a high-school coach. "You knew playing Duke that you'd better be ready physically because they were going to try to wear you down as much as anything else."

Williams, who also speaks freely of lessons learned from North Carolina's Smith, said Bubas was "neat" to study. "He was really innovative," Williams said. "He ran the multiple guards at you. Bud [Millikan] was still playing five, six, maybe seven if you got into foul trouble. Bubas, he platooned his guards. He had great guards. Vacendak was as good as anybody I ever played against. Verga was as good a shooter as there was in the country. Jack Marin was there. He took advantage of his talent."

Bubas set about building and selling a product off the court as well, his innovations becoming familiar over the years as

others emulated them. "Vic taught us all how to recruit," Smith said.

Bubas held a preseason basketball "ladies' clinic for girls from 1 to 101." He visited fraternities and sororities to discuss his teams. He started a coach's TV show. At a time when many ACC home courts were old and poorly illuminated, he insisted on better lighting in the arena, which would be named after Cameron in 1972. Then he made Duke players more easily identifiable. "I think in our section of the country, we were the first ones with the names on the jerseys," Bubas said.

To further improve the atmosphere and presumably his home-court advantage, Bubas started a pep band, copying the "straw hat band" of California-Berkeley. He introduced dancing girls on the sidelines, taking his cue from UCLA. Cameron has been known for its crowds ever since.

Bubas also won. He immediately made his mark as the only first-year head coach to win the ACC Tournament. That meant succeeding with inherited players, the best of the bunch Howard Hurt, an All-ACC second-team selection from 1959-61. "If it were left to me to select the Atlantic Coast Conference basketball team that accomplished the most with the least native talent, I wouldn't hesitate a minute before choosing the 1960 Duke team," said Add Penfield, Duke's radio announcer.

Duke was 12-10 entering the 1960 ACC Tournament, having lost at home by 25 to North Carolina in the regular-season finale. Yet the Blue Devils beat South Carolina, upset the Tar Heels 71-69 in the semifinals and topped Wake for the ACC title. "They got hot in the tournament, had one of those tournaments where, if you played 100 more, maybe you wouldn't be able to duplicate it one time," Bubas said of a squad that reached the NCAA East Regional final.

The '60 tournament also was the first of five straight in which McKinney's teams got to the final, winning in 1961 and again in 1962. Only Duke from 1963-67, North Carolina from 1991-95 and Duke from 1998-2002 reached as many ACC Tournament finals in succession.

By 1962-63, when Bubas and Heyman were in their fourth season together at

LEFT

Duke coach Vic Bubas, who cultivated a home-court advantage, watches as his team is introduced at then-Duke Indoor Stadium. The arena was renamed in 1972 for Eddie Cameron, a former director of athletics who also coached football and basketball at the school. *Sports Illustrated* named Cameron Indoor Stadium fourth on a list of top-10 sporting venues of the 20th century.

Duke, the Blue Devils went undefeated in the ACC, led the nation in field-goal percentage (.511) and reached the Final Four.

By then the ACC was brimming with national-caliber teams. While the 1960s was the only decade in which no ACC squad won a national basketball championship, 10 league teams finished in the top 10 in the polls, seven reached the Final Four and two got to the title game against UCLA — Duke in 1964 and North Carolina in 1968. "I think we helped to advance the ACC to a position to where we were recognized at a pretty good level no matter which ACC team was in there," Bubas said.

For Duke, 1960 would prove the only season in which it won ACC championships in both football and basketball.

The Blue Devils repeated in football in 1961 and '62. Yet the dominant ACC football player at the start of the decade was Roman Gabriel, the 6-foot-4, 200-pound N.C. State quarterback.

In fact, several extraordinarily gifted passers came through the league during its first decade of competition before going on to extended professional careers. First was Duke quarterback Sonny Jurgensen (1954-56), from the same high school in Wilmington, N.C., that produced Gabriel. Wake had Norman Snead, who paced the ACC in passing in 1959 and 1960, breaking ACC records for passing yardage.

Jurgensen was twice voted second-team All-ACC but had a modest impact in college, attempting only 128 passes his junior and senior years combined. He played 18 years in the National Football League and was inducted into the Pro Football Hall of Fame in 1983. (Jurgensen is one of five former ACC players so honored. The others were defensive stalwarts — Maryland tackles Stan Jones and Randy White, Virginia tackle Henry Jordan and UNC linebacker Lawrence Taylor. Jordan, also an ACC heavyweight wrestling champion, failed altogether to win all-conference recognition during his career from 1954-56.)

Gabriel was the best of his era. But he joined an N.C. State program whose coach, Earle Edwards, was noted for a conservative offense typified by the comment, "Most passing records are established in losing causes." Until Gabriel joined the varsity in 1959, Edwards' teams had never passed for more than 804 yards in a season.

Gabriel's sophomore year he passed for 832 yards. His .604 completion percentage on a 1-9 team was best in the nation and

FACING PAGE
N.C. State quarterback Roman Gabriel was a two-time ACC player of the year (1960-61). He led the nation in completion percentage (.604) in 1959. He was also an academic All-American and was named the ACC athlete of the year in 1960. Gabriel set numerous school records in passing before leaving to become a successful professional quarterback in the National Football League. He was named the NFL's most valuable player in 1969.

RIGHT
N.C. State football coach Earle Edwards and star quarterback Roman Gabriel. Edwards' teams won five ACC championships during his time at the school. He had to overcome great odds to do it, too. Edwards began with only 10 scholarships and in the 12 years he coached before Carter-Finley Stadium opened, the Wolfpack played just 41 home games.

remains an N.C. State record for a sophomore. "I was never against passing," Edwards said later. "I was just against poor passing."

The '60 Wolfpack came within a game of catching Duke atop the ACC standings at a time when a single bowl bid went to league clubs. Gabriel was ACC player and athlete of the year and an academic All-American. Playing offense and defense was the custom at the time. Gabriel also helped secure a win over UNC with key defensive plays. During the spring, he led the Wolfpack baseball team in home runs and runs batted in while playing first base and outfield.

Gabriel repeated as ACC football player of the year in 1961, one of only five repeat selections as the league's premier player. (The others were UNC's Don McCauley in 1969 and 1970, UNC's Mike Voight in 1975 and '76, Clemson's Steve Fuller in 1977 and '78 and Florida State's Charlie Ward in 1992 and '93.) The following spring, Oakland picked Gabriel first in the American Football League draft. The Los Angeles Rams made him the second overall pick in the National Football League draft.

The 1961 football season also saw Virginia end an 18-game ACC losing streak with a 28-20 win over South Carolina. Perhaps the highlight of the season for the Gamecocks came against Clemson, and not just because of the result, a 21-14 win secured when USC fumbled, only to have the ball bounce into the hands of quarterback Jimmy Costen, who ran down the sideline for the winning score.

Clemson folks were known to pluck live chickens or wring their necks at games to mock the Gamecocks. A pilot once flew over a baseball game between the schools and dropped a chicken along the right-field line. Such pranks were routine leading up to football meetings between the rivals. "You always looked for the least thing you'd expect," said Bill McLellan, a retired Clemson athletic administrator and former assistant football coach.

One year, to exploit the expectation of shenanigans Howard instructed McLellan to surreptitiously paint the goal posts on Clemson's practice fields in USC's garnet and black. "That got the boys all pepped up," McLellan said. "It didn't hurt anybody. It hurt me because I had to go back the next week and paint it over."

The premier prank, however, occurred at Carolina Stadium on Nov. 11, 1961, just days after John Kennedy was elected president of the United States.

USC's chapter of Sigma Nu fraternity had a number of pledges among the school's freshman football players. Bedecked in uniforms borrowed from nearby Orangeburg High School, the pledges bore an admirable resemblance to the Clemson Tigers. So prior to the game, about two dozen ersatz Clemson players ran onto the field, took up positions in front of the Tiger fans and began performing calisthenics. Seeing them, the Clemson band played "Tiger Rag." Then the fun began.

"They lined up in two rows; one row they cupped their hands with their thumbs down like udders, and the others started acting like they were milking them because Clemson was a cow college," said Tom Price, a historian of South Carolina sports and retired sports information director. Then the ringers started dancing to music they'd brought along. Several blew kisses to the crowd.

"It took a minute or a minute and a half for the Clemson folks to realize they'd been had," Price said. "It was a pretty funny sight, at least to South Carolina it was."

Angry Tiger fans swarmed toward the field, but state police preserved order.

About three weeks later, the 1961-62 basketball season got underway with a new coach at North Carolina. McGuire had resigned in August, taking a job with the Philadelphia Warriors of the National Basketball Association. Replacing the flamboyant McGuire was Dean Smith, an unknown 30-year-old assistant with a flair for tactics.

Smith had served McGuire for three years, but hadn't gotten the teachings of Hall of Fame coach Forrest "Phog" Allen out of his system. Once when McGuire and Smith roomed together on the road, the former Kansas Jayhawk leapt from bed while still asleep and started going through his defensive stances, shouts and all. McGuire awoke with a start, Smith recalled. "He ran in the closet and hit his knee, I think. He thought it was a burglar."

Smith's inherited team went 7-7 in the ACC in 1962 and posted the only losing season of his career, going 8-9 overall. Smith was so nervous for his debut,

TAKE AND GIVE

Played And Served As Men's Head Coach
In Basketball At Schools In ACC

Player/Coach	Played	Coached
Vic Bubas*	NCS	Duke
Bobby Cremins	USC	GT
Matt Doherty	UNC	UNC
Lefty Driesell	Duke	Md
Murray Greason*	Wake	Wake
Jeff Jones	UVa	UVa
Billy McCann*	UVa	UVa
Banks McFadden*	Clem	Clem
Bones McKinney*	NCS,UNC	WF
Dwane Morrison*	USC	GT
Jackie Murdock	Wake	Wake
Les Robinson	NCS	NCS
Bucky Waters	NCS	Duke
Gary Williams	Md	Md

* Played prior to formation of ACC.

an 80-46 defeat of Virginia, he forgot to have a game ball set aside.

Wake Forest emerged as the league's basketball power even as North Carolina went into eclipse. The Deacons first won the ACC title in 1961 behind Packer and 6-8 center Len Chappell, whom Robert Lipsyte of *The New York Times* called "the fastest-moving mountain in North Carolina." Chappell was voted the 1961 ACC player of the year, and McKinney repeated as coach of the year as the Deacons finished one game away from the Final Four.

The 1962 Deacons were picked third nationally in preseason behind Ohio State and Cincinnati. But after posting two wins, Wake Forest hosted Ohio State with John Havlicek and Jerry Lucas. The Buckeyes crushed the Deacons 84-62 before a sellout crowd of 8,600. Wake next traveled to Florida to play Norm Sloan's lowly Gators. According to Barry Lawing's book *Demon Deacon Hoops*, many players got debilitating sunburns hanging around the pool prior to the game, which they lost 71-65.

Back on campus, fellow students hanged Wake players in effigy. The team proceeded to win at Virginia before losing at Maryland and Duke. "I am just as surprised at the inept play as any of our followers," McKinney said.

McKinney might be called a "Big Four" original — he starred on a great high-school team in Durham, played college ball first at N.C. State and later at UNC, and wound up at Wake Forest, doubling as an assistant coach while studying to be a Baptist minister. Body and mouth,

ABOVE
Wake Forest center Len Chappell (50) led the Deacons to their only Final Four appearance. He was twice named the ACC player of the year (1961 and '62), and his 24.8 points per game remains among the top 10 all-time in scoring average. He was the first consensus All-American at the school and was a three-time All-ACC performer.

McKinney was in constant motion on the sidelines. Penfield, the radio announcer, described him as "a gangly, sometimes wild-eyed and often zany showoff." Marvin Francis, a McKinney classmate at Durham High School, called him "on the nutty side" but a good coach and so "great" a storyteller "he'd tell the same stories 100 times, but the way he would tell it you would still laugh."

Once, after Commissioner Weaver criticized McKinney's sideline decorum, Wake fans had a seat belt affixed to his chair on the bench and the coach wore it, at least temporarily. McKinney habitually drank water during games by dipping a ladle into a galvanized bucket by his side. On one occasion, he tossed a dipper full of water over his shoulder to douse an abusive fan; another time he purposely sloshed water onto the court to stop action when his timeouts were exhausted.

After entering February with a 7-7 record, McKinney's Deacons won eight of their next nine to conclude the regular season and then swept to the 1962 ACC title with three straight double-digit victories. Chappell was named ACC player of the year for the second straight season, the first to repeat since Wake's Dickie Hemric in 1954 and '55.

Wake reached the Final Four by beating Villanova, following overtime victories against Yale and St. Joseph's. Riding a 12-game winning streak, the Deacons again faced Ohio State. Again they lost. In the consolation game, they defeated UCLA 82-80 to finish 22-9. That would prove the last

BODY AND MOUTH, MCKINNEY WAS IN **CONSTANT MOTION** ON THE SIDELINES

Wake Forest's Horace "Bones" McKinney always gave an emotional performance along the sideline. In 1962, McKinney directed the Deacons to their only Final Four appearance. As a player, McKinney led the Southern Conference in scoring while playing for N.C. State in 1942. Then he left school and entered the Army during World War II. After the war he enrolled at North Carolina and

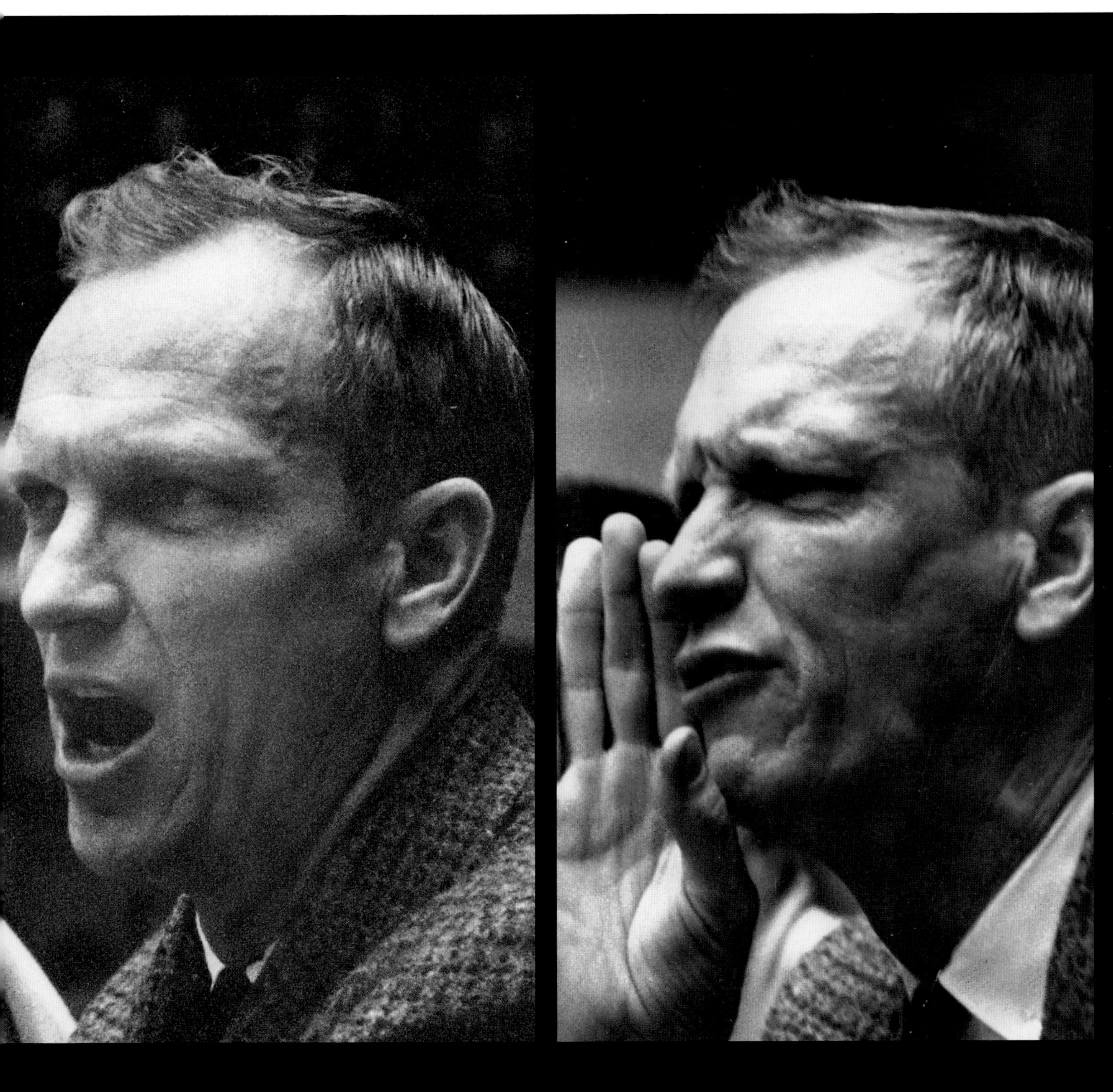

in 1946 helped to lead the Tar Heels to their first Final Four appearance. He became head coach at Wake Forest in 1957. His Demon Deacons played in five consecutive ACC Tournament title games and won the championship in back-to-back years (1961-62). His teams went 122-94 in eight seasons.

time the Bruins dropped an NCAA Tournament game until N.C. State beat them in 1974, and the only time to date a Wake squad reached the Final Four.

The 1962 season became something of a high-water mark for Clemson basketball, too. Despite finishing with a losing record overall in Press Maravich's last year as head coach, the Tigers reached the ACC Tournament final, falling to Wake, 77-66. No Clemson squad since has gotten that close to winning an ACC title, although the 1990 Tigers did finish first during the regular season.

The 1962 NCAA berth was Wake's fourth since the NCAA Tournament started in 1939. Only N.C. State among ACC members had been invited more often. But after '62, the Demon Deacons would not return for 15 years.

Duke, meanwhile, got on a roll in basketball. The Blue Devils won 99 games between 1963 and 1966 and reached the Final Four three times.

The '63 team was 27-3. The leader was Heyman, who paced Duke in scoring and rebounding for three straight years and was league and national player of the year in 1963. Heyman had 40 points, a career high, in a victorious home finale against North Carolina. While Bubas wouldn't pick a best player from his tenure, he tabbed the 6-5 Heyman, the ACC scoring leader in 1963 (24.9), as his choice "if you had 10 seconds to go and you wanted to get the ball to somebody, because if he missed it he had the best chance of going back and getting it."

The 1963 Blue Devils were the first of 13 squads in school history to reach a Final Four, but lost decisively in the semifinals to Loyola, the eventual 1963 national champions and the first to win the title with African-Americans comprising a majority of its starters.

The fall of 1963 saw a change in football leadership as North Carolina and N.C. State tied for the ACC title, a first for the Tar Heels. N.C. State had won in 1957. Both went to bowls, the first pair of ACC teams invited in the same year and the last until 1972.

The suddenly soaring Tar Heels shot down Air Force 35-0 in the Gator Bowl. The Wolfpack fell to Mississippi State in the Liberty Bowl, played in Philadelphia. Frank Weedon, a former N.C. State senior associate athletics director, recalled it was so cold coffee froze in cups and water froze in press box urinals. "There was no crowd, not only because of the cold," Weedon said. "The only publicity we got was protestors, picketers, saying you've got two Southern schools that don't have any black players on your teams."

A single victory highlighted Wake Forest's 1963 football season. "Why has Wake Forest football turned into an Atlantic Coast Conference version of the New York Mets comedy act?" asked Ernie Accorsi of the *Charlotte News*. The Deacons' losing streak reached 18, longest in the

10.8.66
N.C. State opens Carter-Finley Stadium with a 31-21 loss to South Carolina

10.8.66
South Carolina's Bobby Bryant sets an ACC record by returning a punt 98 yards for a touchdown at N.C. State

1967

3.9.67
ACC Tournament played at Greensboro Coliseum, first time outside of Raleigh's Reynolds Coliseum

9.16.67
Duke, UNC, N.C. State and Wake Forest play football doubleheader

9.23.67
Clemson begins tradition of touching Howard's Rock en route to playing field

nation, before they beat South Carolina 20-19 at Columbia. The hero that November day was junior running back Brian Piccolo, who ran for 140 yards, scored the tying touchdown and kicked the game-winning extra point.

Six days later, Wake played N.C. State and dropped a 42-0 decision. Worse, the teams played on Friday, Nov. 22, the same day President Kennedy was assassinated. Given more time to consider, the rest of the league postponed its Saturday games. When a similar situation arose in September 2001 following terrorist attacks on New York's World Trade Center and the Pentagon in Washington, D.C., the ACC took the collegiate lead nationally in spurning business-as-usual and postponed its schedule of football games.

Wake's football fortunes remained in distinct contrast with basketball, which finished second in the league in 1963-64. The Deacons reached the ACC Tournament final for the seventh time in 11 years, but Wake again fell to Duke. Bubas won his third title in his first five seasons. The Blue Devils advanced by beating N.C. State and a North Carolina squad that depended on "The Kangaroo Kid," Billy Cunningham, who led the league in scoring (26.0) and rebounding (15.8).

Ultimately the '64 Blue Devils got to the NCAA final behind seniors Jay Buckley and Jeff Mullins, the ACC player of the year, only to see UCLA's John Wooden capture the first of his 10 titles in 12 years.

That same March, South Carolina announced Frank McGuire as its new basketball coach. "The program was in shambles," said Price, the USC sports historian. McGuire's Gamecocks were competitive within three years, and he was at the center of a bitter league-wide dispute within two. Price praised McGuire as "a great coach and a great recruiter." But, Price said, "He reveled in controversy."

During the summer of '64, Mullins and former Tar Heel Larry Brown (1961-63), initial helmsman of Smith's famed "Four Corners" delay, became the first ACC players to compete for the United States in Olympic basketball. Competing at Tokyo, the United States won the gold medal. Duke's Joel Shankle and Dave Sime, the league's 1956 athlete of the year, had previously competed in the Olympics in track.

N.C. State, lagging in basketball, won its third football title in 1964. Yet the Wolfpack was only 5-5 overall. No ACC squad posted a winning record. In fact, five teams finished 5-5. Surprisingly Wake Forest was among them. That was the school's best effort since 1959, earning newcomer Bill Tate unanimous selection as the 1964 ACC coach of the year.

The player of the year was Piccolo, who led the nation in scoring (111 points) and rushing (1,044 yards). Piccolo remains tied for fifth in ACC history with 17 touchdowns in a season and ranks among the top 10 in rushing attempts per game (25.2)

1968

4.4.68
Martin Luther King Jr. assassinated

6.5.68
Sen. Robert Kennedy mortally wounded by assassin

11.30.68
Clemson opens Littlejohn Coliseum with a 76-72 win over Georgia Tech

7.20.69
Neil Armstrong first human to walk on moon

By Bill Vilona

FSU'S JOANNE GRAF DRIVES ACC INTO FAST LANE

JoAnne Graf's legacy began innocently enough. She was too young and too thrilled to ponder the future. Heck, she was only 24 years old and a graduate student at the University of North Carolina at Greensboro when the telephone rang in 1978.

She interviewed, and the next thing she knew, Florida State wanted her to become its first full-time women's softball coach. Graf leaped at the chance to return to her alma mater, which was also located in her hometown. "I was finishing up my master's and this was my dream job," she said. "And when you're that age, you never really think about what might happen."

She has not left Tallahassee since, but time passed quickly. Along the way, victories accumulated, achievements steadily piled up. Suddenly, Graf became a legend-in-waiting.

On Feb. 23, 2002, she became the all-time winningest coach in NFCA (National Fastpitch Coaches Association) history, earning her 1,125th victory. The accomplishment headlined FSU's best season in more than a decade, which finished with a riveting run at the Women's College World Series in Oklahoma City.

"I don't really dwell on all that too much," said Graf, 48, whose record-setting moment came in her 24th season as Florida State's coach. "Every year, you're trying to equal or surpass what you did the year before. In my case, I've been blessed to have a great staff and a lot of great players along the way."

Her route included experiencing the sport's biggest evolution. In the early 1980s, when women's collegiate athletics broke from the Association of Intercollegiate Athletics for Women (AIAW) to the NCAA, softball changed from slow-pitch to a fast-pitch game.

"I was confident we could make the transition, but I worried if people were going to keep the sport," said Graf, who

LEFT: Florida State softball coach JoAnne Graf helped to bring fast-pitch softball to the East. When FSU joined the ACC, the stature of her teams helped to improve the quality of play in the conference.

RIGHT: FSU catcher Kimmy Carter and her teammates earned a trip to the 2002 Women's College World Series.

led FSU to a pair of (AIAW) national titles in slow pitch. "Many schools started dropping it. Most of your [Southeastern Conference] schools dropped it, and a lot of others in the Southeast."

The Atlantic Coast Conference fell into that category. Recruiting became a major issue because most of the talented fast-pitch players attended high schools in California or lived west of the Mississippi River. Hence, teams on the East Coast were unwilling to fund major recruiting budgets.

When Florida State became a playing member of the ACC in 1992, the softball program's impact mirrored the school's football influence. "We had the longest established program," said Graf, who has earned her doctorate degree. "We were a couple years ahead of the other schools in the ACC who were playing softball. But I knew the teams would catch up to us. That's exactly what has happened.

"The other schools began to fund their programs, build great facilities, hire more full-time coaches. It's progressed exactly as I thought."

The progression continues. North Carolina State will restart its program in 2004. The Wolfpack will become the sixth ACC softball team, thus enabling the league to regain its automatic NCAA Tournament bid for the conference champion. The remaining non-playing schools — Duke, Clemson and Wake Forest — are considering ways to fund softball programs.

Florida State had the league's dominant team for a decade, winning eight ACC Tournament titles and nine regular-season championships. But parity has pushed forward. North Carolina won the 2001 ACC Tournament. Georgia Tech beat the Tar Heels for the 2002 championship on FSU's home field.

Three weeks later, Florida State finished third — equaling its highest finish ever — in the Women's College World Series by staging upset wins against top-seed UCLA and Nebraska.

"That speaks highly for the ACC," said Kimmy Carter, FSU's four-year starting catcher. "It shows the teams in the East are getting much better. When I played my freshman and sophomore years (1999-2000), I wouldn't say it was a cakewalk in the ACC, but I'd say it was a lot easier. We didn't win the ACC Tournament my last two years. The competition definitely was a lot higher."

Carter, a 5-foot-3 dynamo, played in 272 games, including a school-record 247 consecutive starts. If her last name strikes a chord, well, it should. She's the youngest daughter of Gary Carter, an 11-time Major League Baseball All-Star catcher whose career spanned 19 seasons with Hall of Fame-qualifying credentials.

Kimmy Carter was 14 when fast-pitch softball was introduced in Florida high schools. "He taught me how to be a baseball catcher in softball," she said. "He didn't hold back. He could whip that ball in there. When they converted to fast pitch, there was so much more excitement within the girls, the fans, everybody, because the way the game moved in slow pitch was literally slow. The pitching is slow, and there really isn't a lot of action."

Carter grew up in Palm Beach Gardens, Fla. She was lured to Florida State the same way so many other talented players were. Graf's personality became the selling point.

"Coach Graf can't kill a fly," Carter said. "She does not have a mean bone in her body. She's a very generous, compassionate person. But at the same time, she has that competitive fire when you're on the field."

When Florida State entered the ACC, Graf knew a couple of teams, primarily Georgia Tech and North Carolina, would provide competition. There has also been competition for upgraded facilities, prompting Florida State to build its own Seminole Softball Complex, which opened in 1998.

"It's made us work harder to make our program even better," Graf said. "I think we set the standard, and other ACC teams have risen up to meet that standard. I think the sport will continue to grow in our league. When we joined, the ACC was known from a regional perspective, but not nationally. I think what happened [in 2002] showed how competitive our conference has become."

Entering the 2002 season, Graf's winning percentage (.766) was third-best among active Division I coaches. She has taken FSU to 15 NCAA Tournament appearances, advancing six of those years to the Women's College World Series. She's been the ACC coach of the year four times. Most impressive, none of her teams at Florida State has ever sustained a losing season.

"It was a privilege to play for her," said Carter, who had the game-winning RBI for Graf's record-setting win. "To know I played a small part in all of this is awesome. It was a lot of fun and great memories." ✯

and rushing touchdowns in a season (15). In 1964 Wake enjoyed its first win over Duke in 13 years as Piccolo single-handedly outran the Devils with 36 rushes for 115 yards, besting the visitors' 35 rushes for 102 yards. He also scored all of Wake's points in the 20-7 victory.

Remarkably, Piccolo's 1964 achievements came without committing a fumble. "He was so dependable, it was incredible," said Gene Hooks, then starting his tenure as Wake's athletics director.

"Brian could break tackles," said Tate, praising Piccolo's ability to run inside, particularly his instinct for cutting against the flow. "He had that good lower-body strength. He had that good lean. He had good hands. He could catch the football." The man throwing to Piccolo, senior quarterback John Mackovic, led the ACC in total offense in '64 as he finally got to play extensively under Tate.

Piccolo wasn't particularly fast, didn't practice all that hard, and at 5-11 and 198 pounds wasn't highly sought for college ball. The Floridian wasn't drafted by the pros, either. Tough and determined, "Pick" nevertheless earned a spot in the Chicago Bears' backfield. There, he played alongside the great Gale Sayers. The pair formed a biracial friendship unusual for the time, later immortalized in the film *Brian's Song,* that culminated with Piccolo's death of cancer at age 26.

About the time Piccolo's college career ended, prize recruit Larry Miller debuted for North Carolina's freshman basketball team, still called the "Tar Babies." The nickname drew scant attention. Statues of black jockeys still populated American lawns, and teams held awards dinners at segregated country clubs. Southern pep bands routinely played "Dixie." Norm Sloan, who became head basketball coach at N.C. State in 1966, recalled being taught by African-American players to stop referring to players as "boys" and to quit underscoring a point by saying, "And that's in spades."

Miller's presence in Chapel Hill signaled Smith's first major-recruiting victory against Bubas. Smith's program seemed to have arrived, and some preseason polls had the Tar Heels in the top 10 in 1964-65. But it would be departures more than arrivals that characterized the '65 ACC seasons in basketball and football.

Basketball got off to a sad start as a fatigued Everett Case retired immediately after N.C. State's second game of the season. Case would be dead of cancer in a year and a half. In 18 seasons coaching the Wolfpack, his record was 377-134 with 10 league titles, four in the ACC, as well as the seminal role in sparking regional interest in basketball.

Press Maravich, who had become Case's

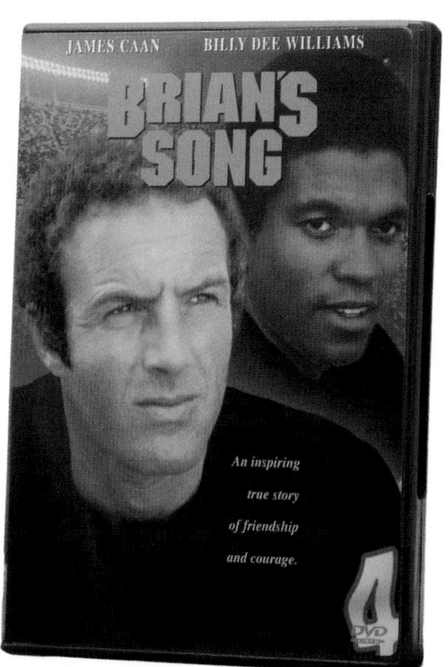

FACING PAGE
Wake Forest running back Brian Piccolo led the nation in rushing in 1964 with 1,044 yards and was named an All-American. He played with the Chicago Bears of the National Football League when he left Winston-Salem, but his life was cut short by cancer. The movie *Brian's Song* was made about him and his relationship with Bears teammate Gale Sayers.

FACING PAGE
North Carolina's Billy "The Kangaroo Kid" Cunningham goes up for the ball against South Carolina. Cunningham led the league in scoring and rebounding in 1964 and 1965 and was named the ACC player of the year in 1965. Cunningham and teammate Larry Brown (far left) were successful coaches after their careers in the ACC. Brown won a national title coaching Kansas and has also been recognized for his excellence as a professional coach. Cunningham's Philadelphia 76ers won the National Basketball Association championship in 1983. Cunningham and Brown are members of the Naismith Basketball Hall of Fame.

chief assistant the previous year, stepped in as head coach and promptly led the Pack to 11 straight wins. N.C. State finished the season tied for second with Maryland and North Carolina, one game behind 11-3 Duke.

UNC's second-place showing in 1965 began a 36-year run in which the Tar Heels never finished lower than third in the ACC standings. Thirty-two of those seasons came under Smith, his program the most consistently excellent over the long haul the college game has seen.

Cunningham again led the ACC in scoring and rebounding in 1965, and he was voted the league's player of the year. His teammate, Bob Lewis, a 6-3 sophomore, emerged as an All-ACC player. Against Vanderbilt, Lewis had 31 points and Cunningham 30, the first ACC teammates to score 30 or more in the same game. Cunningham added 25 points and 16 rebounds in the Tar Heels' finale at Woollen Gym, their home court since 1939, as they defeated Duke for the second time.

Yet in mid-January Smith's popularity, if not his job, appeared in jeopardy. Jack Horner wrote in the *Durham Morning Herald* of "Coach Dean Smith's disappointing Tarheels" and disgruntled students twice hanged the coach in effigy within a week's span. The first time, following a 107-85 defeat at Wake, Cunningham and other players left the team bus to tear down the dummy. The second symbolic hanging followed a three-point home loss to Maravich's surging Wolfpack. About 100 students burned a four-foot-tall effigy of Smith as someone played taps. "I'm just glad they settled for hanging a dummy and not the real thing," Smith said later.

The '65 season culminated at Reynolds Coliseum with N.C. State winning the ACC Tournament behind 6-2 playmaker Eddie Biedenbach and 6-5 forward Larry Worsley. The big surprise was Worsley, a junior who averaged 7.4 points on the year but scored in double figures in all three tournament games. Coming off the bench in the final against Duke, he contributed eight rebounds and 30 points on 14-of-19 shooting.

Worsley's efforts earned the first Everett Case Award as the ACC Tournament's most valuable player. Case, so ill he could not attend the semifinals, was on hand to see his former team win the title. The N.C. State players hoisted Case on their shoulders so he could cut the nets.

McKinney, beset by personal problems, resigned as Wake's head coach in September 1965 following a 12-15 season. McKinney's record was 122-94 over eight seasons, with two ACC titles. He soon worked as an analyst on ACC basketball television broadcasts with Jim Thacker and Billy Packer, his former player.

The '65 football season had its share of farewells. Gone was one-platoon football with limited substitutions. Now teams could employ an offensive unit separate from a defensive unit, broadening the emphasis on squad depth.

On Nov. 13, N.C. State beat Florida State and coach Bill Peterson 3-0 in the final game at Riddick Stadium, the on-campus facility built in 1906. A week later, Duke

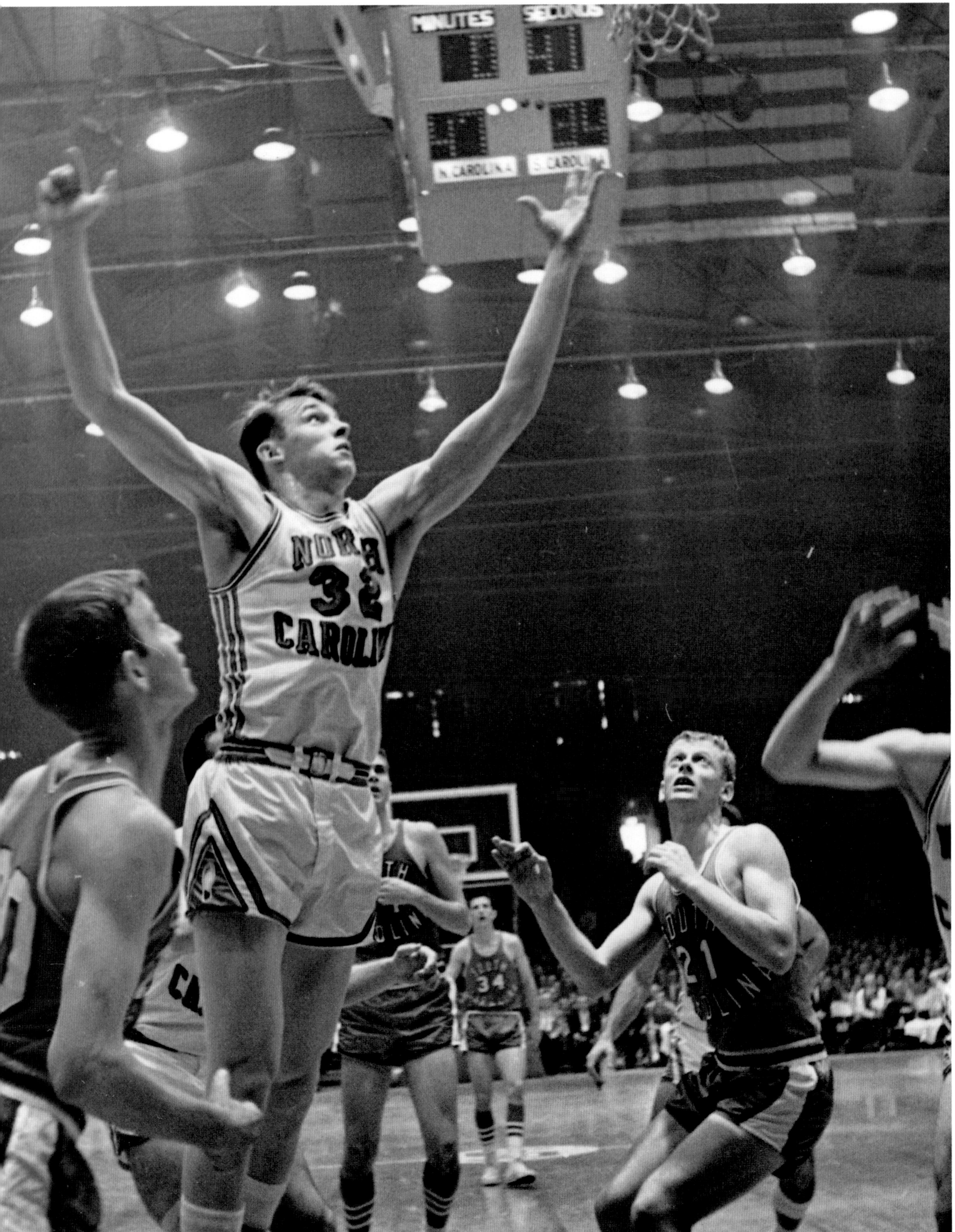
MINUTES
SECONDS
N. CAROLINA

BELOW
Duke offensive lineman Mike McGee, shown here with coach Bill Murray, is one of the most decorated Blue Devils ever. He was a first-team All-American in 1959 and also captured the Outland Trophy, which is awarded to the top interior lineman in the country. He was the 1959 ACC player of the year, a two-time All-ACC choice and is a member of the College Football Hall of Fame.

coach Bill Murray surprised everyone, including his players and staff, by announcing his resignation after a 34-7 win over North Carolina at Wade Stadium, site of the 1942 Rose Bowl.

Five teams entered that final Saturday of the '65 season with a chance for the ACC title, Duke among them. The Blue Devils broke open the UNC game with 22 points in the second quarter, including a 35-yard interception return for a touchdown by All-ACC linebacker Bob Matheson. Thinking he had assured the Blue Devils a piece of the championship, Murray "got a ride off the field he helped dedicate back in 1929 as a star Duke halfback," wrote Dick Herbert, columnist for Raliegh's *The News & Observer*. "A victory made the leaving more pleasant, but it still was a sad day for a happy man."

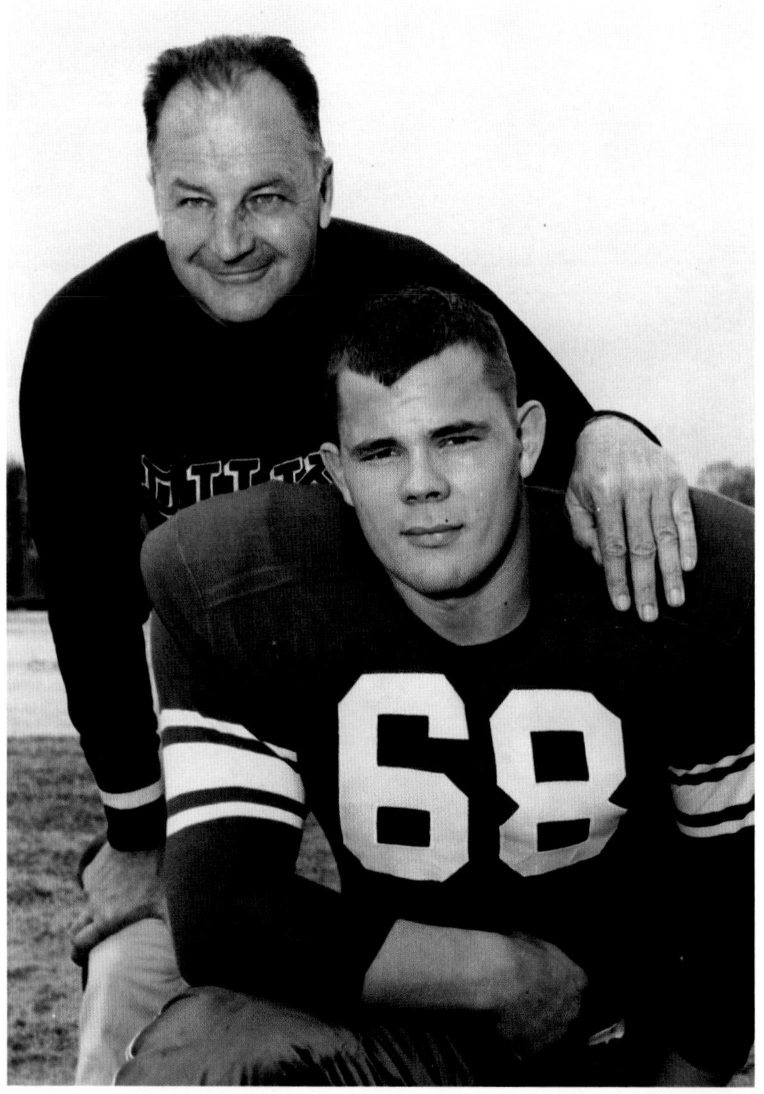

Murray was eventually inducted into the sport's Hall of Fame with a 144-68-12 record in 22 years at Duke and Delaware, including three undefeated seasons with the Blue Hens and three bowls with Duke.

But the final-game victory didn't secure the 1965 title for Duke. The Blue Devils were apparently tied atop the ACC standings with South Carolina, a 17-16 victor over Clemson on the last weekend. The Gamecocks, however, had used two players who received financial aid without scoring 800 on the SAT. Because their board scores made them ineligible under ACC rules, USC forfeited its football wins, vaulting N.C. State and Clemson into first and dropping Duke a game back of the leaders.

The league also fined Clemson and South Carolina $2,500 each for violating scholarships limits. "I know he was a Phi Beta Kappa at the University of Alabama," Commissioner Weaver said of Tiger AD Frank Howard, "but he must not have taken mathematics."

More quietly, conference leaders also put to rest two longstanding initiatives. They tabled a two-year discussion of criteria other than winning the ACC Tournament for determining the recipient of the league's automatic NCAA bid, and turned aside a second attempt to add Virginia Tech as a member.

With Murray gone, Eddie Cameron offered the Duke football job to Homer

Rice, offensive coordinator for Kentucky, the top passing team in the country. "Going back to the airport, Eddie said, 'You're our pick,'" recalled Rice, who went on to success elsewhere as a football coach and athletics director. But Duke President Douglas Knight wanted an Ivy League coach. He hired Tom Harp, who had played at Army and compiled a losing record at Cornell. "A few years later, I wound up at North Carolina, of all places," Rice said of his first AD job.

Duke football went into a tailspin, going 23 years before winning as many as seven games in a season, 24 before winning a piece of another ACC title.

Two more ACC schools had new football coaches in 1966. Maryland added nomadic Lou Saban, who lasted a year and had the privilege of losing at Penn State in the opener, the first win for head coach Joe Paterno. South Carolina hired Paul Dietzel, who doubled as athletics director. Dietzel was a hands-on type who tore a ligament in his knee in 1967 by jumping into a pile of players to demonstrate a point during practice. Flamboyant and extroverted, he immediately clashed with McGuire.

The basketball coach had more than enough problems after signing Mike Grosso, a big man from New Jersey whose uncle's business supposedly paid his way to Columbia despite scholarship offers from about 75 other schools. "This boy is 6-8, 230 pounds and one of the great, great prospects in the country," Duke's Bubas said. "Some say he is as good as Lew Alcindor." McGuire, mixing pros with college, said Grosso was for South Carolina what "Jerry West is to Los Angeles, Billy Cunningham was to North Carolina and Art Heyman to Duke."

Because Grosso's family was paying his tuition and he had met South Carolina's entrance requirements, Commissioner Weaver upheld the player's eligibility, despite a reported 789 score on the SAT. Grosso averaged 26 rebounds and 22.7 points on USC's freshman squad in 1965-66.

Without Grosso the Gamecock varsity finished 11-13 in 1966, and McGuire complained of an ACC officiating bias against teams from outside North Carolina. "These officials are scared to death of Cameron," he said of Duke's AD. "He's the one who

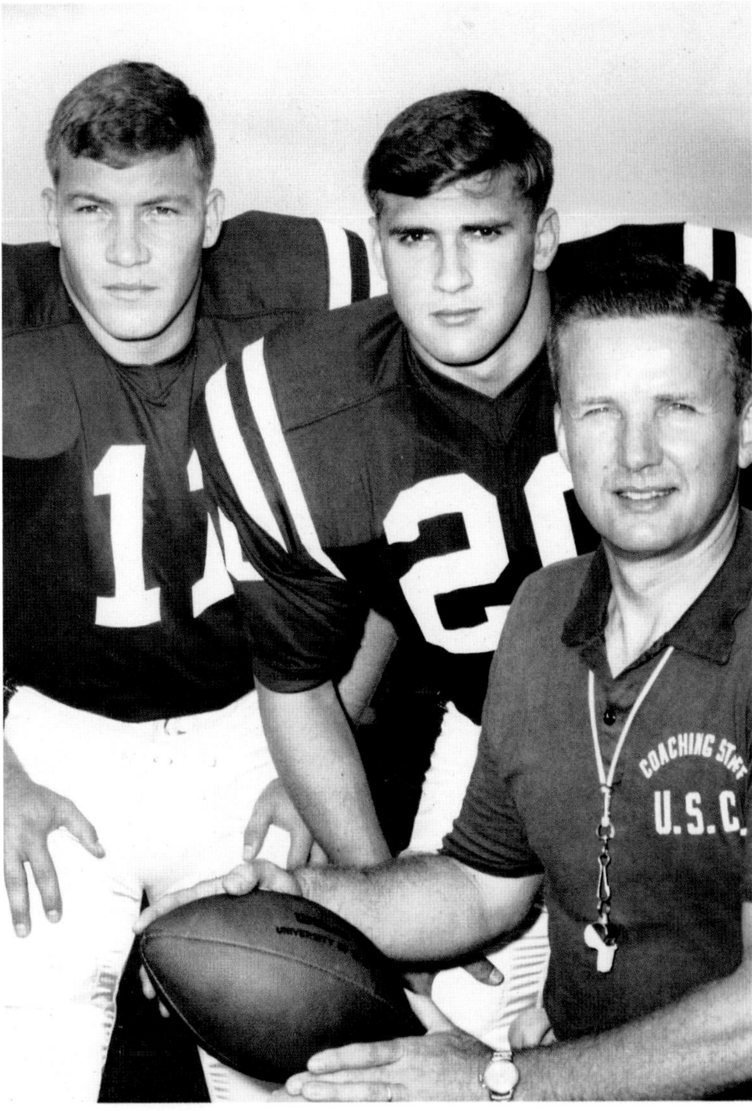

BELOW
Coach Paul Dietzel, kneeling next to Ben Garnto and Benny Galloway, came to South Carolina from Louisiana State after directing the Tigers to a national championship. He coached the Gamecocks from 1966-74, and his teams went 42-53-1.

runs this conference. ... I demand respect for the University of South Carolina."

Animosities simmered as Duke finished first for the fourth straight season, then won the title after enduring a 21-20 slowdown by North Carolina in the ACC Tournament semifinals. Bubas won his third coach of the year award in four seasons; Vacendak was 1966 ACC player of the year, and the Blue Devils again reached the Final Four, losing to Kentucky at Cole Field House. It was UK's second win over an ACC team that season after defeating Virginia in December in the opener at $4 million University Hall.

The Wildcats fell to Texas Western (later Texas-El Paso) in the title game, the first major-college championship won by a squad that started all African-Americans. That Texas Western won with discipline and defense, and upset Adolph Rupp's lily-white Wildcats, hastened the assimilation of African-Americans into the game.

On April 30, 1966, Case died. He left much of his money to former players and coaches and was buried along U.S. Highway 70 between Raleigh and Durham so he could overlook Wolfpack teams en route to face the Blue Devils. The day Case died, in Baton Rouge LSU announced it had hired Maravich as head coach. His son, Pete, went with him.

The ACC returned its attention to Grosso. First the league adjusted its eligibility rule, deciding that participation required an 800 SAT score regardless of a player's source of financial assistance. Grosso was then ruled ineligible.

The worst was yet to come for South Carolina. During August 1966, the school was forced to forfeit its '65 football games and received other punishment after Weaver found evidence "certain athletic personnel" prior to Dietzel's arrival had "deliberately planned and put into effect gross malpractices for the sole purpose of gaining an unfair advantage." Then in January 1967, the NCAA placed the basketball program on two years' probation for recruiting violations involving Grosso.

McGuire, the first coach to take teams from different schools to the NCAA final (St. John's and UNC), now became the first to place two different programs on probation for recruiting violations (UNC and USC).

An outraged McGuire went on the attack, blaming Cameron and Chuck Erickson, the AD at North Carolina, for conspiring against USC. "I have never

BELOW
Former Clemson football coach and director of athletics Frank Howard is shown here in his early years at the school. His teams won six ACC championships and went 165-118-12. He is a member of the College Football Hall of Fame. Howard, who placed tobacco at each corner of Memorial Stadium when it was built, is buried within sight of "Death Valley."

FACING PAGE
Frank Howard stands next to his rock, which he made famous. Memorial Stadium had been nicknamed "Death Valley" by an opposing coach, and the rock was a gift to Howard from a friend, who brought it from Death Valley, Calif. The rock was first placed on its pedestal on Sept. 24, 1966. The Tigers then started a tradition in the first game of the 1967 season of rubbing the rock for good luck before running down the adjoining hill to the field prior to each home game.

Clemson Welcomes You To Death Valley

BELOW
Former N.C. State wrestler Chuck Amato also played linebacker for the Wolfpack. Amato was a member of the "White Shoes Defense" in 1967. As a wrestler, he won ACC titles in two weight classes. The 1967 Wolfpack football team went 9-2, 5-1 in the ACC and enjoyed one of the most successful seasons in school history. Amato coached football under Bobby Bowden at Florida State for 18 years and then returned to N.C. State to become head coach in 2000.

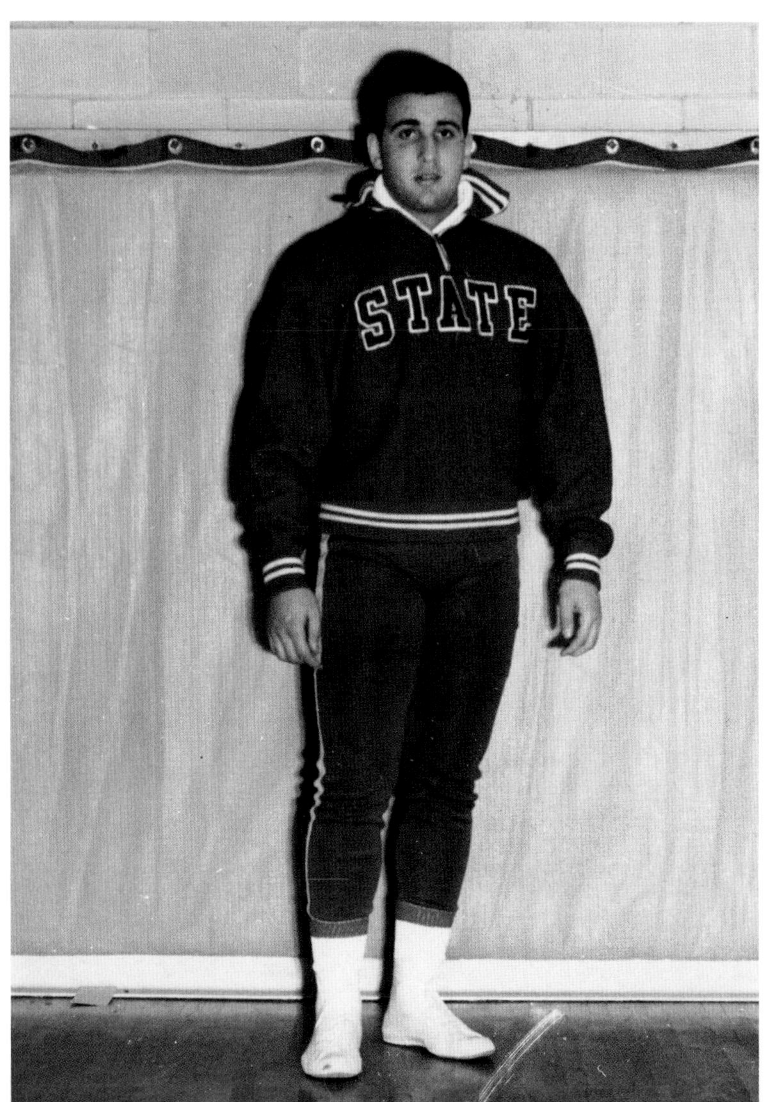

gotten into the gutter with skunks before in my life, but this time I have," McGuire declared. "Not for myself, but to save a boy's life."

McGuire's words became so heated, the president of South Carolina apologized publicly for his coach, whom he muzzled. Grosso transferred to Louisville. ACC rules were temporarily changed to allow teams to reschedule games with South Carolina to a neutral court or to cancel them entirely "because of the climate created by events of the past several months." Gamecock fans began a campaign called "Project GET OUT" to withdraw from the ACC.

The 1966 football season seemed less bruising by comparison. N.C. State opened new 45,000-seat Carter Stadium, later Carter-Finley, near the state fairgrounds west of campus. Clemson finished a game ahead of the Wolfpack as Howard won his fifth ACC title and second coach of the year award.

The season also saw the start of a distinctive tradition at Clemson, where a stone from Death Valley, Calif., was installed at Memorial Stadium.

Clemson's home field had been dubbed "Death Valley" by an opposing coach, and now "Howard's Rock" gave physical testament to the linkage. The rock, a gift to Howard from a friend, was placed atop a pedestal prior to the Sept. 24, 1966, opener against Virginia. "I kind of feel like a June bride," Howard said on game's eve. "I know something's going to happen, but I don't know what."

The Cavaliers, improved under coach George Blackburn, led 35-17 late in the third quarter behind quarterback Bob Davis, the '66 player of the year, and running back Frank Quayle. That's when Clemson quarterback Jimmy Addison got untracked. Hitting 12 of 19 passes for 283 yards and three touchdowns, including a 75-yard toss to Jacky Jackson with 3:49 to go, Addison rallied Clemson to a 40-35 victory.

Christened in triumph, Howard's Rock became a fixture. The next season, as Clemson repeated as ACC champion, Howard added a wrinkle to his rock's symbolic function — touching the stone prior to a game became an affirmation of a commitment to total effort, a tradition that continues to this day.

Clemson had to be perfect to repeat because 1967 saw N.C. State reach its zenith under Earle Edwards. The Wolfpack had 17 senior starters, most notably 6-4, 257-pound defensive tackle Dennis Byrd, an All-American and the first football player three times voted All-ACC.

The Wolfpack built an identity as the "White Shoes Defense," a gimmick spawned by several players including linebacker Chuck Amato, who returned 23 years later as head coach. There was a touch of daring in wearing white footgear, typified by bad-boy Alabama quarterback Joe Willie Namath, among others. (Namath had originally intended to attend Maryland, but he failed to qualify academically.)

Before every game N.C. State players used white shoe polish to transform their black shoes. They did this even with borrowed soccer shoes at the Astrodome, where they faced second-ranked Houston on artificial turf. The defense throttled Houston, the nation's most prolific offensive unit, in a 16-6 victory that C.D. Chesley telecast back to Reynolds Coliseum via closed circuit. Afterward celebrating fans thronged nearby Hillsborough Street and a crowd estimated at 7,000 met the team at the airport.

N.C. State went on to win its first seven games, rising to third in the polls. Included was a Sept. 16 victory over North Carolina as part of the only football doubleheader in ACC history. Duke beat Wake in the nightcap. But with a shot at the No. 1 spot, the Pack lost 13-8 at Penn State, their final chance ending on fourth down at the Nittany Lions' 1-foot line. N.C. State then lost at Clemson, the Tigers sporting shoes painted orange. "If we had won at Penn State, we'd have won at Clemson," Weedon said. "The team and the area were a morgue" after the loss in Pennsylvania.

N.C. State, 8-2 and ranked 17th, earned an invitation to the Liberty Bowl in Memphis, breaking a three-year drought for the ACC, longest in history. The Wolfpack capped a season in which the ACC first surpassed one million in attendance by beating Georgia, 14-7.

Another milestone was recorded that '67

BELOW
North Carolina tailback Don McCauley (left) and coach Bill Dooley walk off the field after a win at Kenan Stadium. McCauley set an ACC record in 1970 that stood for 29 years by rushing for 1,720 yards.

season at Wake Forest. Tate went with Freddie Summers, a junior-college transfer, as his starting quarterback. Summers possessed excellent speed, good size, a strong arm and good judgment making plays out of Wake's option offense. "He was terrific," said John Swofford, a rival quarterback at UNC. "He was a great player, I thought."

Summers was African-American. No other predominantly white university in the South had a black quarterback before Summers arrived on the scene in 1967. Five more years would pass before Tennessee's Condredge Holloway broke the SEC color line at quarterback. This slowness was largely by design. As *Ebony* put it in December 1966, "It was not stated openly, but the consensus of opinion was that tan players were not up to the mental duties demanded of a quarterback — the snap decisions, deft play-calling and overall leadership."

Tate, from Illinois, had other ideas and found an ally in Wake President Tribble. Both saw tremendous opportunity for the school to make inroads while others hesitated. Tate had African-Americans on his varsity squad by 1965.

"I think it's too bad Wake has not enjoyed the credit for being [almost] the first school to recruit blacks," Tate said. "It's gone by the wayside, and people have lost sight of it. I think it's a major, major thing, and Wake Forest should claim credit for this."

The path wasn't always smooth. Feelings often ran high regarding race.

RIGHT
Wake Forest's Freddie Summers (7) became the first African-American quarterback in the ACC. Summers earned all-conference honors that season. He accounted for 28 touchdowns rushing and throwing in his two years as the Deacons' quarterback and set the school record for the longest scoring run from scrimmage with a 90-yard dash in 1968.

Emotions ran even higher over South Carolina basketball, especially after the Grosso incident. Duke drew much of the anger among Gamecock fans. The atmosphere became so heated USC's faculty representative for athletics warned "that he had some misgivings about the Duke-South Carolina game being played in Columbia," according to Commissioner Weaver. At the commissioner's urging, the 1967 series between the schools was canceled.

The '67 Blue Devils faded to second, supplanted by North Carolina, which swept through the ACC Tournament — held for the first time in Greensboro rather than at Reynolds — behind Larry Miller, the player of the year. The Tar Heels advanced to the Final Four, lost twice and finished 26-6. The following season Miller repeated as player of the year, and the Tar Heels repeated as regular-season champion, tournament champion and Final Four entrant. This time they were 28-4, reaching the NCAA title game only to lose 78-55 to UCLA and center Kareem Abdul-Jabbar (Lew Alcindor).

Reflecting a league rule change that expanded postseason participation, Duke went to the 1967 NIT, despite dropping a 12-10 decision to N.C. State in the ACC Tournament semifinals. The deep-freeze evoked the famously dismissive on-air comment from UNC radio voice Bill Currie that the game was "about as exciting as artificial insemination." The Blue Devils lost quickly in the NIT to Southern Illinois and star guard Walt Frazier, a black All-American who had left Atlanta to play his

BELOW
Virginia halfback Frank Quayle (24) led the nation with 1,616 all-purpose yards as a sophomore in 1966. He was the ACC player of the year in 1968 after rushing for 1,213 yards and catching 30 passes for 426 yards.

ball farther north.

An ACC team did win an NCAA championship in 1968, as Maryland captured the men's soccer title. The Terps also won in lacrosse in 1960 and 1967, the only national crowns achieved by ACC squads during the '60s.

Over the summer, many prominent African-American basketball players, including Abdul-Jabbar and Houston's Elvin Hayes, boycotted the 1968 Olympics at Mexico City. One who went was North Carolina's superb sophomore, Charles Scott. The sole ACC representative on the team, Scott helped the U.S. maintain its lock on the gold medal.

Scott's success, as well as his treatment by UNC's Smith, drew notice within the African-American community, according to Ernie Jackson. "I think that helped (Smith) for years to come," the Duke player said. "I think there was a good amount of loyalty toward him for what he did."

As Bill Tate noted, Wake didn't reap such dividends despite a second season with Summers as quarterback. For one thing, Wake didn't win, and Tate was soon gone. The '68 Deacons went 2-7-1, losing four of their first five games by a combined 11 points. The other game ended in a tie. "He was very good," Jackson said of Summers, "and I think his supporting cast wasn't there." Among the defeats was the opener at Groves Stadium, the school's long-awaited football facility near campus.

Wake's fortunes waned even as coach George Blackburn and senior tailback Frank Quayle sparked Virginia to a 7-3 record, its best showing since 1952. Virginia scored at least 41 points in five of its wins, and fewer than 24 points only twice, as it became the first ACC squad to average more than 400 yards in total offense (439.4).

Quayle led the ACC in all-purpose yardage for three straight years, pacing the nation as a sophomore with 1,616 yards. As a senior, Quayle's 1,213 rushing yards led the conference. His all-purpose average that year (186.9) remains the best by an

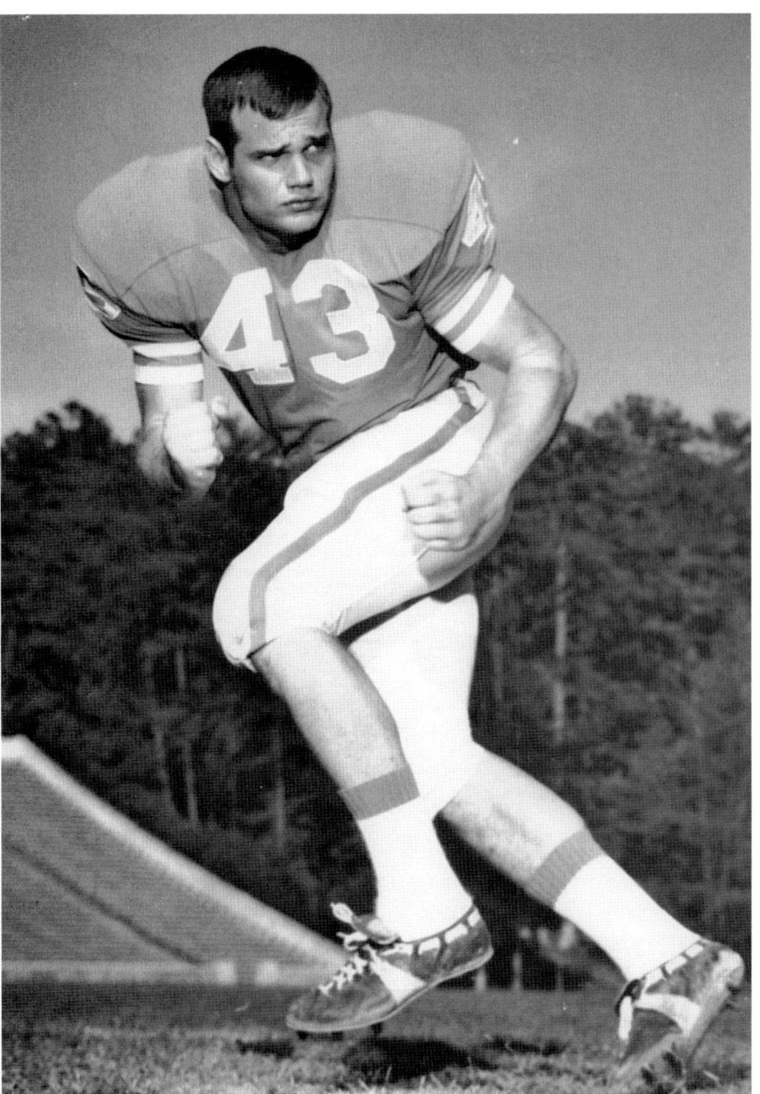

ABOVE
John Bunting played linebacker for North Carolina from 1969-71 and was a member of coach Bill Dooley's first ACC championship team at UNC. From there Bunting moved to the National Football League, playing linebacker for the Philadelphia Eagles from 1972-82. He played two more years in the United States Football League before retiring as a player to become a coach. He returned to UNC in December of 2000 as the Tar Heels' new head coach.

ACC back. The performance earned Quayle honors as 1968 ACC player of the year. Blackburn was named coach of the year. He would be gone after two more seasons.

The big news for Maryland football was the end of a 16-game losing streak. Begun in 1966, the slide ended in 1968 with a 33-24 win over North Carolina, the only team to finish lower in the standings.

The All-ACC quarterback in 1968, Duke's Leo Hart, became the league's first passer to exceed 2,000 yards in a season. The following year Hart became the only ACC quarterback named all-conference three times. He was also a central figure in one of the most pivotal trick plays in ACC history, pulled by the Blue Devils over North Carolina.

Rebuilding under Bill Dooley, the favored Tar Heels were tied with Duke at 7-7 late in the third quarter of their 1969 game. The Blue Devils had the ball on their own 47, third down and nine.

Duke, en route to its worst season in 43 years, lined up to the left of the ball. Hart knelt as if tying his shoe. "I'm the sophomore signalcaller, and I've got my back to everything," recalled John Bunting, then a UNC linebacker and now the school's head coach. "I can hear people talking behind me, and I can hear them telling Leo to get his shoes tied."

Suddenly, with the Tar Heels still in their defensive huddle, Duke ran its "shoestring play," also known as "Killer Left."

Flanker Marcell Courtillet ducked in, grabbed the ball and shoveled it to wide receiver Wes Chesson. No defender was in the vicinity as Chesson ran 53 yards around left end for the go-ahead score in a 17-13 victory. "I would have had to slip on a blade of grass not to score," Chesson said.

"It was an awful feeling," Bunting said. "I cried after that game. I felt miserable that we lost that ball game." Third-year coach Bill Dooley still brought North Carolina in at 5-5, bolstered by the running of Don McCauley, one of the great backs in ACC history and the 1969 ACC player of the year. The junior finished atop the league with 1,092 yards rushing, becoming the first player in school history to run for more than 1,000 yards in a season.

The '69 football season belonged, though, to the other Carolina, which won its only unblemished ACC title. Dietzel increased revenues and spending, and was rewarded with a 7-4 record, the first winning finish at South Carolina since 1959. Six Gamecocks were selected all-conference, led by running back Warren Muir. USC was invited to the Peach Bowl and lost 14-3 to West Virginia.

South Carolina fared nearly as well in basketball, finishing second with an 11-3 ACC record. McGuire upped USC's talent level and league wins each year, and the 1968-69 squad was his best yet. The group featured scrappy off-guard Bobby Cremins and a quartet of sophomores led by 6-10 Tom Owens and 6-2 playmaker John Roche. Owens led the ACC in rebounds

GAMECOCK YEARS (clockwise from top left)
Football coach Paul Dietzel talks to Johnny Gregory. Gamecock guard Bobby Cremins (21) takes a shot. Cremins would return to the ACC eventually as the basketball coach for Georgia Tech. Dietzel celebrates the Gamecocks' 1969 championship in football. USC went 6-0 in the league that season. Two-time ACC player of the year John Roche fires a shot. Frank McGuire, who won a national championship in basketball at UNC, returned to the league to coach the Gamecocks in 1964. He was named the ACC coach of the year at North Carolina (1957) and South Carolina (1970). His teams went undefeated in regular-season conference play both of those years.

GAMECOCKS
88

SOUTH
21
CAROLINA

USC

32

GO TARHEELS GO

with 13.0 per game. Roche led the Gamecocks with a 23.6-point average, second in the league to Clemson's Butch Zatezalo (25.8).

The performances earned McGuire recognition as 1969 ACC coach of the year and Roche as '69 player of the year, the first sophomore so honored.

Virginia was starting to make noise, too, though not in a manner it preferred. Following a quick ACC Tournament loss in Charlotte, the Cavaliers' 10th straight in the first round, junior guards John English and Tony Kinn openly criticized coach Bill "Hoot" Gibson. The *Cavalier Daily*, the Virginia student newspaper, ran a four-part series calling for Gibson's ouster, arguing that players had been "mishandled, misled and in some cases deceived by the coach." But the school stuck with Gibson, his case bolstered by an open letter from members of the 1968-69 freshman squad, who as upperclassmen would take Virginia to new basketball heights.

Intense Maryland football coach Bob Ward wasn't so lucky. A petition calling for his removal was signed by 115 players, and after posting a two-year record of 2-17 he resigned on the eve of the '69 ACC Tournament.

LEFT
North Carolina's 1969 basketball team celebrates its third consecutive ACC championship under coach Dean Smith. The Tar Heels made it to the Final Four all three seasons.

Demonstrative student-athletes were in keeping with the tenor of the time, which saw protests sweep college campuses, most in reaction to the Vietnam War. Militancy had transformed the civil rights movement, particularly after the assassination of Martin Luther King Jr. in April 1968. Takeovers of college administration buildings swept the country. C.B. Claiborne, Duke's first African-American basketball player, participated in such an action as a senior in February 1969.

The Blue Devils ended the 1969 regular season tied for third, yet not only reached the ACC Tournament final but led top-seed North Carolina by 11 points with less than 17 minutes remaining.

That is, until Scott took over. The leading scorer on the ACC's first-place team scored 40 points — 25 in the second half on 12-of-13 shooting — in an 85-74 victory. Scott's performance sparked lavish praise. Typical was Mel Derrick of the *Charlotte Observer*, who wrote: "The man who peeled off the shroud was Charlie Scott. That's 's' as in sensational, 'c' as in confident, 'o' as in oh-h-h, and 'tt' as in terrific twice."

The win sent the Tar Heels to the NCAAs, and UNC advanced to its third consecutive Final Four, a run unmatched by another ACC program until 1990. Scott, fluid and versatile, was excellent in the NCAA Tournament. Most notable were his 32 points in the East Regional final, capped by an 18-foot jumper to beat Davidson 87-85 at the buzzer. "Dean had a nice blend of players who played together," said Terry Holland, a Davidson assistant and later Virginia's head coach and athletics director. "I'd say that was probably the real step up. And for the league, too. The league had put teams in the Final Four before, but not three in a row."

Shortly after UNC eliminated his Wildcats for the second straight year, Lefty Driesell departed Davidson to become Maryland's head coach. "I feel Maryland has the potential to be the UCLA of the East Coast," Driesell proclaimed. He quickly hired as an assistant George Raveling, the first African-American to hold such a job in the ACC.

FACING PAGE
Clemson's Frank Howard retired as football coach in 1969. He served on the coaching staff at the South Carolina school for 39 years, 30 of those as head coach.

WE SALUTE
COACH FRANK HOWARD
1940 1969

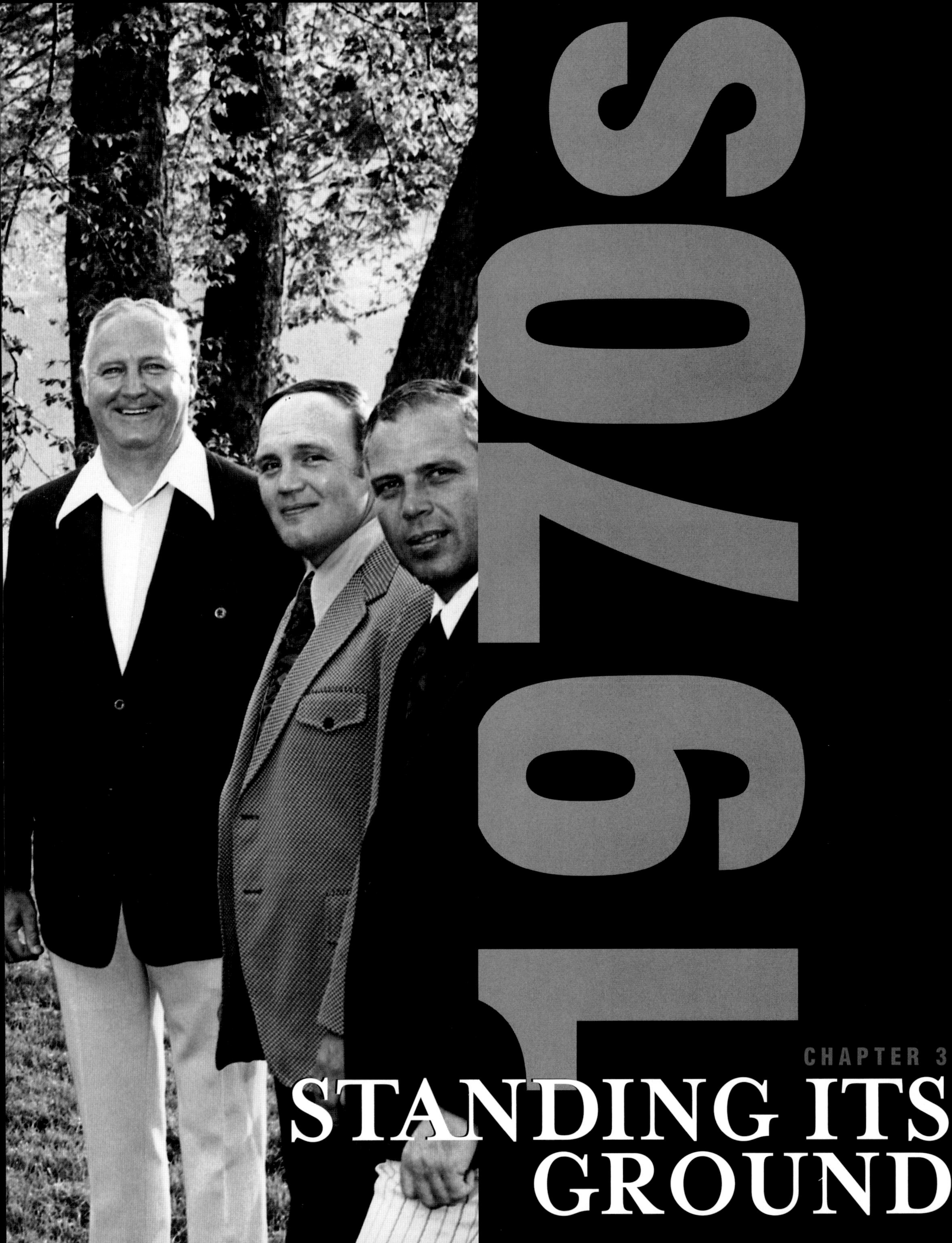

1970s

CHAPTER 3

STANDING ITS GROUND

Handled well, adversity can present opportunity, a lesson the Atlantic Coast Conference learned in the 1970s as it survived painful internal discord to emerge a stronger and more broadly competitive league.

The circumstances that ultimately brought Georgia Tech into the ACC fold had their roots in decisions made in the early '60s, when conference leaders took a strong stand on academic eligibility requirements for athletics. "I think maybe the greatest thing you could say about the ACC is it's achieved national prominence, leadership, without notable sacrifice of its academic integrity," said Irwin Smallwood, longtime editor and writer at the *Greensboro Daily News.*

Some chafed under the academic restrictions, notably South Carolina athletics director Paul Dietzel, who doubled as football coach, and Frank McGuire, his basketball counterpart. "The ACC, the minimum [SAT score] was 800," said Tom Price, South Carolina's sports information director at the time. "Dietzel felt that was a disservice to the entire ACC in recruiting, especially South Carolina and Clemson, because we were on the border of the SEC. We were losing players left and right."

Dietzel, a man with a big smile whom Clemson's Frank Howard called "Pepsodent Paul," was "the driving force" behind USC's 1971 withdrawal, although "no one person made the final decision," Price said. Gene Hooks, Wake's athletics director from 1964-92, agreed the decision was a group effort. "There was no doubt in my mind but what both of them felt like they would be more successful if they got out of the conference," Hooks said of Dietzel and McGuire.

Later, McGuire claimed the impetus came from Dietzel, who in turn insisted no Gamecock coach objected when the 1971 withdrawal was discussed. "Everybody was trying to put the blame on somebody else when they left," recalled Marvin "Skeeter" Francis, the retired ACC publicist.

There's no question the rise of South Carolina basketball, and the acrimony surrounding the squad, helped expedite the separation process.

Typical were McGuire's comments and actions following a devastating loss in the final of the 1970 ACC Tournament with a squad he called "the greatest college team I ever coached." Heavily favored after posting an undefeated ACC regular season, the Gamecocks lost to N.C. State in a slowdown that lasted two overtimes. An ankle injury hobbling star guard John Roche proved a decisive factor.

McGuire wouldn't bring his team out of the locker room after the game to accept the second-place trophy. After 15 years of coaching in the ACC, he claimed he didn't know the awards ceremony required his team's presence. A longtime critic of the tournament, he also blasted the event as "ridiculous" and added: "I don't care anymore. I think stupid people realize what they are doing to me and everyone else. It is plain ridiculous."

The 1969-70 ACC basketball season had been one of the most competitive in history, the first since 1957 in which only two teams — Virginia and Clemson — posted losing records.

Duke, 17-9 under new coach Bucky Waters, finished in the first division, led by big man Randy Denton. The ACC's other new coach, Maryland's Lefty Driesell, finished 13-13, the only non-winning season of his 17-year tenure at College Park.

More important than the record was Driesell's immediate transformation of the atmosphere surrounding the Terrapin program. Driesell was hired around the same time Jim Kehoe, Maryland's new athletics director, brought aboard football coach Roy Lester, a success locally at Montgomery (Md.) High School. When the search for a basketball coach came down to Driesell and Morgan Wootten of nearby DeMatha High School, Kehoe went with the Davidson veteran, who had been considered for the Duke job as well.

"He was obviously fiery," said Terry Holland, who played for, assisted and later succeeded Driesell at Davidson. "He had a great passion for the game and had a competitive nature that was right on the surface ... Lefty's always, you know what you're getting. There's not a lot of guile there. A lot of salesmanship, but even that's upfront."

Driesell was offered substantial support at Maryland, from a full slate of scholarships to a new courtesy car annually to a princely salary of $21,000. In turn he said, "I believe I can produce a national champion at Maryland."

Confidence was understandable because Driesell had achieved four top-10 finishes over the previous six years at cozy Davidson, a school with more limitations than Maryland. But first Driesell had to invigorate a program so out of favor with its own students and fans that writer Kent Baker called Cole "a virtual morgue" during games.

"It was terrible," agreed Gary Williams, who played at Maryland from 1965-67 and stayed close to the situation. "You went down to Tobacco Road and played in those gyms back then; it was such a tough place to play compared to our place. We had no home-court advantage whatsoever when I played there. I think it was the easiest place to play in the league."

The situation had worsened, if anything, by the time Driesell arrived and made his

BELOW
South Carolina's Tom Riker (51) flips the ball toward the basket. The Gamecocks defeated UNC for the ACC Tournament championship in 1971, one year after a bitter defeat to N.C. State in the final of the same event.

FACING PAGE
Maryland coach Charles "Lefty" Driesell, a Duke graduate, instilled great enthusiasm in the Terrapins' basketball program after taking over as head coach in 1969.

pronouncement about becoming "the UCLA of the East." Hyperbole, yes, but Williams applauded it. "That was a marketing move that Lefty did when he came in," said Williams, who led the Terrapins to the national championship in 2002 as their head coach. "It worked. He's been criticized some for it, but it's the old story, he got a lot of attention — whether it was positive or negative — about saying it. Back then, that's what he was looking for. He wanted Maryland to be talked about. It sure worked."

Driesell concentrated on off-court improvement beyond recruiting as Duke's Bubas had done a decade earlier. Maryland redid dressing and training rooms and the media guide, which evolved into a paean to Driesell's achievements. Newspaper ads touted Maryland basketball — attracting the eye of recruit Jim O'Brien — and every game was broadcast on radio. Floor seats were installed, eliminating large open spaces between the court and fans. Driesell connected with students. The coach also became part of the show, flashing a "V for victory" sign like President Richard Nixon as he entered the gym to the strains of "Hail to the Chief."

"At a school where the biggest thrill at basketball games immediately prior to Driesell had been supplied by the race between the two sweepers who cleaned the floor at halftime, the contrast boggled the mind. A revolution had deposed apathy," Kent Baker wrote in his 1979 book *Red, White and Amen* on Maryland basketball.

Also deposed that season was North Carolina, a second-place finisher after three straight ACC titles. The Tar Heels were 18-9, the last time a Dean Smith squad had fewer than 21 wins in a season. UNC was eliminated in the opening round of the 1970 ACC Tournament by Virginia, which earned its first tournament victory since 1959, despite 41 points from Charles Scott, the UNC All-American.

"Scott may just be the best player the Atlantic Coast Conference has ever had," Clemson coach Bobby Roberts said. Said Kentucky's Adolph Rupp: "Scott is such an unsettling player. He destroyed my man [Larry] Steele who was trying to guard him. Maybe we should have sent Scott to Viet Nam. He could terrorize the Viet Cong like he does everyone in this country."

A pair of great scoring match-ups between New Yorkers Scott, a senior, and Charlie Davis, a Wake junior, also marked the 1970 season. The Deacons rallied from a 15-point deficit in the first half at Chapel Hill to win, 91-90. Scott had 43 points to Davis' 34. Wake staged a comeback in the return engagement to win again, 88-85. Davis scored six of his 41 points in the final 90 seconds. Scott had 31 in a losing effort, finishing the year with a 27.1 scoring average, third-highest in UNC history.

N.C. State tied the Tar Heels for second, led by forward Vann Williford, a two-time pick for first team All-ACC. Williford scored 73 points in the '70 ACC Tournament, including 18 of the Wolfpack's 42 in the title game, en route to winning the MVP award.

LE FIELD HOU
HOME OF THE TERRAPINS
PO

Roche didn't start the final against N.C. State because of his sprained left ankle, but he played most of the way. He had repeated as ACC player of the year, barely edging Scott, and it was his team. "There is not the slightest doubt in my mind that Roche is the greatest player in the conference and in the entire country," McGuire said. "I think he is the greatest player I have ever coached."

McGuire wasn't one for cultivating his bench, preferring to employ a gifted iron five. "He always coached from a confidence standpoint," said Smith, McGuire's former assistant, "telling a player, 'What do you think I recruited you for?'"

Roche "was a great clutch player, the type of player who could dominate a game," according to Price, USC sports historian. But Roche was so badly hobbled against the Wolfpack that he shot 4-of-17 from the floor, missing jumpers to win at the end of regulation and the first overtime. The game finally turned with 22 seconds left in the second extra period when guard Ed Leftwich stole the ball from USC senior Bobby Cremins and drove for the decisive basket.

"The game against South Carolina in the tournament gave us some momentum," said N.C. State coach Norman Sloan, an Everett Case disciple. "We got some credibility out of that."

The result crushed the Gamecocks, particularly McGuire and a disconsolate Cremins, who fled to the North Carolina mountains to restore his spirits. What McGuire called "the smartest team I've ever had," a squad he believed could win the national championship, was relegated to sitting out the postseason. Back then, USC was prohibited from making an NIT appearance because it hosted an NCAA Tournament regional.

"All they had to do was win the East Regional and they were in the Final Four," said Bob Cole, a writer with *The State* in Columbia. "That championship that year was their birthright." Soon green bumper stickers urging South Carolina to "Drop the ACC" were common around town.

South Carolina also had a bad time of it in 1970 in football. The Gamecocks were 4-6-1 a year after winning their sole conference title. N.C. State, two years removed from a title, went 3-7 in Earle Edwards' last season.

Clemson, playing for the first time since 1931 without Howard on the sideline as an assistant or head coach, dropped to 3-8, its worst record in 18 years. New coach Cecil "Hootie" Ingram, later athletics director at Florida State (1981-89), did have immediate impact in one area. Ingram "wanted to change the image, try something new," according to Bill McLellan, then an assistant athletics director. So the school hired a Greenville, S.C., advertising firm to come up with a new emblem for its teams. Thus the Tiger paw was born.

While more familiar contenders dropped from the football picture, Wake Forest, under second-year coach Cal Stoll, won its only ACC championship to date. Picked to finish last in 1970, the Deacons dropped their first three games at Nebraska, South Carolina and Florida State. Stoll, the 1970 ACC coach of the year, switched to a veer option offense and didn't lose again in the league.

"They were a rough, tough team; they were a physical team," said John Bunting, a UNC linebacker who returned to become the Tar Heels' head coach. Wake finished 6-5, 5-1 in the ACC, its first winning record overall since 1959. Key to the team's success was a pair of all-conference Larrys: Russell at quarterback and Hopkins at running back.

Player of the year went to North Carolina's Don McCauley, an unassuming 6-foot senior who enjoyed arguably the greatest season ever by an ACC running back.

McCauley came to UNC from Garden City, N.Y., just as taskmaster Bill Dooley took over the program. Decrying a "country club" atmosphere, Dooley put his squad through such rigorous workouts in the spring of 1967 that he instigated wholesale departures among the veterans.

"People told me not to take the job because Carolina was a party school and the atmosphere wasn't right," Dooley said. "I told them we would create our own atmosphere." Come fall, the roster was so decimated that freshmen — who had their own squad and schedule in those days of ineligibility — were needed to practice with the varsity.

McCauley, recruited as a defender, was inserted at tailback sometime during the first scrimmage. "He ran all over the place," recalled a classmate listed as Johnny Swofford, now the ACC commissioner. "The rest of us are just kind of looking at each other like, 'This guy's supposed to be a defensive back?' He was just piling up yardage against the varsity, and that's what he did his entire career."

BELOW
Clemson coach Frank Howard holds a fish while North Carolina coach Bill Dooley looks on. The two were attending a spring golf and fishing outing at Grandfather Mountain in North Carolina.

Bunting tried to stop McCauley in practice. "Don McCauley would be an All-ACC back today," Bunting said. "This guy could run around, over, through. He could juke people. He had good ball skills."

Good speed, better balance and remarkable durability enabled McCauley to lead the ACC in rushing yardage and all-purpose yardage in 1969 and 1970. The league's second repeat player of the year in football, after N.C. State's Roman Gabriel a decade earlier, McCauley gained 1,092 yards on 204 carries as a junior and 1,720 on 324 carries as a senior. His '70 yardage broke what was then the single-season NCAA record, set at Southern Cal by O.J. Simpson. McCauley's record remained the ACC standard for 29 years. He also scored 21 touchdowns in 1970, still the league record.

"He never missed a game," said Swofford, a quarterback. "Of course, in Coach Dooley's offense at the time, we ran him to death. At one point, he carried it eight times in a row, which for a running back in football, that's a lot. He finally, after the eighth carry, walked back to the huddle and said, 'Would you give the ball to somebody else?'" Swofford said, laughing at the memory.

McCauley, the only UNC running back besides Charlie Justice (1948, '49) selected as a consensus All-American, was elected to the College Football Hall of Fame in 2001.

Tied for second in the ACC with Duke, North Carolina was chosen to face Arizona State in the 1970 Peach Bowl. The Tar Heels lost 48-26, finishing 8-4. Wake, the ACC champion, stayed home.

By then the league had confronted several more important losses at its winter meeting in Greensboro. Bob James, a former Maryland student and associate dean, was chosen to replace Jim Weaver, who died in July 1970. South Carolina had announced in October 1970 that it would begin recruiting immediately under less stringent NCAA rules, its trustees arguing that "the ACC cut-off rule is educationally unsound and athletically unwise." Facing the prospect of possible dissolution, with Clemson and Maryland wavering, ACC presidents voted 5-3 to stick with an 800 SAT score and 1.6 grade-point prediction for athletic eligibility.

The ACC's standard "became a handy, all-purpose scapegoat," wrote Frank Barrows in the *Charlotte Observer*. "Football coaches were quick to blame their 2-7-1 records on the 800 rule, citing it as the only thing which stood between them and every player who eventually wound up at Alabama. Basketball coaches were less vocal. But they, too, could grumble about how it hampered recruiting."

Greasing the skids for USC's departure was a gifted basketball squad still smarting from its 1970 disappointment and seemingly at war with the rest of the league. "It was an us-against-the-world thing," said Cole, the Columbia reporter.

Ranked second in preseason, a South

1970

7.11.70
ACC Commissioner Jim Weaver dies while attending a meeting in Colorado

7.21.70
Tiger paw unveiled as new Clemson emblem

12.10.70
Bob James hired as second ACC commissioner, effective March 1, 1971

Carolina team with speed, size, toughness and unaccustomed depth generated great excitement in Columbia, drawing a full house for its first intrasquad scrimmage. "Nobody really cared about basketball down here until Frank McGuire came down here and embarrassed everybody," Frank Howard told Clemson's new basketball coach, Tates Locke.

Most attention from 1969-71 focused on the 6-3 Roche, but Owens, a rugged post player and fellow New Yorker, led the ACC in rebounding all three years and was selected all-conference each season. McGuire believed, with some justification, that New York prep ball was the nation's finest. So it was no surprise that at South Carolina, as at North Carolina, the bulk of his squad hailed from his home turf. Indicative of the fervor for Gamecock basketball, a Charleston columnist called McGuire's players "our South Carolina Yankees." Even Cremins' replacement on the '71 squad, sophomore Kevin Joyce, was a New Yorker.

"I don't think it's fair to say he wouldn't play them unless they were from New York," Smith said of McGuire's player preferences. "That's true, but it's a terrible thing to say."

Worse things were said of McGuire and his 1970-71 squad as it became embroiled in a series of denunciations, scuffles, confrontations and fights. "That was an ugly year, that year," recalled Gene Corrigan, who became Virginia's athletics director on Jan. 1, 1971.

The worst incident occurred less than a week after the ACC's December meeting. A melee broke out in the final five minutes as Maryland was routed at Columbia. While Driesell was on the court trying to act as peacemaker, he was held from behind by USC's Jimmy Powell and punched in the face by Gamecock John Ribock. Newspapers ran the graphic photo the next day, even as McGuire insisted tape showed the Maryland coach had punched himself.

Warning of dire consequences, including deaths, McGuire said South Carolina's game at College Park should be canceled "under any conditions." Driesell predicted, "There will be a riot." Norvell Neve, acting commissioner until James took office March 1, 1971, announced the game would be played, but "only if this office is completely convinced that it is safe and prudent to do so."

As the pot simmered, the Gamecocks beat Clemson to capture their 17th consecutive regular-season ACC win. They then lost their next three league games, all on the road.

North Carolina defeated USC decisively. Next, on Jan. 9 before a sellout crowd at Maryland, South Carolina blew a 30-25 lead with 16 seconds remaining in overtime and lost, 31-30. The score had been 4-3 at halftime as the Terps held the ball for all but 20 seconds in the opening period. Following the incident-free game, celebra-

.16.70
ght at South Carolina
volving Maryland in
ich Terp coach Lefty
iesell is punched in face

1971

3.29.71
South Carolina announces departure from ACC

6.30.71
Voting age lowered to 18 by 26th Amendment to U.S. Constitution

7.1.71
South Carolina officially departs ACC

SOUTH
51
CAROLINA

tory fans carried Driesell on their shoulders. McGuire complained that he and his players were manhandled leaving the court.

The Gamecocks completed their unhappy tour at Charlottesville. The largest crowd in Virginia history to that point witnessed sophomore guard Barry Parkhill hit a 15-foot jumper with seven seconds left to secure a 50-49 Cavalier victory.

Barely two years after a "Boot the Hoot" campaign almost cost Bill Gibson his job, "Hooterville" signs had sprung up, and Virginia was en route to its first winning record in 17 seasons. Attendance jumped nearly 100 percent as fans embraced a squad dubbed the "Amazin' Cavaliers." The team leader was Parkhill, a supposedly marginal prospect from Pennsylvania who led Virginia in scoring with a 15.9 average.

The run of road losses left McGuire publicly bitter. Herman Helms, executive sports editor of *The State* and the coach's friend, took McGuire to task for his attitude.

"It is time the coach got rid of his persecution complex, stopped making excuses and faced the fact that the Gamecocks are only human and sometimes they really do LOSE," Helms wrote. "The officials, the crowd, the ACC are not always to blame. ... As long as he has been coaching, McGuire should have learned by now how to lose with some dignity."

South Carolina's slip on the road cost it in the ACC standings. First place in 1971 belonged to North Carolina, as it would all but once between 1967 and 1972. Smith won his third ACC coach of the year award in five seasons.

Wake's Charlie Davis, a slender guard who led the conference with 26.5 points per game, was voted '71 ACC player of the year. In 1969 UNC's Scott had alleged racial prejudice when the media picked Roche ahead of him. Now Davis, less overtly involved in campus racial politics than Scott, became the first African-American honored as the ACC's top player.

The ultimate honor belonged to South Carolina, however. In its valedictory season, it won the ACC title.

His team trailed UNC by a point with six seconds remaining in the ACC Tournament final when Joyce out-leapt the Heels' taller Lee Dedmon for a jump ball. The plan was for Dedmon to tap the ball to guard George Karl near the USC bench. Instead, Joyce followed McGuire's instruction to, as Owens said, "jump for the moon and not just the ball." The tapped ball went to Owens, who laid it in the basket for a 52-51 South Carolina win. Suddenly, finally, the Gamecocks had secured an NCAA bid and an ACC championship.

Postseason wasn't kind to USC, which lost immediately to Pennsylvania. North Carolina, by contrast, won the NIT, the first of five ACC clubs to do so over the years. (The others were Maryland in 1972, Virginia in 1980 and 1992, and Wake in 2000.)

Two days after UNC beat independent Georgia Tech in New York — the Yellow Jackets left the SEC in 1963 — South Carolina announced it was leaving the

FACING PAGE
Virginia's Barry Parkhill shoots over South Carolina's Tom Riker. Parkhill was the first Cavalier to be named ACC player of the year. He led Virginia to new heights during his career, which ran from 1971-73.He set a school single-game scoring record with 51 points. His 1972 Virginia team went 21-7 and earned the school's first top-10 ranking. Parkhill averaged 21.6 points per game that season.

ACC. The act became official July 1, 1971. "I'm not surprised," Corrigan said at the time. "I don't think anybody is. But I think it's a shame that they have taken this course of action."

South Carolina's president expressed hope its withdrawal would be a short one, and the school later made several overtures to return to the conference. All were rebuffed.

Clemson, resistant to unilaterally high academic standards, remained in the ACC despite fears it might leave. "Our future was better set right where we were," said McLellan, who became AD in February 1971 upon Howard's retirement.

That fall South Carolina remained on most ACC football schedules, although the results didn't count toward league standings.

Wake Forest finished 1971 with its second consecutive winning football season, a feat unmatched at the school until the late 1980s under Bill Dooley. Again led by the backfield duo of Hopkins and Russell, the Deacons set enduring ACC marks for single-game rushes (94 in a win over Tulsa) and season records for rushing attempts (744, 67.6 per game) and most rushing yards gained (3,344). After the season, Stoll rushed to the University of Minnesota to become its head coach.

Duke posted a winning record under new coach Mike McGee, a former Blue Devil tackle who won the 1959 Outland Trophy and ACC player of the year award. The star of the team was Ernie Jackson, a

BELOW
A former ACC player of the year and first-team All-American, Mike McGee returned to Duke as the head football coach. He held that position from 1971-78, posting a 37-47-4 record. He later became the director of athletics at Southern California and then moved to take the same job at the University of South Carolina.

fleet 5-10 defensive back who doubled as a running back when injuries decimated the squad.

Jackson's 54-yard interception return for a touchdown gave Duke all the points it needed in a win at Stanford. He scored two touchdowns in a win over South Carolina, returning a punt and an interception, and saved a score with an interception. Jackson rushed for 181 yards on 17 carries against Navy and rushed for two touchdowns in a win over N.C. State.

The multifaceted performance in an age of specialization earned Jackson All-America and 1971 ACC player of the year honors. Spurned by South Carolina, his hometown team, and caught in what he called a "love-hate relationship" with Duke and its racial attitudes, Jackson was the first African-American to win the ACC award. He's also the first of eight predominantly defensive performers voted league player of the year.

The 1971 ACC football championship went to North Carolina, clearly the best team with a 6-0 league mark, 9-3 overall after losing to Georgia in the Gator Bowl. That game pitted brothers against each other as coaches for the first time — the Bulldogs' Vince Dooley against the Tar Heels' Bill Dooley, the '71 ACC coach of the year.

That same December the ACC found itself pitted against two prospective Clemson students in another contest, this one in federal court in South Carolina. Joey Edward Beach, a prospective football player, and James Marion Vickery, a diving hopeful, filed a motion to enjoin the ACC and Clemson from withholding grants-in-aid based on the 800 eligibility requirement.

The ACC argued the academic threshold represented a safeguard "to reduce the exploitation of young athletes." Beach and Vickery, joined later in the class-action suit by a pair of football aspirants, claimed the restriction was unconstitutional.

By the time the case was decided, the 1971-72 basketball season had come and gone. North Carolina was 26-5 and advanced to the Final Four for the fourth time in six years. Maryland was 27-5 and won the NIT, the second straight ACC team to do so. Virginia, behind 1972 ACC player of the year Barry Parkhill, went 21-7, the

BELOW
Ernie Jackson is one of four Duke players to earn consensus All-America honors. The defensive back played for the Blue Devils from 1969-71. When injuries depleted the squad, Jackson doubled as a running back. He became the first African-American to be named the ACC player of the year in football. He is the only player in conference history to earn the league's player of the week honors on offense and defense.

ELMORE
41
BURLESON
24
54

school's first 20-win season since 1927-28.

The ACC was moving into a pinnacle period in its basketball history, with great classes accumulating at Chapel Hill, College Park and Raleigh.

Bob McAdoo, a North Carolinian who went to Vincennes College in Indiana, returned to become one of two junior-college products ever to play for UNC's Smith. (The other was Jeb Barlow, a deep reserve on Smith's first NCAA championship squad in 1982.) McAdoo was the top scorer (19.5) and rebounder (10.1) on a '72 team with seniors Dennis Wuycik and Bill Chamberlain, junior George Karl and sophomore forward Bobby Jones.

The Tar Heels finished first in the seven-team league and got a bye in the opening round of the ACC Tournament. They won twice in Greensboro, capturing the ACC's automatic bid to the NCAAs, and advanced until Florida State beat them 79-75 in the national semifinals.

That spring McAdoo left school with a year's eligibility remaining to play professional basketball. Maryland's Barry Yates became the first ACC player to take that route the previous year.

The Terrapins apparently didn't miss Yates, the ACC's No. 6 rebounder in '71, thanks to a 1971-72 sophomore class featuring big men Len Elmore and Tom McMillen. The 6-11 McMillen was the center of a fierce recruiting battle involving Virginia, North Carolina and Maryland that received extensive national coverage. McMillen topped the Terps with a 20.8-point average, while Elmore led in rebounding (11.0).

Another recruiting battle over David Thompson, a far less-touted prospect from outside Shelby, N.C., landed both N.C. State, the school he attended, and Duke on a year's NCAA probation effective in 1972-73. Thompson joined a program — albeit as an ineligible freshman — that boasted Tom Burleson, a 7-4, 230-pound center who was the ACC's top rebounder (14.0) and No. 2 scorer (21.3) behind Parkhill.

Virginia returned four starters and won its first dozen games in 1972, its best debut since 1915, and climbed to 18-1 and sixth in the polls before settling to earth. Along the way, the Cavaliers won for the first time at Duke, ending a 27-game losing streak on the road in the ACC. Home attendance

FACING PAGE
N.C. State's David Thompson soars for a shot while teammate Tom Burleson and Maryland's Len Elmore and Tom McMillen work for position to rebound. The Maryland and N.C. State teams from that era competed in some of the league's most famous games.

FAR LEFT
N.C. State's David Thompson (44), a member of the Naismith Basketball Hall of Fame, guards North Carolina's Walter Davis. Both players are members of the league's 50th anniversary team.

IMMEDIATE LEFT
Tom McMillen was at the center of one of the nation's toughest recruiting battles. In the end, he chose Maryland over North Carolina and Virginia. He became a three-time All-American and a three-time academic All-American. When his professional basketball career ended, he ran successfully for the U.S. Congress.

surged. Fans chanted "Hoot! Hoot! Hoot!" to welcome Gibson onto the court. Parkhill became so popular, "BP 4 President" signs sprouted on campus. "I've never enjoyed a season more," Gibson told Paul Attner of the *Washington Post.* "This is delightful. I hope it never comes to an end."

Not every turnaround in 1972 was welcome.

Burleson, McMillen and UNC's Jones made the U.S. Olympic basketball team and thought they had won the gold medal. Instead, in Games marred by the terrorist massacre of 11 Israeli athletes, officials twice put back three seconds on the game clock, allowing the Soviet Union's Aleksander Belov to score the decisive layup in a 51-50 victory that ended the Americans' Olympic winning streak at 62 games. Infuriated by the Munich result, the Americans refused to accept their silver medals, which remain in an International Olympic Committee vault in Lausanne, Switzerland.

An adverse judgment of a different sort hit the ACC in August 1972, when Judge Robert W. Hemphill ruled the league's athletic eligibility requirements to be "denial of equal protection of the law" under the 14th Amendment, the same constitutional standard upon which the U.S. Supreme Court relied in its 1954 ruling in *Brown v. Board of Education* that doomed segregation.

Hemphill's 23-page decision found that the 800 minimum for participation was "not based on valid reasoning." The ACC decided to appeal the decision, then reversed course. Commissioner James noted the opinion raised "some concerns not related to athletics" and these apparently convinced the remaining seven schools to drop the 800 rule, causing the judge to vacate his order.

The SAT was not designed as a predictor of performance. Some argued the ACC's standard was too low, anyway. There were concerns the test's cultural bias was a barrier to recruitment of minority students and might attract unwanted enforcement

NATIONAL CHAMPIONSHIPS

YEAR	SPORT	CHAMPION
1953	Football	Maryland
1955	Men's Lacrosse	Maryland
1955	Baseball	Wake Forest
1956	Men's Lacrosse	Maryland
1957	Men's Basketball	North Carolina
1960	Men's Lacrosse	Maryland
1967	Men's Lacrosse	Maryland
1968	Men's Soccer	Maryland
1968	Men's Lacrosse	Maryland
1970	Men's Lacrosse	Virginia
1972	Men's Lacrosse	Virginia
1973	Men's Lacrosse	Maryland
1974	Men's Basketball	N.C. State
1974	Men's Golf	Wake Forest
1975	Men's Golf	Wake Forest

YEAR	SPORT	CHAMPION
1975	Men's Lacrosse	Maryland
1979	Women's Cross Country	N.C. State
1980	Women's Cross Country	N.C. State
1981	Men's Lacrosse	North Carolina
1981	Women's Indoor Track	Virginia
1981	Football	Clemson
1981	Women's Cross Country	Virginia
1981	Women's Soccer	North Carolina
1982	Men's Basketball	North Carolina
1982	Men's Lacrosse	North Carolina
1982	Women's Soccer	North Carolina
1982	Women's Cross Country	Virginia
1983	Men's Basketball	N.C. State
1983	Women's Soccer	North Carolina
1984	Men's Soccer	Clemson

YEAR	SPORT	CHAMPION
1984	Women's Soccer	North Carolina
1986	Men's Golf	Wake Forest
1986	Women's Lacrosse	Maryland
1986	Men's Lacrosse	North Carolina
1986	Men's Soccer	Duke
1986	Women's Soccer	North Carolina
1987	Men's Soccer	Clemson
1987	Women's Soccer	North Carolina
1987	Women's Field Hockey	Maryland
1988	Women's Soccer	North Carolina
1989	Men's Soccer	Virginia
1989	Women's Field Hockey	North Carolina
1989	Women's Soccer	North Carolina
1990	Football	Georgia Tech
1990	Women's Soccer	North Carolina

action from the federal government. Competitive pressures to recruit African-American athletes were on the rise as well. Even Alabama football coach Bear Bryant began recruiting black players after his team couldn't stop Southern Cal's Sam Cunningham in a 1970 defeat.

Compelled to retreat, the ACC adopted the NCAA's 1.6 projected grade-point average based on class standing and SAT score, the standard South Carolina had sought all along.

Vickery and Beach never did play the sports of their choice at Clemson.

By 1973 the NCAA had dropped even the 1.6 (a "C" was equal to a 2.0) in favor of a simple and easily manipulated 2.0 high school grade-point average, and the ACC followed suit. "I thought from that time on ... football began to improve," Clemson's McLellan said.

Further sparking ACC improvement were the changes wrought by North Carolina's Dooley, who had worked for his brother at Georgia and brought an SEC mentality to his first head coaching job. "The entire Atlantic Coast Conference is tougher now than it has ever been," said Don Lawrence, coach at Virginia from 1971-73. "I hate to admit it, but Bill Dooley is responsible for it all. He came into this league and worked around the clock to build a fine program. Now everybody else has started working overtime to catch up. Dooley turned ACC football around."

Bunting, who played for Dooley, agreed. "I think he was the Bobby Bowden of the '60s and '70s. I think he changed recruiting. He was coming out of the SEC, where recruiting was becoming year-round."

Dooley's relentless work ethic, no-frills style and I-formation offense led North Carolina football on an upward march from 2-8 in 1967 to 11-1 in 1972, when the Tar Heels repeated as ACC champs. UNC ran its conference winning streak to 16 games in '72, a season that culminated with a 32-28 win over Texas Tech in the Sun Bowl. In the eight years from 1970 through 1977, when Dooley left for Virginia Tech,

NATIONAL CHAMPIONSHIPS

YEAR	SPORT	CHAMPION
1991	Men's Basketball	Duke
1991	Men's Lacrosse	North Carolina
1991	Women's Lacrosse	Virginia
1991	Men's Soccer	Virginia
1991	Women's Soccer	North Carolina
1992	Men's Basketball	Duke
1992	Women's Lacrosse	Maryland
1992	Men's Soccer	Virginia
1992	Women's Soccer	North Carolina
1993	Men's Basketball	North Carolina
1993	Women's Lacrosse	Virginia
1993	Football	Florida State
1993	Men's Soccer	Virginia
1993	Women's Soccer	North Carolina
1993	Women's Field Hockey	Maryland

YEAR	SPORT	CHAMPION
1994	Women's Basketball	North Carolina
1994	Men's Soccer	Virginia
1994	Women's Soccer	North Carolina
1995	Women's Lacrosse	Maryland
1995	Women's Field Hockey	North Carolina
1996	Women's Lacrosse	Maryland
1996	Women's Soccer	North Carolina
1997	Women's Lacrosse	Maryland
1997	Women's Field Hockey	North Carolina
1997	Women's Soccer	North Carolina
1998	Women's Lacrosse	Maryland
1999	Women's Golf	Duke
1999	Women's Lacrosse	Maryland
1999	Men's Lacrosse	Virginia
1999	Football	Florida State

YEAR	SPORT	CHAMPION
1999	Women's Field Hockey	Maryland
1999	Women's Soccer	North Carolina
2000	Women's Lacrosse	Maryland
2000	Women's Soccer	North Carolina
2001	Men's Basketball	Duke
2001	Women's Lacrosse	Maryland
2001	Men's Soccer	North Carolina
2002	Men's Basketball	Maryland
2002	Women's Golf	Duke

NATIONAL TITLES BY SCHOOL

School	Titles	School	Titles
Clemson	3	North Carolina	30
Duke	6	N.C. State	4
Florida State	2	Virginia	13
Georgia Tech	1	Wake Forest	4
Maryland	22		

By Tony Barnhart

ACC EXCELLENCE

GEORGIA TECH'S TRACK ATHLETES CONQUER WORLD

Track and field at the collegiate level is a different kind of athletic animal. There are no polls or preseason television specials. There is no Final Four to generate national interest. There are no bowl games. The championships, for the most part, are conducted far from the media spotlight.

Nevertheless, the athletes are special because of the incredible dedication and personal sacrifice necessary to rise to the highest level of their sport. The Atlantic Coast Conference has produced more than its fair share of great track and field athletes as it heads into its 50th season:

- The wonderful Renaldo Nehemiah of Maryland, a two-time NCAA indoor champion (1978, '79) in the 60-yard high hurdles. He still holds the NCAA record in that event (6.90). He also won an NCAA title in the outdoor 110-meter hurdles.
- James Trapp, the Clemson sprinter who won the 1993 World Championship in the 200 meters. He made the Olympic team in 1992 before heading into professional football.
- Jim Beatty of North Carolina, the first man to break the four-minute mark in the indoor mile. Beatty would be named the nation's top amateur athlete in 1962, when he set world records in the mile, two miles, 1,500 meters and 5,000 meters.
- Virginia's Paul Ereng, who won the 1988 national championship in the 800 meters. He was a four-time All-American.
- Marion Jones of North Carolina, the first female track and field athlete to win five medals at a single Olympics. She won three gold and two bronze medals at the 2000 Games in Sydney, Australia.

And the list goes on.

While most track and field stars spend their college years in relative obscurity, there is always the hope for one moment when the years of hard work will be fulfilled on an international stage. That moment also gives the athlete's school its time in the spotlight.

That stage is the Olympic Games, in which the color of the day is always gold. And when it comes to bringing home the gold, no school in the ACC has done it quite like Georgia Tech.

Georgia Tech did not participate in its first ACC meet until 1979, but since then four different Yellow Jacket performers have won six gold medals in Olympic competition:

- Antonio McKay was a member of the 4x400 championship teams in both the 1984 Games in Los Angeles and the 1988 Games in Seoul, South Korea.
- Derrick Adkins won the 400 intermediate hurdles in the 1996 Games in Atlanta.
- Derek Mills gave Georgia Tech its second hometown gold when he was a member of the winning 4x400 championship relay team in Atlanta.
- Angelo Taylor, a native of Atlanta, won two gold medals in the 2000 Games in Sydney by taking the 400 intermediate hurdles and running on the winning team in the 4x400 relay team.

All totaled, Georgia Tech has seven gold medals, as Ed Hamm won in the broad jump in 1928.

FACING PAGE: Andria King (1996-99) was a two-time All-American in the 55-meter hurdles (1998) and 60-meter hurdles (1999). She also earned ACC titles in the 60 meters and 60-meter hurdles in 1999, earning all-conference honors in these two events as well as the conference indoor MVP award. She is a member of the ACC's 50th anniversary team.

LEFT: Angelo Taylor, coach Grover Hinsdale and Derrick Adkins. Taylor won two gold medals in the 2000 Olympic Games. Hinsdale has continued a tradition of successful track and field at Georgia Tech. Adkins won a gold medal in the 1996 Olympic Games in Atlanta.

BELOW: Derek Mills won a gold medal in his hometown of Atlanta in the 1996 Summer Games in the U.S. 4x400 relay team.

The credit for this success at Georgia Tech goes to two men: Buddy Fowlkes, who built the program into a national power, and Grover Hinsdale, his assistant and eventual successor. Fowlkes stepped down in 1992 after 30 seasons as head coach and turned the program over to Hinsdale, who has kept things going strong ever since.

Each of the great athletes brought something different to his ACC and international experience. But they all had one thing in common — a burning desire to be the best in the world at what they did.

McKay, Hinsdale said, never walked onto a track expecting to finish second.

"Tony never gave any thought to what might happen if he lost," Hinsdale said. "He expected to win and focused on how fast he was going to run. I've never met a man who had a deeper passion for winning. He didn't lose much, and he was always gracious in defeat. But he never accepted losing well."

Adkins was Hinsdale's first protégé as a head coach to win the gold. But the real pride comes not from the gold, but what Adkins had to overcome to win it.

Adkins was the heavy favorite to win the 400 intermediate hurdles at the NCAA Championships in 1992 as a senior. In the championship race, he led the field by 15 meters at the seventh hurdle. He fell on the eighth hurdle and finished eighth.

Then on the Monday of the Olympic trials, he fell down a flight of stairs and twisted his ankle. He finished fourth and missed the team.

"So in the span of two weeks, two of the biggest goals in his life are gone," Hinsdale said. "Now he has to decide if he wants to take his engineering degree and go into the real world or train four more years for another shot."

Adkins chose the latter and four years later, Hinsdale was sitting at the Olympic Stadium in Atlanta, preparing to watch Adkins run in the gold-medal race.

"When the gun sounded, I blocked everything out of my mind and followed Derrick every step of the way," Hinsdale said. "It was like watching a silent movie."

Adkins may have been silent, but he wasn't slow. He finished first and won the gold. "I am so proud of him it is hard to describe," Hinsdale said.

Taylor was a sophomore in high school when Hinsdale came into his life. He had just won the state championship, and Hinsdale saw a star in the making. The two men bonded, and Taylor went on to become a star in the ACC, as he was crowned champion seven times.

In 2000, when he was but five hours away from the Olympic championship race in the 400-meter hurdles in Sydney, Taylor was concerned about his starting position, which was lane one. He called his old coach back in Atlanta and got some reassurance.

Hinsdale told Taylor that he should not worry because others had won from that position. Then he told Taylor to relax and find his rhythm, because "rhythm is everything in the hurdles."

"I just told him to run his own race," Hinsdale said. "I told him to just make sure he was still in the race at 300 meters because there was nobody in the world that could hang with him in the final 100. He was just too tough."

Taylor won the gold with a personal best of 47.50. Because of the time difference between Atlanta and Sydney, Hinsdale did not learn the news until he was driving his children to school the next morning.

"I couldn't believe what I heard on the radio," said. "It was just so wonderful. Angelo is just a special guy."

The Georgia Tech gold rush may not be over. David Krummenacker, who dominated the 800 and 1,500 meters during his time at Tech (1994-98), has in 2002 elevated his performances and is one of the best middle-distance runners in the world. So don't be surprised if Georgia Tech and the ACC will be panning for more gold come 2004 in Athens, Greece.

the Tar Heels made six bowl appearances.

Yet even at 11-1, UNC couldn't crack the Top 10, finishing 12th in the Associated Press poll and 14th according to United Press International.

"I don't think it was getting the respect it was due, at one count," Homer Rice, then North Carolina's athletics director, said of ACC football. "But also, I think that we didn't play a lot of the big, top schools outside the conference. We really didn't seem to have a lot of competition, so we really didn't know."

Rice arrived at Chapel Hill in 1969 as UNC's third athletics director, straight from a job as head football coach at the University of Cincinnati. "I went into the office," he recalled of his first day. "I closed the door, sat in the big chair and waited for the phone to ring. That's about what I knew about athletic administration."

Rice learned quickly, infusing the school's multitude of sports with the resources necessary to fund scholarships and compete for championships. By 1971 North Carolina captured the Carmichael Cup, emblematic of the ACC's top overall athletic program, and repeated in 1972 and 1973. (Competition for the cup was discontinued in the 1980s.) Rice, among the first to embrace women's sports as they reached varsity status, nearly took a pioneering role of a different sort when Wolfpack athletics director Willis Casey, a UNC alumnus, asked his advice about candidates for N.C. State football coach.

"I don't know how I got into it, but he said, 'You wouldn't be interested, would you?'" Rice said. Once before, when Jim Tatum was at Maryland, N.C. State unsuccessfully sought to raid another ACC program for a head coach. Now, Rice tentatively accepted the offer to switch. Word got to UNC Chancellor J.C. Sitterson that Rice might go to Raleigh. "He called me in," Rice said with perhaps the slightest bit of embellishment, "and got down on his knees and says, 'Go anywhere, anywhere but North Carolina State as football coach.'"

Based in part on Rice's recommendation, N.C. State hired Lou Holtz in 1972. The fast-talking Holtz was immediately successful after arriving from William & Mary, winning '72 coach of the year honors as the Wolfpack jumped from 3-8 to 8-3, a second-place ACC finish, and a 49-13 Peach Bowl victory over West Virginia. N.C. State then got better in 1973, finishing atop the league with an undefeated mark and a 9-3 record after beating Kansas 31-18 in the Liberty Bowl.

Running back Willie Burden, among the school's pioneer black football players, was named the 1973 ACC player of the year.

Good as those performances were, they

BELOW
Coach Bill Dooley directs traffic along the North Carolina sideline. Dooley took over a downtrodden UNC program in 1967 and built it into a champion. His Tar Heels captured three conference titles before he departed. He left Chapel Hill to coach at Virginia Tech following the 1977 season, and later returned to the ACC to coach Wake Forest. He led the Deacons to a bowl victory in his final season there in 1992.

paled in comparison with the Wolfpack's basketball season. The 1972-73 squad, led by Thompson, Burleson and playmaker Monte Towe, went 27-0, the only ACC squad to go undefeated besides North Carolina's 1957 national champs. In those days before the shot clock and 3-pointer, the '73 Wolfpack set an enduring ACC single-season scoring mark, overwhelming opponents by averaging 92.9 points.

Competition was fierce within the league in 1973, with N.C. State ranked second nationally behind UCLA, Maryland eighth and North Carolina No. 11. Virginia faded to 13-12, which still gave it an unprecedented three winning seasons in a row with Parkhill on the varsity.

The 1971-73 teams laid the foundation for a viable program at Virginia, according to Terry Holland, the Cavaliers' head basketball coach from 1975-90. "The Parkhill phenomenon really was what it was, which more than anything else got people in the seats," Holland said. "Without Parkhill and those teams coached by Bill Gibson, nobody could have turned this place around."

The battles between the '73 Wolfpack and Terrapins were especially heated and well-played, with two of three meetings decided by a basket. The defining game occurred at College Park on Jan. 14, 1973. N.C. State was 11-0, Maryland 10-0 with guard John Lucas at the controls in the first year freshmen were eligible. Played as a prelude to Super Bowl VII, the first ACC game ever televised nationally came down to a final shot. Burleson missed, but here came Thompson soaring in to lay the ball in the hoop — dunks were prohibited by NCAA rules — for an 87-85 victory.

Thompson scored 37 points that day and averaged 24.7 to lead the league, a feat he managed in each of his varsity seasons. His average rose every year. By his senior season, Thompson scored 29.9 points per game.

Thompson was named ACC player of the year for three straight seasons, beginning in 1973. Only Virginia's Ralph Sampson (1981-83) matched this feat. N.C. State went 57-1 during the two years Thompson and Burleson played together, the best two-season mark by any ACC program.

BELOW
Lou Holtz was an instant success at N.C. State. His Wolfpack football teams packed the stands and went 33-12-3 during his four seasons in Raleigh. Three of his teams finished the season ranked in the top 20 in the national polls. His teams were particularly tough at home. The Wolfpack went 20-1-1 at Carter-Finley Stadium under Holtz, and N.C. State won all six conference games in 1973 to capture the ACC championship.

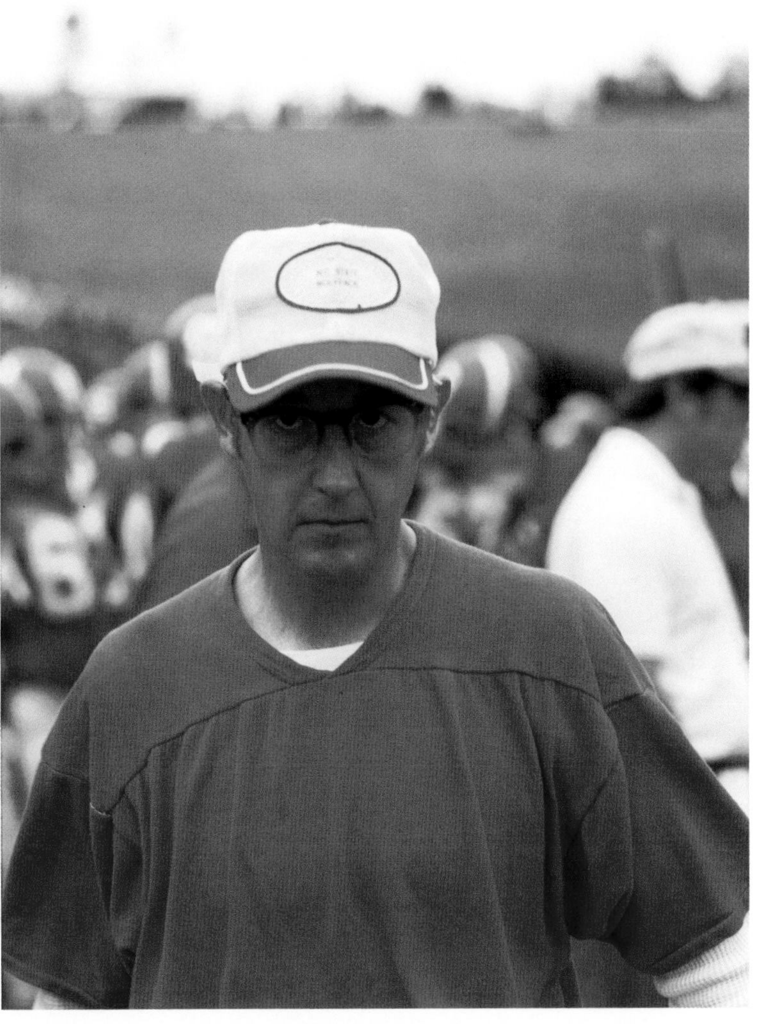

BELOW
Monte Towe of N.C. State passes the ball around North Carolina's Bobby Jones (34) as George Karl (22) watches from the other side of the court. Towe ran the team for the Wolfpack, which went undefeated in league play in 1973 and '74. Jones led the ACC in field goal percentage three times and went on to become an eight-time member of the National Basketball Association's all-defensive team. Karl became a successful head coach in the NBA.

Statistics inadequately define Thompson's contributions. His was a constant presence. At 6-4 he had fine perimeter skills and the ability to score on jump shots or drives. He was a good passer, defender, rebounder and shot blocker. He had exceptional hands. His will to win was fierce. "He just will not let them lose," UNC's Jones said. "If State needs something, Thompson will get it for them. He's just the best I've ever been around."

More than anything, though, Thompson's game was revolutionary. "It seemed like gravity didn't affect him," teammate Phil Spence said. Washington, D.C.-product Elgin Baylor soared for Seattle in the 1950s and Julius Erving did likewise for Massachusetts and then the American Basketball Association in the 1970s. But Thompson and his above-the-rim performance occurred at the highest levels of competition just as national TV discovered college basketball, and he produced copious victories and admirers.

The unassuming Thompson, youngest of 11 children, grew up a fan of Charles Scott, the ACC's first great African-American wing player. Now others emulated the player some nicknamed "Skywalker" but most knew simply as "David," echoing the perfection of Michelangelo's famous sculpture. Among those modeling their game after Thompson's was a youngster in Wilmington, N.C., named Michael Jordan.

Finding athletic role models or athletic opportunities was more difficult for young girls. "You weren't a women's basketball fan when I was coming up in high school," said Bernadette McGlade, who played the sport at North Carolina from 1977-80 and later coached at Georgia Tech.

Women's athletics was slow to take hold nationally beyond country club-type sports such as tennis and golf. The NCAA repeatedly refused to sponsor women's championships. Funding for college teams was minimal. Chris Weller played basketball at Maryland from 1963-66 as a member of a club team because there were no varsity sports for women. The squad had no uniforms, drove its own vehicles to games and received no expense money for food or travel. "I was just so thrilled to play because I didn't

FACING PAGE
N.C. State's David Thompson soars in an attempt to block a shot during the semifinals of the 1974 Final Four against UCLA at the Greensboro Coliseum. The Wolfpack won the game and snapped the Bruins' string of national titles. N.C. State then defeated Marquette to win the national championship. Many people still consider Thompson to be the greatest ACC basketball player ever.

THOMPSON
44
52
UCLA
34

have a team in high school," said Weller, later Maryland's women's head coach.

ACC bylaws restricted athletic grants-in-aid to males until 1973, a year after passage of Title IX, part of a package of education amendments that prohibited federal funds from going to schools that practiced racial, sexual, religious or other discrimination.

"The advent of Title IX got a little bit of backing and support for those who were trying to develop the opportunity for people, not just for women," Weller said. "I'd always tell people, 'I don't want you to think I'm trying to be a women's libber or anything. What I'm just trying to do is liberate people. We happen to be a significant part of the population.'"

Starting in 1971, women banded together to form their own national organization, the Association of Intercollegiate Athletics for Women (AIAW). "The AIAW philosophy was, you should have a team comprised of the students on your campus," said Nora Lynn Finch, Wake Forest's first women's basketball coach and now an associate director of athletics at N.C. State. "Recruiting was one of the things the AIAW very seriously frowned on. Scholarships were viewed to be the root of most evil in men's athletics."

RIGHT
Former Maryland basketball coach Chris Weller was a pioneer in women's athletics. She also made the Terrapins a consistent winner on the court. She played club basketball at Maryland before women could compete in official ACC intercollegiate sports.

By 1972 the AIAW held its first national basketball championship tournament, and Maryland and Wake had varsity women's teams. Not until 1974 was a scholarship awarded to an ACC female athlete, Camey Timberlake, a UNC tennis player. (Rice also awarded the first women's scholarship at Georgia Tech in 1981, where he served as AD from 1980-97.)

As it turned out, 1974 was a benchmark year for the ACC in many respects.

Wake Forest won the first of two consecutive national golf titles under coach Jesse Haddock, who had league championship squads for 10 straight years from 1967-76 and 15 overall. Tony Waldrop, a UNC miler, captured the 1974 NCAA indoor title in his event in San Diego, set an ACC mark of 3:53.2 in the mile, and was the McKevlin Award winner as the conference's top athlete.

For the first time ever, the conference sent three teams to bowl games in 1974 — Maryland, North Carolina and N.C. State.

Holtz took the Wolfpack to four bowls in his four years. The Wolfpack had been to a total of three previously. The '74 squad went 9-2-1 behind senior fullback Stan Fritts and the Buckey twins, quarterback

ABOVE
From left to right, the 1974 Wake Forest golf team: Jay Haas, Lex Alexander, Bill Argabrite, Curtis Strange, coach Jesse Haddock, Bob Byman, David Thore. The Deacons won back-to-back national titles in 1974 and '75. Strange clinched the team title in 1974 and grabbed medallist honors with an eagle on the final hole. Haas won the individual championship in '75, and the team ran away from the field, winning by 33 strokes.

Dave and receiver Don. Fritts was the ACC's top rusher with 1,169 yards. "Stan is the most complete football player that I've ever been around in my entire life," said Holtz, taking especial note of Fritts' balance, strength, peripheral vision and blocking. "He has amazing mental discipline and understands that he has to do the little things to get victories."

Just as Driesell quickly turned around basketball's fortunes at Maryland, so Jerry Claiborne transformed football after arriving in 1972. The former Kentucky player under Bear Bryant improved the Terps' record virtually every year until peaking with an 11-1 mark in 1976. Claiborne won ACC coach of the year three times from 1973 through 1976, a period in which the Terps were 21-1 in ACC competition.

Few ACC teams ever boasted leaders on both sides of the ball to surpass the '74 Terps, who won the first of three straight ACC titles at the school. The offense revolved around quarterback Bob Avellini, who led the ACC in total offense and passing. But a regimented wide-tackle six defense was the key to Maryland's fortunes, and in 1974 the linchpin was Randy White, alias "Manster," according to N.C. State's Fritts. "That's what everybody called him — half man, half monster," Fritts told Chip Alexander of Raleigh's *The News & Observer.*

The mustachioed White was large at 6-4 and 250 pounds, yet lightning quick for a defensive tackle and unusually strong thanks to weight-training, a regimen Claiborne was among the first to embrace. "He catches enemy runners from behind with regularity," Paul Attner wrote of White in the *Washington Post,* "frightens opponents so much they frequently run away from him, never tires and just loves to hit anything that moves."

White, considered by some the best performer in ACC football history, was the league's 1974 player of the year and won both the '74 Lombardi and Outland trophies emblematic of the nation's top lineman. He went on to a career with the Dallas Cowboys that landed him in the Pro Football Hall of Fame.

Even as White rampaged across the ACC landscape, David Thompson soared above it, taking N.C. State to the 1974 NCAA basketball title.

The '74 Wolfpack won 30 and lost once. UCLA, the colossus that stood astride the college game as champion for nine of the previous 10 years, defeated N.C. State 84-66 on a neutral court. One or the other team held the top spot in the polls all season.

Competition was again fierce within the ACC. Maryland (23-5) rose as high as second in the polls and never dropped below fifth, continuing to engage the Wolfpack in spirited combat behind playmaker Lucas (20.1 points, 5.7 assists) and seniors McMillen and Elmore. Talent-laden North Carolina (22-6), the ACC's third-place finisher, was in the top 10 for most of the season. The Tar Heels led the league in field goal accuracy for the fourth straight year with seniors Jones and Darrell Elston, sophomore Mitch Kupchak and freshman Walter Davis.

Davis proved central to a victory at Carmichael Auditorium that forever cemented Smith's reputation for coaching legerdemain. Over the years every North

BELOW
Dave Buckey (11) played quarterback for N.C. State from 1972-75. He still ranks among school leaders in total offense with 4,787 yards. He played in three consecutive bowl games as the Wolfpack reached a new level of consistency. N.C. State won the league title in 1973.

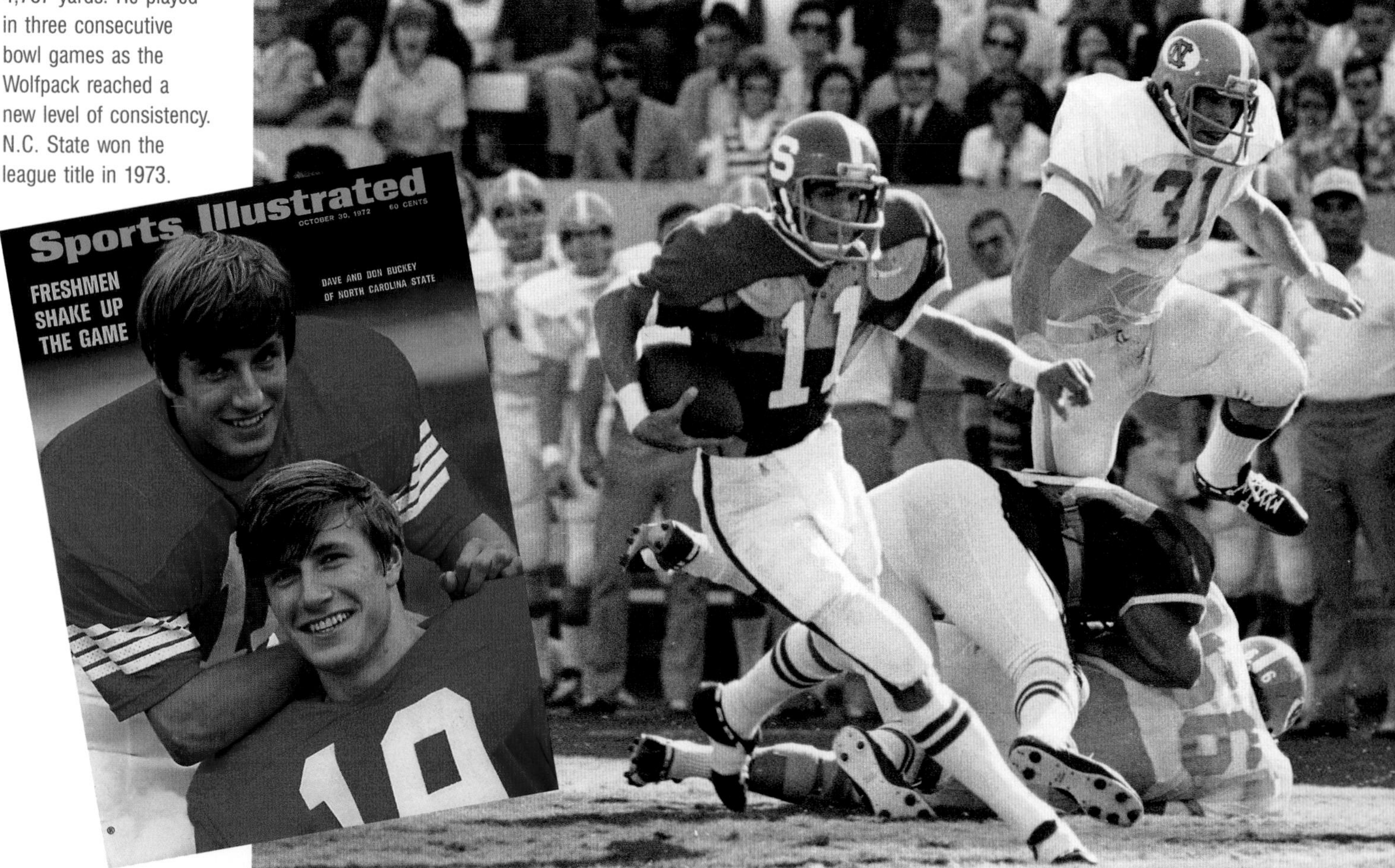
Sports Illustrated
OCTOBER 30, 1972 60 CENTS
FRESHMEN SHAKE UP THE GAME
DAVE AND DON BUCKEY OF NORTH CAROLINA STATE

Carolina media guide came to include a section on comebacks, and none was more famous than the eight-point deficit the Tar Heels overcame in the final 17 seconds against Duke. It was Davis' 30-foot bank shot at the buzzer that forced overtime, producing a 96-92 UNC win in an era before shot clocks or 3-pointers.

Good as they were, no ACC teams could match N.C. State, which recorded its second consecutive undefeated season in the league, a run yet to be duplicated. The '74 squad had improved its supporting cast, and had the incentive of being eligible for NCAA competition. Mo Rivers now plied the backcourt alongside Towe, and Phil Spence joined a frontcourt mix with Burleson and Tim Stoddard, a star baseball pitcher during the spring. And always there was Thompson.

Yet it was Burleson, sixth in all-conference voting, who emerged as the star in the 1974 ACC Tournament final against Maryland. The senior scored 38 points on 18-of-25 shooting and had 13 rebounds in a game generally regarded as the greatest in conference history and one of the best ever in the college game.

The 1974 season would be the last in which leagues were restricted to a single entrant in the NCAA Tournament, a decision spurred by what happened in Greensboro that March day in 1974.

The ACC Tournament was a grand stage, riveting the region and drawing national attention. After leaving Reynolds Coliseum, the event became a perennial sellout. The tournament generated revenue not only from TV rights and ticket sales but also from boosters contributing to their favorite schools in order to qualify to attend.

The tournament offered fans intrigue, excitement and a social focal point. Every game was televised, starting in 1974. People threw tournament parties or gathered around television sets to watch at work or school. For front-running teams, the three-day affair offered the pressures of single-elimination competition: Lose and there would be no NCAA bid. For also-rans, it offered a last chance to redeem a season.

"That was the greatest pressure, to win the regular season and then have to win the tournament to even go to the NCAA," UNC's Smith said in 1987. "Up until 1975, we started talking about the ACC Tournament as our goal. It was our long-range goal; it was everything. What we really have now at the NCAA level is a glorified old ACC Tournament, the one-game-and-you're-out. We knew it wasn't fair. And that's why there's so much interest in the national tournament because

BELOW
Maryland defensive lineman Randy White, a member of the Pro Football Hall of Fame and the College Football Hall of Fame, captured the Outland and Lombardi trophies as the top lineman in the country in 1974. He was the ACC player of the year and a consensus All-American. White is still remembered as one of the finest football players ever in the ACC. His school record for single-season tackles for loss (24) stood from 1974 until 2001.

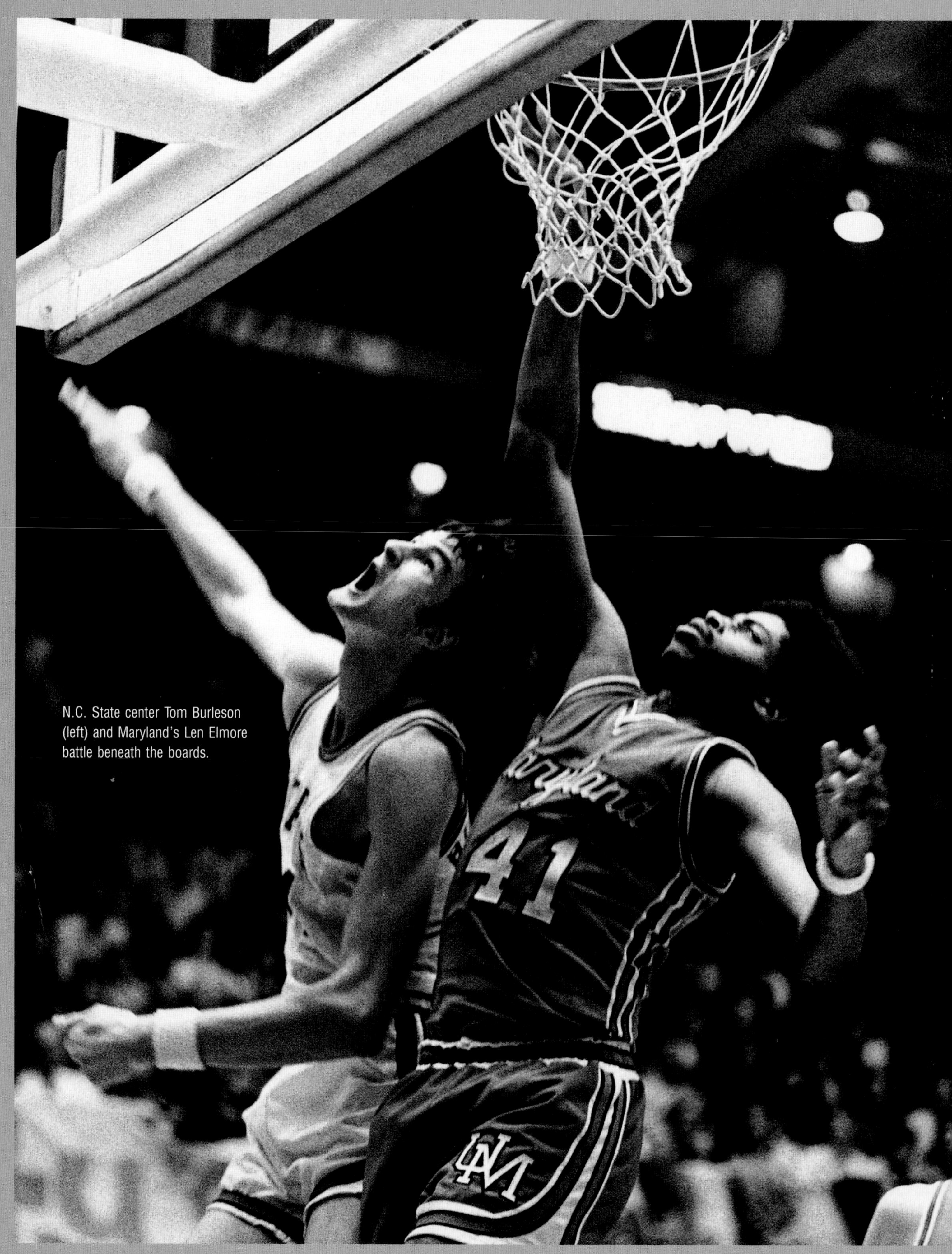

N.C. State center Tom Burleson (left) and Maryland's Len Elmore battle beneath the boards.

Burleson shoots over Elmore at the 1974 ACC Tournament championship game, which is viewed by many as the best conference game ever played. Five members of the two teams from that game made the 50th anniversary team: Burleson, Elmore, David Thompson, John Lucas and Tom McMillen. N.C. State won the game 103-100 and advanced to capture the national championship.

it's the same format, almost."

The ACC Tournament, once derided for sapping ACC squads' strength entering NCAA play, became so respected that by the mid-1980s a majority of collegiate leagues had their own postseason event. Now virtually everyone does.

"There is one thing about the ACC Tournament, as I saw when I was with the Big Eight, when it had a preseason tournament," said Wayne Duke, then commissioner of the Big Ten. "It's the same thing I see with the ACC, a great intangible factor, that the tournament built such great conference pride and camaraderie."

The '74 championship game, which went to overtime before N.C. State secured a 103-100 victory, elevated the event's already-impressive stature.

BELOW
North Carolina's Phil Ford (12) and Walter Davis (24) stand with the nets around their necks after winning the ACC Tournament. The pair captured two conference tournament titles (1975 and '77) together and played in the national championship game in 1977. Ford was the national player of the year in 1978.

Five of 10 starters went on to become first-round NBA draft choices. The contest was not only close but also superbly played. Legend has the game devoid of turnovers, when in fact there were 29. There's no need to exaggerate the efficiency of both teams. Maryland made 61 percent of its shots, N.C. State 55 percent. Eight players scored in double figures. Thompson had 29, while McMillen and Mo Howard, among four Terrapins who played every minute, had 22 each.

The game came down to a missed one-and-one free throw and an errant pass from Lucas, a Spence layup off a Towe feed and a pair of Towe foul shots.

As victor, N.C. State received the ACC bid to play in Reynolds Coliseum in the NCAA East Regional. Maryland, disheartened in defeat, declined a bid to the NIT, an event it won two years previously. The Terps had gone to the NCAAs in 1973 while the Wolfpack was on probation, but made an early exit.

Claiming the Terps were ACC "outcasts," McMillen called for his school to quit the league. "Just for once I'd like to see the roles reversed," the senior and Rhodes scholar said. "I'd like to see everything going for us with the crowd behind us and see what they would do. It's got to make a difference."

A similar sense of injustice fueled alumnus Gary Williams nearly three decades later. "It's kind of been skewed a certain way for a long time," he said. "I was thinking about this: If you played the ACC Tournament, say 43 out of the 50 years in the league, in Baltimore and Ocean City, I think we would have won a few more, probably."

Certainly N.C. State enjoyed familiar turf en route to the NCAA title. First it won twice on its home court, surviving a frightful fall by Thompson against Pittsburgh that left him unconscious for four minutes and spectators stunned and fearing the worst. Thompson was rushed to a hospital but returned before game's end, head wrapped in a bandage that covered 15 stitches.

Next came UCLA and center Bill Walton in the Final Four at Greensboro. The Bruins had won 38 straight NCAA contests. But the ACC champions won 80-77, rallying twice from major deficits, the second a seven-point hole in overtime. An anticlimactic 76-64 victory over Marquette secured the title, the first for N.C. State and the ACC's second.

Thompson, courted avidly by the pros, decided to return for his senior year. Apparently matching the Wolfpack stride for stride, in June Driesell signed 6-11 Moses Malone. Sought by about 300 colleges, Malone was so prized a prospect some schools stationed recruiters full-time in motels in his hometown of Petersburg, Va. "I'd be mighty surprised if we don't win a national championship before Moses leaves," Driesell said.

Allegations of misconduct flew so thick, ACC Commissioner Bob James called the situation "the worst recruiting mess I've ever seen." Maryland wasn't charged with wrongdoing, but it lost Malone anyway when he signed with the American Basketball Association's Utah Stars.

Thompson, the first of the great ACC players to spurn professional options for a four-year college career, led N.C. State to a 22-6 record in 1975, and won national player of the year honors. But the Pack wasn't the same without Burleson, and it was Maryland that finished atop the ACC standings, a first for the Terrapins. Maryland, N.C. State and UNC made the final top 10, a first for the league.

N.C. State beat Maryland in the '75 ACC Tournament semifinals, and North Carolina went to overtime to eliminate Clemson and star freshman Skip Wise. Then the Tar Heels and freshman point guard Phil Ford beat N.C. State, with Ford winning MVP honors. UNC and Maryland

BELOW
North Carolina's Phil Ford (right) passes the ball as Clemson's Tree Rollins guards the lane. Ford is recognized as one of the finest point guards in league history. He made coach Dean Smith's Four Corners offense famous and became the leading scorer in school history. Rollins is the career leader in rebounds at Clemson. He is the only Tiger to average double figures in two statistical categories for four consecutive years.

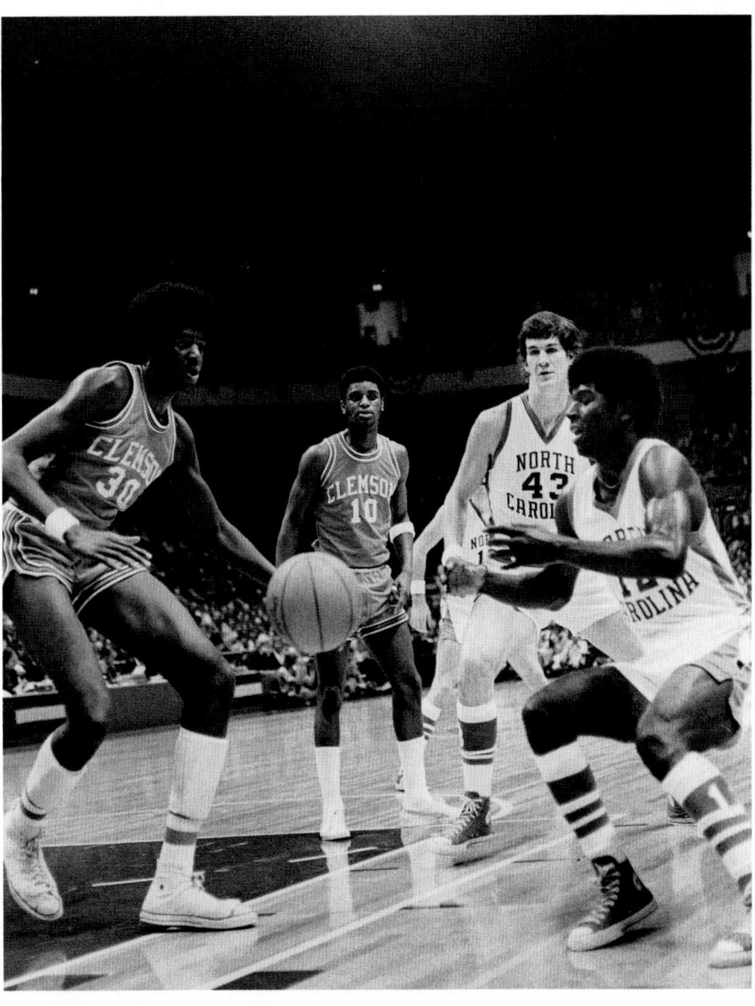

got NCAA bids as the national tournament began taking multiple entrants from the same league.

N.C. State, as Maryland the year before, disdained the NIT. Clemson, on the other hand, readily accepted, and earned its first postseason basketball appearance ever. Clemson coach Jess Neely turned down the school's first chance at postseason play, rejecting a bid to the 1939 NIT, then the game's most prestigious event.

"He merely said that he didn't have any money for a basketball team to go sit up in New York for a week when football practice had already started," said Banks McFadden, one of seven squad members who played both sports.

The 1975 Tigers finished tied with UNC for second in the ACC, new heights for the program. Seven-foot-one center Wayne "Tree" Rollins was a force inside, leading the ACC in rebounding (11.7). Wise was the only freshman voted first team All-ACC until Georgia Tech's Kenny Anderson in 1990.

BELOW
North Carolina tailback Mike Voight played from 1973-76 and won ACC player of the year honors his junior and senior seasons. He rushed for better than 1,000 yards three consecutive years and twice led the conference in rushing. He ended his senior season with 261 yards rushing against Duke. Voight is a member of the 50th anniversary team.

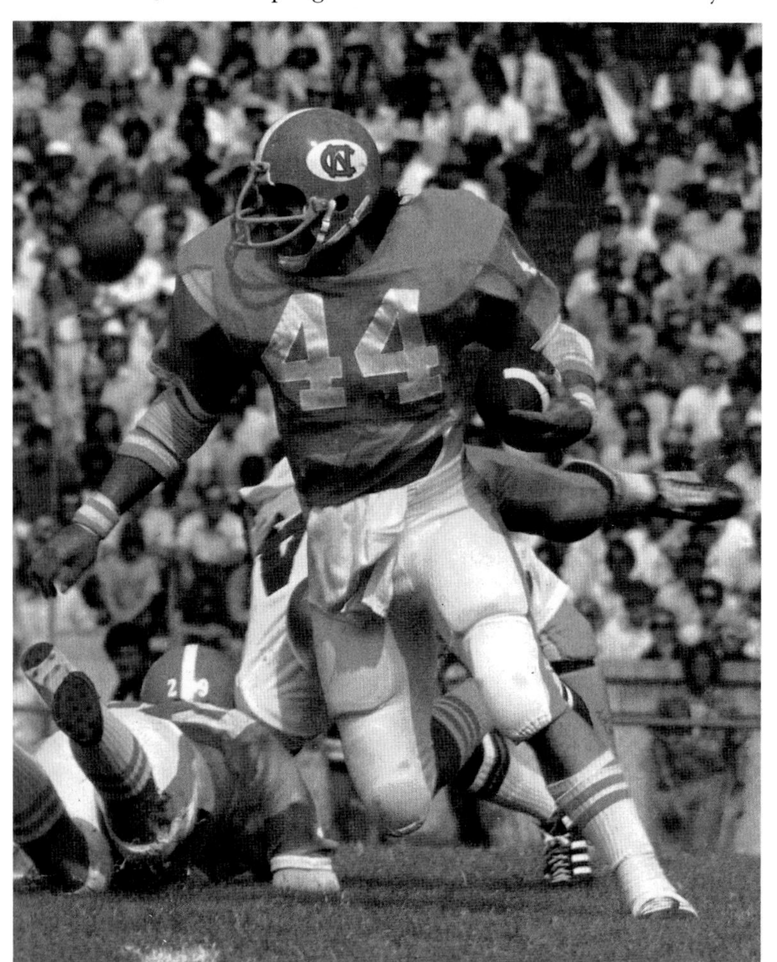

Clemson's bright outlook dimmed in a hurry, and not just because the Tigers were bounced in their NIT opener. Locke was fired for cheating. Wise went pro. In October 1975 the NCAA handed down a three-year probation for a wide range of violations, the punishment lessened due to "assurances from the institution that the university intends to comply fully with the governing regulations in the future."

Maryland and N.C. State also topped ACC football in 1975, posting the only winning records overall. Duke was undefeated in the ACC, but had a 4-5-2 record. The Terrapins beat Virginia to clinch the league title as five players from both teams rushed for 100 or more yards, an ACC single-game record. Soon afterward Virginia fired alumnus Sonny Randle. Hired the previous season, Randle said he could turn things around because "I think I'm something special." But he won only five games in two years, including a 1-10 mark in 1975 when three teams, Maryland among them, scored at least 61 points against the Cavaliers.

North Carolina tailback Mike Voight, the ACC rushing leader with 125 yards per game, was voted 1975 player of the year. Running back Ted Brown won the league's first rookie of the year award as N.C. State went 7-4-1. Wake dealt the Wolfpack its only home loss of the Holtz era, 30-22. Both Maryland and N.C. State went to bowls, the Terps beating Florida 13-0 in the Gator, while the Wolfpack lost 13-10 in the Peach against West Virginia.

Virginia had far better luck in 1976 behind another second-year coach, Terry Holland, who provided "the state's biggest moment since the Declaration of Independence," declared the *Atlanta Journal-Constitution* in a bit of bicentennial bombast.

Holland instilled a hard-nosed, man-to-man defensive system that from 1975 through 1979 was annually the ACC's stingiest at yielding points. Dominated by underclassmen, the '76 group finished 18-12 during the regular season, Virginia's second-highest victory total since the conference began. That was merely good enough for fifth in a league in which only Duke had a losing overall record.

Everyone trailed North Carolina. The Tar Heels built a 25-4 record, 11-1 in the ACC, on the strength of multiple, shifting defenses and a disciplined, intricately calculated, relentlessly unselfish offense that led the league in field-goal accuracy for 10 of 14 years between 1966 and 1979. Talents such as Ford, Davis, Tom LaGarde and Mitch Kupchak, the 1976 ACC player of the year, led the way.

The '76 ACC Tournament was moved from the state of North Carolina, a first, and played at the Capital Centre in Landover, Md., not far from College Park.

BELOW
N.C. State running back Ted Brown (23) was a consensus first-team All-American in 1978. He was the rookie of the year in 1975, and he set the conference record for rushing with 4,602 yards. He scored 51 touchdowns in his four-year career. He enjoyed a successful seven-year career as a professional football player and is a member of the 50th anniversary team.

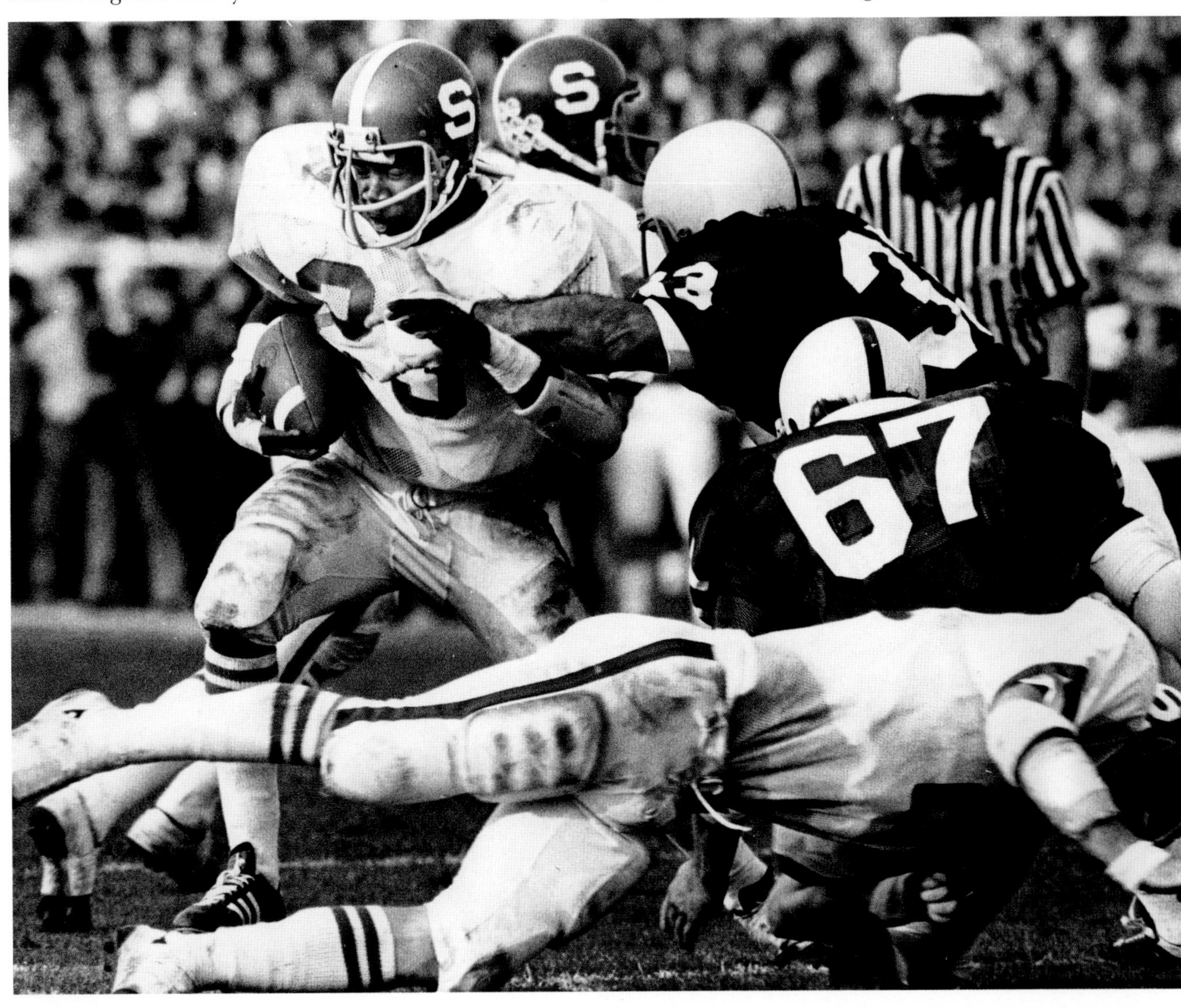

BELOW LEFT
Wally Walker (1973-76) led Virginia to its first ACC Tournament championship and its first NCAA Tournament appearance in 1976 when the Cavaliers upset North Carolina in the championship game. He earned the Everett Case award as the tournament's MVP for his efforts. He averaged 22.1 points his senior season and 17.8 over his career.

BELOW RIGHT
Walker and coach Terry Holland embrace after winning the 1976 ACC Tournament. The Cavaliers were seeded sixth, but upset three ranked opponents, including defending champion North Carolina.

The tournament was no longer do-or-die, but it remained the proud path to the league's automatic bid and official championship.

Senior forward Wally Walker, or "Wally Wonderful" to his fans, led the Cavaliers. Walker, as with Burleson two years earlier, derived motivation from being left off the first unit of the all-conference team. Walker got his revenge by leading his team to the conference title, winning selection as the ACC Tournament MVP as he scored 73 points on 68 percent shooting, made all but one of 18 foul shots, paced Virginia with 21 rebounds and supplied solid defense.

To win, the Cavaliers beat 17th-ranked N.C. State and star forward Kenny Carr, and then dispatched ninth-ranked Maryland and John Lucas, who would be the top pick in the 1976 National Basketball Association draft. Finally Virginia ended UNC's 13-game winning streak, 67-62. Guard Billy Langloh's one-and-one free throws gave the Cavs their final edge with 34 seconds to go. "We all had made plans to go to Florida next week for spring vacation," Walker said. "But we'll gladly change that."

No ACC basketball team fared well in postseason, unless you count the U.S. Olympic squad at the Montreal Games. Coached by North Carolina's Smith, the team engendered criticism because seven of its 12 players hailed from the ACC: Duke's Tate Armstrong, Maryland's Steve Sheppard, N.C. State's Carr, and UNC's Davis, Ford, Kupchak and LaGarde. Objections muted when the Americans won the gold medal.

Postseason wasn't kind to ACC football in 1976, either. Both Maryland and North Carolina lost bowl games. The 11-1 Terps, undefeated in the league a third straight time, did scale heights not seen in the ACC since 1960, finishing in the top 10 in the Associated Press poll. Maryland's Jerry Claiborne repeated as ACC coach of the year, but his No. 8 squad lost its final game 30-21 against No. 4 Houston in the Cotton Bowl. UNC's Mike Voight repeated as player of the year in 1976, leading the league in rushing, all-purpose yardage and scoring as the Tar Heels rebounded from a losing effort in '75 that had fans grumbling. Voight ranks second all-time at UNC in rushing (3,971 yards) and third in scoring. He ended his career with a suitable flourish, rushing for 261 yards and scoring 26 points in the regular-season finale against Duke. North Carolina went to the Peach Bowl. But with Voight injured, Kentucky shut out UNC, 21-0.

Wake finished third and, in safety Bill Armstrong, boasted its first football consensus All-American. N.C. State tied Duke for fourth, but endured a losing record overall in Robert "Bo" Rein's first year replacing Holtz, gone to pro football's New York Jets. Down in Tallahassee, independent Florida State handed the reins to Bobby Bowden, who had coached West Virginia to victory over the Wolfpack in the '75 Peach Bowl.

When basketball resumed, Smith continued the roll he had started with the Olympics, nearly winning the 1976-77 NCAA title. The Tar Heels made their fifth trip to the Final Four within an 11-year span but, plagued by injuries and thwarted by their own delay tactics, fell 67-59 to

BELOW
Wallace Wade (left), Hall of Fame football coach at Alabama and Duke and the man who served as commissioner in the ACC's first year of existence, meets UNC basketball coach Dean Smith (right), a member of the Naismith Basketball Hall of Fame. Former Blue Devil football great Ace Parker, also a member of the College Football Hall of Fame, stands between the two.

Marquette in the championship game.

League-wide balance marked the 1977 basketball season. Only Virginia posted a losing record, and the Cavaliers still reached the ACC Tournament final.

Clemson finished 22-6 under second-year coach Bill Foster, its first 20-win season ever. Duke, with its own coach Bill Foster, lost Armstrong to injury in January, but the Blue Devils ended the school's 27-game ACC road losing streak behind guard Jim Spanarkel and co-rookie of the year Mike Gminski. The Devils had endured three coaching changes since Vic Bubas retired in 1969, at one point trying to lure Kentucky's Adolph Rupp out of retirement.

Wake tied Clemson for second and also registered 22 wins. Coach Carl Tacy's club had a strong perimeter with Skip Brown, Jerry Schellenberg and Frank Johnson, and in 6-6 power forward Rod Griffin a human piston chosen as 1977 ACC player of the year.

Ranked as high as fourth during the regular season, the Deacons returned to the NCAA Tournament for the first time since the Final Four of 1962 and reached the Midwest Regional final, losing to Marquette, the eventual champion.

Good as Griffin was, the most feared performer in the league was doubtless Ford, especially when directing Smith's "Four Corners" delay, an offense that spread the court and isolated the ball-handler one-on-one so he could drive, pass or shoot. The stratagem, although not original to Smith, is one he and Ford made famous.

"Ford was terrific," Holland said. "Point guard does control the show, and they allowed him to do that right from his first year on. He knew the game, knew how to make others better and was such a threat himself."

During Ford's career, North Carolina was a perennial threat both nationally and within the ACC. The 1977 squad did its part, finishing 28-5 and fifth in the AP poll. The Heels were first during the ACC regular season, as happened eight of 12 years

RIGHT
Wake Forest's Rod Griffin fit the prototype for a power forward. He was named ACC player of the year his junior season. He led the Deacons to an NCAA Tournament region final for the first time in 15 seasons and paced the ACC in scoring and rebounding in 1978. He averaged 18.6 points and 8.9 rebounds for his career.

1972

8.7.72
Federal Judge Robert Hemphill invalidates an 800 SAT score as standard for eligibility to compete in ACC

1973

2.73
ACC bylaws changed to allow women to receive grants-in-aid

1974

3.25.74
N.C. State defeats Marquette 76-64 to win NCAA men's basketball titl

from 1967-78. They also won the '77 ACC Tournament, the school's sixth league title in 11 seasons.

UNC's customary depth was never more useful than in 1977, when injuries struck LaGarde's knee, then the index finger on Davis' shooting hand, and, finally, Ford's elbow. Turning to players such as freshman forward Mike O'Koren, sophomore wing Dudley Bradley and senior guard John Kuester, the Tar Heels survived and advanced through postseason play. In the ACC Tournament final, they weathered extensive foul trouble, rallying to a 75-69 victory over a seven-seeded Virginia squad looking to repeat as ACC champs.

Riding a 15-game winning streak, UNC reached the NCAA championship contest against a Marquette squad led by guard Butch Lee and big man Bo Ellis. The Heels fell behind at halftime, but scored 14 of the first 16 points in the second period to tie the score at 41. Just when the momentum seemed theirs, the wounded Tar Heels went to the Four Corners. Al McGuire's club caught its breath, regained the advantage and held on at the foul line for his first and only championship. McGuire promptly retired.

Later that spring Virginia Tech made its third bid in three decades to join the ACC. Sponsored by three members, the application was rejected. "North Carolina and those schools, they would tell them they were going to vote for them, but when they went to the damn meeting none of them voted for them," said Clemson's Bill McLellan, representing a sponsoring institution.

The Gobblers got the last laugh in one respect: Following the '77 football season they hired away Dooley. The North Carolina coach exited on a high note. His 8-3 team went to the 1977 Liberty Bowl after finishing atop the ACC standings. It was the second time in six years the Tar Heels won both the league basketball and football titles.

UNC led the nation in scoring defense, yielding 7.4 points per game. Dooley also added to his collection of superior running backs with freshman Amos Lawrence, the 1977 ACC rookie of the year. "Famous Amos" became the only ACC back ever to rush for at least 1,000 yards in each of his four seasons, and is the No. 2 career rusher in ACC history (4,391 yards).

The man Lawrence trails, N.C. State's Ted Brown, joined him on the All-ACC squad in 1977. Brown made all-conference every year he was in the league. "He combined tremendous lower body power with speed, agility and a competitive heart," Doug Herakovich wrote of Brown in his book *Touchdown Wolfpack!* "He played to win, but he also reveled in the personal challenge."

The 5-11 Brown received only four scholarship offers coming out of High Point, N.C., because of his size. His freshman season he carried once in the first four games, losing 2 yards. He considered transferring.

1976

2.4.76
Former Maryland basketball player Owen Brown dies of heart problem in a pickup game

3.6.76
Virginia wins its only ACC Tournament, defeating UNC 67-62 at Landover, Md., first time event held outside North Carolina

4.1.76
Maryland basketball player Chris Patton dies of cardiac arrest on campus

By John Evans

ACC EXCELLENCE

MARYLAND CASTS MOLD FOR WOMEN'S LACROSSE

Women's lacrosse at Maryland is what every other program in the nation aspires to become.

"Maryland is the premier women's lacrosse program in the country," said Duke women's lacrosse coach Kerstin Kimel, a former Maryland player and a member of the 1992 championship team. "Their program is different from any other program in the country. The culture at Maryland takes good athletes and creates great players."

No school has dominated women's lacrosse the way the Terrapins have. As the program entered its 30th year of existence in 2003, Maryland had won more games (404) and had a higher winning percentage (81.5 percent) than any other club in the country.

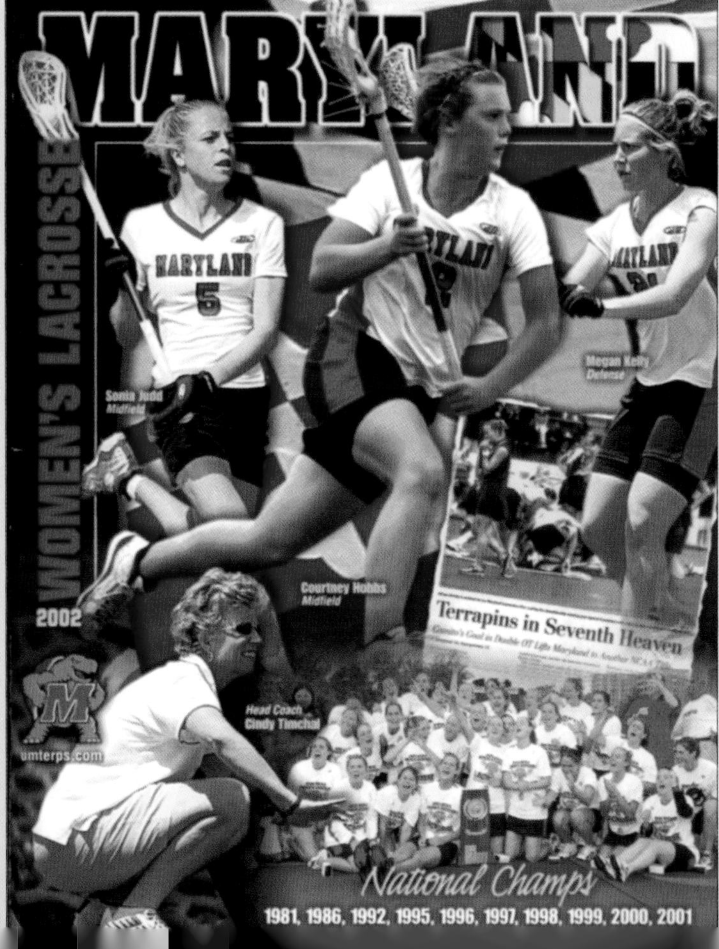

MARYLAND
WOMEN'S LACROSSE
2002
Sonia Judd
Midfield
Megan Kelly
Defense
Courtney Hobbs
Midfield
Head Coach
Cindy Timchal
umterps.com
Terrapins in Seventh Heaven
National Champs
1981, 1986, 1992, 1995, 1996, 1997, 1998, 1999, 2000, 2001

The Terrapins have won nine NCAA titles (plus one Association of Intercollegiate Athletics for Women title). Maryland has appeared in 23 national tournaments and has played 17 times for the national championship. The Terps had made 13 straight NCAA Tournament appearances through the 2002 season.

Eleven Terrapins have been named national players of the year, and at least one Maryland player has been an All-America selection every season since 1980. Then there is the streak of seven straight national championships from 1995-2001, which stands as a stunning achievement.

"I've tried to empower my athletes to focus on what we can control and don't get caught up in what we can't," coach Cindy Timchal said. "We don't try to prove that we are the best team; we just try to be the best team we can be."

Maryland has had three coaches in its history. Two of them — Dr. Sue Tyler and Timchal — have directed the team for 28 of its 29 seasons.

Under Tyler, the Terps were an established national power, winning 195 games in 16 seasons and two national titles (AIAW 1981, NCAA 1986). After leading the Terps to the NCAA final in 1990, Tyler resigned to become a full-time administrator at the school.

Timchal is credited with taking the program and women's lacrosse to greater heights. Under Timchal, the Terrapins have won eight national titles and posted a 203-22 record. Timchal and Maryland also have been trendsetters.

"When Maryland hired Cindy as coach, they knew what they were doing," said Kimel, who had played under Tyler as a freshman in 1990. "But we wondered at the time if they had done the right thing by hiring her, if she could keep us at the national level. Well, she did more than that. She made us national champions and has done it over and over again."

After reaching the NCAA final in 1991, the Terps won two overtime games to win the NCAA tournament in 1992, upsetting Virginia and Harvard (11-10 in the final) for a Cinderella finish to a 14-1 season.

Maryland lost to Princeton in the NCAA semifinals in 1993 and again in the 1994 final, but the long reign of championships began in 1995 with a 13-5 win over Princeton to complete a 17-0 season.

During the seven-title run, Maryland went 140-5 and had win streaks of 50 and 43 games. The Terrapins also had four undefeated seasons: 1995, 1996, 1999 and 2001.

Four-time All-American Kelly Amonte-Hiller, now the head coach at Northwestern, played on the 1995 and '96 teams. She said Timchal's approach to coaching is why the program remains successful.

"She allows the players to really feel like they are the ones who make it happen, that it is their team, and everyone feels they are important," Amonte-Hiller said. "She instills a confidence in her players that makes them make the most of their talents and makes them believe they can handle any game situation. It is a calculated coaching style, but she has managed the right mix."

Another reason for Maryland's success has been Timchal's willingness to take a chance with new ideas. She hired former Syracuse All-American Gary Gait as an assistant coach in 1994, and he brought a new style of play to the women's game.

"We've always tried to be the trendsetter instead of the trend follower," said Timchal, who has also employed sports psychologist Dr. Jerry Lynch as an advisor for the team. "I've always tried to do what's different. I felt Gary Gait would bring fresh ideas to our sport. He taught us his game.

"Not just the men's style of play, but his. He was the best lacrosse player in the world at the time, and he shared his ideas with me and helped teach the girls in such a way that it was an easy transition. It was a great fit for us and still is."

Gait ended his nine-year coaching affiliation with the program after the 2002 season.

"Cindy really thought outside the box when she brought in Gary Gait," Kimel said. "Nobody had ever thought about that before, hiring a man to coach a women's team. Cindy really took a chance in hiring him and showed a lot of courage. But then, she's never been afraid to take the bold step."

Revolutionary at the time, the style of play Gait introduced is now the norm in the women's game.

"He brought advanced stickwork, deception and new defensive skills to the game, and he taught us in such a way it was easy for us to pick up," said Amonte-Hiller, who was there for Gait's first seasons at Maryland. "A lot of it was just pushing us to our limits athletically. What you see women's teams doing in lacrosse today, he introduced."

Timchal was also the first coach to extensively recruit foreign players, tapping into Australia and establishing a pipeline of talent that has developed four All-Americans: Sarah Forbes, Sascha Newmarch, Jen Adams and Courtney Hobbs.

Forbes was national offensive player of the year in 1997 and was named the ACC female athlete of the year. Adams finished her career as the all-time NCAA leader in points and assists, was a three-time player of the year and twice was ACC female athlete of the year.

Maryland has helped to improve play in the ACC as well. Of the five losses during the championship streak, three were to North Carolina and one to Duke. Maryland's 14-13 triple-overtime loss to the Tar Heels in 2000 is still one of the sport's most memorable moments. Maryland defeated Virginia in three national championship games: 1996, '98 and '99.

"We have managed to stay on top while always playing the best schedule in the country," Timchal said. "ACC teams have become so good that within our own conference we've developed strong, intense rivalries to go along with the traditional teams we've played."

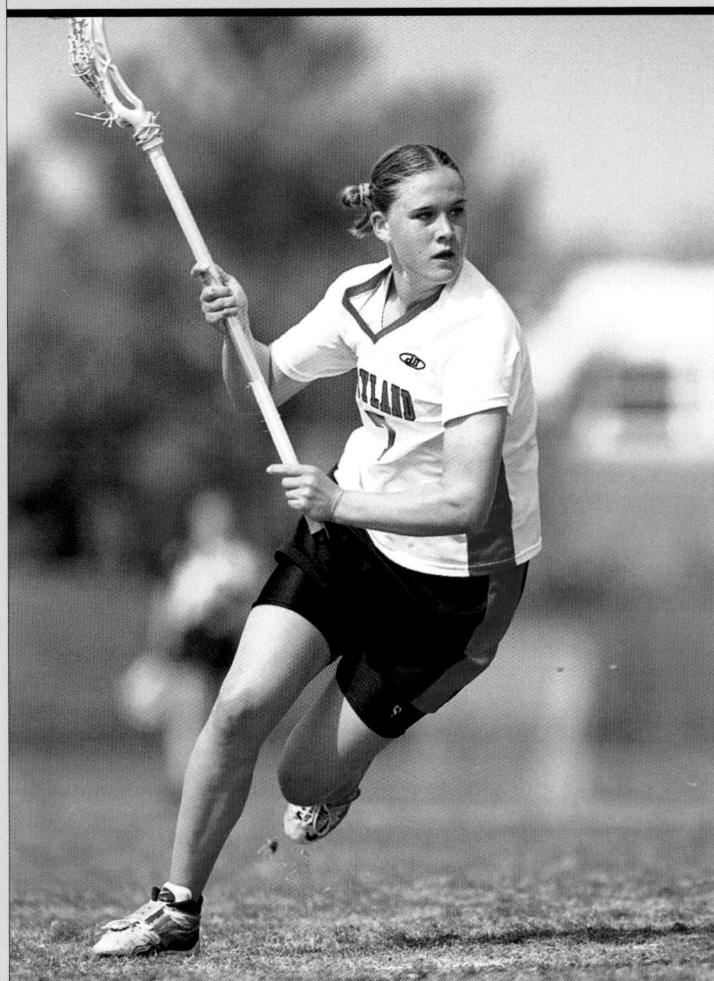

Above: Former All-American Jen Adams is one of the players who made Maryland the dominant force in NCAA women's lacrosse. The Terrapins have won 10 national championships, including seven consecutive titles in the 1990s and at the turn of the century.

Kimel credits Maryland's success with improving the ACC as a whole.

"Due to Maryland's success and the efforts of the other three schools to build their programs to compete, the ACC is now the top women's conference in the country," Kimel said. "The conference has had a great amount of success in a short period of time."

"Obviously, it's been a great journey for all of us," Timchal said.

Maryland men's lacrosse also ranks among the best in NCAA history, winning more than 600 games dating back to 1924.

Although the Terps men have not won an NCAA title since the 1970s (1973 and '75), the program ranks second only to Johns Hopkins in NCAA appearances, with 25. The Terps have also won or shared 24 ACC titles and advanced to the NCAA championship game nine times.

Under Dick Edell, Maryland went to the NCAA finals three times in four seasons in 1995, 1997 and 1998 and made it into the NCAA tournament 13 times in 18 seasons. His 1998 team won a school-record 14 games.

Edell retired as Maryland coach prior to the 2002 season, having guided Maryland to a 171-76 record — the most wins ever by an ACC men's lacrosse coach.

But after other Wolfpack runners fumbled six times in a 31-31 tie with Michigan State, Brown got a start at Indiana and gained 121 yards. He remained a fixture in the N.C. State backfield for the remainder of a career that concluded in 1978 with 27 100-yard games and 4,602 yards rushing.

In a home loss in '77, Brown set a school record by gaining 251 yards. He did so against a Penn State defense that entered the contest yielding just 90 yards per game on the ground. "Brown is better than Tony Dorsett," said one Nittany Lion defender, referring to the previous year's Heisman Trophy winner from Pittsburgh. "He runs harder than Dorsett."

Nevertheless, Brown never won ACC player of the year honors. His last two seasons, 1977 and '78, the award went to Clemson quarterback Steve Fuller.

Clemson was the ACC's rising power in 1977. Coach Charley Pell joined the Tigers in December 1976, arriving from service as assistant head coach at Virginia Tech of all places. Pell immediately won 1977 ACC coach of the year honors as the Tigers went 8-3 and played in the Gator Bowl, their first postseason appearance since 1959.

Maryland slipped a bit and finished tied for third with the Wolfpack, which broke the Terps' 21-game ACC winning streak on Oct. 1. Claiborne's squad still finished 8-4, beating Minnesota 17-7 in the Hall of Fame Bowl. N.C. State, also 8-4, beat Iowa State 24-14 in the Peach Bowl.

Four ACC squads earned bowl bids in 1977, most in a single year to that point and a majority of the seven-team league. Similarly, basketball enjoyed unprecedented prosperity in 1977-78. For the first time, every ACC team had a winning record overall, a feat duplicated only in 1985. Also for the first time, four squads won at least 20 games.

North Carolina, of course, was one of them, finishing first at 9-3 and 23-8 overall. N.C. State, paced in scoring by forward Charles "Hawkeye" Whitney, went 21-10. Virginia finished 20-8 a year after tying for last place, led by Jeff Lamp and Lee Raker,

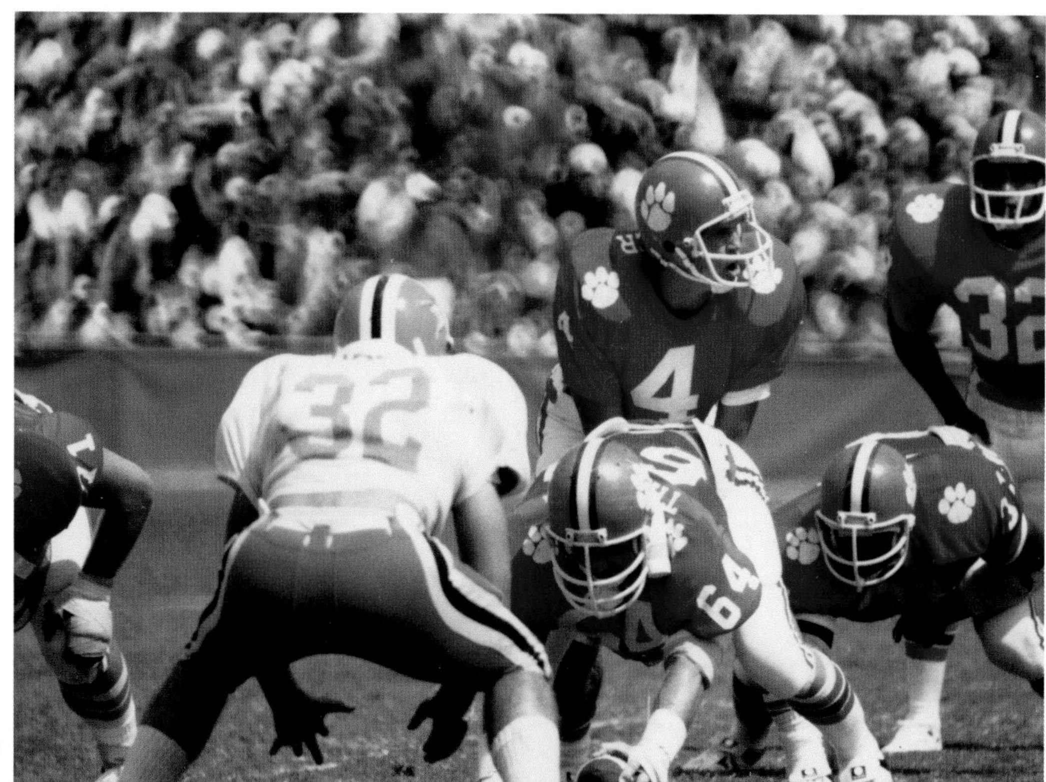

BOTH PAGES
Clemson quarterback Steve Fuller became the first player in school history to have his jersey retired. He excelled as a student and athlete, earning first-team academic All-America honors while twice being named the ACC player of the year. In his senior season of 1978, the Tigers went 6-0 in the ACC, 11-1 overall and were No. 6 in the final Associated Press poll after defeating Ohio State 17-15 in the Gator Bowl.

3

20
CAMERON
HOME OF THE

freshmen from the same high school in Louisville, Ky.

Duke, the team the Cavaliers tied for sixth in '77, was the big surprise in 1978. Not only did the 27-7 Blue Devils post their first 20-win season since 1968, they captured the ACC title and advanced to the national championship game, losing 94-88 to top-ranked Kentucky.

Just a few years earlier, coach Bill Foster, who had previously won at Rutgers and Utah, admitted his Duke program was struggling to make a dent in the ACC. "We're just going 'glub, glub, glub' trying to keep our heads above water, let alone swim," he said. That began to change when Foster landed consecutive ACC rookies of the year in Spanarkel (1976), Gminski ('77) and forward Gene Banks ('78).

Banks, a highly recruited prospect from Philadelphia, was the first prominent African-American basketball player signed by Duke, which had trailed only Maryland in integrating its squad during the mid-'60s with C.B. Claiborne.

Nicknamed "Tinkerbell," Banks was brash and exuberant. So was classmate Kenny Dennard, a rugged forward from North Carolina. As with Brian Piccolo and Gayle Sayers a decade earlier in the NFL, the pair's overt bond, including boyish embraces on the court, provided an uncommon expression of racial harmony. "On the court we're all brothers," Banks said. A sense of fun permeated the squad. "It surprised me that they're so young, yet they play so well together," said Kentucky veteran Rick Robey. "And they have that

LEFT

Duke coach Bill Foster (right) cheers on his team and forward Gene "Tinkerbell" Banks (20). Banks played a big role as Foster revitalized Blue Devil basketball in the late 1970s. The 1978 club won the ACC Tournament and then made a run to the NCAA title game. Banks was a member of two ACC championship teams, scoring 21 points in the title contest his junior season (1980) to lead the Blue Devils to a 73-72 victory over Maryland.

young enthusiasm."

Also joining the Blue Devils in 1978 were a pair of transfer point guards, John Harrell from North Carolina Central and Bob Bender from Indiana. Bender had been a member of the Hoosiers' undefeated 1976 NCAA championship squad, and he became the only player ever to reach the title game with two different teams.

The makeover of Duke basketball extended to a $650,000 renovation of Cameron Indoor Stadium, renamed in 1972 in honor of Eddie Cameron, one of the ACC's founding fathers. Lobbies in the 1940-vintage Gothic structure were redone. A new floor, a Hall of Fame Room and suspended baskets were installed.

The Blue Devils didn't crack the polls until beating UNC at home in mid-January, their second win over the Tar Heels in 17 tries. The regular-season race came down to the last game, another meeting between the archrivals. Just as Duke senior Art Heyman did 15 years earlier in his home finale against UNC, so senior Phil Ford enjoyed a career-best scoring effort (34 points) in his curtain call at Carmichael, leading the Tar Heels to an 87-83 win. Asked what he would do without Ford after the '78 season, Smith said simply, "Resign."

The ACC's spotty success in the NCAAs, blamed on being a finesse league, motivated Commissioner James to hire outside officials to work the conference tournament. Television caused the event to be spread over four days, a first. Unfazed, Duke beat Wake for the title and rolled to the NCAA final, only to see its zone

BELOW
Clemson guard Billy Williams (24) was first-team All-ACC in 1980. Jim Spanarkel (34) was the ACC Tournament MVP in 1978, a two-time all-conference selection and an All-American. The veteran of the group, Spanarkel guided Duke to the national championship game in 1978. He is among the school's career leaders in scoring and assists.

defense plucked for 41 points by UK's Jack "Goose" Givens. Banks was informed after the game that two threats had been made on his life.

Maryland also reached the 1978 Women's Final Four, though the AIAW version. That meant the team had to pay its own way to Los Angeles and fork over an entry fee to participate.

Scrounging for funds was a way of life for women's teams. "You had to, in that day and age, figure out creative ways to finance these opportunities," said Chris Weller, Maryland's head women's basketball coach from 1975 to 2002.

At North Carolina, Bernadette McGlade said funding increased annually during her playing career. But the stark differences between men's and women's resources were manifest when both squads went to a holiday tournament in London, England, in late 1979. "The men and the women were both invited as Carolina basketball," McGlade said. "The men, of course, jet-setted over, and we were raising money like for a road race." Finally, a student newspaper article "shamed" the school into footing the bulk of the bill, said McGlade, now an ACC associate commissioner.

Weller stayed up nights prior to road games making 50 sandwiches for her players, trying to stretch the peanut butter and jelly and the mustard and mayonnaise that went with the cheese and bologna. A program goal was to afford two sets of uniforms and a set of warm-ups. "We had one set of uniforms, the red uniforms, so if we went to a tournament we had to always be

BELOW

Mike Gminski (43) set Duke records for scoring and rebounding before he graduated in 1980. He helped rebuild the proud program and played a huge role in the Blue Devils earning a trip to the Final Four in 1978. A two-time All-American, Gminski averaged double figures in scoring and rebounding in three of his four years.

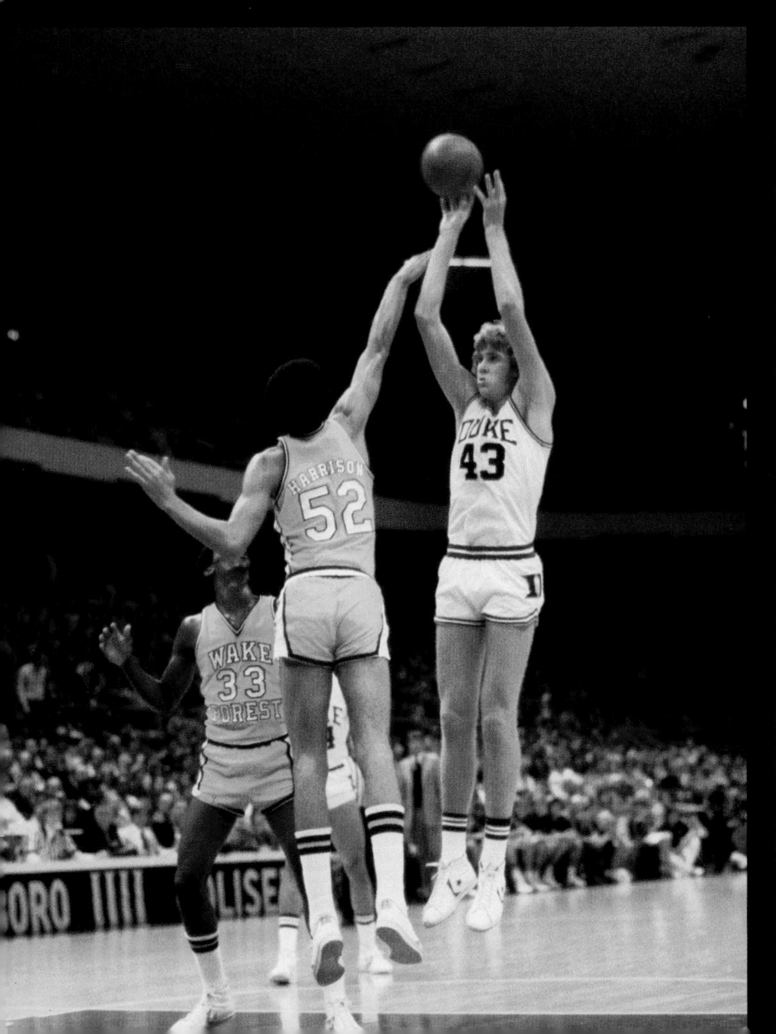

the away team," Weller said.

The ACC held its first tournament for female athletes in Winston-Salem in the fall of 1977, with North Carolina emerging the tennis champion. The inaugural ACC women's basketball tournament was held in early February 1978 at Virginia. "We need to build up fan interest," said Barbara Kelly, director of women's athletics at Virginia, which first added women undergraduates in 1970. The event, the oldest in Division I for women, was moved off campus and to a neutral site in 1983.

Weller's Terrapins, led by Tara Weiss, won that first tournament, beating N.C. State 89-82 in the final in a battle of top-10 squads. Both teams had a single loss to that point, with Kay Yow's Wolfpack the victor in their only previous meeting. "I remember that we stressed to our team that they had a chance to be a part of history," Weller said. "It was terribly exciting to win that tournament, and it was definitely an honor to be the first."

Maryland reached the AIAW final, losing 90-74 to UCLA and All-American Ann Meyers.

Two days after basketball concluded its business for the 1977-78 season, the ACC balanced its books at eight, adding a member for the first time since its earliest days. Georgia Tech formally applied for league membership March 30, 1978, drawn by the prospects of regional compatibility, stabilized revenues and sharing in conference and ACC Tournament competition. Four days later, the ACC's Executive Committee accepted the Atlanta engineering and technology school into the fold.

"It opens up a new fan interest area for us," James said. "It's also attractive from a TV standpoint because of the strong market in Atlanta, and it also adds balance geographically." Writing in Raleigh's *The News & Observer*, Joe Tiede noted: "South Carolina left the ACC in 1971 without looking back. It's hard to imagine anyone doing that now. The league's stature is higher than ever."

Yellow Jacket basketball coach Dwane Morrison played at South Carolina just prior to the ACC's advent. He knew what lay in store when conference play began in 1979-80. "Our basketball is going to take a beating for a couple of years, I believe," he said, an accurate forecast.

Conversely, the *Charlotte Observer*'s Bob Quincy expected the ACC to benefit from the addition of a football program that claimed national championships in 1917, 1928 and 1952 and boasted Hall of Famers in coaches John Heisman, William Alexander and Bobby Dodd. "The Yellow Jackets add immense prestige to the conference football segment," Quincy said.

League football was already on the upswing. Three teams got postseason bids — N.C. State, which beat Pittsburgh 30-17 in the Tangerine Bowl; Maryland, which lost the Sun Bowl 42-0 to Texas; and Clemson, which defeated Ohio State 17-15 in a Gator Bowl that saw one notable

1977

10.1.77
Maryland's 21-game ACC football winning streak broken 24-20 by N.C. State

10.8.77
North Carolina wins the ACC tennis tournament, the first league title contested in a women's sport

1978

2.11.78
Maryland wins first women's ACC basketball tournament, 89-82 over N.C. State at Charlottesville, Va.

3.25.78
Maryland first ACC basketball team to reach a women's Final Four, losing 90-74 to UCLA in the AIAW final

4.3.78
Georgia Tech admitted to ACC as eighth member

coaching career begin and another come to an abrupt end.

Maryland and N.C. State finished 9-3, fueled by impressive running backs. The second-place Terps boasted Steve Adkins, their first back to rush for 1,000 yards. Adkins had 1,261 yards, but he trailed the Wolfpack's Ted Brown, whose 1,350 yards (122.7 per game) led the conference.

Other than Georgia in the second week, nobody caught Clemson, which finished 11-1 in '78. The Tigers led the ACC in scoring offense, total offense, rushing offense and total defense. Their mobile 6-4 quarterback, senior Steve Fuller, repeated as the league's total offense leader and ACC player of the year. Yet the 12th-ranked Tigers didn't secure their first conference title in 11 years until the regular-season finale at 11th-ranked Maryland, beating the Terrapins, 28-24.

Then things got interesting. Pell, the 1978 ACC coach of the year, resigned Dec. 4 to take over at Florida. Offensive line coach Danny Ford was named Pell's replacement the next day, at age 30 the nation's youngest Division I-A coach.

Ford, not Pell, coached the sixth-ranked Tigers in the Gator Bowl against a No. 20 Ohio State squad with quarterback Art Schlichter. Clemson held a 10-9 edge at halftime, the lead changing for the third time on Obed Ariri's 47-yard field goal with five seconds remaining in the second quarter.

Each team scored a touchdown in the second half. Trailing 17-15 late in the game, the Buckeyes mounted a final drive, reaching the Clemson 24. On third-and-five, second-stringer Charlie Bauman intercepted Schlichter, the only pick of the middle guard's four-year career.

Bauman was run out of bounds by the OSU bench, where coach Woody Hayes took a swing at the Clemson lineman. Consecutive unsportsmanlike-conduct penalties were assessed against Ohio State. The Tigers ran out the clock for the program's first win over a Big 10 team, and Hayes was soon out of a job.

LEFT
Norman Sloan (left) and Dean Smith (right) sit alongside Bill Guthridge. All three men would become ACC head basketball coaches and lead their teams to the Final Four. Sloan won the national championship with N.C. State in 1974. Smith won the national title at North Carolina in 1982 and '93. Guthridge, longtime assistant to Smith, succeeded him as the Tar Heels' head coach in 1997 when Smith retired. Guthridge directed UNC to two Final Fours before retiring after just three seasons as the head coach. Guthridge won more games (58) in two years than any previous coach in the NCAA, and he tied former N.C. State coach Everett Case with the most Division I victories after three seasons (80).

The drama during the 1978-79 ACC basketball season was every bit as compelling, although for the league the denouement was nearly as dark as Hayes'.

Every team except Wake posted a winning record and at least 18 victories. Among the winners, only N.C. State failed to get a postseason invitation. The Pack's near-miss could be traced to a haunting 70-69 home loss to North Carolina. N.C. State rallied from a 40-19 halftime deficit, only to see guard Clyde "The Glide" Austin pick-pocketed near mid-court by master thief Dudley Bradley, whose layup with seven seconds to go won the game for the Tar Heels.

Maryland, Virginia and Clemson went to the NIT. All three were bumped in the second round. Virginia finished third in the ACC, its 7-5 league mark the best at the school since 1972. Maryland finished fourth, fortunes buoyed by a 67-66 win over top-ranked Notre Dame on a 3-point play by big man Larry Gibson with a second remaining.

Duke and North Carolina, the first-place finishers, received NCAA bids. As in 1978, the regular-season race boiled down to the final game between the two, this one at Cameron. Clemson had won by 21 points using slowdown tactics in Duke's prior outing, so Smith contentedly had his team hold the ball throughout the first half. "It was a strange game because they didn't choose to chase us," Smith said of the high-intensity, low-action opening period. "Their fans were chanting, 'We want basketball.' ... We didn't want to let them sit back in their zone because that's their strength."

UNC trailed almost from the outset and tried just two shots in the half. The Heels were behind 7-0 at intermission, the first time an ACC team failed to score in a half. During one stretch, the Tar Heels ran nearly 12-and-a-half minutes off the clock before 6-9 Rich Yonaker missed the basket and backboard with a jumper. The resulting chant of "Airball! Airball!" that arose spontaneously remains a campus staple nationwide.

BELOW
Clyde Austin (3) and Kenny Carr (32) race down the court for N.C. State. Carr was one of the finest players in N.C. State history. He made several All-America teams and was a member of the U.S. Olympic team that won the gold medal in 1976. He was named to the All-ACC Tournament team twice. He led the conference in scoring in 1976 as a junior (26.6 points per game) and in 1977 as a senior (21 ppg).

"AIRBALL! AIRBALL!"

ABOVE
Virginia tailback Tommy Vigorito (22) topped the Cavaliers in rushing from 1978-80. In 1979, Vigorito led Virginia to its second winning season since the inception of the ACC. He gained 1,045 yards rushing and averaged 5.7 yards per carry and made first-team All-ACC.

Duke won 47-40 as the teams essentially played to a draw in the second half. "It should have been 2-0 or something like that at the half," Smith said. "I wanted to win the game 2-0. That's just as good as 82-80."

The Tar Heels got a measure of revenge a week later, topping Duke and Gminski, the league's 1979 player of the year, in the ACC Tournament final, 71-63. Bradley was voted MVP. "I think this is a great basketball team," Smith said. "I think Duke is a great basketball team, and either of us could go all the way this year."

All the way to Reynolds Coliseum, that is. Both ACC entrants were sent to the NCAA East Regional and given first-round byes. Each had to win once at Raleigh to advance to the regional semifinals on the same Greensboro court that again hosted the ACC Tournament from 1976-80.

But North Carolina lost 72-71 to Pennsylvania, one of only three programs (with Kentucky and Marquette) to surpass the Tar Heels in victories during the 1970s. Then Duke lost 75-70 to St. John's. March 11, 1979, became known as "Black Sunday" and marked the last time the ACC failed to have at least two teams advance to the Sweet 16.

"Only two events could lure 10,000 North Carolinians into a smoky room on a bright March afternoon — a state funeral or a college basketball game," wrote Lenox Rawlings in the *Winston-Salem Journal*. "In Reynolds Coliseum yesterday you could get both for the price of one."

The decade ended for ACC basketball with one NCAA title, four trips to the Final Four and three appearances in the title

game. Since 1962 the ACC had sent 11 teams to the Final Four, impressive representation in the game's increasingly visible showcase event.

Renaldo Nehemiah, a two-time All-American in the hurdles at Maryland, won the McKevlin Award for the league's top athlete in the summer of 1969. No male track and field athlete has won the award since.

The ACC's upward trajectory in football continued the following fall, even as it encountered a hurdle that would plague the league for years to come.

Five of seven ACC teams enjoyed winning records in 1979, the best showing in five seasons. The biggest surprise was Wake Forest at 8-4, more wins than in the previous three years combined and a stunning turnaround from 1-10 in '78. Since 1888, when Wake won the first collegiate football game played in North Carolina under so-called "scientific" or official rules, no squad at the school has surpassed that eight-victory total.

John Mackovic, the former Deacon quarterback in his second season back at Winston-Salem, was voted 1979 ACC coach of the year. His quarterback, Jay Venuto, was ACC player of the year, the last of three Deacons to win the award. Wake's reward was a berth in the Tangerine Bowl, the school's first postseason bid since 1949.

Virginia was 6-5, only its second winning

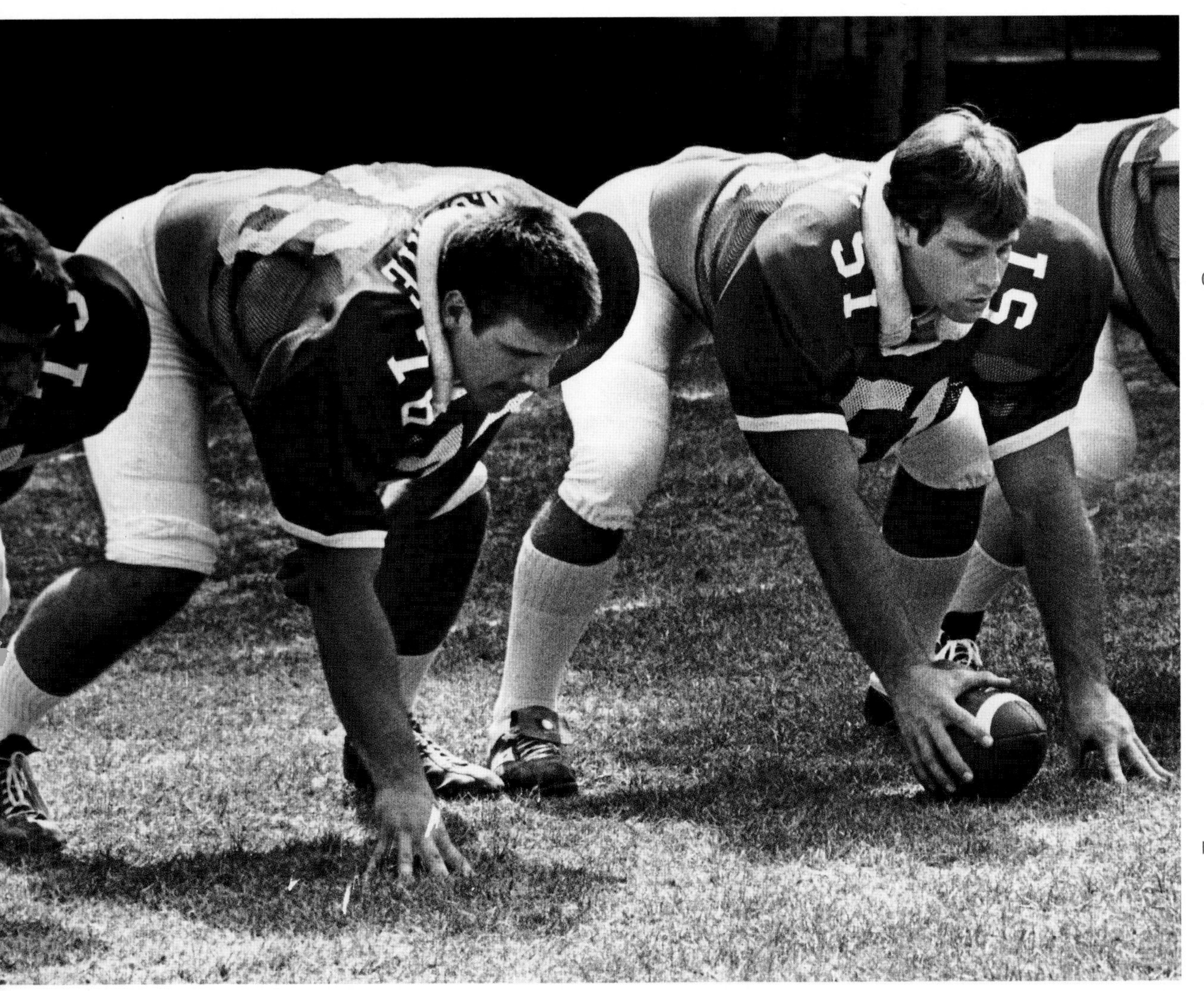

BOTH PAGES
Jim Ritcher (51) separated himself as one of the finest football players in the history of the ACC. He was a two-time consensus All-American, twice won the conference's Jacobs' Blocking Trophy and captured the Outland Trophy in 1979, which goes to the top interior lineman in the nation. He enjoyed a long, successful career as a professional football player, too. He participated in four Super Bowls with the Buffalo Bills. N.C. State retired his jersey number, and Ritcher is a member of the College Football Hall of Fame and the ACC's 50th anniversary team.

football record as an ACC member and more victories than in the previous three years combined. Included was a stunning 31-0 triumph at Georgia hailed among the greatest moments in Cavalier football history. Coach Dick Bestwick's squad was led by running back Tommy Vigorito, who had 1,044 yards, and 170-pound quarterback Todd Kirtley, who said wryly, "I may not be big or strong, but I'm slow."

North Carolina quickly returned to prominence with an 8-3 showing under second-year coach Dick Crum. The No. 15 Tar Heels, the ACC's only ranked team, ended the season following almost exactly in Clemson's 1978 cleat prints, playing in the Gator Bowl and winning 17-15 over a Big 10 squad (Michigan). The Tigers were also 8-4 and tied Maryland and Wake for second in the league.

The champion was N.C. State, 5-1 in the ACC and 7-4 overall under Bo Rein.

The Wolfpack opened the year by beating East Carolina at Carter-Finley Stadium. Early planning had focused on a domed facility; a far simpler design still cost $3.7 million when the stadium opened in 1966. "Earle Edwards built our program and the stadium," Frank Weedon said. "Lou Holtz paid for the stadium, and created the aura of quote bigger football or better football."

About half the construction money came from the Carter brothers, N.C. State alumni and textile manufacturers. The name of A.E. Finley, a Raleigh philanthropist, was added in 1979. The remainder of the funding was secured through a loan to be repaid by 2004. But the excitement of the Holtz era attracted unprecedented crowds, and AD Willis Casey froze departmental salaries for six years, according to Weedon, and didn't spend home football gate receipts for 12. As a result, the stadium was paid off by 1979, the mortgage burned symbolically at halftime of the ECU game.

The Wolfpack's most prominent player that year was Jim Ritcher, a retiring, 6-3 Ohioan who won the Outland Trophy as the nation's top interior lineman. "I honestly think State may have in Ritcher the best offensive center that's ever lined up to play a college football game," said Pat Dye, the ECU coach. "Add Charley Pell's name to the not-so-secret admirer list of Jim Ritcher," wrote Abe Hardesty in the *Greenville* (S.C.) *Piedmont.* "He can do things that can't be done," said Pell, shaking his head.

What the Wolfpack couldn't do was secure a bowl bid, the first exclusion for the ACC champ since Wake in 1970. N.C. State couldn't keep the imaginative and enthusiastic Rein, either. Shortly after Thanksgiving, Rein became head coach at LSU.

Barely six weeks later, the 34-year-old was dead when his plane flew from Louisiana into the Atlantic Ocean. The plane crashed after running out of gas, the coach and his pilot apparently succumbing to hypoxia, the same blackout caused by lack of oxygen suspected in the death nearly 20 years later of professional golfer Payne Stewart. ✴

FACING PAGE
Wake Forest alumnus and football coach John Mackovic (left) and quarterback Jay Venuto survey the field. In 1979, the pair led the Demon Deacons to an 8-4 record, a tie for second in the league standings and a bid to the Tangerine Bowl. Venuto was the ACC player of the year in '79 and was the first-team All-ACC quarterback in 1979 and '80.

J. VENUTO
14

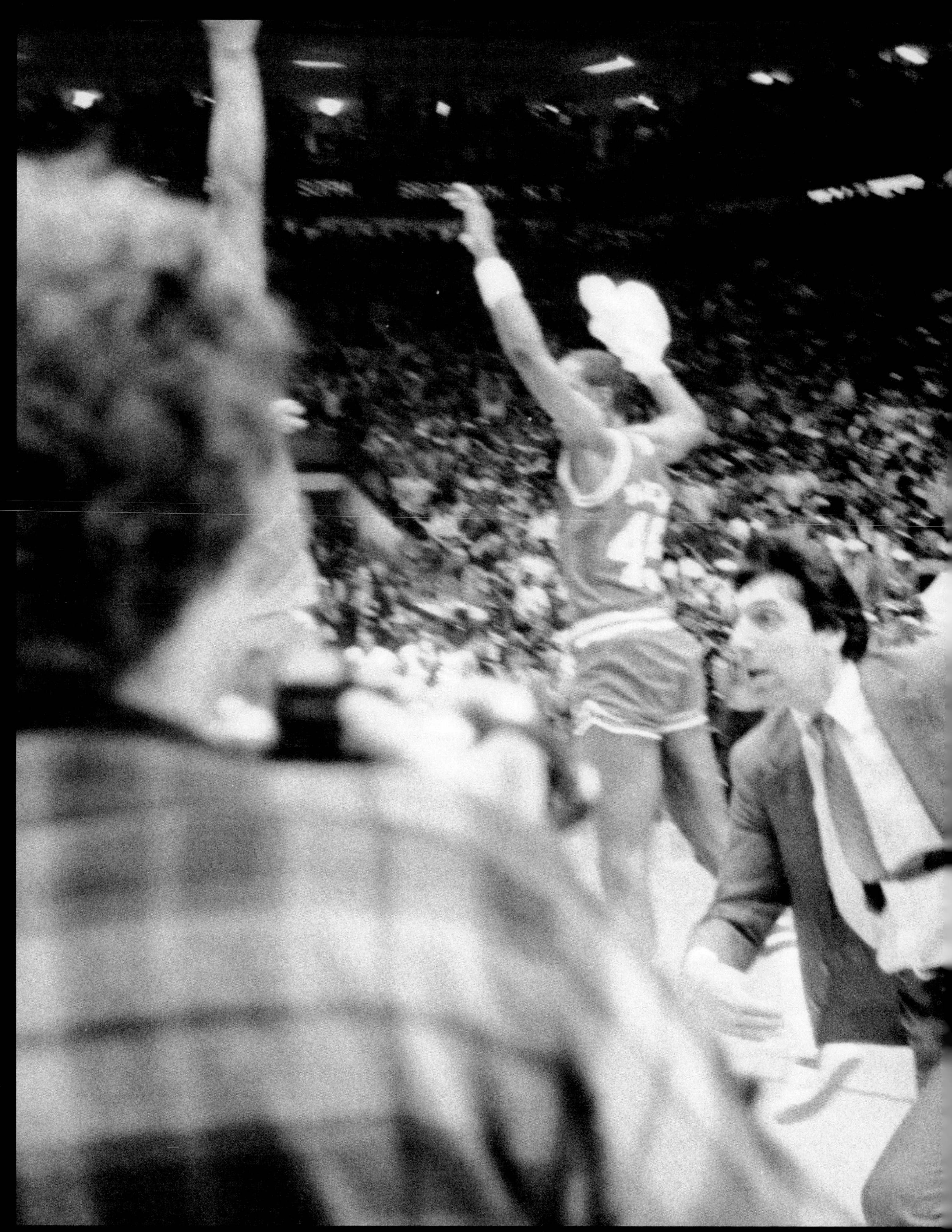

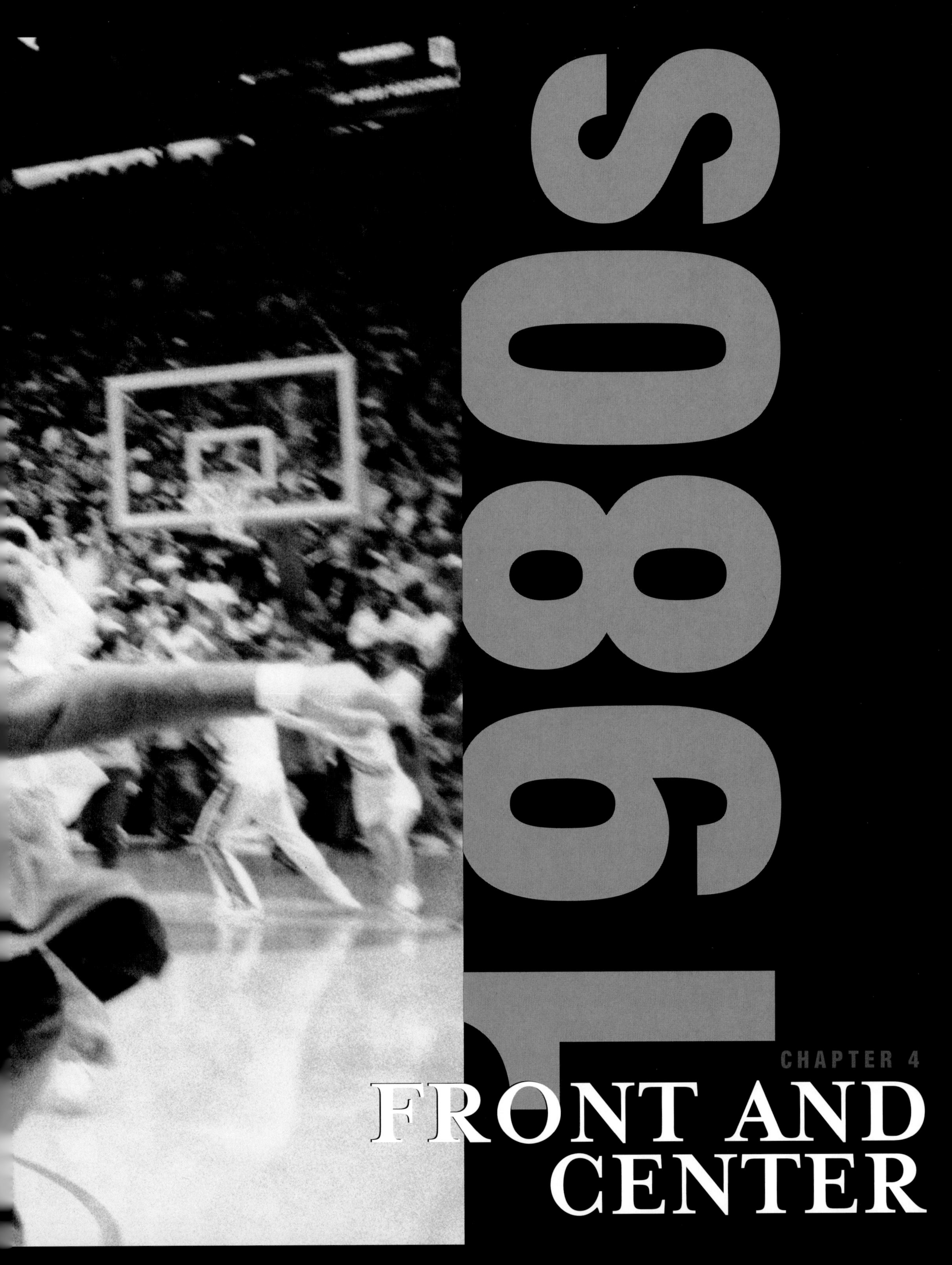

1980s

CHAPTER 4

FRONT AND CENTER

Extraordinary success came swiftly and in abundance to the ACC during the 1980s. Three league teams won major national championships in the decade's first four years. Football was on the rise from Clemson to Chapel Hill to Charlottesville to College Park. ACC men's basketball squads reached the Final Four in all but three seasons, a reprise of the prosperous '60s. Women's athletics made major strides.

Yet success may contain within it seeds of discontent, or worse.

Jim Valvano, the entrepreneurial head basketball coach at N.C. State from 1980 through 1990, was fond of author Ambrose Bierce's icy warning that success is "the one unpardonable sin against one's fellows." Dean Smith fretted that perennial success raised unrealistic expectations at North Carolina, where a prodigious new basketball arena inadvertently sapped the home-court edge even as it increased attendance and revenue.

Too often during the '80s success was also accompanied by self-destructive acts that were variously tragic, controversial or plain disappointing. This occurred even as the ACC blossomed and matured competitively.

ACC men's basketball entered the decade widely regarded as the nation's best. The performance in 1980 was emblematic, as six of eight teams won at least 20 games. Five received NCAA bids, a majority of the league's membership, and far more than in any previous season. Four were ranked at season's end.

Thirteen players active in the conference in 1979-80 would be first-round National Basketball Association draft picks. Seven were named first- or second-team All-Americans during their careers. Two were chosen for the 1980 U.S. Olympic squad that didn't play because of a boycott of the Moscow Games. Two others were considered the nation's top prospect the year they concluded high school.

Wake Forest was a temporary exception to the prosperity. Georgia Tech's problems went deeper. The new ACC member was in another league when it came to resources and facilities. "We were at the bottom of the league in every sport, not just bottom, but being beaten," said Homer Rice, who became the school's director of athletics in February 1980. "The facilities, I'll never forget reading a report — somebody had picked the top 10 and the bottom 10. And the bottom 10 had just one school, and that was Georgia Tech."

Rice was head coach of the National Football League's Cincinnati Bengals as the '80s dawned. While at North Carolina from 1969 to 1975, he had also served as a consultant on athletics to Tech President Joseph Pettit. Three times Rice was offered the AD job at Georgia Tech, he said, and three times he turned it down. After finally accepting the position with the Yellow Jackets, upon close inspection Rice found shower-room facilities shared by teams and officials, a cinder track and virtually no women's program.

"It was pathetic," Rice said. "I thought, 'Boy, what have I gotten myself into?'"

Rice was soon offered a National Football League assistant's job with Denver coach Dan Reeves, a quarterback at South Carolina from 1962-64 and twice second team All-ACC. Rice nearly took it. Instead he stayed at Georgia Tech for 17 years, raising more than $100 million for facilities for the ACC's newest program.

Rice worked in half-decade increments. The first five-year plan aimed to earn ACC competitiveness and respect. By 1986, the Jackets had won the ACC men's basketball tournament and league titles in baseball and golf. The second five-year segment sought national respect, earned as the football team won a share of the 1990 national championship and the basketball squad reached the Final Four. The third phase of Rice's efforts was capped by Georgia Tech's inclusion as the site of the Olympic Village and swimming events at the 1996 Olympic Games in Atlanta.

"When he went in, they stunk at everything," said Gene Corrigan, then athletics director at Virginia and later ACC commissioner. "Homer came in and built that place up. What he did at Georgia Tech ... he did one of the best all-time jobs ever."

Of course Tech wasn't built in a day. The early Yellow Jackets, fighting merely to survive, went 8-18 overall, 1-13 in the league in their debut ACC men's basketball season. The 1980 regular season belonged to Maryland, led by Albert King, the league's top scorer (21.7) and the ACC player of the year. King, a 6-6 junior from Brooklyn, N.Y., keyed a squad that included classmates Ernest Graham and Greg Manning and sophomore rebounding maven Charles "Buck" Williams, the 1979 ACC rookie of the year. Coach of the year Lefty Driesell directed the Terrapins to a finish atop the ACC at 11-3, two games ahead of North Carolina and N.C. State.

Clemson was fourth, but had a banner year. The Tigers compiled a 23-8 record, their second 20-win season in history, both under coach Bill Foster. The performance earned an NCAA invitation, the school's first. Seizing the opportunity, the Tigers advanced further than any Clemson squad since. Behind senior guard Billy Williams, the only junior-college transfer to make first team All-ACC since UNC's Bob McAdoo in 1972, and big men Larry Nance and John "Moose" Campbell, they reached the 1980 West Region final, losing 85-74 to UCLA.

By contrast, veteran NCAA participants North Carolina and N.C. State, which finished a game ahead of Clemson in the standings, each went out in the first round. Maryland lasted two rounds.

The Tar Heels fell in double-overtime to Texas A&M, their third consecutive defeat in an NCAA opener. This provoked grumbling about Dean Smith's coaching. The criticism ignored what had been a handsome recovery from a staggering blow, the loss of freshman forward James Worthy. UNC's leading rebounder and top inside threat broke his ankle against Maryland on Jan. 20, yet the Tar Heels won 11 of their last 15 behind Mike O'Koren and Al Wood.

For N.C. State, less notable than its quick NCAA exit against Iowa was the fact the contest was Norm Sloan's last with the Wolfpack before going to the University of Florida.

BELOW
Homer Rice, shown here with his wife, Phyllis, served as the director of athletics at North Carolina and Georgia Tech. In Atlanta, he improved facilities and rebuilt the athletic programs into winners after the Yellow Jackets joined the ACC.

One reason Sloan gave for leaving was a wish to escape the shadow of Smith and his program. "If you're in a beauty contest, you want to win," Sloan said. "But when the same contestant always wins, it's time to find a new contest." Sloan took the rivalry personally, refusing to shake hands with Smith at league meetings or in public. "Why the hell should we shake hands after the game?" the intense Sloan, nicknamed "Stormin' Norman," asked a colleague. "Everybody knows we don't like each other."

Duke also lost its head coach following the 1980 season, which began with the Blue Devils ranked third in the country and saw them finish fifth in the ACC. Jim Spanarkel, the knock-kneed, pigeon-toed leader of previous seasons, had graduated. But in Mike Gminksi, Gene Banks and Kenny Dennard, the Blue Devils boasted a frontline as good as any.

Come the ACC Tournament, Duke reached the final for the third consecutive year. The opponent was Maryland, which survived an overtime game against deliberate Georgia Tech before subduing Clemson. While a snowstorm raged outside the Greensboro Coliseum, the Terrapins and Blue Devils staged a closely fought contest that came down to a last, controversial play.

Duke took a 73-72 lead with eight seconds left as Gminski tapped in a shot. King, the Case Award winner as the tournament MVP, missed a long jumper. Williams' tapped follow fell off the rim, his legs taken out from under him by Dennard on a move that, however questionable, failed to elicit a foul call.

The next day, Foster announced he was headed to South Carolina. Differences with Tom Butters — the school's athletics director was "absolutely heartless in a negotiation," said Corrigan — and a wish to forge the independent Gamecocks into a national presence via cable television, an infant medium, motivated the move. Before Foster was done, the Blue Devils upset top-seed Kentucky and reached the Mideast Regional final, losing 68-60 to Purdue.

The other ACC squad that broke the 20-victory barrier in 1980 was Virginia, which advanced to win the NIT, a third title in that event within a decade for an ACC team.

The key to Virginia's fortunes — on and off the court — was freshman Ralph Sampson. The 7-4 center from nearby Harrisonburg, Va., was the nation's most highly sought prospect in 1979. His final choice of schools came down to North Carolina, Virginia and Virginia Tech. "We had the toughest time recruiting against Virginia Tech because the visibility of their athletic program projected that Blacksburg was a great place for black athletes," said Terry Holland, Virginia's coach from 1975-90 and later its athletics director. Minority students were few at Charlottesville. Virginia "was a prep school for all intents and purposes until we admitted women in 1970," Holland said.

Academic requirements remained strin-

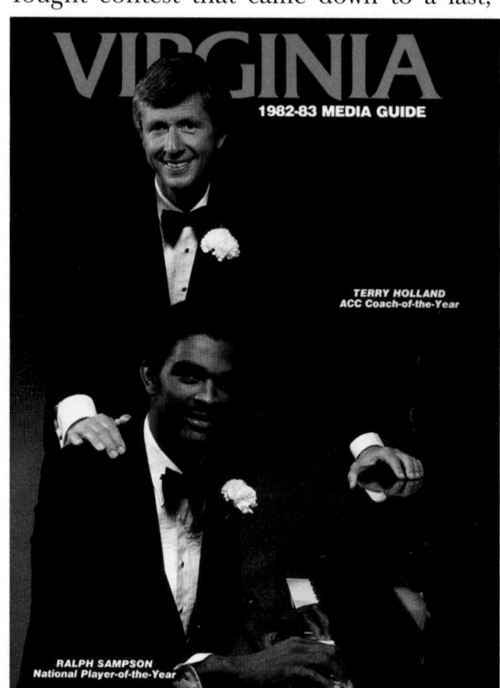

RIGHT
The 1983 Virginia basketball media guide shows basketball coach Terry Holland (top) and star center Ralph Sampson getting ready to make some sweet music. Sampson's presence helped Holland build a top-10 team and first Final Four participant from UVa.

gent, resources scarce and minority recruitment minimal at Virginia through most of the 1970s. Finally, in 1979 Corrigan challenged the university administration to decide whether it wanted an ACC-caliber athletic program. "Unless we make a decision to do that," he recalled telling a superior, "I'm not going to stay here."

Even as Virginia intensified efforts to diversify its student body and to bolster its athletic enterprise, Sampson picked the Cavaliers. "He wanted to play in a program that could win a national championship," Holland said. The coach recalled telling Sampson, "'We're going to be good, but we need somebody to get us over the hump.'"

Once Sampson accepted that challenge, Holland believed it transformed Virginia's image. "This is a young black male that could go anywhere, and he chose to go to the University of Virginia." That Sampson was an in-state signee was significant as well. Making inroads with top Virginia athletes, particularly African-Americans, had been a problem for the school. For instance, eight members of the ACC's 1979 preseason football team came from Virginia, twice as many as any other state. None played for the Cavaliers.

"Ralph coming to Virginia, doing as well as he had for the basketball program, what he did for the whole university in terms of exposure and perception, led the way for the University of Virginia," said John Swofford, the current ACC commissioner whose administrative career started at Charlottesville in 1973. Holland noted a similar effect. "As we enjoyed some success in basketball, I think everybody became convinced we could be successful across the board."

Coaching changes at Duke and N.C. State in early 1980 had similarly salutary effects on those basketball programs' competitive standing, although not immediately.

Butters consulted on his choice with Indiana coach Bob Knight, who had once accepted the Maryland job for a day and then changed his mind. The field of candidates ultimately narrowed to four, among them Knight disciple Mike Krzyzewski, the Army head coach. "It was obvious to me that Mike's teams were well-coached, organized, intense competitors, and they played up to their abilities," said Steve Vacendak, the former Duke player who helped Butters research candidates. "That trademark was so obvious to those who saw Army play."

Krzyzewski's wife, Mickie, was so impressed with Duke's campus and with the opportunity she admonished the young coach, "Don't screw this up." Krzyzewski apparently followed instructions. Despite a 9-17 record in 1979-80, his

BELOW
Mike Krzyzewski came to Duke as head basketball coach in 1980. By 1986, he had taken the Blue Devils to the Final Four and the national championship game. As the years progressed, Krzyzewski and the Blue Devils would construct one of the elite programs in America.

fifth season at his alma mater, he became Duke's coach on March 18, 1980. He brought with him a strict commitment to man-to-man defense and motion offense, and a wish to escape Knight's shadow.

Nine days later, N.C. State hired its new coach, Jim Valvano, at 34 a year older than Krzyzewski. Coming off a 29-5 season and consecutive NCAA appearances at Iona, including a 17-point win over Louisville, the 1980 national champion, Valvano was a hot coaching commodity. He was a proven recruiter and a flexible, daring sideline improviser.

"Jim was a hell of a coach, and he was a motivator," said Frank Weedon, the longtime N.C. State athletics official. "If we were in a game at the very end, Valvano had a much better than 50 percent chance of winning."

Valvano insisted he had no playing "system" to speak of. "I really play, in a sense, with the players that I have," he said. "My coaching is more visceral, shall we say. My system depends more on the emotion of the moment. You ask about my vision. Consistency is not as important to me as building towards championships."

The Wolfpack retained one head basketball coach through this period of transition who had already seen success at Raleigh. Kay Yow was hired in 1976, the second year the school had a women's team, and immediately embarked on a run of a dozen straight winning seasons. In 1978, the first year of official ACC women's competition, N.C. State was undefeated within the league and 29-5 overall. The future Hall of Famer's teams reached 11 of the first 14 ACC Tournament finals, including all but one from 1978 through 1985.

The first five championship contests matched N.C. State and Maryland, with the Terrapins winning all but once. The exception was 1980, when center Genia Beasley, the tournament MVP, and All-American Trudy Lacey led the Wolfpack to the title.

Women's sports were going through a painful transition. The AIAW, the national organization governing women's athletics, attempted to steer a course that avoided the shoals of NCAA men's competition, perceived as rife with ethical compromise caused by an overemphasis on winning. "A lot of women resisted becoming a so-called competitive Division I sport," Rice said. "They had heard all the horror stories of recruiting and all that."

But many women wanted to embrace competition, not just participation. "The athletic model is not a men's model," said Chris Weller, the former Maryland coach. "It's a model of competition for people."

That went against both the AIAW ethic and social stereotypes of women. N.C. State's Nora Lynn Finch recalled that in the early '70s, it was customary for women's teams to share punch and cookies after a game. "It was a social event, not just a competitive event," Finch said. When she was head coach at Wake Forest and Yow was at Elon, they struck up a friendship upon noticing they were more interested in comparing out-of-bounds plays than in socializing.

Attitudes changed slowly. As late as July 1984, *USA Today* ran an article that discussed women's need to overcome empathy for competitors if they were to learn how to win. "If women are worried about

1980

10.25.80
Maryland's Charlie Wysocki sets an ACC record with 50 rushes in a game against Duke

1981

9.12.81
North Carolina's Kelvin Bryant sets an ACC football record by scoring 36 points on six touchdown runs versus East Carolina

10.31.81
Clemson sets ACC football record for most points scored in an 82-24 win over Wake Forest

11.7.81
Clemson wins 10-8 at North Carolina in first match of top-1[cut off] ACC football squad[cut off]

hurting someone's feelings by beating them, or wanting approval from others, it keeps them from doing their best," said Dr. Dorothy Harris, director of the Center for Women in Sports at Pennsylvania State University.

ACC schools began putting money into women's programs in part to meet the requirements of Title IX, a section of the federal Education Act of 1972 banning discrimination in institutions using federal funding. But some ADs — notably Maryland's Jim Kehoe, Homer Rice at North Carolina and Willis Casey at N.C. State — were quick to broaden their vision.

"Jim Kehoe, he's a man who's always embraced the concept of excellence," Weller said. "If he's going to have a program, he's going to have the best." A Maryland-Immaculata game in 1975 was the first nationally televised women's basketball contest.

Finch, who moved to N.C. State in 1977 as associate head basketball coach and women's administrator, said Casey was "a power broker" and "an intimidator" who was also creative, persistent and proud. "He wasn't going to wait," Finch said of the former N.C. State swim coach, who between 1946 and 1969 won 11 conference championships and coached 33 All-Americans, among them 1968 Olympic gold medallist Steve Rerych. "He was probably the strongest advocate for women's athletics among the ACC ADs. He coached women's swimming and married one of his swimmers."

One sign of the growing impact of women's athletics was that in 1980 and again in 1981 the ACC athlete of the year was Julie Shea, a cross-country runner who helped N.C. State to a pair of AIAW national titles. The league started separate awards for the top male and female athletes in 1990. Shea remains the only woman to win the McKevlin Award in the ACC's first 36 years.

Casey also enjoyed good luck with football coaches, hiring Lou Holtz and Bo Rein during the '70s. After both left for higher-profile jobs, in 1980 Casey turned to Monte Kiffin, a defensive specialist and first-time head coach.

The outgoing Kiffin engaged in a mock boxing match with Joe Frazier to enliven one N.C. State pep rally. But Kiffin's most famous stunt was his first, undertaken to drum up interest in the Red and White intrasquad football scrimmage that capped spring practice in 1980. The Nebraska grad wore a Lone Ranger outfit complete with mask and cowboy hat and rode a white horse across campus to the student union. Unfortunately, Kiffin had never ridden a horse. When his arrival was greeted with the Lone Ranger's theme, from Gioacchino Rossini's "William Tell" overture, the crash of cymbals caused the horse to rear and Kiffin was hard-pressed to keep his seat.

Kiffin's 1980 squad finished third in the ACC and 6-5 overall. He did no better in the following two seasons and was replaced.

Maryland was second in football in 1980, the seventh time in eight seasons Jerry Claiborne brought a team in among the ACC's top two. The Terrapins were 8-4 and went to the Tangerine Bowl, losing 35-20 to Florida. Charlie Wysocki, a bruising and

1.29.81
lorida State wins 81-67
ver Florida A&M to open
eon County Civic Center

1982

3.26.82
Maryland reaches first NCAA women's basketball Final Four, losing 76-66 to Cheyney State

3.29.82
UNC beats Georgetown 63-62 for NCAA men's basketball title

10.9.82
Duke's Chris Castor sets an ACC record with 283 receiving yards against Wake Forest

12.23.82
Top-ranked Virginia loses 77-72 to NAIA-member Chaminade

durable tailback, rushed for 1,359 yards, the single-season record at College Park until 1999. Running from a multiple-I offense, the 5-11, 205-pound Pennsylvanian set enduring Maryland standards with eight 100-yard games and 334 rushes in 1980. Wysocki's 50 rushing attempts in a 17-14 win at Duke remain the ACC record.

The top team, though, was North Carolina, which won the league race for the fourth time in 10 years. Dick Crum's Tar Heels were 11-1, matching the school's best record ever. They finished 10th in the polls, their sole defeat a 41-7 disappointment at Oklahoma, and beat Texas 16-7 in the Bluebonnet Bowl.

Crum was voted 1980 coach of the year in his third season after arriving from Miami of Ohio, the so-called "Cradle of Coaches." UNC led the ACC in scoring offense (25.5 points), paced on the ground by senior Amos Lawrence, and in scoring defense (11.2), led by outside linebacker Lawrence Taylor, the '80 ACC player of the year and a consensus All-American.

"Famous Amos" had an impact that was immediate and enduring. Lawrence, Pittsburgh's Tony Dorsett and New Mexico's Denvis Manns remain the only major-college backs to rush for 1,000 or more yards in each of their four seasons.

Taylor's start was more modest. He played sparingly as a freshman, and out of position at nose guard and inside linebacker as a sophomore. As a junior, Taylor returned to outside linebacker, but Crum publicly questioned his intensity. Not until 1980, Taylor's senior season, did he emerge as a dominating presence, registering 16 quarterback sacks for losses totaling 127 yards. He made game-saving plays to beat Texas Tech and Clemson, his tackle of quarterback Homer Jordan handing the Tigers their last home loss until 1984.

"He could accelerate out of his stance as well as anybody," said Bill Dooley, who recruited Taylor to Chapel Hill. Ultimately Taylor was named to 10 consecutive Pro Bowls with the New York Giants, was the NFL's most valuable player in 1986, and in 1999 was voted into the Pro Football Hall of Fame, one of only five ACC players so honored.

"Some real national prominence came to that program during that period," said John Swofford, who became UNC's athletics director in 1980, "and then things started to backslide from a competitive standpoint."

Booed at home in 1978 after losing 7-3 to Miami of Ohio, Crum took the Tar Heels to five straight bowls from 1979 through 1983, never winning fewer than eight games. The Heels cracked the top 10 intermittently during every season from 1980

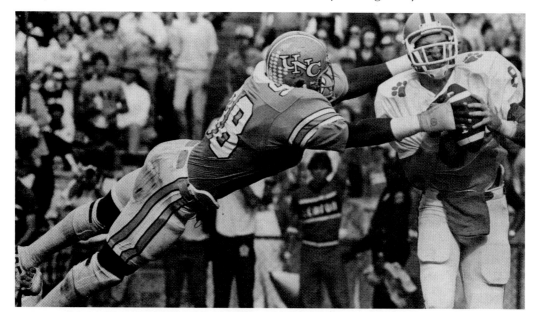

RIGHT
Lawrence Taylor (left) was the 1980 ACC player of the year. He still holds the school single-season record with 16 quarterback sacks. He is in the Pro Football Hall of Fame.

through 1983, the top 5 from 1981 through 1983. They won four straight bowls from 1979 through 1982, finally dropping the Peach Bowl to Florida State and coach Bobby Bowden in 1983.

Yet a sense of unmet expectation grew as Crum's teams never won another ACC title after 1980, never finished in the top 10 again after 1981, and compiled an overall mark of 5-19-1 against ranked teams. Three of Crum's final four seasons produced losing records and his contract was bought out with alumni help in 1987.

Unfulfilled promise, or the perception of same, had become something of a curse for UNC men's basketball as well.

Dean Smith's program was a stunning model of consistent excellence. During the 14 seasons between 1967 and 1980, his teams posted 13 20-win seasons, enjoyed nine first-place finishes in the ACC, ranked eight times in the AP top 10, won seven ACC titles, advanced to five Final Fours and two NCAA championship games. So far, however, Smith had no national titles to his credit. This led critics to say his system limited individual achievement and the ability to rise to an occasion.

Smith, a man fighting a lifelong battle to balance humility with intense competitiveness, alternately defended his record and shrugged it off. "Some years I didn't think we'd make the Final Four, and we did," he said. "Some years we were knocked out in the first round when I thought we were the better team. Each time I felt, 'Life goes on.'"

The 1980-81 season, coming on the heels of three straight early NCAA departures, found UNC rated the conference's third-best squad after Maryland and Virginia. That's not how things turned out.

The favored Terrapins finished fourth, surpassed by resurgent Wake Forest and playmaker Frank Johnson, the Deacons' top scorer, passer and foul shooter. The Deacons started strong en route to a 22-7 record, winning the final Big Four Tournament. An early season event held annually in Greensboro for a dozen years, the Big Four matched Duke, North Carolina, N.C. State and Wake over two nights. Quite popular with fans, in 1981 the tournament was surpassed by other revenue sources and done in by coaches' reticence to participate. At the end, only Wake

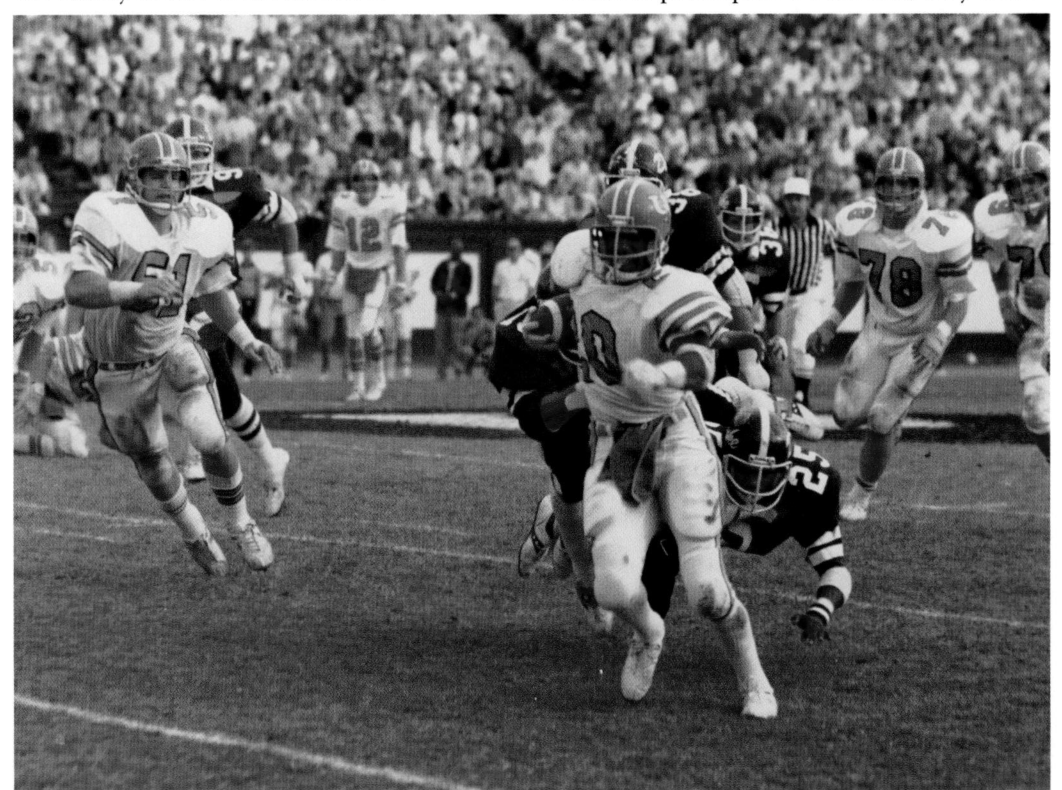

LEFT
Amos Lawrence rushed for more than 1,000 yards all four seasons of his career at North Carolina. He finished as the second-leading rusher in ACC history. Lawrence rushed for better than 100 yards in back-to-back bowl games in 1979 and '80.

By Tim Peeler

ACC EXCELLENCE

CHESLEY FILLED NATION'S AIRWAVES WITH ACC BASKETBALL

CASTLEMAN DETOLLEY CHESLEY
JUNE 13, 1913-APRIL 21, 1983

An impressive 154 Atlantic Coast Conference men's basketball games would be televised during the 2002-03 season, with 135 of those appearances scheduled for various national networks.

Castleman DeTolley Chesley is no doubt smiling from above.

He never scored a point or defended a shooter, and his name may not be recognizable to many fans today, but Chesley did as much for the game and the ACC as any single individual. He lifted basketball from small, hot gymnasiums along the Eastern Seaboard and placed it in living rooms across the nation.

"He put ACC basketball on the map, about 10 years ahead of everyone else," said Hugh Morton, a longtime photographer of ACC sports, owner of Grandfather Mountain in North Carolina and close friend of Chesley. "And they are still trying to catch up."

Chesley, once a producer of regional college football telecasts for national networks NBC and CBS, had a simple idea — put the passion of the ACC on the airwaves.

He started with a few football games in 1956, until the NCAA took over the broadcast rights for all college games. In 1957, he became enthralled with Frank McGuire's undefeated North Carolina men's basketball team. Chesley knew he could convince a handful of television stations in North Carolina and Kansas to broadcast the games from the Final Four.

There was no March Madness back then, no Selection Sunday, no Dick Vitale. Fans who could not be at the games listened to Ray Reeve describe the action on the Tobacco Sports Network on radio, or read the stories in the next morning's newspaper.

Chesley's broadcast of the 1957 championship from Municipal Auditorium in Kansas City went to five stations in North Carolina. The broadcast captivated the state as it watched the Tar Heels beat Michigan State in the semifinals in triple overtime. The next night, against the most famous player in the country, Kansas center Wilt Chamberlain, McGuire's Tar Heels outlasted the Jayhawks in three more overtimes to win the ACC's first basketball national championship.

The players didn't realize the game had been broadcast back home, but they discovered it when they arrived at Raleigh-Durham Airport. Ten thousand people greeted them on the runway. Looking back, that broadcast was a seminal moment for the four-year-old conference.

"They were renting TV sets for hospitals," Chesley told the *Greensboro Daily News*. "It was the damnedest thing you ever heard of. I knew right then and there that ACC basketball could be as popular as any TV show that was shown in North Carolina."

Chesley, a former assistant athletics director at the University of Pennsylvania, may have known he had a product that could make money and entertain viewers, but when he first began his weekly broadcasts in 1958, the basketball coaches were opposed.

"You can't convince me that TV will not hurt the attendance," Bones McKinney, head men's basketball coach at Wake Forest, said of Chesley's weekly package of games. McKinney never lived this prediction down, even after he joined Chesley's collection of all-star announcers that included Jim Thacker, Billy Packer, Jim Simpson, Charlie Harville and Dan Daniels.

"If they had kept ratings back then, the ratings for [the ACC] area would have been through the roof," former ACC Commissioner Gene Corrigan said. "Everybody in the winter at one o'clock on Saturday afternoon watched ACC basketball. There was no alternative."

Recruits watched those games as well. "There's no doubt that the reason the ACC kept getting the best talent was because of all those games on television," Corrigan said. "If you think kids like being on television now, you can imagine what it was like back then, when there was only one or two games on a week."

Chesley had a background in football and the theater, and he knew how to put on a good show. A native of Washington, D.C., he played football at North Carolina before transferring to the University of Pennsylvania. He became captain of the football team at Penn and was the lead actor for the Wig and Mask Society. During an opening night performance in 1935, Chesley's booming baritone answered 17 curtain calls.

"He really was an amazing man," said his stepson, James Porter, who lives in Westchester, Pa. "He decided he could produce sports on his own better than the networks."

He did, too. Chesley produced a variety of sports, from ACC basketball to Sunday afternoon rebroadcasts of Notre Dame football. He also produced the first television broadcast of the Greater Greensboro Open and helped organize and televise the first Liberty Bowl. He even produced the Miss North Carolina beauty pageant for several years in Greensboro.

He was a fairly simple businessman, despite owning a degree from Penn's Wharton School of Business. He operated without an advertising rate card and on a limited budget.

"It was very simple," said Billy Packer, who began his broadcast career with Chesley's company. "He figured out how much he wanted to make. He figured out how much he had to pay in rights fees and production costs, and that determined the advertising price."

"Every check I ever got from him was handwritten," said Woody Durham, who got his start with Chesley before moving on to become the "Voice of the Tar Heels" for the radio broadcasts of UNC sports.

LEFT: C.D. Chesley, flanked by Marvin "Skeeter" Francis (left) and Commissioner Bob James, pioneered television coverage of collegiate sports in the Atlantic Coast Conference. His efforts helped to make ACC men's basketball tops in the country by putting the league's teams on television regularly, well ahead of other conferences around the nation.

FACING PAGE: Television announcers for Chesley's college-basketball broadcasts — Bones McKinney (left), Billy Packer and Jim Thacker — listen to Chesley.

Chesley knew how to take care of his advertisers, whether it was his longstanding partnership with Pilot Life Insurance Company or the string of other sponsors who supported the infant stages of college basketball, from Pabst Blue Ribbon Beer to Piedmont Airlines to Holly Farms and Food Lion. Now the string of the league's "corporate partners" could fill a page.

He also took care of the station managers who aired the weekly games, even if it was just a few rounds of golf and several hands of poker during an annual spring retreat at Grandfather Mountain.

Soon after Chesley began televising ACC games on a regular basis, he developed throat cancer. He survived, but doctors had to perform a laryngectomy that silenced his showman's voice. He was forced to speak through a hole in his throat for the remainder of his life.

The effects didn't keep Chesley from screaming at the top of his tube when production went wrong or from moaning when the league wanted to add more games on television.

"Every time we ever mentioned showing more games on TV, he would say 'You're killing me; it can't be done,'" Corrigan said. "But he always did it. He was very protective of the product, and he didn't want it to be overexposed. Ches deserves a lot of credit for the caliber of ACC basketball because he set the standard."

That standard included regionally televised regular-season and tournament games. He went national in 1973 and '74, when he strung together a network of stations to broadcast a pair of Super Bowl Sunday games between N.C. State and Maryland, two of the best teams in the nation and the league during that era.

"It wasn't just his initial broadcast, but his idea of taking the league and exposing it, and in the quality way that he did it," Packer said. "It really put the ACC in a special category ... because of his exposure, the ability of the league to recruit beyond its natural territories, way beyond any other conference. That separated [the ACC] from other leagues when you started talking about the rise of its quality."

Through the 1970s, Chesley made the ACC and its players famous, well before the advent of cable television sports network ESPN. Even McKinney finally became convinced. "He presented the ACC with a goldmine," McKinney said in 1983. "They ought to put a statue in front of the ACC office."

Chesley was never immortalized in marble or granite. He is buried in a public cemetery at the base of Grandfather Mountain. "He was so wonderful, so happy, so funny," said his widow, Ruthie, who still lives only a few miles from where her husband is buried.

Chesley died from the advanced effects of Alzheimer's disease on April 21, 1983, just weeks after N.C. State coach Jim Valvano and his Wolfpack captured the league's fourth national championship in basketball.

Fans across the country watched every moment on television, just as the folks around the ACC had been doing for years — thanks to C.D. Chesley. ✶

cared to continue.

Clemson enjoyed another 20-win season in 1981, the only time in history the Tigers won 20 games twice in a row. They were invited to the NIT, their third straight post-season bid. An NIT invitation also went to Duke, which was 17-13 in Krzyzewski's first year, paced by Banks, the ACC's top scorer (18.5).

Georgia Tech was the sole ACC squad with a losing record, and so far outclassed by the competition it went 4-23 and winless in the league, a first since Clemson in 1955. The Yellow Jackets' four victories came against lowly Flagler, University of the South, Presbyterian and Newberry. The '81 season would be the last for coach Dwane Morrison, best known both for finishing interviews with a folksy "Bless you, brother" and for a subsequent career as a professional golf caddy.

BELOW
N.C. State's Dereck Whittenburg reaches for the ball against North Carolina's Michael Jordan. Both players were important to their teams winning a national championship.

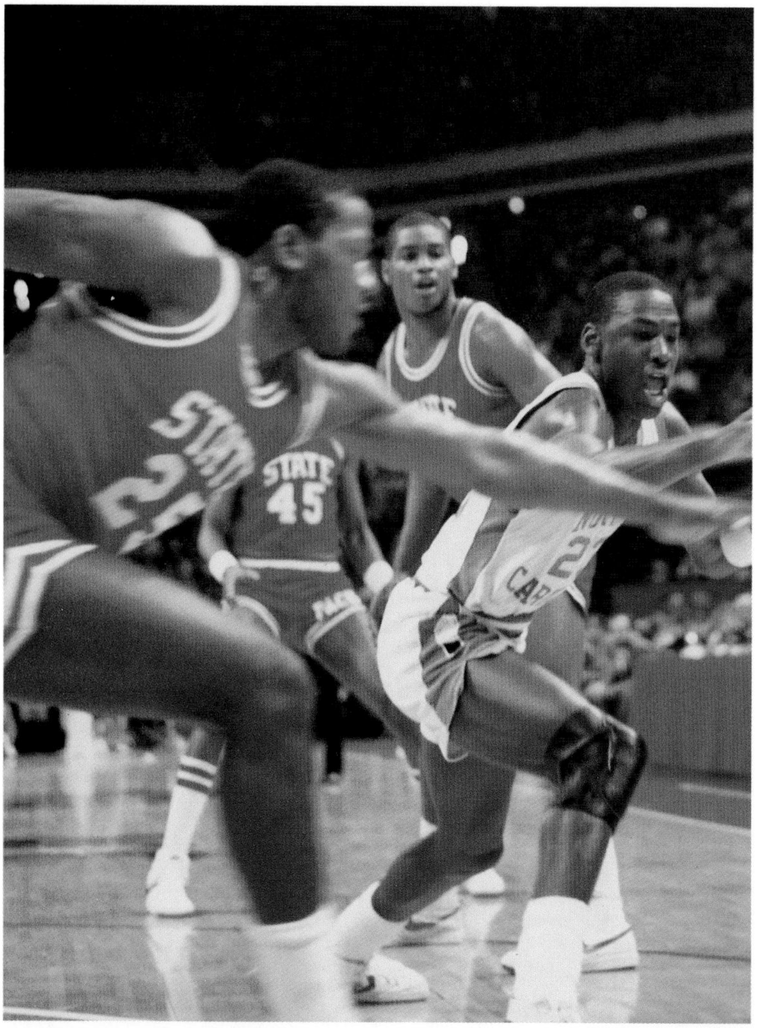

Just as Tech followed form, so did Virginia, finishing 13-1, the only time to date the Cavaliers enjoyed sole possession of first place in the ACC.

Sampson won the first of three straight awards as ACC and national player of the year, becoming the most honored player in conference history. "Sampson competed so hard," UNC's Smith said admiringly. The very big man's interior presence changed the character of a game, reflected by his leading the ACC in rebounding in 1981 and in blocked shots throughout his four seasons at UVa.

Virginia (29-5) was much more than a starring vehicle for Sampson. Senior wing Jeff Lamp, one of the great clutch performers in ACC annals, paced the '81 squad with 18.2 points per game and made his third all-conference team. Forwards Lee Raker and Craig Robinson did much of the supportive work. The backcourt was bolstered by a pair of freshmen, starter Othell Wilson and reserve Ricky Stokes, and anchored by junior Jeff Jones, the league's premier assist man for the second straight year.

Good as they were, the Cavaliers couldn't shake one contender. In fact, what evolved over the course of the 1981 season and continued through 1983 was a rivalry with North Carolina that was as rich in talent, as heated in intensity and as significant in impact as the N.C. State-Maryland match-ups of the mid-'70s.

The stellar trio of All-ACC senior Al Wood, sophomore forward James Worthy and center Sam Perkins, the 1981 ACC rookie of the year, led the Tar Heels. "James has a unique talent for a guy his size," Smith said of the future All-Pro. "In Worthy you have a 6-9, 220-pound ball-handler. I think that's exciting basketball." Complementary talents rounded out the roster, most prominently playmaker Jimmy Black, guard Mike Pepper, originally a walk-on, and 6-7 freshman Matt Doherty, the future UNC head coach.

Virginia twice beat the Tar Heels during the 1981 regular season, each time rallying from a deficit. The comeback at Chapel Hill was from 16 points down in the second half, the Cavaliers' 80-79 overtime victory solidifying their No. 1 ranking. UVa's winning streak over two seasons extended to 28 games until ended 57-56 by Notre Dame in Chicago on an errant inbounds play. Virginia lost its next outing, too, 73-66 in overtime at Wake Forest.

The ACC Tournament returned to Landover, Md., where Virginia earned its only league title in 1976. This time Maryland beat the Cavaliers 85-62 in the semifinals. The Terrapins advanced to the title game for the fifth time in a decade, and came up short for the fifth time. North Carolina won 61-60, and Perkins earned the MVP award.

Virginia and North Carolina met one last time in 1981, and on the game's biggest stage. The first pair of ACC teams to reach the same Final Four, they began a trend that saw the conference send 23 teams to the national semifinals over a 22-year span through 2002.

The Tar Heels won 78-65 this time, fueled by Wood's 39 points — a career high, an enduring record for an NCAA semifinal and a neat refutation of Smith's supposed penchant for preventing players from rising to an occasion. Sampson, guarded primarily by Perkins, was held to one basket in the second half. "They can have those two regular-season wins," Wood said. "We'll take this one."

Indiana rose to the occasion two nights later, beating UNC 63-50 in a title game almost canceled because of the wounding of President Ronald Reagan earlier in the day by a would-be assassin.

Both Virginia and North Carolina did win national championships in 1981, however. The UVa women won in indoor track and field and in cross country. The Tar Heel men won the NCAA lacrosse title. And, in the third year after establishing the UNC women's soccer program, coach Anson Dorrance led his soccer squad to a 23-0 record and an AIAW title. Dorrance's program, perhaps the most dominant ever in a collegiate sport, would win 16 more championships and appear in every Final Four sanctioned by the NCAA or AIAW through 2002.

The ACC managed another national championship in 1981, the league's first in football since its founding season.

The '81 football season was also the first in which a pair of ACC teams ranked in the

BELOW

Virginia's Jeff Lamp celebrates the Cavaliers' victory in the 1981 NCAA Tournament East Region championship, which put the school into its first Final Four.

TOP
Coach Danny Ford, the head Tiger, was voted the national coach of the year in 1981 as well as the ACC coach of the year.

BOTTOM
Defensive back Terry Kinard, honored at Clemson's Memorial Stadium, was a first-team All-American in '81. Kinard is a member of the College Football Hall of Fame

top 10 and enjoyed double-digit wins. That North Carolina was 10-2 was no surprise after its 11-1 record in 1980. That the other high-achieving squad was Clemson, coming off a 6-5 season, was unexpected. Even more unexpected was where the Tigers finished.

Well, not entirely unexpected. A sign that hung all year long in Clemson's training room read: "Tigers 11-0. In the Orange Bowl vs. Nebraska." Which is exactly what happened in Danny Ford's third full season as head coach.

The 1981 ACC and national coach of the year had 53 returning lettermen, among them eight players who enjoyed all-conference seasons. Half were on offense, half on defense, bespeaking a 12-0 team that set records on both sides of the ball. Ultimately 22 players on the squad enjoyed NFL careers.

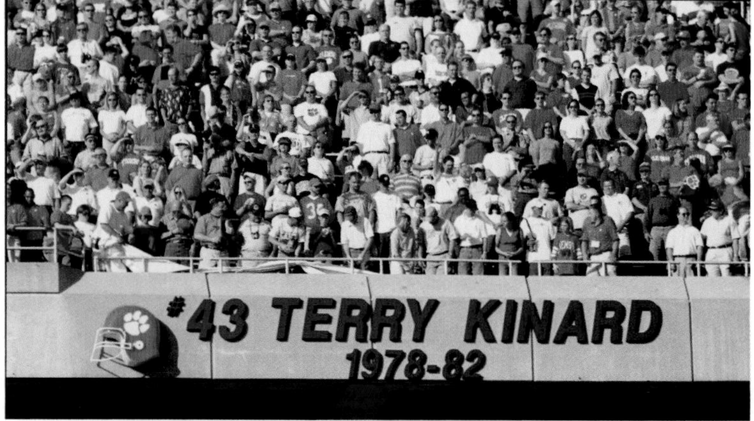

The '81 Tigers led the ACC in scoring defense at 8.2 points allowed per game. Seven opponents, including a pair ranked in the top 10, failed to reach double digits in scoring. Spearheading a defense that forced a school-record 41 turnovers was senior linebacker Jeff Davis, nicknamed "The Judge." The All-American from Greensboro, N.C., was the 1981 ACC player of the year after making 175 total tackles. Davis' relentless passion for the game became an odd lullaby for Perry Tuttle, a four-year roommate. "When we were in the room at night, he would talk about the defense and what it was going to do until I fell asleep," the All-American wide receiver said.

The defense also boasted free safety Terry Kinard, the second-leading tackler on the 1981 squad. A 2001 inductee into the College Football Hall of Fame, Kinard's 17 career interceptions remain the Clemson record and are tied for second in ACC history behind UNC's Dre' Bly, who had 20 from 1996 to 1998. "I haven't seen a player who could dominate a game from the secondary like he could," Ford said of Kinard. "He covered a lot of ground. He made a coach feel secure about the secondary."

The offense was directed by All-ACC quarterback Homer Jordan. The junior led the league in passing in 1981 and hit 62 percent of his throws against the three ranked teams the Tigers faced. Against Wake Forest and new coach Al Groh on Halloween, Jordan helped Clemson to an 82-24 victory that saw the home team amass 756 total yards, score 12 touchdowns, convert every one of its dozen third-down chances and set 22 league, school and stadium records, including the most points ever scored by an ACC team.

Jordan, from Athens, Ga., surely relished the Tigers' third win of 1981, a 13-3 conquest of Georgia that catapulted Clemson into the polls. The fourth-ranked Bulldogs, coming off a national championship season, had a 15-game winning streak end at Clemson as running back Herschel Walker fumbled twice, new Tiger kicker Donald Igwebuike, recruited from the soccer team, booted a pair of field goals, and Jordan threw to Tuttle for a score. "This is the best I've ever felt after a football game," said Dan Benish, an All-ACC defensive tackle.

A win at Kentucky followed, then a shutout of Virginia, on the way to a 1-10 record in Dick Bestwick's last year as head coach. Next came Duke, which would go 6-5 under coach Shirley "Red" Wilson, its best record since 1974. The Blue Devils had a prolific passer in sophomore quarterback Ben Bennett, an exciting All-ACC wide receiver in Cedric Jones and an innovative young offensive coordinator named Steve Spurrier. Bennett did throw for a touchdown, the first yielded by Clemson in 18 quarters, but the Tigers won 38-10 and moved to third in the polls.

N.C. State was the seventh victim, 17-7. The Wolfpack managed the first rushing touchdown against Clemson. Wake's record drubbing came next, followed by the greatest regular-season showdown the ACC had witnessed to that point.

UNC was 7-1 and ranked ninth as it hosted No. 2 Clemson in the first game involving a pair of ACC teams rated in the top 10. The Tar Heels boasted elusive tailback Kelvin Bryant, whose six touchdowns and 36 points against East Carolina set single-game ACC records earlier in the year. Bryant was among seven All-ACC performers for UNC, including defensive leaders William Fuller, a tackle, and linebacker Lee Shaffer.

Clemson fullback Jeff McCall rushed for the game's decisive touchdown in a 10-8 victory. The verdict wasn't secured until Tiger defensive tackle Jeff Bryant recovered a mishandled lateral with 57 seconds left. The All-ACC lineman was apparently the only player who recognized the errant toss was in play.

Triumphs over Maryland and South

BELOW
Quarterback Homer Jordan (3) led Clemson to the 1981 national championship with a victory over Nebraska in the Orange Bowl. Jordan completed 11 of 22 passes and had 180 yards of total offense.

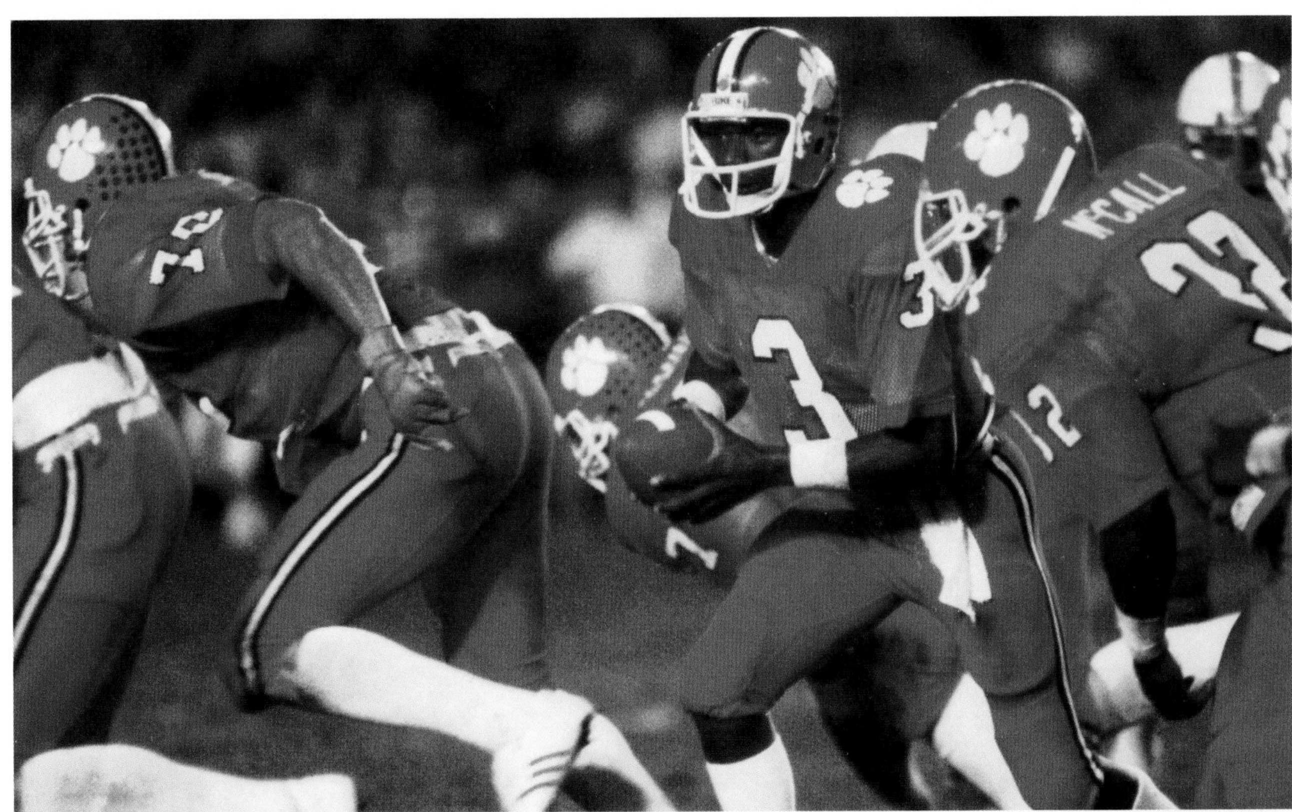

BELOW
The 1982 national championship North Carolina basketball team is interviewed by former Wake Forest player Billy Packer (far right). The Tar Heels, left-to-right: Sam Perkins, Jimmy Black, Michael Jordan, Matt Doherty and James Worthy. Worthy, who scored 28 points, was named the most outstanding player after the 1982 national championship game against Georgetown. Doherty returned to UNC in 2000 as the Tar Heels' head coach.

Carolina followed. When Penn State beat Pittsburgh and quarterback Dan Marino, the Tigers were the nation's only remaining undefeated squad and moved atop the polls. Clemson had twice previously posted perfect regular seasons, in 1900 and 1948. This third unblemished effort earned a trip to the Orange Bowl to face No. 4 Nebraska, in its 16th bowl in 17 seasons. "It's not like they are a childhood bride or anything," Ford said.

The tone was set early in a 22-15 Clemson victory. On the fourth play, the Huskers' Mark Mauer fumbled, and the Tigers capitalized. Igwebuike's field goal put them ahead, 3-0. Another fumble set up Clemson's first touchdown, a 2-yard run by Cliff Austin, who had been stuck in the hotel elevator for two hours earlier in the day.

The 12-7 halftime lead grew to 22-7 in the third quarter as Jordan, the game's offensive MVP, hit Tuttle for his eighth touchdown reception of the season. Then Clemson held on for the victory and the championship, its first in any sport, making Ford the youngest coach to win a national football title.

Clemson's success was apparently contagious, because in 1982 and 1983 ACC teams responded with consecutive NCAA men's basketball championships. The league would mount similar bookend runs in each of the next two decades. In each case one title laid to rest doubts about the most successful coach in the program's history.

The '82 beneficiary was Dean Smith, whose Tar Heels were 32-2, tied Virginia for first during the regular season, endured an ACC Tournament final that ignited a firestorm of criticism and survived an NCAA championship contest that turned on a freshman's jump shot and a Georgetown player's bonehead pass.

The Tar Heels had replaced Wood in the lineup with a freshman listed as Mike Jordan, a 6-4 guard from Wilmington, N.C., who finished behind teammate Robert "Buzz" Peterson in voting for the state's 1981 prep player of the year. Jordan wound up third on UNC in scoring (13.5), second to James Worthy in steals and was voted the 1982 ACC rookie of the year. Worthy, Sam Perkins and Jordan all ranked among the league's top scorers. The trio,

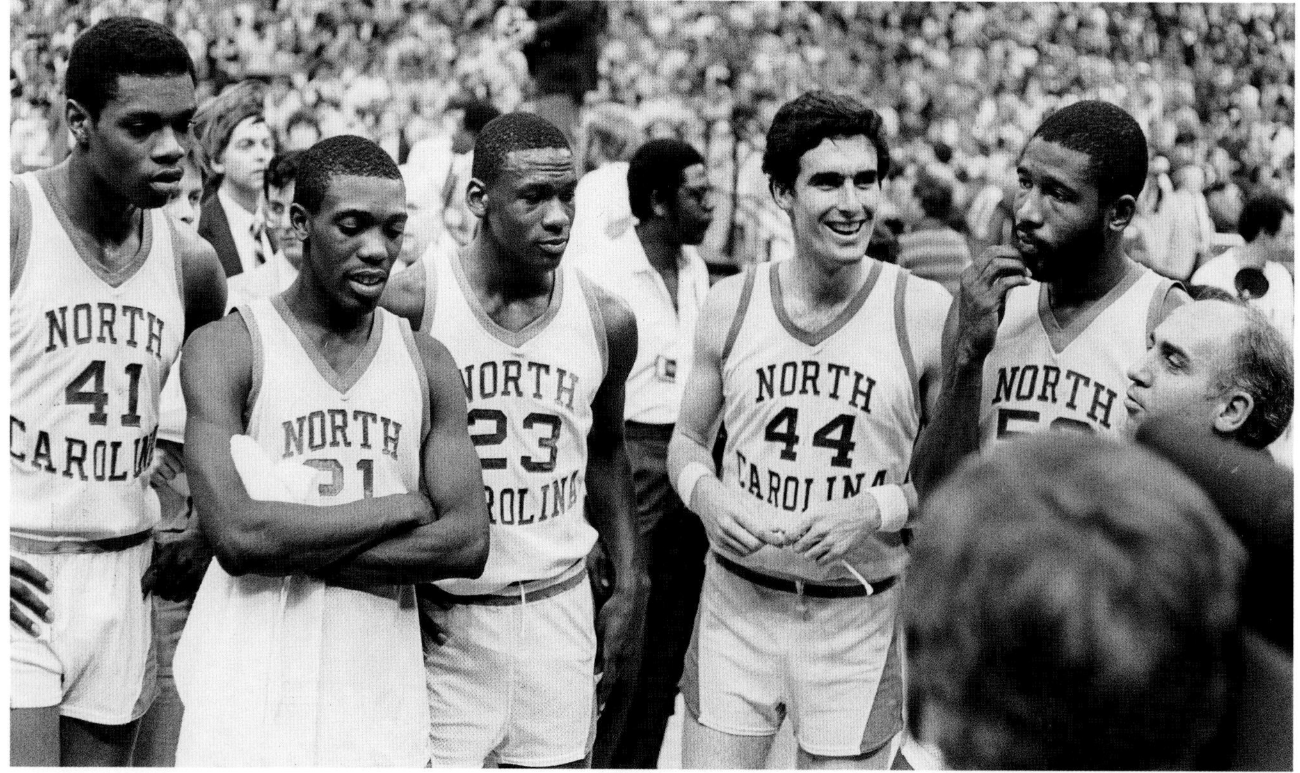

along with point guard Jimmy Black and forward Matt Doherty, each played at least 1,000 minutes on what was essentially a five-man squad.

UNC's sole home loss came to Wake Forest 55-48 while Perkins was in the infirmary. The Deacons, bolstered by sophomores Danny Young and Anthony Teachey, finished third in the league at 9-5. They were 21-9 overall, giving the school its first consecutive 20-win seasons.

The Tar Heels' other defeat came at Charlottesville, 74-58. North Carolina already had held service at home 65-60 against Virginia. When the Cavaliers lost in overtime at Maryland to conclude the regular season, they finished tied with UNC at 12-2 atop the ACC.

The 1982 ACC Tournament returned to Greensboro, televised as part of a new arrangement that marked the end of C.D. Chesley's pioneering regional network. Chesley, who built ACC basketball into a valuable television commodity, was a fixture at league meetings for a quarter-century, smoking his cigar even after cancer forced the removal of his larynx. "It was a family," recalled Nancy Thompson, who attended the ACC get-togethers as the commissioner's secretary. "It wasn't a dog-eat-dog situation."

Chesley, according to Bill McLellan, Clemson's AD at the time, had charmed earlier athletics directors and "kind of got them to do whatever he wanted." But changing economic circumstances and looming legal action overtook Chesley's collegial hold on ACC television rights. National networks had increasingly gotten into the picture, broadcasting regular season and ACC Tournament action. Other regional packagers were interested.

Chesley paid $1 million in rights fees for the entire 1980-81 season. McLellan was among those who voted to open up bidding the following spring. The ACC soon signed multi-year agreements with national networks NBC and CBS and, after a year with Metrosports, found a new regional partner in Raycom/Jefferson-Pilot, which still televises league games. The combined packages were soon worth more than $10 million annually. A fledgling cable network, ESPN, also embraced ACC action.

The '82 ACC Tournament proved quite a show, especially where Virginia was concerned. Top-ranked North Carolina breezed to the final. The Tar Heels easily handled Georgia Tech, in last place again under new coach Bobby Cremins, and then N.C. State, which would finish 22-10 and get an NCAA bid.

The third-ranked Cavaliers, meanwhile, fought desperately to reach the final.

First they defeated Clemson 56-54, suffering a blow late in the first half when guard Othell Wilson sustained a badly bruised thigh in a collision with the Tigers' Mike Eppley, the combination basketball guard/football quarterback.

The semifinal against Wake on the Deacons' homecourt went to overtime before the Cavaliers prevailed, 51-49. (Following 1976 and 1979 defeats of bond referenda for a new arena in Winston-Salem, Wake moved its home games 30 miles east to the Greensboro Coliseum. They remained there until the 1989-90 season.) Virginia, playing without Wilson, beat Carl Tacy's club when 5-10 Ricky Stokes, the ACC's shortest player, banked in a 10-foot jumper with one second remaining.

The final was comparably close, with North Carolina leading 34-31 at halftime. "You had two really powerful teams, and in spite of the fact we were playing without Wilson it was a terrific game," Virginia coach Terry Holland said. "It was tremendous back and forth."

The Tar Heels still had a 44-43 edge with 7:33 remaining when Smith decided to go to a full-fledged delay to bring Sampson away from the basket. Virginia had successfully handled the Four Corners in previous meetings by resisting the urge to cover too much floor area. Depriving UNC of easy layups took "a lot of wind out of their sails," Holland said, and put the pressure on the Tar Heels. Besides, the defense was handicapped by Wilson's absence.

So while a national TV audience watched on NBC, two of the best teams in the country stalled to a 47-45 finish. UNC scored the deciding points on Doherty's free throws after Virginia began fouling intentionally.

Coaches and players defended the slowdown, saying it was within the rules and consistent with playing to win. Such arguments didn't stem the torrent of criticism that followed. "It was decided in typical ACC fashion," wrote Frank Vehorn in the *Virginian-Pilot*. "The men sitting in the coaching chairs on the opposite benches decided the outcome. Strategy, not fast breaks or slam dunks, would win this one."

Maryland athletics director Jim Kehoe was even blunter. "I can't believe that we watched two of the greatest teams in college basketball — teams with four All-Americans — play this way," Kehoe said. "All this talent, all those millions of people watching on national television, all the millions of dollars involved in running this tournament, and we get this."

The outcry sparked widespread experiments with a shot clock and 3-pointer the following season, and ultimately led to permanent rule changes that preclude such dilatory tactics. "I think everybody said, 'God, we really don't want that,'" Holland said.

Virginia and a hobbled Wilson lasted two rounds in the 1982 NCAA Tournament. North Carolina survived a 52-50 scare against James Madison in its opener as Worthy took over in the final minute, then advanced to New Orleans and its second straight NCAA championship contest.

The opponent was Georgetown, led by intimidating center Patrick Ewing and coached by John Thompson, a Smith friend. For the second consecutive year, a North Carolina upperclassman enjoyed a career-high effort in the Final Four, with Worthy scoring 28 points. But the decisive score, with 17 seconds left, came on an 18-foot jumper from the left wing by Jordan after a timeout. "Knock it in, Michael," Smith said as the team broke its huddle.

The shot not only catapulted Jordan to stardom but established the final score, 63-62. The issue was settled when Hoya guard Fred Brown inexplicably passed the ball to Worthy against UNC's scramble defense. "I

BELOW
Center Ralph Sampson of Virginia, a three-time national player of the year, posts up against Georgetown's Patrick Ewing in a December 1982 contest billed as "the game of the century."

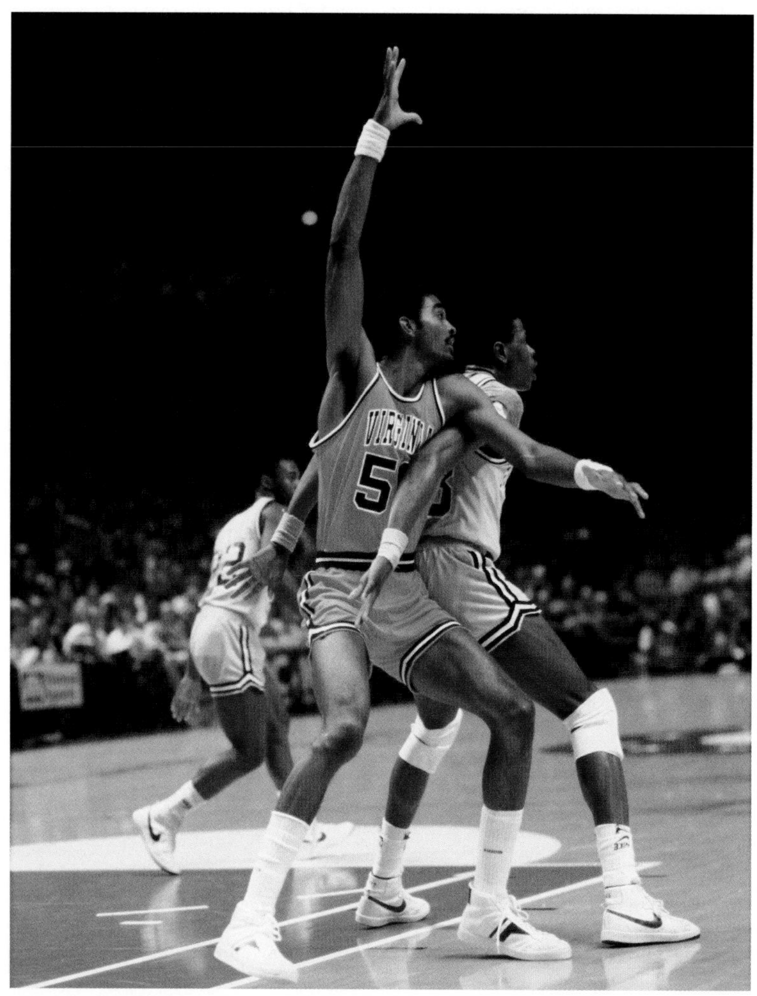

was pretty surprised because it hit me right in the chest," said Worthy, the Final Four's most outstanding player.

"I think I was out-coached tonight, but fortunately I had players that played extremely well," said Smith, whose post-game comments included chiding one media critic for questioning the coach's approach. "I'm not sure we were the best team tonight. I think we were the lucky team."

The ACC had another team in a basketball Final Four that spring — Maryland, which won its fourth ACC women's title in five years, beating Clemson 93-81 in the ACC Tournament final. "This is the best yet," said the Terrapins' Weller. Clemson's Barbara Kennedy was co-MVP with Maryland's Marcia Richardson after posting a 33-point, 21-rebound game against UNC in the semifinals, followed by another 33-point effort in the title game. Kennedy finished her career in her next game, an NCAA loss to Penn State. She remains the ACC career women's leader in total points (3113), points per game (24.5) and total rebounds (1,252).

The 1982 season was the first in which the NCAA took over women's college athletics after "doing all it could to battle Title IX," according to N.C. State's Finch. The Terrapins got to the national semifinals for the second time in five years, but lost to Cheyney State, 76-66.

Not all ACC news was good in 1982. Clemson repeated as the league football champion, running its ACC winning streak to 12 straight as it finished 9-1-1 and eighth in the polls. But Ford's Tigers could not defend their title, their '81 championship tainted by a two-year NCAA probation and a three-year ACC bowl ban.

The NCAA punishment ranked with the most severe to that time. The program was found guilty of numerous violations related to "a pattern of improper recruiting activities" over a five-year period dating to 1976. Most occurred under Ford. Some involved quarterback Homer Jordan, who was suspended, allowing Mike Eppley to become the nation's only starter in football and basketball in 1982.

The penalty reduced Clemson's scholarships to 10 in both 1983 and 1984, seasons in which it was prohibited from postseason play or live television. The school did not contest the penalties, including the ACC's addition of another year to the bowl ban.

"The chief executive officers of colleges too long have allowed the pressure and

FOUR-FRONT

ACC Women In NCAA Final Four
(Since 1982, When NCAA Began Women's Tournament)

2002	Duke
1999	Duke*
1998	N.C. State
1994	North Carolina**
1992	Virginia
1991	Virginia*
1990	Virginia
1989	Maryland
1982	Maryland

* Reached title game
** Won national championship

TEN-ACIOUS

ACC Women's Basketball Teams Ranked In Top 10 In Final Poll
(Rankings Started in 1976-77 Season)

School	Seasons Finished Top 10
Clemson	1999, 1991*
Duke	2002, 2001, 2000, 1999, 1998
Maryland	1992, 1989, 1988, 1983, 1982, 1981, 1980, 1979, 1978
No. Carolina	1998, 1997, 1994
N.C. State	1998, 1991, 1990*, 1989*, 1980, 1978, 1977
Virginia	1996*, 1995, 1994, 1993, 1992, 1991, 1990*, 1988, 1987*, 1986

* USA Today poll only

NORTH
44
33
50
NCAA

Freshman Michael Jordan of North Carolina (23) takes the shot that won the national championship for the Tar Heels and catapulted him into the limelight. UNC beat Georgetown 63-62 in New Orleans to secure coach Dean Smith's first national title. Jordan would go on to win six National Basketball Association championships and take many more game-winning shots during his professional career.

importance of athletics to dominate the college," declared Clemson President William Atchley. "There is no place in this community for cheating, in the classroom, the laboratory, or on the playing field. Clemson can be superior, Clemson will be superior, and remain a champion — both academically and athletically — and can do it without breaking rules."

With the Tigers removed from the picture, bowl bids went to the ACC's second- and third-place finishers, Maryland and North Carolina, respectively. The Tar Heels (8-4) beat Texas 26-10 in the Sun Bowl, UNC's fourth straight bowl appearance. More surprising was Maryland's leap from 4-6 to 8-4 under Bobby Ross, earning the newcomer honors as 1982 ACC coach of the year.

Ross was aboard because, for the second time in history, Maryland watched a future football Hall of Famer leave to coach the University of Kentucky. The first instance followed the 1945 season, when Bear Bryant departed College Park after a year. This time Jerry Claiborne returned to his alma mater and was replaced by Ross, an NFL assistant with college coaching experience at Maryland, among other places.

The Terrapins, tough against the run and adept with the pass, went to the inaugural Aloha Bowl, losing 21-20 to Washington. The '82 season was the third straight in which Maryland led the ACC in rushing defense (87.2 yards). Over one three-win stretch the Terrapins yielded nine points. Included was a 23-6 victory against N.C. State in which the Wolfpack failed to gain a yard on the ground.

The Terrapin offense depended upon junior quarterback Norman "Boomer" Esiason, tight end John Tice and All-ACC place-kicker Jess Atkinson. Yet good as Esiason was, Duke's Bennett overshadowed him throughout his career. The quarterback from California led the ACC in 1982 in passing and in total offense (262.3 yards per game). Chris Castor, a 6-foot senior, took advantage of Bennett's throws to score 13 touchdowns, lead the league in receiving yards (86.5 average) and earn recognition as the 1982 ACC player of the year.

BELOW
Coach Bobby Ross turned Maryland into a consistent power during the 1980s. Ross' Terps won the ACC championship three consecutive seasons (1983-85). One player who helped the Terrapins gain that status was quarterback Boomer Esiason (right), who threw 42 touchdown passes during his career.

Spurrier's exciting attack set what was then an ACC record for total offense (4,990 yards). The '82 Blue Devils became the first league squad since Maryland in 1953 to average more than 300 passing yards per game. They finished 6-5, giving Duke consecutive winning seasons for the first time in more than a decade. Wilson still got fired following a 23-17 win over North Carolina in the season finale.

Two other squads finished 6-5 — N.C. State in Monte Kiffin's last season as head coach and Georgia Tech under Bill Curry, matching the Yellow Jackets' win total for the previous three seasons combined.

Tech's basketball fortunes also improved during the 1982-83 academic year, the second with Cremins as head coach. Cremins, the former South Carolina guard under Frank McGuire, had been hired from Appalachian State prior to the 1982 season after a protracted process in which Gary Williams, then at American University, was a finalist. "I wanted somebody like Bobby," said Rice, the Georgia Tech AD. "I thought he would know how to recruit the Eastern Seaboard, and he understood Atlantic Coast Conference basketball. He was my choice. It turned out well."

Cremins, a Bronx native, had emulated McGuire in mining the veins of New York City talent, establishing a "Bronx to Boone Express" that brought 100 wins in six seasons at Appalachian. Upon arrival in Atlanta, Cremins again tapped New York for talent. Brooklyn's John "Spider" Salley, a spindly but smooth big man, was an important member of his first full recruiting class. "They're my kind of kids — aggressive, hungry and they play hard," Cremins said of the New Yorkers.

But Tech's key freshman in 1983 was guard Mark Price from Enid, Okla., the same town that produced Clemson quarterback Steve Fuller, the ACC's 1977 and 1978 player of the year in football.

Price, a 6-foot guard, didn't readily accept a playmaker's harness. He preferred to shoot, a skill emphasized in 1983 when the ACC adopted an experimental 30-second shot clock and a 3-pointer from an arc located just 19 feet from the backboard,

BELOW
Quarterback Ben Bennett (left) and Steve Spurrier combined to make Duke a winner again in football. With Spurrier directing the show as offensive coordinator and Bennett executing the plans as starting quarterback, Duke went 6-5 in 1980 and '81 for the school's first back-to-back winning seasons since 1970-71. Bennett was named the 1983 ACC player of the year after throwing for 3,086 yards and 17 touchdowns. He was a first-team All-ACC quarterback in 1982 and '83. He was the rookie of the year in 1980. Spurrier left Duke in 1982, but returned in 1987 as the Blue Devils head coach.

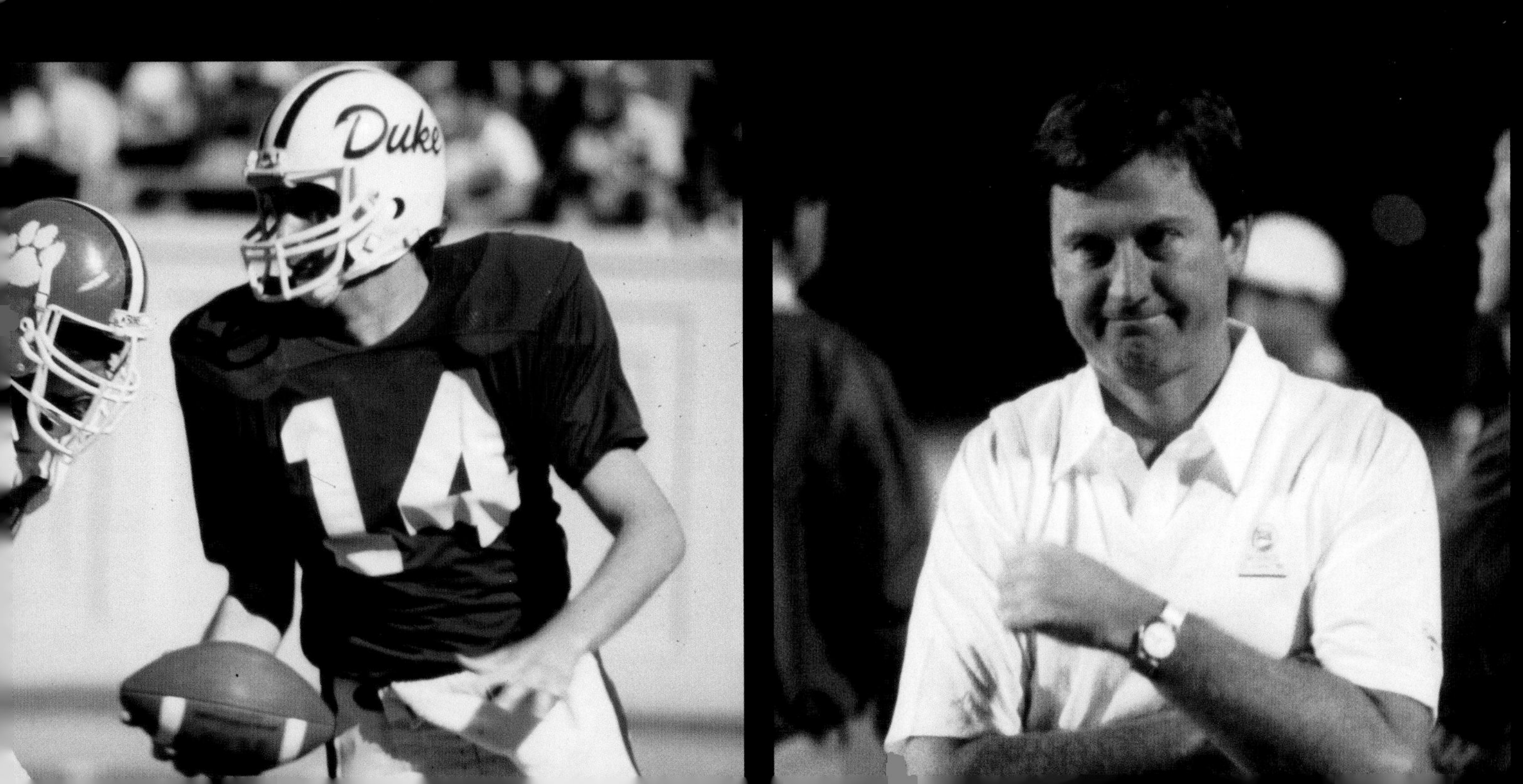

two feet closer than the current line, measured 19-9 from the center of the basket. Even that is considered too close by many.

Team scoring averages jumped league-wide under the experimental rules, from 64.96 points per game in 1982 to 77.82 in 1983. Even so, Wake's Tacy and Virginia's Holland eschewed the 3-pointer. Duke's struggling Mike Krzyzewski chewed out those who supported the change.

Yet it was the ACC's other two young coaches who embraced the rule most fully. N.C. State averaged more 3-point attempts (10.6) than any other ACC squad. "I'm not saying it's too close," Jim Valvano said of the line, "but last night my mom came out of the stands at halftime and knocked in three of four."

Cremins, whose squad averaged 9.5 attempts, gave Price a green light from the bonusphere. Price responded by hitting 3-pointers with 44 percent efficiency, his 73 bonus baskets more than the entire output at Virginia or Wake. He averaged 20.3 points, the only time a freshman paced the ACC in scoring, and was voted 1983 ACC rookie of the year. That distinction started quite a trend — counting Price, Georgia Tech freshmen won four straight rookie of the year awards and six between 1983 and 1990.

Behind Price and Salley, the Yellow Jackets finished 13-15 with four ACC wins, more than Duke or Clemson. Voted 1983 ACC coach of the year, Cremins beat both Maryland and Wake, among five 20-game winners in the ACC. "Bobby was a very good coach," Rice said. "He was a heck of a recruiter and one of the finest persons I ever worked with. He was always upbeat. He was a fighter."

Tech actually beat Maryland twice in 1983, including an overtime decision in the ACC Tournament. The Terrapins got an NCAA invitation, anyway, one of four to ACC squads.

North Carolina and Virginia also got NCAA bids after tying for first at 12-2. Again Sampson was ACC player of the year, matching N.C. State's David Thompson as the only three-time winners.

There were significant differences in the upper-echelon rivalry, however. Worthy left a year early to go pro. Point guards Jimmy Black and Jeff Jones graduated. UNC added big man Brad Daugherty, ultimately the top pick in the 1986 NBA draft, and UVa added transfer Rick Carlisle, a guard.

North Carolina swept the series in 1983 for the only time during Sampson's tenure. First the Heels ended Virginia's 34-game home winning streak. A month later Jordan tipped in a shot, then stole the ball from Carlisle in the backcourt and dunked it to secure a 64-63 comeback at Chapel Hill. UNC, which got off to an 0-2 start for the first time since 1929, finished 29-9, ending the season with an 82-77 loss to Georgia in the NCAA East Region final.

The 29-5 Cavaliers also lost twice to N.C. State: 81-78 in the ACC Tournament title game and 63-62 in the NCAA West Region final.

The Cavaliers' other loss ranked among the great regular-season upsets in college history. Top-ranked and undefeated, UVa stopped in Hawaii on its return from two games in Tokyo, Japan, and lost to Chaminade, an NAIA school, 77-72.

Ultimately, though, the Chaminade upset was mild compared with what N.C. State pulled off, starting with the 1983 ACC Tournament and culminating in a 54-52 win over Houston in the national championship game.

A trio of seniors inherited from Norm Sloan led the Wolfpack — graceful 6-11 forward Thurl Bailey and a pair of burly guards from Maryland's powerful DeMatha High, shooter Dereck Whittenburg and

Sidney Lowe, a "consummate" point guard, according to Valvano. The other starters were sophomores: left-handed center Cozell McQueen, a South Carolinian famous for remarking he had fled north across the border to N.C. State to escape the South, and sophomore Lorenzo Charles, an evolving power forward from Brooklyn.

Whittenburg broke his foot in January and was presumably lost for the season. Freshman Ernie Myers, a prep All-American, stepped in to replace him, and sharpshooter Terry Gannon lent punch from the perimeter.

The Wolfpack was only 14-8 when powerful North Carolina came to Raleigh in mid-February. But the so-called "Cardiac Pack" built a one-point lead at halftime and pulled away to a 70-63 victory punctuated by Bailey's late dunk, setting off wild celebrations in Raleigh. That was just the beginning for Valvano, who had signed a 10-year contract earlier in the season. The gregarious coach did not always know where his team practiced, but was a master gamesman whether playing darts or pachinko in his office or strolling the sideline calculating how to exploit his team's strengths, an opponent's weaknesses, and soft spots in the rules.

N.C. State won 10 straight soon after Whittenburg's early return to the lineup. The run began with a pair of triumphs over Wake, a 130-89 thumping in the regular-season finale and a 71-70 victory in the opening round of the ACC Tournament, this time in Atlanta, on a free throw by Charles with three seconds left. Then came a 91-84 overtime win over North Carolina to reach the tournament final.

The opponent was Virginia, looking for its first ACC title of the Sampson era. The big man had concluded the regular season in style, his 14-footer with four seconds to go sinking Maryland, 83-81. But the Cavaliers couldn't get past N.C. State, which at 20-10 earned the ACC's automatic bid to the NCAAs.

Nobody else got past the Wolfpack,

BELOW
Georgia Tech won its first ACC championship in basketball in 1985. John Salley (left), coach Bobby Cremins and guard Mark Price (right) carried Yellow Jacket athletics to new heights that day. Price was a four-time All-ACC pick and a first-team All-American in '85. Cremins' teams captured three ACC titles before he stepped aside in 2000.

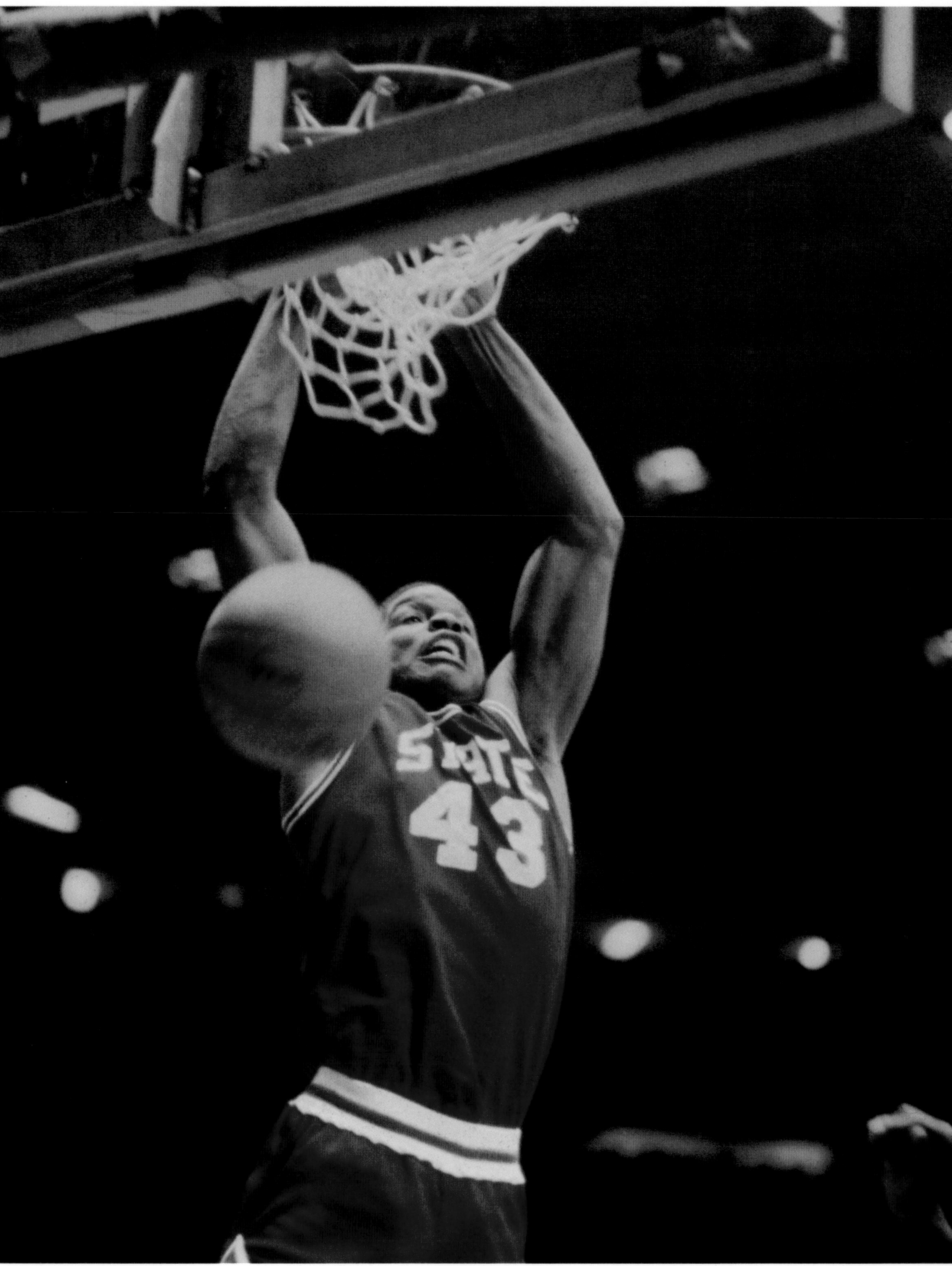
43

either, as solid play, strategic fouling and plain luck intervened. "Survive and advance" and putting a team "in a position to win" became watchwords for N.C. State. The tone was set in the Pack's NCAA opener, a double-overtime win over Pepperdine. The Wolfpack rallied from six down in the final minute of the first extra period as Dane Suttle, the third-best foul shooter in Division I, missed a pair of one-and-one opportunities. "Hey, we may be destined to win this thing," Valvano said in the locker room.

The penultimate magic came in the title game against top-ranked Houston and its potent "Phi Slamma Jamma" lineup led by center Akeem Olajuwon and forward Clyde Drexler. N.C. State was expected to delay but took the attack to the Cougars, got an early lead and then controlled the tempo. The defense virtually eliminated the fastbreak chances that fueled coach Guy Lewis' team. Drexler drew four first-half fouls. The Wolfpack weathered a Houston rally, then exploited the Cougars' unaccustomed stall to forge a tie at 52-all in the final minutes on consecutive jumpers by Whittenburg.

The game came down to a last shot, as famous as any in Final Four history. Whittenburg rushed a long jumper after six-seeded N.C. State ran down the clock. The shot fell short, but Charles caught the ball and dunked it as time expired. Suddenly the game was over and the Wolfpack had its second national championship within a decade.

"We got bent out of shape on the last play," said Valvano, who jubilantly ran the Albuquerque court seeking someone to hug after the buzzer sounded. "Then we lost track of how much time was left. All our receivers were covered, so we went to the tight end over the middle."

During the real 1983 football season Maryland recaptured first place in the ACC behind the passing of Esiason, starting a run of three straight titles. The 6-4 lefty remains among the school's career leaders in numerous offensive categories. Yet 1983 player of the year honors went to Duke's Bennett, who threw for a record 3,086

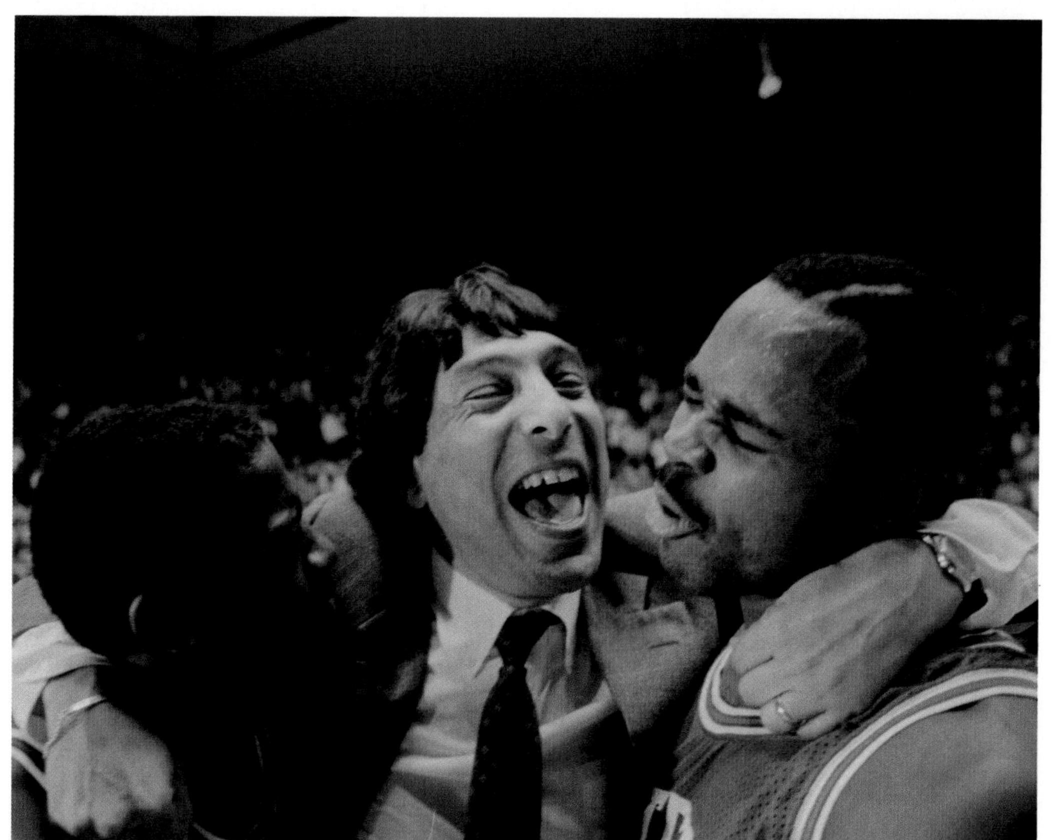

FACING PAGE
Lorenzo Charles made the most famous shot in N.C. State history when he grabbed an errant jumper by Dereck Whittenburg and dunked the ball at the buzzer against Houston to win the 1983 national championship. That team was known as the "Cardiac Pack" for the way it made so many stirring comebacks during its run through the NCAA Tournament.

LEFT
Coach Jim Valvano (center) hugs Dereck Whittenburg (left) and Sidney Lowe as they celebrate in 1983.

BELOW
Coach George Welsh turned Virginia into a consistent winner. When he arrived in 1982, the Cavaliers had just two winning seasons in the preceding 29 years. All that changed when the former Navy quarterback took over. Welsh retired in 2000 after becoming the winningest coach in Virginia and ACC history with a 134-86-3 record.

yards and concluded his career as the ACC's all-time passing leader (9,614 yards) to that point. He was tops at the time in the NCAA as well, passing Brigham Young's Jim McMahon (9,536).

North Carolina, which matched Maryland at 8-4 and finished second in the ACC, led the conference in total offense. Both the Terrapins and Tar Heels got bowl bids, and lost. Clemson was 9-1-1 but remained on probation. Georgia Tech finally counted in the league standings and finished tied for third with Virginia at 3-2. Those were the Jackets' only victories in 11 games.

The 1983 coach of the year was George Welsh, who took Virginia to a 6-5 record in his second season on the job. That was the first tangible evidence of one of the great turnarounds in college football history.

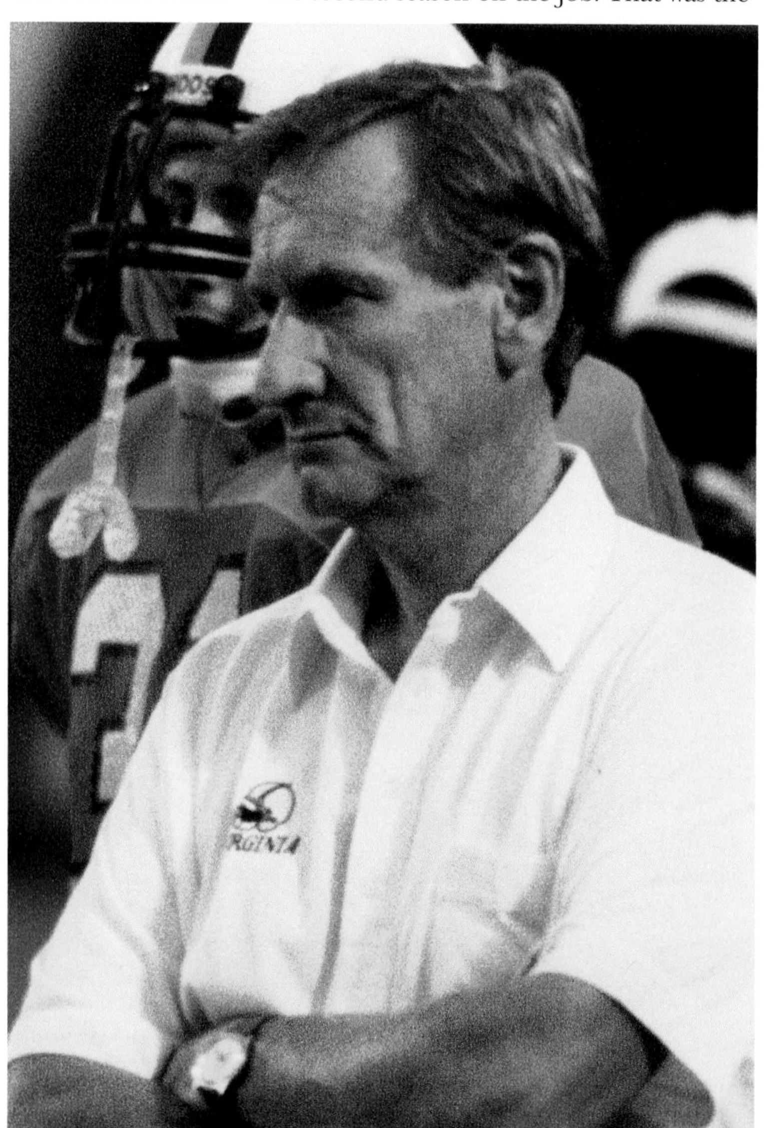

Welsh was accustomed to success. The native of Coaldale, Pa., had finished third in the 1955 Heisman Trophy voting, leading the nation in passing and total offense as Navy's quarterback. Welsh became head coach at his alma mater in 1973 and rejuvenated the program after working as an assistant under Rip Engle and Joe Paterno at Penn State. "George is the best judge of football talent I have ever seen," Paterno said. "He has always been a guy who smelled of confidence."

When Virginia offered him its head coaching job, friends told Welsh the idea simply smelled. The program had two major handicaps, Welsh recalled. "One of them was, there were very poor facilities. The other was, they had no winning tradition."

The effects of only two winning seasons in 29 years were immediately evident upon arrival in Charlottesville. "Players here did not know what it took to win when I first came," Welsh told writer Robert Viccellio of *Albemarle* magazine. "I was appalled by the attitude. In fact, some players came to me after I got here and said that I was working them too hard." The Cavaliers soon learned to work harder. Among them were tackle Jim Dombrowski and defensive back Lester Lyles, both All-ACC in '83. "We got lucky," Welsh said. "I inherited some good players from a previous regime." Dombrowski went on to consensus All-America honors in 1985.

Fortune smiled on Welsh in other ways. Sampson's presence broke the ice with the state's African-American athletes, and criticisms leveled internally by Corrigan led to an infusion of resources. "You keep changing football coaches and suddenly you realize maybe it wasn't the coaches," Corrigan said. "Maybe those other guys didn't have a chance. George was the first guy who ever had a chance here."

Welsh brought the Cavaliers in at 8-2-2 and second in the ACC in 1984, the first time since the early '50s the program posted consecutive winning seasons. The '84 unit also got invited to the Peach Bowl, the school's first postseason appearance.

Postseason was good to Virginia in 1984. Not only did the football squad defeat Purdue 27-24, but the basketball team made a surprise return to the Final Four a year after Sampson graduated. "I can honestly say we shouldn't have been invited," Holland said of his club, which finished the regular season unranked and 17-10.

That the Cavaliers got bumped in the opening round of the 1984 ACC Tournament and still received an NCAA bid reflected the league's overall strength and the respect it commanded. "The ACC appears to be the overwhelming number one," said Dave Gavitt, commissioner of the Big East.

No ACC team posted a losing record. Only N.C. State dropped a home game against a non-conference opponent. Five ACC schools were invited to the NCAAs, tying the best showing to that point.

North Carolina was undefeated in the conference and lost just three times all year. Five previous teams had gone through the ACC season without a loss, most recently N.C. State in 1974. Jordan, a junior and one of five eventual first-round NBA draft choices on the squad, led the league in scoring (19.6) and was voted 1984 ACC and national player of the year. That summer he and Perkins played on the 1984 U.S. Olympic basketball team that won the gold in Los Angeles under Indiana coach Bob Knight.

The Tar Heels won their first 21 games and concluded the regular season atop the polls. But Kenny Smith, their stellar freshman playmaker, broke his left wrist when fouled from behind against LSU in late January. Steve Hale was an able fill-in, and Kenny Smith returned to the lineup late in the season. But a squad considered among Dean Smith's best failed to regain its earlier chemistry and suffered a pair of quick losses in postseason play. Upstart Duke eliminated the Heels 77-75 in the semifinals of the ACC Tournament, and Indiana ousted UNC in an NCAA regional semifinal as Jordan was held in check.

Duke, the team that ended North Carolina's 1984 run at 15 straight ACC wins, finished 24-10 and got to the NCAA Tournament, sweet redemption for Krzyzewski.

BELOW

George Welsh hoists the trophy after Virginia defeated Purdue 27-24 in the 1984 Peach Bowl. This was the first bowl appearance in school history. By the time Welsh retired, the Cavaliers had played in 12 bowls, and he would be named the ACC coach of the year a record four times.

Stubbornly clinging to his preferred man-to-man defense even when a zone might salvage a few wins, Krzyzewski posted consecutive 17-loss seasons in 1982 and '83. Included was a humiliating home defeat by Wagner that served as a haunting benchmark. "What motivates me is losing," Krzyzewski said a decade and two NCAA titles later. "To me, that's the motivation — I'm afraid. I don't want to lose the competitive edge I have right now. And the memory of what it was like to lose helps me."

The 1983 squad had perhaps the country's best freshman class, featuring big men Mark Alarie and Jay Bilas, wing forward David Henderson and guard Johnny Dawkins. By '84 Alarie was first-team All-ACC, Dawkins second. Dawkins led Duke in scoring for four years and ranks as the ACC's second-most prolific scorer with 2,556 points. (He trails only Wake's Dickie Hemric, who scored 2,587 from 1952-55.)

The 1983 season had ended on a bitter note for Duke, a 109-66 defeat against Virginia in the opening round of the ACC Tournament. The margin remains the largest ever in the event. Afterward accusations of dirty play and running up the score swirled through The Omni in Atlanta. "I didn't think much of the incident at the time," Holland said. Krzyzewski apparently did. "He really had a vendetta against Virginia," said a confidant. The Blue Devils won the next 16 meetings between the schools, a streak that lasted until 1990.

The 1984 Blue Devils added a single recruit, point guard Tommy Amaker, and immediately improved, earning Krzyzewski a contract extension at mid-year. The Duke coach also made a splash when, following a home loss to UNC in January, he angrily decried a "double standard" in officiating that benefited Smith. Fred Barakat, the ACC's reform-minded officiating supervisor, found no basis for the claim. Yet subsequent ACC action grew more physical, to Duke's advantage, and league teams held their own in greater numbers in rugged NCAA competition.

Duke's defeat of North Carolina in the ACC Tournament earned a trip to the title game against Maryland. Finally, on his sixth try, former Blue Devil Lefty Driesell came away with the crown. Terrapin sophomore Len Bias was tournament MVP. The following two seasons Bias would be ACC player of the year.

BELOW
Lefty Driesell coached Maryland from 1969 to 1986. He won 122 ACC games and the 1984 conference championship. He produced numerous All-Americans, All-ACC players and some of the league's most competitive teams.

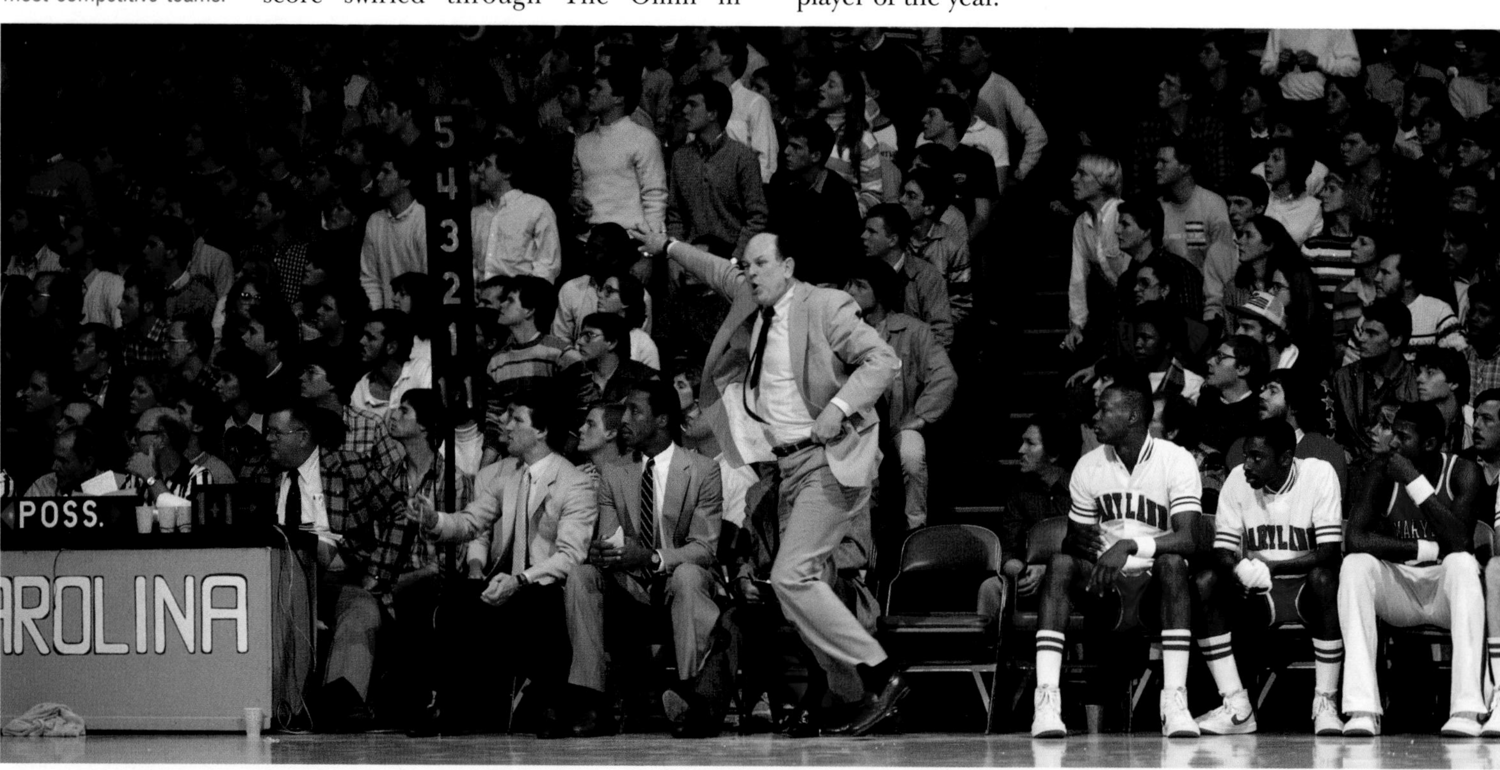

"Back when I first started out, I wanted to win that thing real bad," Driesell said of the title. "I said, 'If we win that thing I'm going to have my car in here, and I'm going to get that trophy and screw it on the hood and ride all around the state of North Carolina for a week.' I really was going to do that. Now, I'm too old for that. I've got to get home and get some sleep."

Neither ACC Tournament finalist fared well in the NCAAs. That was left to Virginia and Wake Forest, among five ACC squads that were invited. Every year from 1984 through 1994 a majority of ACC teams received NCAA Tournament bids.

Wake, led by guards Delaney Rudd and Danny Young and frontcourt players Anthony Teachey and Kenny Green, reached the Midwest Region final. There the Deacons concluded their fourth straight 20-win season with a 68-63 loss to Houston. Along the way Young's layup helped the Deacons to a 73-71 overtime victory against top-seed DePaul, ending Ray Meyers' 42-year coaching career at the Chicago school. It was Wake's sixth win in seven overtime games in 1984, each total tops in ACC history.

Virginia got a step further relying primarily on guards Wilson, Carlisle and Stokes. The Cavaliers reached the Final Four, losing 49-47 to Houston in overtime.

Proficiency in both basketball and football was unprecedented at Virginia. Welsh's squad was in contention for the 1984 conference title until the final game of the season, when Maryland came to Charlottesville and collected a 45-34 win.

Only two ACC football teams had losing records in 1984, the best overall showing since the league returned to eight members. The timing couldn't have been better, since thanks to a lawsuit the NCAA's stranglehold on TV rights had been broken. The ACC got more national exposure and built its own regional network to showcase an improved product.

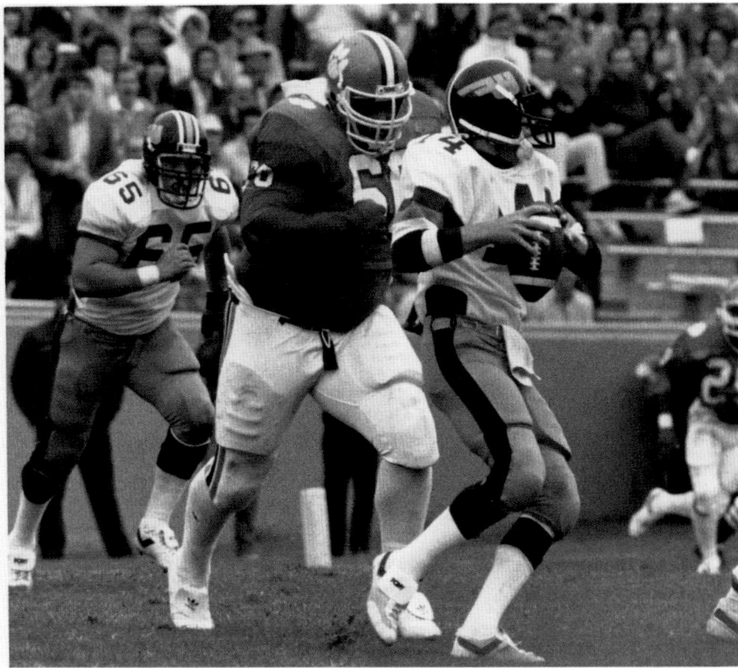

ABOVE
William "The Refrigerator" Perry of Clemson rumbles toward another quarterback sack. He set a school record in 1984 with 25 career sacks. The defensive lineman was named the ACC player of the year that season. Perry was the first three-time All-American at Clemson. He was a consensus All-American twice. Perry went on to a successful career with the Chicago Bears of the National Football League.

North Carolina finished third with star running back Ethan Horton. Fourth-place Wake Forest was 6-5, its first winning season in five years. Georgia Tech, paced by running back Robert Lavette, was 6-4-1 and ended Clemson's streak of 20 straight wins over ACC rivals.

The Tigers, in their final year on probation, were 7-4 and boasted the 1984 ACC player of the year in middle guard William "The Refrigerator" Perry. The mobile 6-3, 320-pound senior, who could dunk a basketball, was the first ACC defensive player chosen consensus All-American two years in a row.

The big winner, though, was Maryland. The '84 Terrapins finished atop the football standings for the second straight season, giving the school matching titles in the major men's sports. Only Georgia Tech in 1990 has since won both official titles in the same year.

The Terrapins replaced Esiason with a pair of quarterbacks, Stan Gelbaugh and Frank Reich, and didn't miss a beat. Having a relief pitcher proved especially valuable in a game at Miami that resulted in the greatest comeback in NCAA history.

Maryland fell behind 31-0 at halftime against the defending national champions, but it was the Hurricanes who were blown away. Reich, a senior, came off the bench and completed 12 of 16 passes for 260 yards and three touchdowns as the Terrapins rallied for six second-half scores in a 42-40 victory.

But few comebacks could match the turnaround completed in 1984-85 by Georgia Tech basketball.

Just four years removed from a winless ACC season, the Yellow Jackets finished in a three-way tie for first with North Carolina and N.C. State. Then, with the ACC Tournament back in Atlanta, they beat the Tar Heels 57-54 for the conference championship. The '85 Jackets initiated a run of consecutive NCAA Tournament bids that continued through 1993. Tech's only previous NCAA appearance occurred in 1960.

Tech forward Duane Ferrell was voted 1985 rookie of the year. Add sophomore guard Bruce Dalrymple and Price, the tournament MVP, and the majority of the Jackets' starters were rookies of the year. Cremins, the man who recruited them, was voted ACC coach of the year for the second time in three seasons.

"That kind of got us going in everything," Rice said of the basketball title. "Bobby, I give him a lot of credit for the overall success of our program."

The ACC's much-vaunted internal competitiveness and balance peaked during the 1985 basketball season, as every men's team had a winning record. Three tied for first at 9-5, two tied for fourth at 8-6.

Wake Forest, an also-ran during the season, enjoyed its biggest victory in June with Winston-Salem's passage of a bond referendum to build a new $26 million arena, to be named after hometown hero Lawrence Joel, a Medal of Honor winner during the Vietnam War.

Good as the ACC was in 1985, no league squad reached the Final Four. Five teams were invited to the NCAAs and the three first-place finishers all were bumped in regional finals. Tech (27-8) lost to top-seed Georgetown, the defending champ. UNC (27-9) lost to Villanova, which advanced to an upset championship. And N.C. State lost to St. John's as the Big East made a splash in the Final Four.

The Wolfpack's strong finish was welcome tonic for a 1984-85 season soured when freshman Chris Washburn was arrested in December for taking an $800 stereo system from a teammate's dorm room. Assiduously recruited, acclaimed as the best big man in his class, the 6-11 Washburn was suspended for the season by Valvano and pleaded guilty to three misdemeanors.

Washburn's 470 SAT score (70 points above minimum and 530 below the school's freshman average) was revealed in court documents. The disclosure was explosive. N.C. State and the 16-campus North Carolina university system reacted by re-evaluating admissions policies. Criticism mounted regarding Valvano's stewardship, which was marked by numerous outside commercial ventures, in-season network television commentary and an avowed goal to parlay his prominence into millionaire's status.

"I came at about the time when the circumstances of athletics really rose to the top of higher education's agenda," said Dr. Thomas Hearn, president of Wake Forest

1983

3.11.83
Virginia defeats Duke 109-66, the largest winning margin in ACC Tournament history

4.4.83
N.C. State upsets Houston 54-52 to win NCAA men's basketball title

4.21.83
ACC television pioneer C.D. Chesley dies

1984

11.10.84
Frank Reich rallies Maryland at Miami to a record comeback from a 31-0 halftime deficit to a 42-40 victory

1986

1.18.86
Smith Center opens as No.1 North Carolina beats No.3 Duke, 95-92

since 1983. He cited a severe NCAA penalty handed to Southern Methodist, academic scandal at Georgia, and the removal of Clemson's Atchley and other presidents over failures involving athletics. "All of a sudden it wasn't going to work to have athletics outside the domain of academic control. ... This is not a war with an external enemy. This is a civil war because these coaches are making these absurd amounts of money, and we have trustees who are telling presidents this is an appropriate thing to do."

Amidst turmoil, the '85 Wolfpack coalesced as a team. Convinced winning would soothe troubled waters, Valvano conjured a squad capable of mounting another title run. "Hey, you're looking at the original dreamer," he said. The Wolfpack eventually produced a 23-10 record, blending three seniors from the '83 championship squad with junior college guards Nate McMillan and Anthony "Spud" Webb.

Duke and Maryland tied for fourth, each enjoying a 20-win season. The Blue Devils even won at Chapel Hill for the first time in 19 years. Two games later Georgia Tech beat UNC for the first time in 20 games.

Georgia Tech football, as with its basketball counterpart, was gaining traction. Powered by the ACC's toughest scoring defense, coach Bill Curry's 1985 squad finished 9-2-1, the Jackets' best record since 1966, Bobby Dodd's last season. The defensive leaders were end Pat Swilling, who set a school record with 15 sacks, including seven in a win over N.C. State, and linebacker Ted Roof, whose 25 tackles in a 6-6 tie at Tennessee are second-best in Tech history.

The No. 19 Yellow Jackets, ranked for the first time since 1972, finished second to No. 18 Maryland in the ACC. They got their only postseason bid of the decade and beat Michigan State 17-14 in the All-American Bowl. Curry was voted 1985 ACC coach of the year.

The Cavaliers tied Clemson for third at 4-3. Each had six victories overall. UVa running back Barry Word was the '85 ACC player of the year and the league's leading rusher (1,224 yards, 5.9 per carry). Virginia extended its streak of winning seasons to three, unprecedented prosperity. Welsh already had more winning seasons in four years on the job than his eight Virginia predecessors had combined to achieve in 29.

BELOW
Virginia's Barry Word won 1985 ACC player of the year honors after rushing for 1,224 yards. He averaged 5.9 yards per carry and scored six touchdowns.

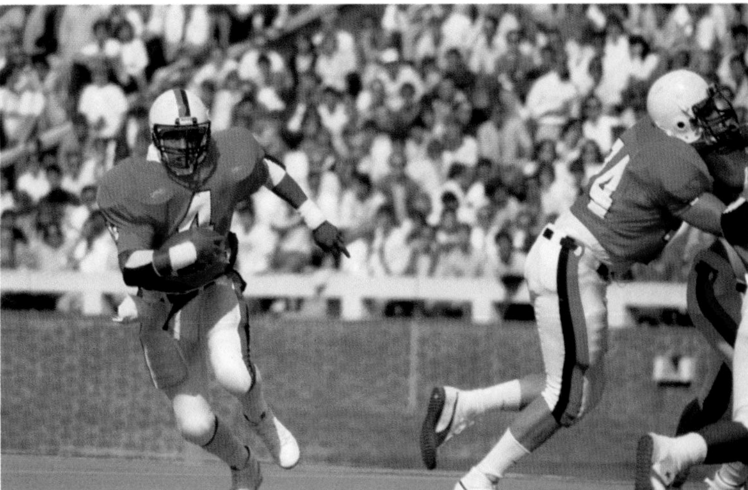

Clemson earned a bowl bid, its first since winning the '81 title. Four Tigers made All-ACC (fewest since 1980), most prominently running back Kenny Flowers. Ford's squad lost to Minnesota in the Independence Bowl, 20-13. President Bill Atchley wasn't there to see the game — after a seven-hour trustees meeting in March, he had been forced to resign because of differences over handling ath-

1987

5.12.87
ACC commissioner Bob James dies abruptly of stomach cancer

9.1.87
Gene Corrigan becomes third ACC commissioner

1988

8.12.88
Four-year deal signed with Florida Citrus Bowl assuring berths for ACC football champion

12.10.88
Duke's Danny Ferry scores an ACC-record 58 points in a 117-102 win at Miami

1989

11.11.89
Lawrence Joel Coliseum opens as Wake Forest wins 84-65 against Davidson

By Tim Crothers

ACC EXCELLENCE

UNC WOMEN CLAIM WORLD OF SOCCER TO THEMSELVES

In the summer of 1997, a sportswriter questioned legendary North Carolina basketball coach Dean Smith about the Tar Heels' preseason No. 1 ranking in football.

"What's it like for a sport other than basketball to be in the spotlight at UNC?"

Smith responded: "This is a women's soccer school. We're just trying to keep up with them."

Huh? *North Carolina? A women's soccer school?*

Smith insisted that he had been propagating the same claim around the UNC athletic department for years, and he supports his argument simply by counting the rings. North Carolina women's soccer is the most relentless dynasty in the history of collegiate sports.

Coach Anson Dorrance's Tar Heels won 17 of the 21 national championships contested as of 2001, including 16 NCAA titles, more than any other women's Division I sports program in the country. Inside the McCaskill Soccer Center on the Chapel Hill campus, the program's NCAA championship plaques are filed sideways into an overstuffed trophy case like a set of encyclopedias.

Anything less than a national title is considered disappointing. The Tar Heels' NCAA runner-up trophies have historically been utilized as doorstops.

The numbers are beyond gaudy. Heading into the 2002 season, UNC had produced an overall record of 511-23-11, or an average of exactly one loss for each of its 23 seasons. The Tar Heels have captured 15 of the 16 ACC titles since league play began in 1987, suffering just one conference defeat in the first 13 years of competition. North Carolina once ran off a streak of 103 consecutive matches without a loss and then, less than a month later, began another string of 92 straight victories. UNC had outscored its opponents 2,370-244 through 2001.

"I am just in awe at how they've been able to consistently win and win and win without any lulls," said Julie Foudy, who played for Dorrance with the U.S. National team and against him at Stanford. "Every team has games when you come out flat or you outshoot an opponent 300-1, and they beat you on one counterattack. But that never happens at Carolina. It goes against the logic of soccer."

Logic has absolutely nothing to do with the evolution of North Carolina women's soccer. When Dorrance first got the job as the men's soccer coach at UNC in 1976 at age 25, he was a law student who had never coached a soccer game above the club level. Three years later, when he was asked to add the school's new women's program to his coaching duties, he admitted that he had no clue how to train females. Fortunately, UNC athletics director Bill Cobey possessed the foresight to allow Dorrance to grant women's soccer scholarships before any other school in the South, a critical head start for the Tar Heels in recruiting the most talented players in the country.

Dorrance discovered many of the coaching techniques that he still employs today while watching UNC basketball practices in the early '80s, studying as Smith taught his vaunted system. Inventing his own buzz phrases, Dorrance then soccer-ized what he learned into what he calls "the competitive cauldron," a system where his Tar Heels compete tenaciously against one another in various training drills and all the results are recorded and posted.

Dorrance said his goal is to transform his women into "Natural Born Killers." He asks each one to strive for some way to be the "margin of victory" in every game. The attitude is illustrated in a quote from George Bernard Shaw's *Man and Superman* that Dorrance shares with his team each season. "Be a force of fortune instead of a feverish, selfish, little clod of ailments and grievances complaining that the world will not devote itself to making you happy."

The North Carolina coach believes that championships are earned through dedicated year-round training. He summed up his philosophy in a brief note he once wrote to his greatest player, Mia Hamm, after stumbling upon her

pushing through a self-imposed off-season individual workout in a local park. The note read, "The vision of a champion is someone who is bent over, drenched in sweat, at the point of exhaustion when no one else is watching."

Dorrance's most celebrated protégés are the 11 Tar Heels who have been selected as national players of the year, including Hamm, April Heinrichs, Kristine Lilly, Tisha Venturini, Cindy Parlow and Lorrie Fair, all of whose names are peppered throughout the NCAA record books. Yet North Carolina's legacy extends beyond the college ranks. Eight of the 20 players on the United States' 1999 World Cup championship team played at UNC, and there were 24 former Tar Heels on WUSA rosters in 2002, twice the number from any other school.

"We never really planned for all this success," Dorrance said. "All of a sudden you look back and something good has happened."

Among Dorrance's fondest memories during his coaching career is the unexpected public compliment from Smith, validating words from history's winningest college basketball coach to history's winningest college soccer coach. "When I called us a women's soccer school," Smith said, "I wanted to honor what they had accomplished. No team has ever won as much as they have. It's hard to compare to anything, anywhere."

But is North Carolina really a women's soccer school? No, it is *the* women's soccer school.

ABOVE: Mia Hamm, a former national player of the year and All-American, went on to become the No. 1 women's soccer player in the world after her career at North Carolina.
LEFT: UNC women's soccer coach Anson Dorrance built the most successful collegiate sports program in the ACC and the nation. As the Tar Heels entered the 2002 season, they had won 17 of the 21 national championships contested in the sport.

FACING PAGE
N.C. State coach Jim Valvano takes the last shot. The Wolfpack played UNC in the final men's basketball game at Carmichael Auditorium in 1986 before the Tar Heels moved to a new on-campus arena. Valvano grabbed the ball after the game and made what he said was the last basket at Carmichael. The Wolfpack's Nate McMillan made the last official basket at Carmichael.

BELOW
Clemson coach Danny Ford talks with Georgia Tech coach Bill Curry before a game. Curry rebuilt the Yellow Jackets into a winner in the 1980s.

letics. McLellan, the athletics director, went too.

Maryland didn't miss a beat, capturing its third straight ACC title at 6-0. Senior quarterback Stan Gelbaugh led the league in passing with 216.8 yards per game, and tackle John Maarleveld was a consensus All-American. In the dozen years since 1974, the Terrapins had won half the ACC championships. And, for the 11th time in 13 seasons and the fourth year in a row, Maryland went to a bowl, defeating Syracuse 35-18 in the Cherry Bowl in Michigan's Pontiac Silverdome.

But a storm was about to engulf College Park, and as part of the collateral damage coach Bobby Ross would resign following the 1986 season.

The 1985-86 academic year got off to a sterling start for the ACC. A single men's basketball team had a losing record, with the remainder winning at least 19 games each. The ACC Tournament final was a cliffhanger, as Duke beat Georgia Tech, 68-67. An unprecedented six men's squads got NCAA bids.

Duke finished atop the polls and reached the national championship game.

North Carolina had expected to open the '86 season in its new 21,572-seat Dean E. Smith Student Activities Center. Instead the Tar Heels played their first five games of the 1986 season in Carmichael Auditorium, concluding their tenure in the building with a 169-20 record in 22 seasons. The last basket at Carmichael was a symbolic layup by N.C. State coach Jim Valvano, following his team's loss to the Tar Heels.

UNC's 300,000-square-foot domed arena broke new ground figuratively as well as literally. Despite its location at a public university, the building was privately funded by 2,262 donors, the most generous contributors securing perpetual rights to courtside seats as an inducement to give. Beautiful, spacious and quite blue (sky version), the "Dean Dome" became a standard of measure for on-campus basketball arenas, although it infrequently matched Carmichael's home-court atmosphere.

"In an ideal world, would you do it differently?" asked John Swofford, then the school's athletics director. "I think the answer to that is yes. In the real world, at that time to raise $35 million to build something of that nature was quite an achievement for that university."

Third-ranked Duke came to Chapel Hill on Jan. 18, 1986, and opened the Smith Center, the largest on-campus arena of its kind. The Tar Heels were top-ranked, the event much-celebrated as the teams were a combined 33-0. "It was like being in the main event, like a big boxing match," Duke's Billy King said.

UNC won, 95-92. The third-ranked Blue Devils lost again in their next outing, at Wake Forest, in its first season under coach Bob Staak. The veteran Blue Devils would

CAROLI

not suffer another defeat until falling 72-69 to Louisville in the NCAA title game. Krzyzewski, whose team finished 37-3, was voted 1986 ACC coach of the year.

Both Georgia Tech (27-7) and North Carolina (28-6) finished in the top 10 in '86. The Tar Heels were third in the ACC, the first time in 19 seasons they did not finish with a share of first or second place.

For the only time ever, the ACC player of the year came from a squad with a losing league record, sixth-place Maryland.

Senior Len Bias was strong, tough, aggressive, mobile and skilled. The 6-8 forward led the ACC in scoring (23.2) for the second straight season. He had 41 points in a losing effort at Duke and rallied the Terrapins to an overtime win at the Smith Center, the Tar Heels' first defeat in their new home. Bias would also win the McKevlin Award as the ACC's top athlete of 1986.

That spring, while Bias awaited the NBA draft, Wake Forest won its third national golf title, rallying from 12 strokes down on the back nine at Bermuda Run in Winston-Salem. In mid-June Bias went second in the draft to the Boston Celtics. Four of the top nine picks, including UNC's Brad Daugherty at No. 1 and Washburn at No. 3, came from the ACC. "Len would have been a star," Boston general manager Arnold "Red" Auerbach said later. "He was highly competitive. He could shoot and rebound and run."

Bias, an instant millionaire, returned to his College Park apartment and free-based cocaine, something he had done previously. This time Bias went into cardiac arrest and, despite resuscitation efforts by Terry Long, a teammate and friend, died June 19, 1986, at 8:50 a.m.

Drug problems were commonplace in society and sports. The example of Bias' death, occurring on the doorstep of the nation's capital, spurred a concerted anti-drug campaign that swept the country. "The Len Bias death was a tremendous shock to the athletic community," said William Friday, retired president of the University of North Carolina system. "It is a supreme tragedy that he had to die to have the impact he did."

Tragedy mixed with outrage, though, when it was revealed Bias was 21 credits short of graduation after four years at Maryland. "Len was under an incredible pressure that was totally inconsistent with studying and finishing his degree," athletics director Dick Dull said of stardom's demands.

Further investigation found four others on the 11-man basketball squad had flunked out during the spring semester. A second straight academic advisor quit, citing an emphasis on eligibility and not education. The average SAT scores for Lefty Driesell's recruits over the previous six

BELOW
Maryland's Len Bias (left) guards UNC's Steve Bucknall. Bias was a two-time ACC player of the year. Bias died of drug-induced cardiac arrest before he could realize his dream of playing professional basketball.

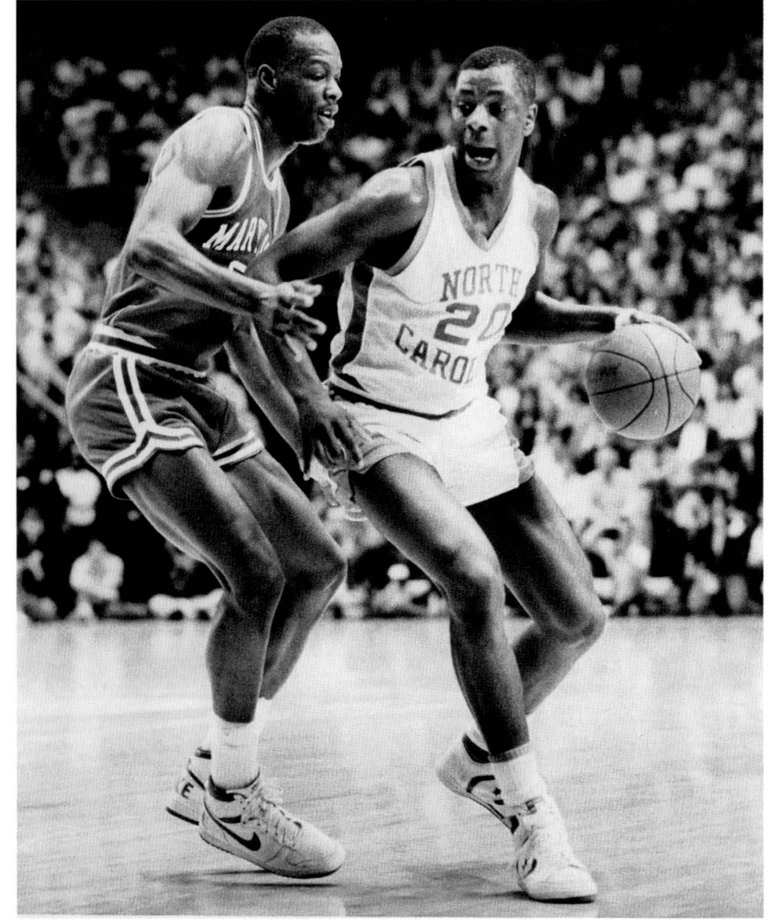

years were 100 points lower than for football and 338 below the 1985 average for all UM freshmen.

"For decades, athletics dominated this university," said Allen Schwait, head of the school's Board of Regents. "Now we're interested in a better balance."

Driesell insisted his program was "wonderful" and "beautiful" and "clean," while Dull decried a mixed message asking for "an athletic department on the scale of Oklahoma or Texas, while maintaining the academic prestige on a level close to Harvard or Yale."

Soon Driesell and Dull were gone. Players transferred. Credibility besmirched, the academic community struck back at sports. "It was horrible, but I'm a Maryland grad so I stayed," said Chris Weller, the women's basketball coach. "It was very difficult. It was completely, unfairly difficult. ... We got hammered in recruiting. We never got completely back to the powerful position of recruiting that we had before that."

The travails affected football as well. Maryland fell from first to fifth, its worst ACC finish in 15 years. The Terrapins went 5-5-1, their only non-winning record under Bobby Ross, who resigned and took an assistant's job with the NFL's Buffalo Bills.

Clemson immediately filled the void at the top in ACC football, starting a run of three consecutive titles. And run it was — the Tigers had the league's best rushing attack six times in seven seasons from 1986-92. They also led in scoring defense and rushing defense for most of those years.

The power game enabled Clemson's Terrence Flagler, a 6-1 All-ACC tailback, to pace the ACC with 13 touchdowns and 78 points in 1986. An 8-2-2 season was capped by a Gator Bowl appearance, a 27-21 victory over Stanford.

The league's leading ground gainer was the other All-ACC running back, North Carolina's Derrick Fenner (1,372 yards), one of seven different Tar Heels to lead in rushing from 1970 through 1991. UNC finished tied for second, concluding the year at 7-5 after losing 30-21 to Arizona in the Aloha Bowl.

N.C. State was 8-3-1, the only other ACC squad with a winning overall record in 1986. First-year coach Dick Sheridan directed the Wolfpack to more victories

LEFT
Dick Sheridan (left) came to N.C. State in 1986 and immediately turned around Wolfpack football. Sheridan coached until 1992, when he resigned for health considerations. His teams went 52-29-3 and lost to rival North Carolina just once.

than in the previous three seasons combined and was voted '86 ACC coach of the year. Quarterback Erik Kramer was player of the year. The reward for the Wolfpack was its first postseason appearance since 1978, resulting in a 25-24 loss to Virginia Tech, coached by Bill Dooley, in the Peach Bowl.

N.C. State fell off the pace in football in 1987, as did Maryland with Joe Krivak at the helm. Both were 4-7. Maryland's Krivak was one of four new coaches in the league, unusual turnover that immediately produced impressive results at Duke and Wake Forest.

Spurrier, Duke's former offensive coordinator, returned to replace Steve Sloan as head coach and installed a wide-open, pass-oriented attack. The Blue Devils promptly led the ACC in total offense, scoring offense (27.4 points per game) and passing offense. Quarterback Steve Slayden was the league's total offense leader with 269.8 yards per game.

BELOW
The Perry brothers, William on the left and Michael Dean on the right, made life tough for opposing quarterbacks and ball carriers. William set the school record in 1984 with 25 career quarterback sacks, and then his brother broke it in 1987 with 28. Michael Dean also broke his brother's ACC record for tackles for loss with 61, edging William by one.

The '87 coach of the year was Dooley, who returned to the ACC after nearly a decade at Virginia Tech. He promptly lifted Wake Forest to a 7-4 record, its best in eight years. "I think he mellowed a lot with time," said Swofford, who played for Dooley at North Carolina almost two decades earlier, "and I think he changed with the times in terms of player relations and so forth."

What didn't change, according to Rice, the AD at Chapel Hill for much of Dooley's first ACC tour of duty, was the coach's emphasis. "Bill Dooley was a very sound, basic, fundamental football coach, and his teams displayed that," said Rice, himself an ex-football coach.

Virginia finished second. The Cavaliers recovered from their 1986 stumble to go 8-4 overall, capped by a 22-16 triumph over Brigham Young in the All-American Bowl.

The champion, again, was Clemson. The Tiger defense dominated, allowing 80 yards per game on the ground, fewest in the league since 1955. Thus it was no surprise that, for the second time in four seasons, a Clemson defender was ACC player of the year. Actually, for the second time in four seasons the award went to a member of the same family, in this case tackle Michael Dean Perry, at 6-2 and 275 pounds truly the baby brother of massive William Perry, the '84 player of the year.

The honor accorded Michael Dean Perry gave 10-2 Clemson a double unmatched before or since at the school. Horace Grant was earlier chosen ACC player of the year in basketball, a unique achievement by a Tiger. Grant was the first player since Wake's Rod Griffin in 1978 to lead the league in scoring (21.0) and rebounding (9.6) in the same season.

In fact, 1987 was a very good year for Clemson athletics. The school won a second national title in men's soccer under coach I.M. Ibrahim. Men's basketball earned 25 victories, a new high, as was a No. 13 ranking, the school's first appearance in a final top 20. The strong showing by the basketball squad, second in the league at 10-4, earned Cliff Ellis the 1987 ACC coach of the year award.

The Tigers suffered only six basketball losses. None stung more than their defeat in the quarterfinals of the '87 ACC Tournament, the result of a fired-up underdog and a restless Capital Centre crowd.

Clemson, the No. 2 seed, held a commanding 17-point lead over Wake Forest when the public address announcer exhorted somnolent spectators to make noise, promising a light show keyed to a sound meter. Quickly, a "Go to hell, Carolina!" chant filled the arena; the Tar Heels had finished the season 14-0 for the second time in four years. At the very instant the crowd awakened Wake's 5-4 guard Tyrone Bogues, the smallest player in ACC history and one of the quickest, converted a steal for a layup. Bogues, All-ACC in 1987, ranks fourth in career steals (275) in the roughly quarter-century the ACC has kept the statistic, fifth in assists (781).

Bogues' steal and spectators' zeal sparked the Deacons, who halved their deficit within two minutes. Wake eventually came away with a stunning 69-62 win, solace for a 2-12 ACC regular season. That was two more wins than Maryland earned under new coach Bob Wade. The 1987 Terrapins joined Clemson in 1954 and '55, Georgia Tech in '81 and Wake Forest in '86 as the only teams to be shut out for an entire ACC season.

Wade, the first African-American head coach in a major ACC sport, was hired directly from Dunbar High School in Baltimore, where he had coached Wake's Bogues, among others. "I don't look at this as a color situation," he said. "It's just an

BELOW

Thanks to performers such as 1987 ACC player of the year Horace Grant (left), coach Cliff Ellis was able to make Tiger basketball roar.

opportunity to coach at the college level."

Wade would last three years and leave the school primed for NCAA probation.

Great drama attended that 1987 ACC Tournament. Both semifinals went to double overtime as first North Carolina ousted Virginia 84-82 and then N.C. State outlasted the undaunted Deacons, 77-73. That was the second straight overtime game for the sixth-seeded Wolfpack, which beat Duke 71-64 in its tournament opener.

N.C. State's Valvano long insisted that, given the ACC's strength, a breakeven record during any regular season would command an NCAA berth. But his '87 Wolfpack, compensating for the loss of Washburn, who went pro two years early, fell short at 6-8. An enduring value of the ACC Tournament came into play, as the automatic bid due the champion became N.C. State's avenue to the NCAAs.

Standing in the way was North Carolina, led by seniors Kenny Smith and Joe Wolf, both All-ACC, and a pair of highly touted underclassmen, sophomore guard Jeff Lebo and freshman big man J.R. Reid, the '87 ACC rookie of the year. Smith also took advantage of new rules that made a shot clock and 3-pointer permanent parts of the game. Only Clemson fired more threes per game than UNC, or was more accurate from that range.

The Heels finished 32-4, evoking harsh criticism when they lost to Syracuse in the East Region final, 79-75. Vinny Del Negro's MVP performance in the ACC Tournament added to Smith's woes. The junior guard, a reserve much of the season, hit the deciding free throws with 14 seconds left in a 68-67 N.C. State victory.

The win gave the Wolfpack its NCAA trip, one of six taken by ACC squads in 1987. Only UNC and Duke, eliminated in the Sweet 16 by Indiana, survived the first round.

Less than two months later, ACC commissioner Bob James died of stomach cancer after 16 years on the job. "Mr. James had that knack for bringing people together," noted Thompson, secretary to the ACC's first three commissioners. Under James' leadership the league had repaired the wounds of South Carolina's departure, improved its internal and national competitiveness, bolstered its television profile and overall revenues, added Georgia Tech and fostered enviable collegiality within its ranks.

Consistent with the ACC's family preferences, James was replaced by Gene Corrigan, a Duke graduate who had coached several sports at Virginia and served there as AD before taking a similar post at Notre Dame. Corrigan was a "real people person," said Thompson, noting his open-door policy extended to fielding

BELOW
Duke's Danny Ferry (35) was ACC player of the year in 1988 and '89. He led the Blue Devils to the Final Four both years. He also played on coach Mike Krzyzewski's first Final Four team in 1986. Ferry became the first player in ACC history to score 2,000 points, grab 1,000 rebounds and officially collect 500 assists.

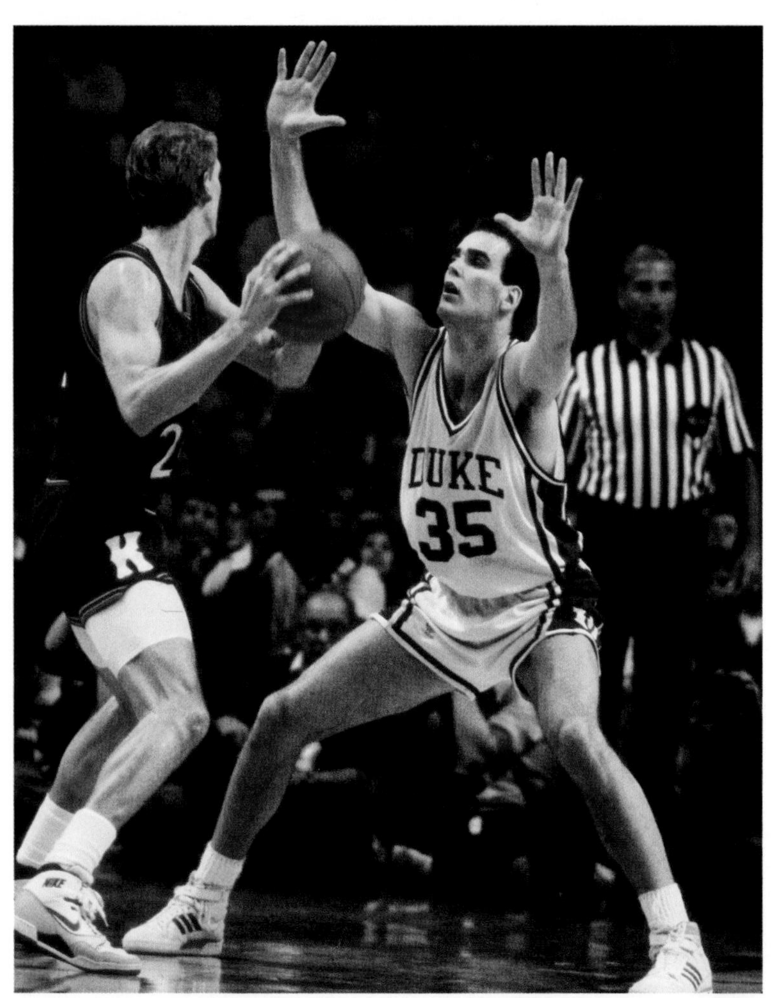

fans' gripes about officiating. "When I look back," Thompson said, "every man was the right man for the time that he was here."

Corrigan arrived in time to witness the men's basketball team at his alma mater embark on one of the most remarkable runs in NCAA history. Mike Krzyzewski's Blue Devils finished third during the ACC regular season, but went 28-7, had the league's 1988 player of the year in versatile big man Danny Ferry, ranked fifth nationally, won the ACC title and reached the Final Four. Kansas, the eventual champion, eliminated Duke, 66-59.

Duke would go to every Final Four from 1988 through 1992, a run that pales only compared to UCLA's hegemony more than a decade earlier. From 1986 through 1994, a span of nine seasons, the Blue Devils made seven Final Fours and four championship games and won a pair of NCAA titles. The program Vic Bubas once built into a national power was again a perennial contender, and then some.

Not that North Carolina disappeared. The enduringly efficient Tar Heels again led the ACC regular season race in 1988 and finished 27-7. They made the ACC Tournament final for the sixth time since 1981, losing 65-61 to Duke at Greensboro. Smith was voted ACC coach of the year.

UNC's J.R. Reid was the only ACC repre-

BELOW
Relentlessly supportive, frequently creative and occasionally cruel, Duke basketball fans, known as the "Cameron Crazies," have become a consistent sixth-man for the Blue Devils through the years.

BELOW
Duke wide receiver Clarkston Hines (left) and coach Steve Spurrier took the ACC by storm in 1989. Hines was a consensus All-American. He set numerous school and ACC records. He was the conference player of the year and won the McKevlin Award as the league's top athlete. The Blue Devils tied Virginia for first place in the conference standings at 6-1, finished 8-4 and played in their first bowl game since 1961. Spurrier's teams went 20-13-1 in his three seasons at Duke.

sentative on the third-place 1988 U.S. Olympic squad at Seoul, Korea. N.C. State's Kay Yow did even better, coaching the American women to a gold medal.

Come football season, Clemson was again on top. The 10-2 Tigers won their fifth title during an eight-year span and third in a row. They completed the '88 season with five straight victories, including a 13-6 Citrus Bowl win over Oklahoma. The Tigers finished ninth in the polls, the first top-10 finish for an ACC squad since Clemson last did it in 1982.

The Citrus appearance reflected a four-year deal engineered by Corrigan, the new commissioner, that assured the ACC champion a postseason berth. "When I got there, we had nowhere for our champion to go," Corrigan said. "We would just hope for somebody to pick us up."

Virginia again came in second in football and was 7-4 overall, but stayed home. Third-place N.C. State, 8-4, went to the Peach Bowl and beat Iowa, 28-23. The 1988 Wolfpack paced the league in total defense (264.3 yards) and rushing defense and placed four players on the All-ACC defensive squad led by tackle Ray Agnew and strong safety Jesse Campbell.

On the other side of the ball, Duke's record-setting offense lifted the Blue Devils to a 7-3-1 finish, best at the school since 1962, when Bill Murray was winning the last of three straight ACC titles. The Devils

led the ACC in total offense, their passing alone producing 351.6 yards per game, best in the conference until 2000. Spurrier, architect of that offense, was named 1988 ACC coach of the year, and Anthony Dilweg, Duke's quarterback, was player of the year.

The Blue Devils again captured both player of the year awards in calendar year 1989 — Ferry repeated in basketball and Clarkston Hines, a 6-1 receiver, was the pick in football. The 6-10 Ferry also set an ACC single-game mark with 58 points in a win at Miami, with only two of his baskets from 3-point range.

Spurrier repeated as coach of the year as his 1989 team tied Virginia for first, the Blue Devils' only taste of a football title since 1962. Spurrier, at 20-13-1 over three years, has the sole winning career mark achieved at Duke since Murray retired in 1965.

The '89 basketball coach of the year was Valvano, a first for him. N.C. State was 22-9 and finished alone atop the ACC standings, which last happened in 1974. Still, 1989 was not a vintage season for Valvano.

His top-seeded squad became the first to lose to No. 8 in the ACC Tournament, dropping an embarrassingly decisive 71-49 verdict to Maryland. Wade collapsed outside the locker room after the game and was rushed to a hospital. The exhausted coach was not at Atlanta's Omni the next

BELOW
Quarterback Shawn Moore (12) directed Virginia to a share of its first ACC championship in 1989. He guided the Cavaliers to 23 victories in his last 28 career starts. He became the first ACC quarterback to lead the nation in pass efficiency and led Virginia to a berth in the Sugar Bowl and a brief No. 1 ranking in the nation. Moore finished fourth in the balloting for the Heisman Trophy.

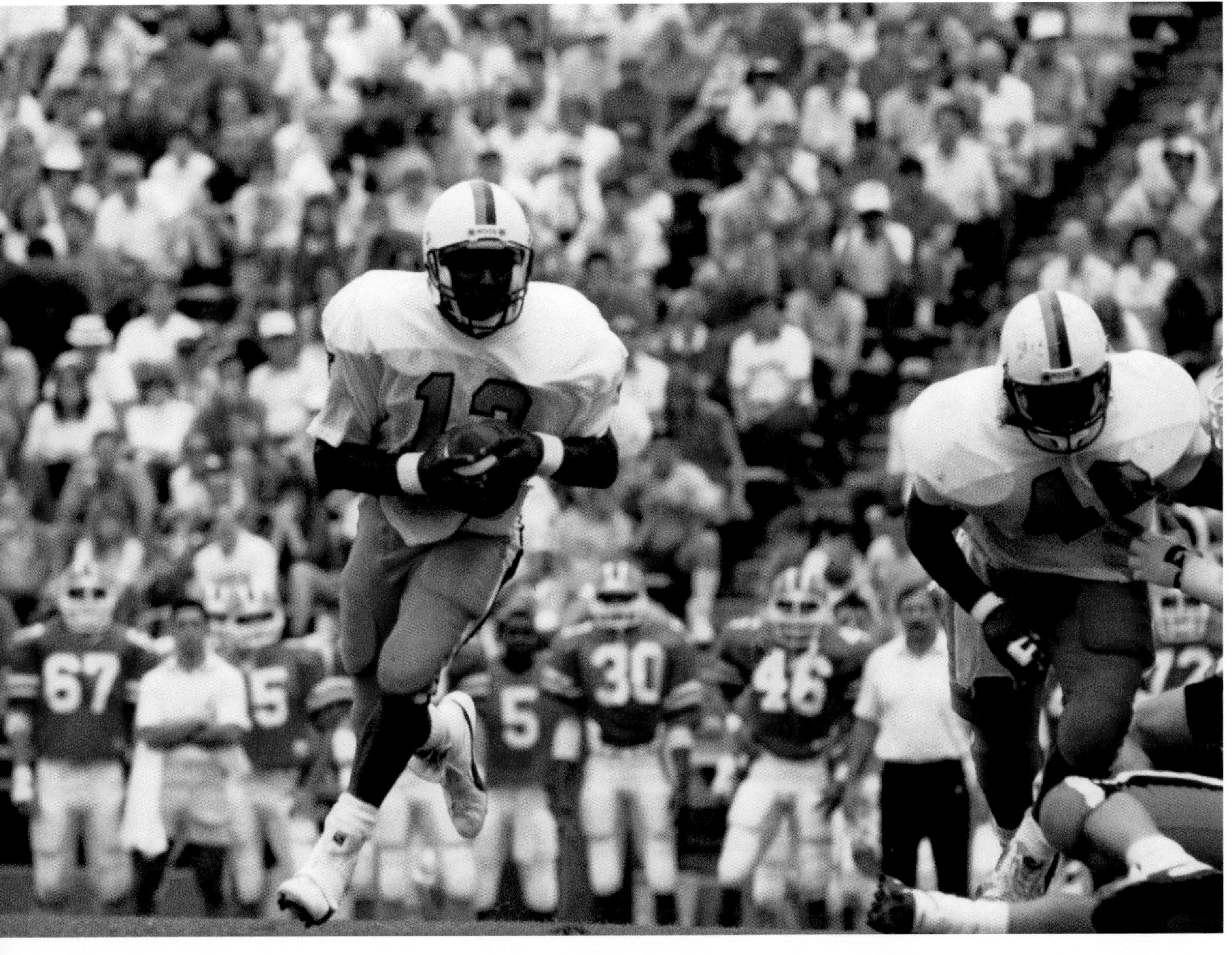

BELOW
Georgia Tech's Riccardo Ingram excelled in two sports. He is a member of the ACC's 50th anniversary baseball team and was an All-American outfielder and the ACC player of the year in baseball in 1987. He also started at safety for the football team and made All-ACC in that sport in 1986. He is flanked by the McKevlin Award, which he won as the ACC's top overall athlete in 1987.

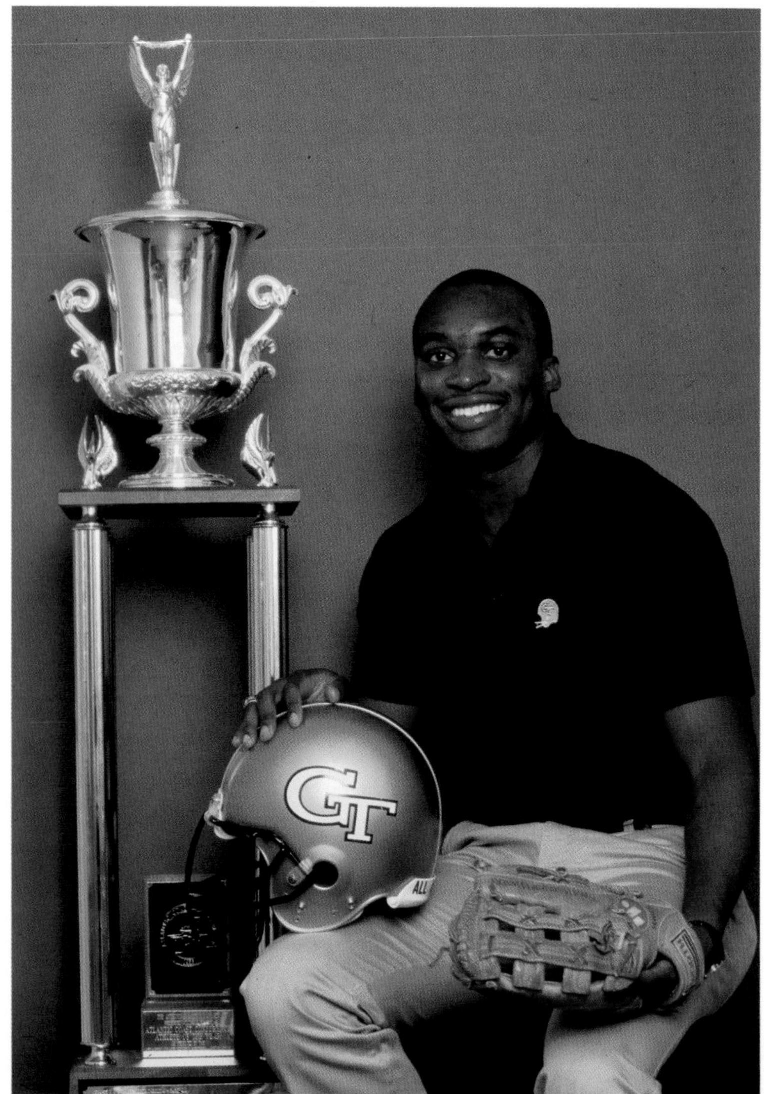

day as UNC routed his final UM team. North Carolina beat Duke 77-74 in the ACC Tournament final, a game notable for a mid-court shouting match between Smith and Krzyzewski.

Six ACC teams went to the NCAA Tournament. Four reached the Sweet 16. Among them was N.C. State, eliminated by Georgetown, the game's pivotal call one for which the official later apologized. Michigan, the eventual champ, beat UNC in the regional semifinals, then knocked off Virginia. Duke again reached the Final Four, losing this time to Seton Hall, 95-78.

N.C. State's on-court miseries were overshadowed by another controversy that engulfed the program. This time the storm was caused by a book, Peter Golenback's *Personal Fouls*, subtitled *The Broken Promises and Shattered Dreams of Big Money Basketball at Jim Valvano's North Carolina State.*

Whatever the merits of a sloppily researched book, it spurred investigations by the national and local media, the NCAA and the University of North Carolina system. When the smoke cleared, the school was on NCAA probation for relatively minor infractions. Valvano was first stripped of his dual role as coach and athletics director and then paid handsomely to leave in the spring of 1990. In 1991 his book appeared, entitled *They Gave Me A Lifetime Contract, And Then They Declared Me Dead.*

A report to the university system's Board of Governors found "clear" evidence "that the academic processes and standards of North Carolina State University have been misused in a number of instances to benefit some individual basketball players." Valvano's program brought in many players with SATs below 700. Players pursued courses of study designed to retain eligibility rather to achieve a degree; academic suspensions were high, and graduation rates only 32 percent.

"Historically, it has been, it is, and it will continue to be a constant struggle to maintain academic integrity," stated the August 1989 report. "Athletics and academic (sic) are in <u>tension</u> by the nature of their time demands, but athletics and academics cannot be allowed to be in <u>conflict</u> in a great university."

Smith commented after Valvano was ousted: "He was hired by Willis Casey to win basketball games, and he did that pretty well.

They never said to graduate players."

The 1989 basketball season ended on a more pleasant note for the ACC's other afflicted athletic department. Maryland's women were 29-3 and ranked fifth, best by an ACC club since the Terrapins of 1982. As with its predecessors, the '89 squad finished first during the regular season, won the ACC Tournament and reached the Final Four. Vicky Bullett, one of three women whose jerseys are retired at Maryland, was named the league's player of the year. Weller was coach of the year.

"I think that was one of the best teams I had," Weller said of her third Final Four squad, which lost to Tennessee, 77-65. "Look at it. I keep telling people, if I could coach we could have won a national championship."

There were no 1989 championships for ACC football teams, either. But the league was bursting with talent, promise and success.

Seven of the eight head coaches won ACC coach of the year honors at some point during their careers. Two league squads reached double digits in wins, a first since 1981, as Virginia was 10-3 and Clemson 10-2. Five teams won at least seven games, including Georgia Tech, 4-3 in the ACC after posting consecutive winless league marks. For only the second time in history four ACC teams went to bowls — with Clemson the sole winner, 27-7 over West Virginia in the Gator.

Virginia tied Duke for first at 6-1 and went to its third bowl under George Welsh, losing 31-21 to Illinois in the renamed Florida Citrus Bowl. Duke was 8-4 after losing 49-21 to Texas Tech in the All-American Bowl, the Blue Devils' first postseason appearance since January 1961.

Duke started the season 1-3 and began its turnaround with a 21-17 home victory over seventh-ranked Clemson. For the third straight year the Blue Devils had a different quarterback, and for the third straight year wide receiver Clarkston Hines paced the ACC in receiving yards. The All-American remains the only player to lead the ACC in receptions, or to account for more than 1,000 passing yards, in three straight seasons. His 3,318 career receiving yards were the league standard until 1998. His 38 touchdown catches remain the ACC record and were a national best at the time.

BELOW
Jim Valvano was known for his sense of humor as much as for his ability to coach winning basketball teams. He also wrote a cookbook during his time at N.C. State.

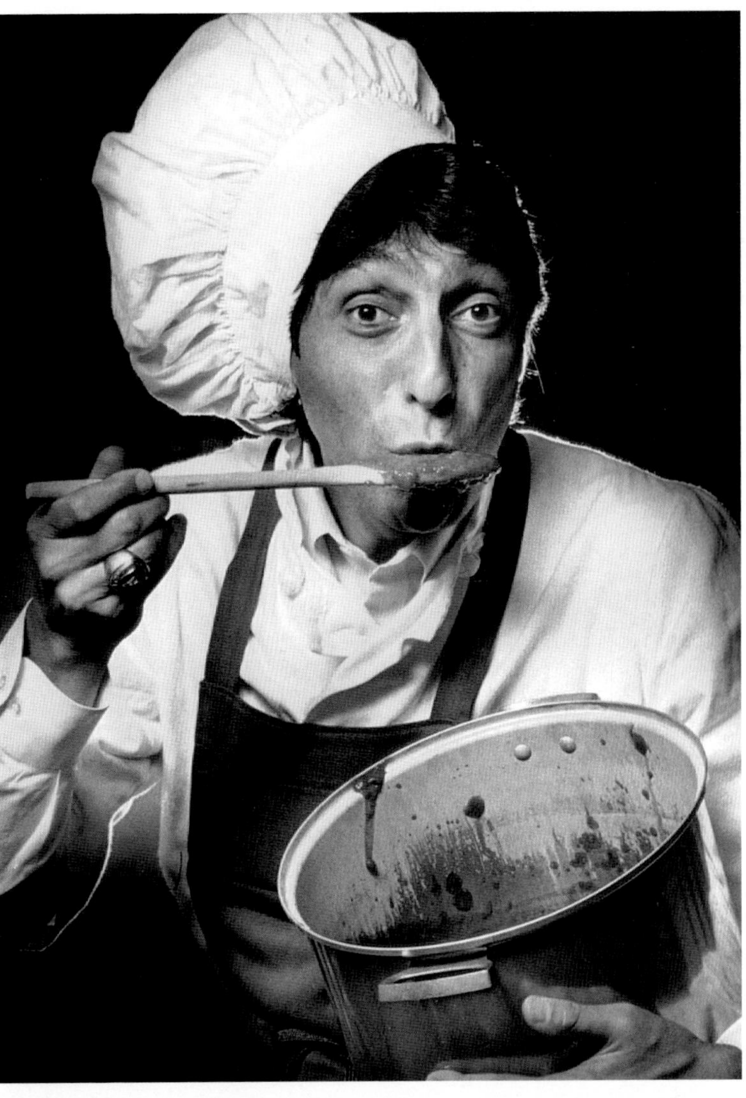

Hines caught three scoring passes from quarterback Dave Brown in the '89 season finale, a 41-0 shellacking of North Carolina, where second-year coach Mack Brown completed his second consecutive 1-10 season.

The Blue Devils' first shutout of UNC in 34 years saw them score on five of their first seven possessions. The large margin didn't prevent Spurrier, the former Heisman winner at Florida, from calling for a reverse, a fleaflicker and a pass from Duke's own end zone in the final five minutes. Tight end Dave Colonna kicked the final extra point.

"Without so much as pointing a finger, Duke taunted and teased UNC to no end," wrote Ron Morris in the *Durham Morning Herald.* Spurrier found something better than tossing words or waving digits. Following the game, in a move sure to charm Duke's archrival, he had the Blue Devils pose for a quick photograph in front of the Kenan Stadium scoreboard. Then, after the squad went to the locker room, it returned to the field and posed carefully for another photo opportunity. ✯

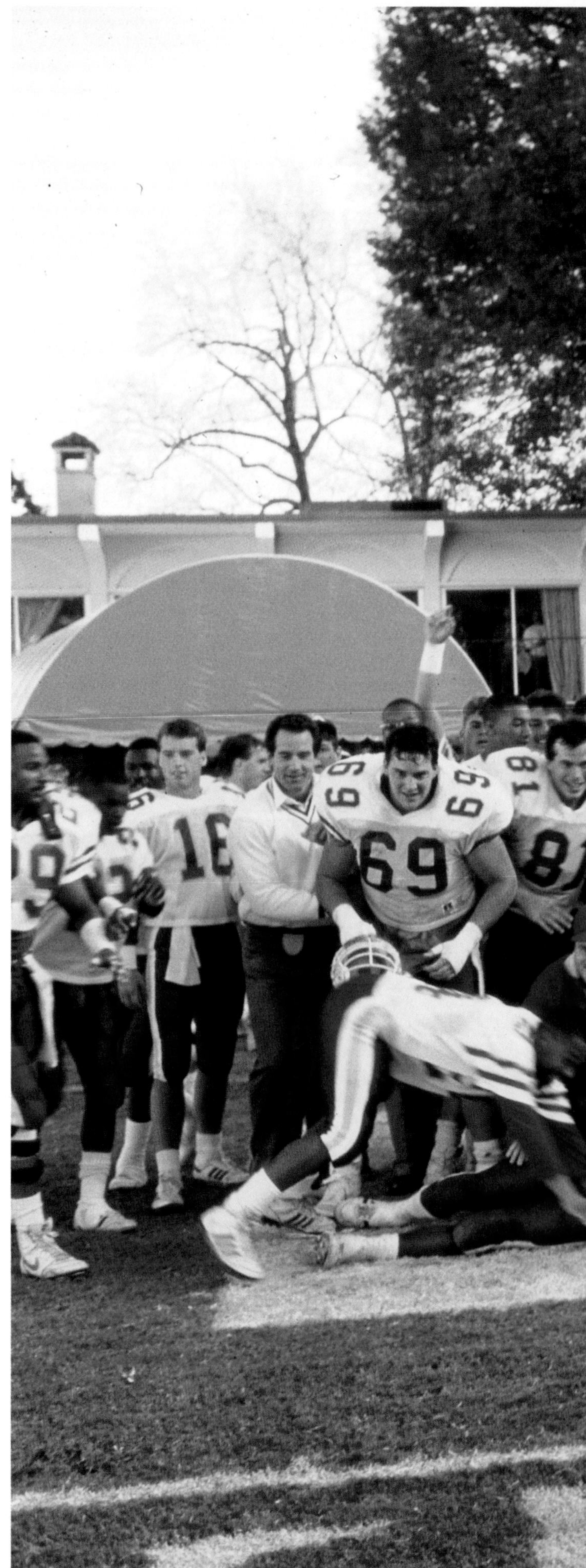

RIGHT
The Duke football team poses beneath the scoreboard at Kenan Stadium in Chapel Hill after defeating North Carolina 41-0 in 1989. Duke ended the regular season that day with seven straight victories and a share of the ACC championship. Quarterback Dave Brown threw for a school-record 479 yards in the game.

CAROLINA
0:00
GUEST
0
41
DOWN
TO GO
BALL ON
QTR
GO TAR HEELS
DUKE
DUKE

EVERY
SEMINOLE'S
PERSONAL
NIGHTMARE
MIRACLE

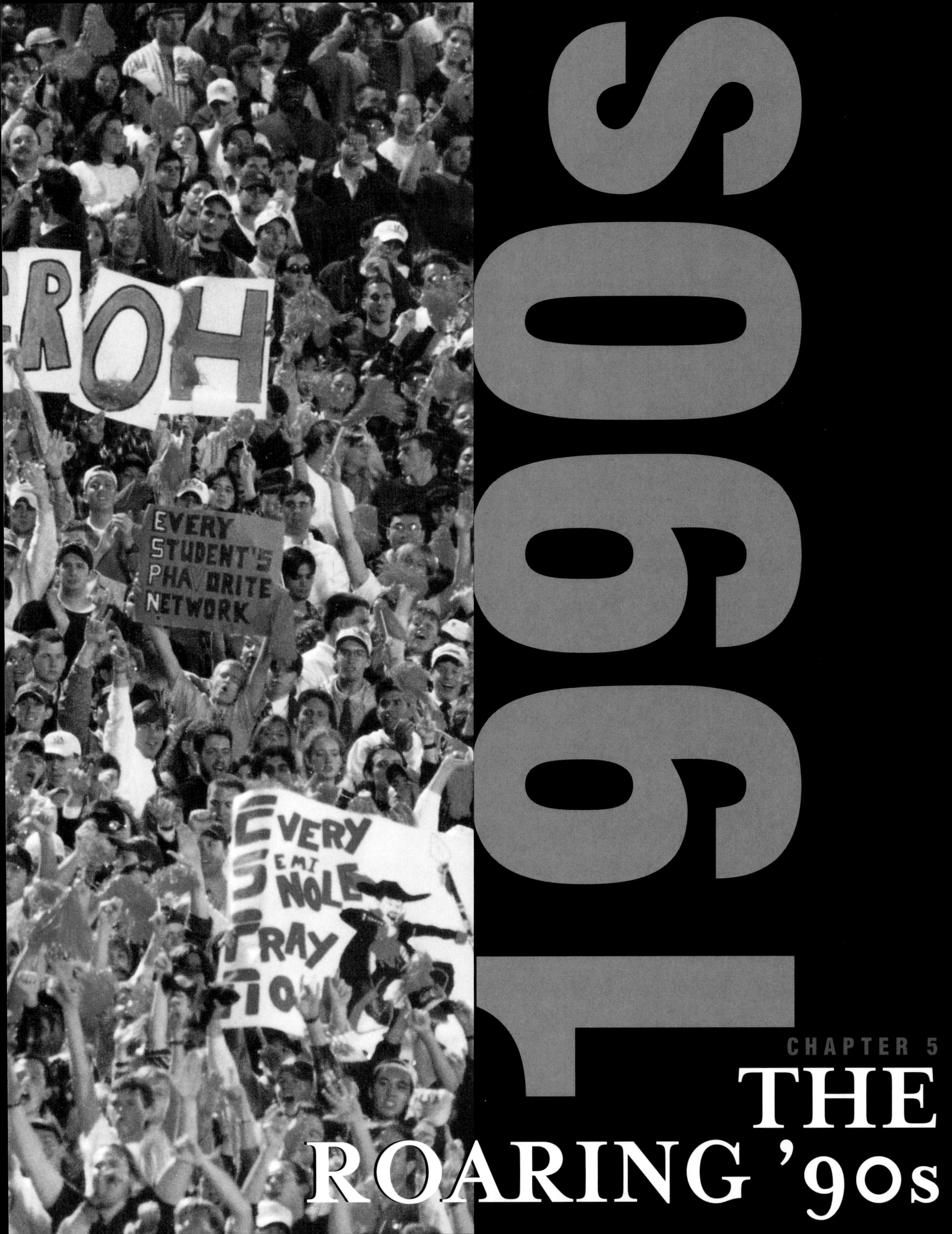

CHAPTER 5

THE ROARING '90s

The 1990s ended as they began, with an undefeated ACC squad capturing a national football title and ACC men's and women's basketball teams competing in NCAA Tournament championship games. This was not only stunningly symmetrical, but characteristic. During the course of the decade, the ACC won four national titles in basketball, three football championships, 17 Final Four berths shared among men and women, a leadership role in injecting order into football's postseason chaos and enough championships in men's and women's Olympic sports to be the envy of any conference.

The ACC's achievements during the '90s ratified its position at the forefront of college athletics. Key to that prosperity at a time expansion fever gripped college sports was the addition of Florida State, a move rightly calculated to improve the ACC's football credibility.

The decade also witnessed a surge in efforts to upgrade facilities, neatly bracketed by the debut of large new off-campus arenas for two basketball programs. The last was N.C. State's Entertainment and Sports Arena (later named the RBC Center), a 19,722-seat facility that cost in excess of $158 million and opened on Nov. 19, 1999. The first was Wake Forest's 14,500-seat Joel Coliseum, opened 10 years earlier almost to the day.

The Demon Deacons further changed the program's tenor to open the 1989-90 season by hiring a new head coach, Dave Odom. He was an assistant to Virginia's Terry Holland for the previous seven seasons, a former Wake assistant under Carl Tacy and briefly head coach at East Carolina.

Odom was talkative, thoughtful, conservative and adaptable. He inherited a program coming off four straight losing seasons and extended the dubious run with a last-place ACC finish in 1990. But Wake would not suffer another losing record during Odom's 12-year tenure. Instead the Deacons embarked in 1991 on a run of seven consecutive trips to the NCAA Tournament, easily the best streak in school history. By mid-decade, the Deacons were atop the ACC for the first time in more than 30 years, boasting one of the great players ever in the conference.

The league's other basketball coaching change in 1989-90 occurred at College Park, Md., as alumnus Gary Williams took over a program still reeling from Len Bias' death four seasons earlier. The '90 Terrapins were picked to finish last in the ACC. Instead they swept North Carolina for the first time in a decade, scored more points than any previous Maryland squad and went 19-14.

Then the NCAA lowered the boom.

Maryland got hit with a three-year probation, including a reduction in scholarships and bans on postseason and television participation, because of 27 rules violations under Bob Wade, Williams' predecessor. The punishment was intensified by Wade's attempts to deceive NCAA investigators, and to encourage subordinates to do likewise. "I knew even when I came to Maryland that there were some things that were going to have to be done," said Williams, former head coach at American, Boston College and Ohio State. "I didn't know the severity of the situation."

The Terrapins settled for an appearance in the NIT, an event Maryland spurned twice in happier days. By the summer of 1990, Lew Perkins, Maryland's athletics director, was gone, the league had voted to exclude the TV-less Terps from the '91 ACC Tournament, and the athletic department faced a deficit that elicited talk of eliminating some sports.

Clemson, too, was rocked by NCAA difficulties, again involving coach Danny Ford's football program. Amidst an investigation, Ford abruptly resigned in January 1990, taking with him a handsome buyout and a 96-29-4 career record, including 6-2 in bowl games. Into the breach sprang Clemson basketball, reaching unprecedented heights in coach Cliff Ellis' sixth season. "The basketball program literally lifted the smoke away from Clemson," Ellis said proudly.

For the first and only time in ACC history, the Tigers finished alone atop the league standings. When they beat Duke — securing their 10th victory and with it first place — fans happily rushed the court at Littlejohn Coliseum. Clemson went 26-9, most wins ever at the school. Big men Elden Campbell and Dale Davis, the latter being the best offensive rebounder in modern ACC play, were voted first-team All-ACC, the only Clemson pair so honored. "Most people think the job we've done has been phenomenal," said Ellis, the 1990 ACC coach of the year. "From the commissioner's office to our athletic director, they'll tell you: This is the toughest job in the league." When the Tigers defeated Wake in the opening round of the '90 ACC Tournament, their first win in the event since '80, Ellis declared, "Tradition's been kicked in the butt again."

Ellis even attributed the relatively low seeds accorded ACC teams in the '90 NCAAs to Clemson's modest basketball tradition. "People were saying, 'Clemson wins the league; it's a down year.'"

Certainly North Carolina experienced a down year by its standards. After finishing tied for third with Georgia Tech, the 1990 Tar Heels lost their ACC Tournament opener against Virginia and entered NCAA play with 19 wins. That endangered their record streak of 20-win seasons and threatened to leave them with their fewest victories in two decades. The Tar Heels already had 12 losses, most since 1964.

Tellingly, for the only time until 2002, no Tar Heel made first- or second-team All-ACC. Critics said the game had passed by Dean Smith, who last directed a squad to the Final Four in 1982. They got their response when Smith took UNC to the Sweet 16 and to 21 victories, knocking off top-seed Oklahoma in the process on a late basket by small forward Rick Fox.

Clemson, too, reached the Sweet 16, only to lose 71-70 to Connecticut on a perhaps-too-late basket by guard Tate George after the Tigers failed to secure the win at the foul line. The '90 season proved the high-water mark of Ellis' 10-year stay (1985-94) at the Clemson helm.

Only Virginia among five ACC entrants failed to advance at least to an NCAA

BELOW
Clemson's Dale Davis (left) and Cliff Ellis hold the trophy they earned by finishing atop the 1990 regular-season basketball standings. The Tigers went 10-4 in the ACC, 22-9 overall and made it to the round of 16 in the NCAA Tournament. Ellis was voted coach of the year in the conference. Davis led the league in field goal percentage for two seasons of his career and in rebounding for three consecutive years.

RIGHT
Virginia women's basketball coach Debbie Ryan (right) turned the Cavaliers into a national power in the early 1990s. UVa finished first in the ACC from 1991-96. Virginia made three consecutive appearances in the Final Four from 1990-92.

Tournament regional semifinal. Behind forward Bryant Stith, the previous season's ACC rookie of the year, the Cavaliers lasted two rounds in Terry Holland's final outing before resigning. He soon became director of athletics at Davidson, his alma mater. (The other third-place team was N.C. State, on probation in Jim Valvano's last season.)

Ultimately, though, the 1990 NCAA Tournament belonged to Georgia Tech and Duke on the men's side, and to Virginia on the women's.

Debbie Ryan's Cavaliers were emerging as the premier ACC women's program. Led by sophomores Dawn Staley and Tammi Reiss, Virginia finished second to N.C. State in 1990. Staley went on to win ACC player of the year awards in 1991 and '92 before having her jersey retired. UVa finished in first place each year from 1991 through 1996, losing a total of eight ACC regular-season games during those six years. The Cavs also made three straight Final Four appearances from 1990 through 1992, a run no ACC women's program has duplicated.

The 1990 Virginia squad won the women's ACC Tournament, topping N.C. State and player of the year Andrea Stinson in overtime, 67-64. Ranked No. 12 in the last regular-season poll, the Cavaliers clinched a Final Four berth with an overtime upset of Tennessee, the defending champ. Then Stanford eliminated Virginia 75-66 in the national semifinals.

When it came to pinnacle years, though, no one could touch Georgia Tech in 1990.

Bobby Cremins' Yellow Jackets played an up-tempo, free-wheeling style fueled by New Yorker Kenny Anderson's ball-handling and flair, Brian Oliver's leadership and toughness and Dennis Scott's scoring and dash. The so-called "Lethal Weapon

III" accounted for 79 percent of Tech's scoring and became the first trio of 20-point scorers on one ACC team.

The Jackets finished 28-7, most victories by a Tech squad. Scott led the ACC in scoring with a 27.7-point average, highest in 15 years, and was voted 1990 ACC player of the year. He's the only winner so far from Georgia Tech. Anderson was '90 rookie of the year and the second freshman, after Clemson's Skip Wise in 1975, voted first-team All-ACC. Oliver was MVP of the 1990 ACC Tournament.

"They're fun to watch play, unless you have to be on the other sideline," said Holland after Tech beat Virginia 70-61 in the tournament final. That remains the only ACC title game in which no North Carolina member was involved.

Cremins, whom Anderson described as "a little bit crazy at times," visibly enjoyed the ride. So did his players. "I just wish we could bottle it and save it," Oliver said of the fun as Cremins guided his thin squad to the school's only Final Four appearance to date.

The ride ended with a 90-81 defeat by the University of Nevada-Las Vegas (UNLV) after 17 straight non-conference wins. Then the Runnin' Rebels routed Duke 103-73 for the championship, the largest winning margin in any final.

Duke's Final Four appearance was its fourth in five years. Duke and Georgia Tech gave the ACC half the berths in the Final Four, a feat it duplicated in 1981 and later in 1991 and 2001.

The Blue Devils, as the Yellow Jackets, were paced by a freshman point guard from the New York area. Bobby Hurley would finish his career with more assists than any modern player (1,076). But he would also finish as the ACC's unofficial career leader in turnovers (534), testament to high-octane daring and wildness that only time and experience would tame.

BELOW
Georgia Tech's Dennis Scott (left), Kenny Anderson (center) and Brian Oliver were known as "Lethal Weapon III." They captured the hearts of fans around the conference with their fast-paced and skilled play as they made their way to the 1990 Final Four. Scott was named the ACC player of the year, Anderson the rookie of the year. Oliver was not as highly decorated, but served as the leader for a team that won the ACC Tournament and finished 28-7, the most victories in school history.

The Blue Devil scoring leaders were All-ACC selections, senior guard Phil Henderson and sophomore forward Christian Laettner, a lineal descendent of versatile big men Mark Alarie and Danny Ferry. The 6-11 Laettner, a fierce and uncompromising competitor, began cementing a reputation for clutch plays in the '90 East Region final. His leaning shot in overtime on a play called "Special" was the difference in a 79-78 overtime win over UConn.

Then came a second Krzyzewski trip to the title game (1986 was the first), and the decisive UNLV loss that left the Duke coach "in awe" of how well Jerry Tarkanian's team played. Some now cast Krzyzewski — as UNC's Smith before him — as a choke artist unable to win the big one.

ACC leaders had more fundamental concerns as the winter ended. In January, Penn State announced it would join the Big Ten. In February, Notre Dame cut its own television deal, undermining the viability of the College Football Association's 65-school national package that included the ACC. Suddenly talk of realignments and mega-conferences surged. Independents scrambled to forge alliances. Revenue sources for Division I-A football programs were jeopardized.

"We're not going to expand," Gene Corrigan, the ACC commissioner, said on the eve of the 1990 Final Four. "It would be the most shocking thing in the world to me if we did. It's not that we're not expanding because we don't like somebody. We're not expanding because eight is the right number for a conference."

Behind the scenes, though, expansion picked up steam. The Big East inquired about forming a football-only alliance between the ACC and three of its Division I-A members — Pittsburgh, Syracuse and Boston College. The two leagues already had initiated an "ACC-Big East Challenge" in basketball during the 1989-90 season. Corrigan found "I just couldn't sell it" when the football deal was proposed to conference leaders.

So when the commissioner ventured a secret-ballot vote of ACC athletics directors on adding either Syracuse or Florida State as full members, he didn't expect the 4-4 vote. "It shocked me," he said. "They were shocked."

Syracuse already belonged to the Big East, and word came it needed to be wooed. Florida State, a football independent, had a different response, according to Corrigan. "God, we were praying for something like this," he recalled the reaction of Bob Goin, FSU's athletics director, when the possibility of joining the ACC was mentioned.

Southeastern Conference officials held discussions with Florida State, which had repeatedly requested membership and been rejected. Homer Rice, Georgia Tech's athletics director, was quoted that summer saying his school should also be receptive to SEC overtures. "I think all of our people are in line with the ACC, but if something came along, you'd have to listen," he told the *Atlanta Journal-Constitution*. Football coach Bobby Ross was similarly receptive. Cremins and, more important, Tech President John P. Crecine, were not. "We are in the ACC to stay," Crecine said.

1990

3.31.90
Georgia Tech loses 90-81 to Nevada-Las Vegas in the Yellow Jackets' only Final Four appearance

9.8.90
Virginia beats Clemson 20-7, ending a 29-game losing streak against the Tigers that was the longest in NCAA Division I-A football

9.15.90
Florida State admitted to ACC as ninth member

11.3.90
Georgia Tech tops No.1 Virginia 41-38 in football

"We've had schools in some trouble lately, but I still feel extremely good about the overall health of the conference and its commitment to academics. We are in union with first-rate academic schools."

ACC leaders insisted more than money was at stake as they contemplated expansion. "The primary concern has to be compatibility if we expand," Todd Turner, N.C. State's athletics director, told Chip Alexander of Raleigh's *The News & Observer*. "A new school would have to embrace the same academic and athletic philosophies that the ACC always has stood for." Duke AD Tom Butters, initially opposed to expansion, cautioned against upsetting a dynamic in which "the ACC has been as much of a family as it has been a conference."

According to Tom Mickle, then an assistant ACC commissioner, "the number-one item" in judging a prospective new member "was a commitment from prospective institutions to the NCAA reform package, i.e., shorter hours of practice for student-athletes, no athletic dorms, reduced schedules, etc." But "the opportunity to improve football," the "potential to enhance post-season revenue" and the market to be gained were also prime considerations. By those measures, Mickle said, it was "quite obvious" after several extended meetings that Florida State was "an ideal match."

Miami, also under consideration, fell out of the picture and joined the Big East. FSU, after an initial vote of 4-2-2, got the necessary support to be invited into the ACC and became a member September 15, 1990.

Football coaches, many of whom agreed with Wake's Bill Dooley that expansion was "inevitable," were happy. "They raised the level by far; they raised the bar," Virginia coach George Welsh said of a Florida State program that finished in the top five in the Associated Press poll every year from 1987 through 2000. "I knew they were very good. I was for them coming into the league."

Leaders such as Corrigan, keen on keeping the ACC competitive in football and finances, were pleased. "That's a whole state with seven major markets in it," he said of Florida, which had double the population of any state in the ACC region and twice the growth rate. "Our whole thing was: This has so much value for us down the road."

That value was manifest within a year as Corrigan helped engineer an alliance binding the ACC, Big East, Notre Dame and four New Year's Day bowls (excluding the Rose) in an arrangement designed to produce a clear champion as often as possible.

"Having Florida State with us without question gave us a place at the table," said John Swofford, then the AD at North Carolina and later ACC commissioner. "Would we have still been there without Florida State? Hopefully, but [the ACC's role] would have been less valuable and more marginal. ... Bringing Florida State into the league was a very wise thing to do. And I think it's been terrific for Florida State. It's been a great marriage."

FSU football coach Bobby Bowden said the move worked because it was made for the right reasons. "Our administration and our president, they studied that thing pretty good and felt like the best conference

1991

1.1.91
Georgia Tech beats Nebraska 45-21 in Citrus Bowl for share of national football title

3.31.91
Virginia loses 70-67 in overtime to Tennessee in NCAA women's basketball final

4.1.91
Duke beats Kansas 72-65 for NCAA men's basketball title

7.1.91
Florida State becomes playing member of ACC

12.15.91
Florida State wins its first ACC basketball game, 86-74 at North Carolina

for us to join was the Atlantic Coast Conference," he said. "I think the thing that persuaded them the most was the high academic standards."

Bowden wasn't indifferent to the financial considerations, however. "We never made a penny in basketball," he said. "Now, all of a sudden we join a conference and we're making millions even though we haven't been very successful in basketball. We're making millions on what North Carolina and Duke and Maryland are doing. ... On the other side of the ledger, our football has helped bring everybody else up."

ACC football actually was on the upswing even as FSU joined the conference, its eligibility to compete for ACC titles delayed until the 1991-92 basketball and '92 football seasons.

Clemson and Virginia were ranked to start the football season, a first since 1983 for an ACC pair. The league won 77 percent of its 1990 games against non-conference foes, the best success rate to date. Five teams went to bowls, a new high for the ACC.

Most notably, unheralded Georgia Tech not only crashed the 1990 polls but also embarked on a meteoric rise that ended in a national title, reflected by the top spot in the final coaches' poll.

Georgia Tech had returned to respectability after a slow start under Bobby Ross, who took over in 1987 when Bill Curry went to Alabama. Ross had early trouble with holdover players. Losing his first 15 ACC games didn't help. As the program struggled, Ross several times contemplated resigning.

"I've never known a guy who wanted to win more than Bobby Ross," said Rice, who hired him. "When we lost, he'd die a slow death until he could get on the field again."

Tech's fortunes began changing after an 0-3 start in 1989. The Yellow Jackets rallied behind quarterback Shawn Jones, the ACC rookie of the year, to finish 7-4.

"Bobby Ross, he was in my opinion a genius in the football business," Rice said. "Bobby was very clever, very methodical in his planning and decision-making and play-calling."

The '90 football team derived additional inspiration from its basketball counterparts, according to offensive tackle Mike Mooney. "Basketball going to the Final Four really helped us," he told Jack Wilkinson, author of *Focused on the Top,* which chronicled Tech's football season. "I really believe that turned the whole thing around here. We wanted some attention, too. Everybody wants it — positive attention."

BELOW
Coach Bobby Ross, who led Maryland to three consecutive ACC titles in football (1983-85), took over the Georgia Tech program in 1987. He was named national coach of the year in 1990 after the Yellow Jackets won a share of the national championship.

The Yellow Jackets got off to a 3-0 start, best at the school in 20 years, enabling them to crack the polls for the first time since 1985.

The ascent continued with a victory at Maryland in which All-ACC outside linebacker Marco Coleman, a 6-4, 250-pound sophomore, registered five quarterback sacks. On the day, Tech had 11 sacks as a defense directed by George O'Leary, Tech's future head coach, held Maryland to minus-20 yards rushing. Over the first four games, the Jacket defense didn't yield a touchdown.

Next came a 21-19 win over Clemson that wasn't secure until Chris Gardocki, the Tigers' all-conference place-kicker, missed a late field goal. "Good Guys 21 Bad Guys 19" said the scoreboard at refurbished and expanded Grant Field. Clemson finished the year 10-2 and ninth-ranked under new coach Ken Hatfield after routing Illinois 31-0 in the Hall of Fame Bowl.

The Jackets barely averted disaster at North Carolina. Stopped twice inside the 5-yard line without a score, Tech settled for a 13-13 score when Scott Sisson kicked a 27-yard field goal with 61 seconds remaining. The tie with the Tar Heels, 6-4-1 as coach Mack Brown posted his first winning season, proved the only blemish on Georgia Tech's record.

Tech rebounded with a win against Duke. Ranked 16th, its record 7-0, Georgia Tech next traveled 517 miles to Charlottesville to face Virginia in one of the most anticipated matches in ACC history. "I think everybody just feels like it's good for everybody," Commissioner Corrigan said for the ACC. "We've been a whipping boy for a while."

The top-rated Cavaliers, once perennial doormats, matched Tech at 7-0. End Chris Slade led Virginia's defense. The offense — fueled by 6-5 receiver Herman Moore, running back Terry Kirby and quarterback Shawn Moore — entered the game leading the nation in scoring (48.1 points) and total offense (544.9). Moore, the 1990 ACC player of the year, was the top-rated quarterback in Division I-A at the time.

Virginia reached uncharted territory even before rising to No. 1, as it defeated Clemson 20-7 in the second game of the season. Clemson coach Frank Howard once reputedly called the Cavaliers "white meat" for his Tigers, whose winning streak against their league rivals was the longest in the NCAA. Finally "the 30th time was the charm for Virginia," as Tom Perrin wrote in his 1992 book *Atlantic Coast Conference Football.*

Once Clemson was out of the way, Virginia pitched two shutouts in four games, wins over Duke and N.C. State. The

BELOW
Outside linebacker Marco Coleman was a two-time All-American and one of the reasons Georgia Tech shared the 1990 national championship with Colorado. He was a two-time All-ACC player and a finalist for the Butkus Award in 1991, which goes to the nation's outstanding linebacker. He finished his career with 27.5 quarterback sacks.

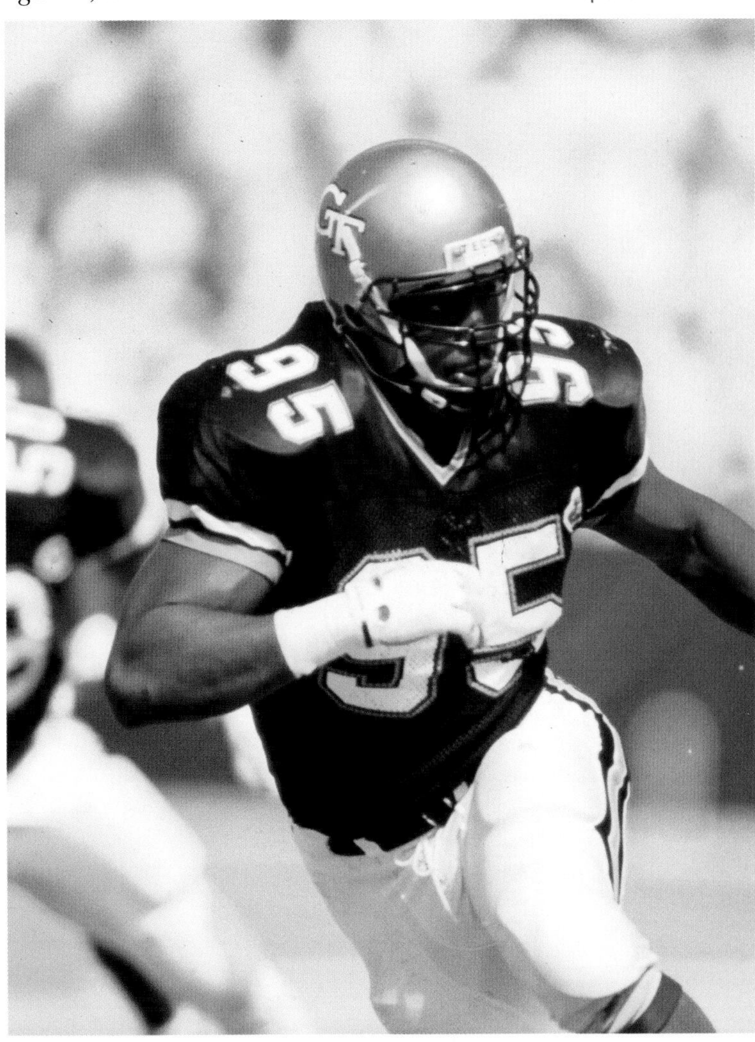

BELOW
Scott Sisson ended his career at Georgia Tech as the school's leader in scoring and field goals. He booted six game-winning field goals during his career, including the kick that defeated No. 1 Virginia in 1990. He was a finalist for the 1992 Lou Groza Award, which goes to the nation's top kicker. He went 60-for-88 on field goal attempts from 1989-92.

Wolfpack, although sixth in the ACC, posted their third straight winning season under Dick Sheridan. They finished 7-5 after topping Southern Miss in the All-American Bowl, 31-27.

The ACC's big showdown, televised nationally by CBS, came on Nov. 3 before a boisterous record crowd of 49,700. In what one newspaper called "The Brawl For It All," the teams produced one of the great games in league history.

There was brief concern on game day that playing conditions might cause a postponement. Vandals had sneaked into Scott Stadium overnight and burned a section of artificial turf. But Virginia groundskeepers repaired the damage with leftover turf from the school's baseball field and the show went on. "We would have played this game on cement," Ross said.

For a time it appeared the Yellow Jackets were stuck in cement. They had one first down in the opening quarter, while Virginia jumped to a 13-0 lead. The Cavaliers built a 28-14 halftime advantage. Herman Moore, who wound up with nine catches for 234 yards, caught bombs to set up the first and third touchdowns, and Shawn Moore ran for three scores in the opening half.

But, in a game of big plays, Ralph Friedgen's Tech offense rose to the occasion. Shawn Jones scored on a 23-yard touchdown run and threw for a 43-yard score to flanker Jerry Gilchrist in the first half. Then, on the first play from scrimmage in the second half, All-ACC linebacker Calvin Tiggle added luster to his 18-tackle day by recovering a UVa fumble. Quickly Gilchrist scored again on a flanker reverse, and Jones tied it at 28-28 on a post-pattern pass to Emmett Merchant.

Virginia regained the lead, this time on a 63-yard Moore-to-Moore touchdown toss. Again Tech tied it, the final 8 yards coming on a burst through the left side by running back William Bell.

The Jackets finally seized the advantage 38-35 on a Sisson field goal. The Tech defense held on first-and-goal inside its own 1-yard line, forcing the Cavaliers to kick a tying field goal with 2:34 left. Jones then drove the Jackets into field goal range, and Sisson came through yet again, his 37-yard kick with seven seconds to go the difference in a 41-38 victory.

"I think we're back," Ross said of Tech football. "I'll admit it; we're finally back. I've been reluctant to say that."

The loss deflated Virginia, which dropped four of its five final games, including a 23-22 decision to Tennessee in the Sugar Bowl. "I think we lost something physically and mentally when we lost that game," Welsh said. The Cavs finished 8-4 and tied with Clemson for second in the ACC.

Tech marched on, or rather kicked ahead. Sisson spelled the difference in the next game, a 6-3 win over Virginia Tech. Then came decisive triumphs at Wake and Georgia and a 45-21 New Year's Day victory over Nebraska in the Florida Citrus Bowl. As with Clemson in 1981, Tech led all the way in beating the Cornhuskers, completing an improbable, undefeated run to a national championship.

The Jackets were the pick by a single vote in the coaches' poll and finished second in the AP poll to Colorado, which had a loss, a tie and a victory over Missouri when erroneously allowed a fifth down.

"Georgia Tech is the best-balanced football team in America," Wake Forest coach Bill Dooley said. "Offense, defense, every way."

Ross won nine professional awards, including 1990 ACC coach of the year. He became the only man besides Dooley honored for his work at two league schools and is the only coach to win the ACC title at two schools, having done it three times with Maryland (1983-85). By 1992 he was coaching in the National Football League.

Georgia Tech's national championship started a trend. ACC teams won titles in football and basketball every year from 1990 through 1994, an unmatched run in conference history.

Next up — and up and up — was men's basketball.

Discussing expansion, a Big East AD told Austin Murphy of *Sports Illustrated*: "The ACC needs to jazz up its football, and it would get great football coverage in New England. What the hell would it want with our basketball? It already has the world." In 1990-91, the ACC went about proving the man right.

Six of eight ACC teams received NCAA bids, 75 percent representation that has yet to be surpassed. For the second straight season a pair of ACC teams reached the men's Final Four.

Seven of eight men's teams had winning records. The exception, Clemson, plunged from first to last in a season's span.

Wake tied for third with N.C. State a season after coming in last, earning Dave Odom ACC coach of the year recognition. Rodney Rogers, Wake's power forward, was rookie of the year. Two seasons later he graduated to player of the year and went pro. Another Rodney was 1991 player of the year. N.C. State's Rodney Monroe led the ACC at 27.0 points per game and became the top career scorer in Wolfpack history.

Virginia returned to the women's Final Four, and Duke returned to the men's. The

BELOW

Quarterback Shawn Jones (10) of Georgia Tech was named the ACC's rookie of the year in 1989. The next season he directed the Yellow Jackets to a share of the national championship. Jones finished his career as the ACC's leader in total offense, a record since surpassed. He threw for 50 touchdown passes in four seasons and ran for another 19.

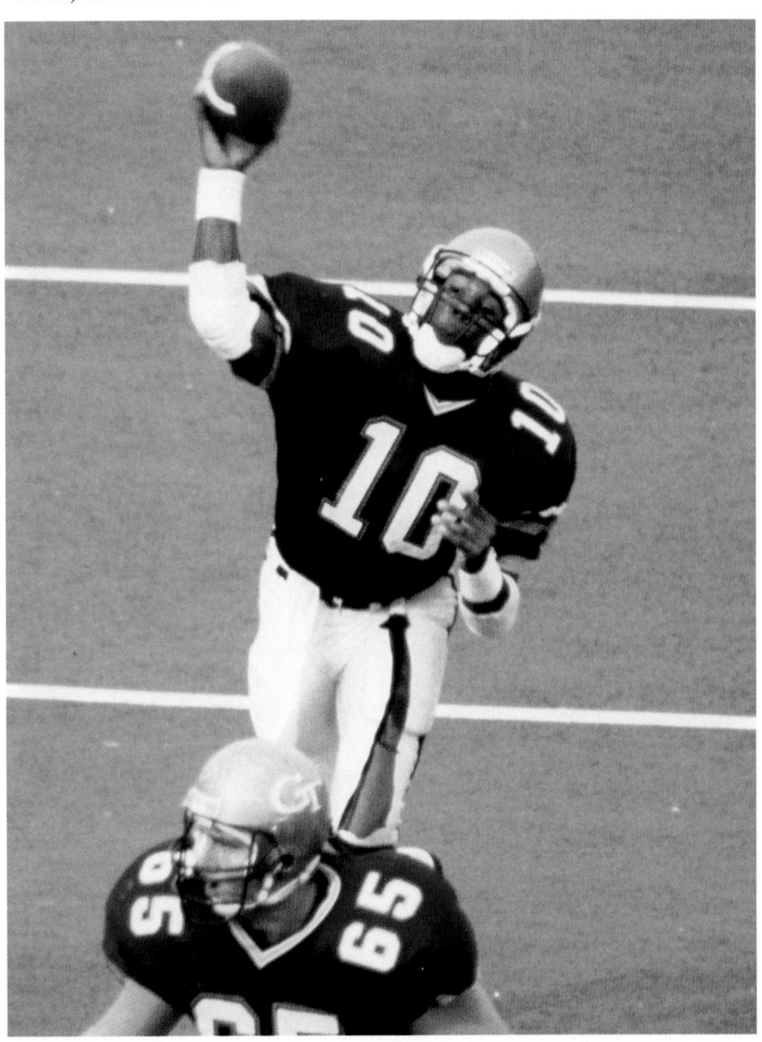

Blue Devils finished first during the regular season, boasting five double-figure scorers. Three would eventually have their jersey numbers retired by the school: Christian Laettner, Bobby Hurley and Grant Hill, then a 6-7 freshman.

The league's other Final Four squad was North Carolina, back for its eighth visit under Smith but first in nine years. The Tar Heels of Rick Fox, Hubert Davis, George Lynch, Pete Chilcutt and King Rice, bolstered by a freshman class touted as the most-balanced ever, finished second during the regular season. Then they beat Duke in the ACC Tournament final and, as the top seed in the East, advanced to meet Kansas in the Final Four.

Duke's route to the title was a tad more daunting. The Devils faced top-ranked and undefeated UNLV, already conceded a repeat national title in popular estimation. Featuring seniors Larry Johnson and Stacey Augmon, it was essentially the same squad that beat Duke by 30 in the '90 championship game. "That's their show: 'Who can beat Vegas?'" Duke's Krzyzewski said of CBS. "It's like a mini-series."

Duke answered the rhetorical question, defeating UNLV 79-77 in the biggest Final Four shocker since Villanova upset heavily favored Georgetown in 1985.

Laettner had 28 points, 20 in the first half, and made the decisive free throws with 12.7 seconds to go. Hurley hit a crucial 3-pointer with Duke trailing 76-71 at the 2:16 mark; some count it the biggest shot of Krzyzewski's tenure. Senior Greg Koubek helped hold Johnson, generally regarded as the nation's best player, to 13 points, 10 below his average.

"I'm not sure we could beat them again," Krzyzewski said afterward. "But, like last

BELOW
N.C. State's Chris Corchiani (left) and Duke's Bobby Hurley (11) are among the finest point guards to play ACC basketball. Hurley was named first-team All-ACC in 1993 and left school as the NCAA's modern career leader in assists, with Corchiani ranking second. Hurley led the Blue Devils to back-to-back national championships in 1991 and '92, and he was the most outstanding player in the '92 Final Four.

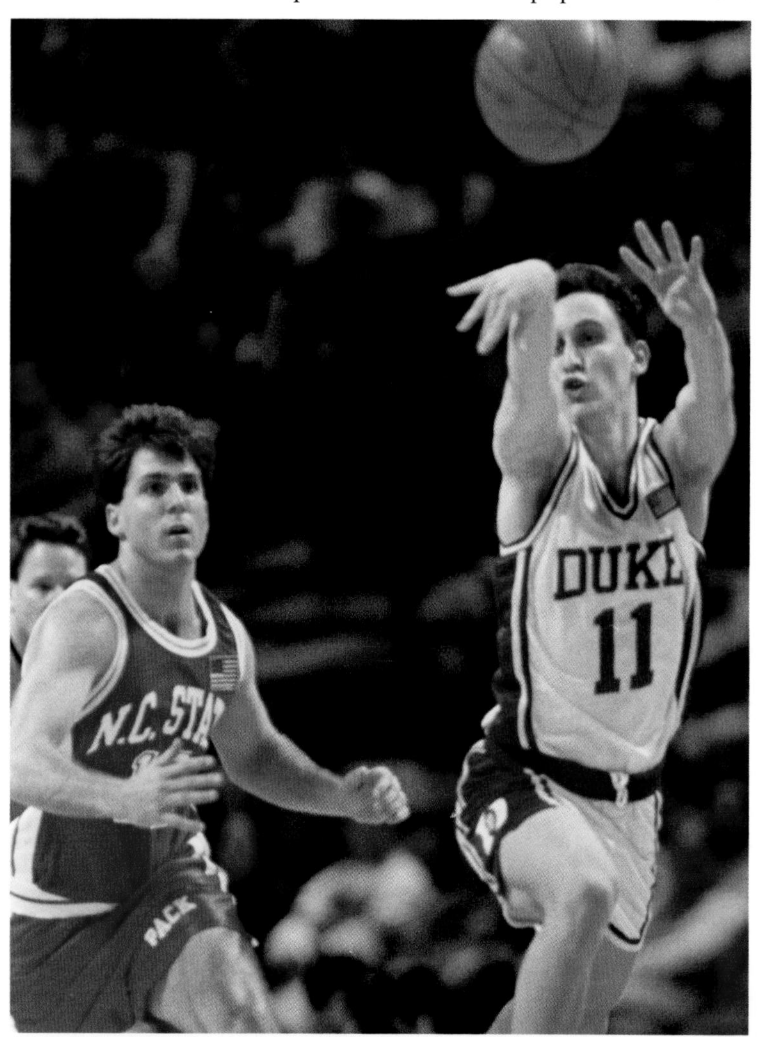

BELOW
Grant Hill (33) soars for two of the 1,924 points he scored during his four-year career at Duke. Hill went on to play for the 1996 U.S. Olympic team that won a gold medal.

year, we only play once."

UNC played once in the '91 Final Four, losing to a Kansas squad coached by Smith protégé Roy Williams. The 79-73 Jayhawk victory was marred when official Pete Pavia ejected Smith in the final seconds. The UNC loss did avert an athletic civil war in North Carolina had the Tar Heels met the Blue Devils for the national title. Duke instead dispatched Kansas 72-65 in a title contest as anticlimactic as N.C. State's '74 triumph over Marquette after ousting UCLA, that era's colossus.

There was considerably more drama in the women's final.

Half the ACC women's teams reached the NCAA Tournament for the sixth straight year. Virginia had dominated the regular season, its 14-0 mark the first undefeated record in ACC play since 1978, the inaugural women's season. Clemson posted its fourth winning season in four years under Jim Davis. The Tigers upset the Cavaliers in the ACC Tournament semifinals, then fell 84-61 to N.C. State in the title game.

Still, it was Ryan's club that reached the Final Four, the third straight appearance for an ACC squad and the second straight for Virginia. The second-ranked Cavs eliminated Connecticut, the decisive points a pair of free throws by senior forward Tonya Cardoza. Then they got close enough to pay dirt to feel the grit under their fingernails in the championship contest. But after leading Tennessee by five points with 1:15 remaining in regulation play, Virginia frittered away its advantage and fell 70-67 in overtime.

No ACC football teams got that close to the ultimate end zone in 1991, although Florida State, rumbling just over the horizon a year prior to entering league play, was top-ranked much of the season.

Bowden's squad won its first 10 games and spent 12 weeks at No. 1. Linebacker Marvin Jones and defensive back Terrell Buckley were consensus All-Americans. The magic was dissipated somewhat by consecutive losses to Miami at Tallahassee (17-16 when Gerry Thomas' 34-yard field goal try went wide right) and to Florida at Gainesville. FSU still ended the year ranked fifth after a 10-2 victory over Texas A&M in the Cotton Bowl.

Four ACC teams earned bowl bids in 1991, although only Georgia Tech emerged triumphant, 18-17 over Stanford in the Aloha Bowl. The Yellow Jackets (8-5) finished tied for second in the league with N.C. State. Dick Sheridan's Wolfpack was 9-3 overall, the school's best record since 1978, even after a 37-34 loss to East Carolina in the Peach Bowl.

Clemson led the league at 6-0-1 in

BELOW

N.C. State's Tom Gugliotta (24) shoots over North Carolina's George Lynch. Gugliotta was not a highly recruited player, but he became one of the top performers in the ACC. He was named first-team all-conference in 1992. Lynch was the most outstanding player of the NCAA Tournament East Region in 1993, which came during the Tar Heels' run to the national championship.

Hatfield's second season. The Tigers' rushing defense was best in the ACC, allowing a paltry 53.4 yards per game. Their only losses in a 9-2-1 campaign were at Georgia and against California in the Citrus Bowl.

Virginia finished fourth, but ended the regular season with a 7-1 rush, the tie coming against Clemson. That earned 1991 ACC coach of the year honors for George Welsh and player of the year for quarterback Matt Blundin. Welsh, whose four football coach of the year awards are tops in ACC history, said Blundin "just couldn't have been a better quarterback when he played, except the first game."

The 6-7 senior, who served double duty as a basketball forward, set an ACC and national record by going the entire 1991 regular season without throwing an interception. Blundin threw 224 times in his sole season as a regular starter, completing 135 passes for 19 touchdowns and 1,902 yards, including a league-best 159.6 per game. He finally threw an interception in Virginia's 48-14 Gator Bowl loss to Oklahoma. "To have the kind of year he had, I never would have said that," Welsh admitted.

Blundin started a bit of a trend for ACC players of the year. Over a three-season span the football award went each time to a quarterback who doubled as a basketball starter. Of course that's because in both 1992 and 1993 the ACC player of the year was Charlie Ward, the elusive 6-1 quarterback at Florida State and starting point guard on coach Pat Kennedy's basketball squad.

With Ward running the offense, and a defense led by a trio of All-ACC players — linebackers Jones and Derrick Brooks and defensive back Corey Sawyer — FSU hit ACC football in the fall of '92 like a 300-pound lineman meeting a 180-pound wide receiver. Bobby Bowden's squad marched through the ACC without a loss, its 8-0 record echoed in 1993, 1994, 1996, 1997, 1999 and 2000.

FSU finished the '92 season 11-1 and third-ranked, its sole loss at Miami, 19-16, after Dan Mowry's attempt at a tying field goal went wide right. The season ended with a 27-14 win over Nebraska in the Orange Bowl, the ACC's first appearance in that event since 1981.

Florida State had several close calls within the league. Ward, shaky early in a September visit to Clemson, rallied his team to a 24-20 victory, capped by a 9-yard pass to Kevin Knox with 2:08 to go. There was also a five-point escape at Georgia Tech after trailing by two touchdowns entering the fourth quarter, and a 13-3 victory over Virginia.

RIGHT
Virginia coach George Welsh (left) shakes hands with then-Florida State assistant coach Chuck Amato as FSU coach Bobby Bowden (center) watches. Amato became the head coach at N.C. State in 2000.

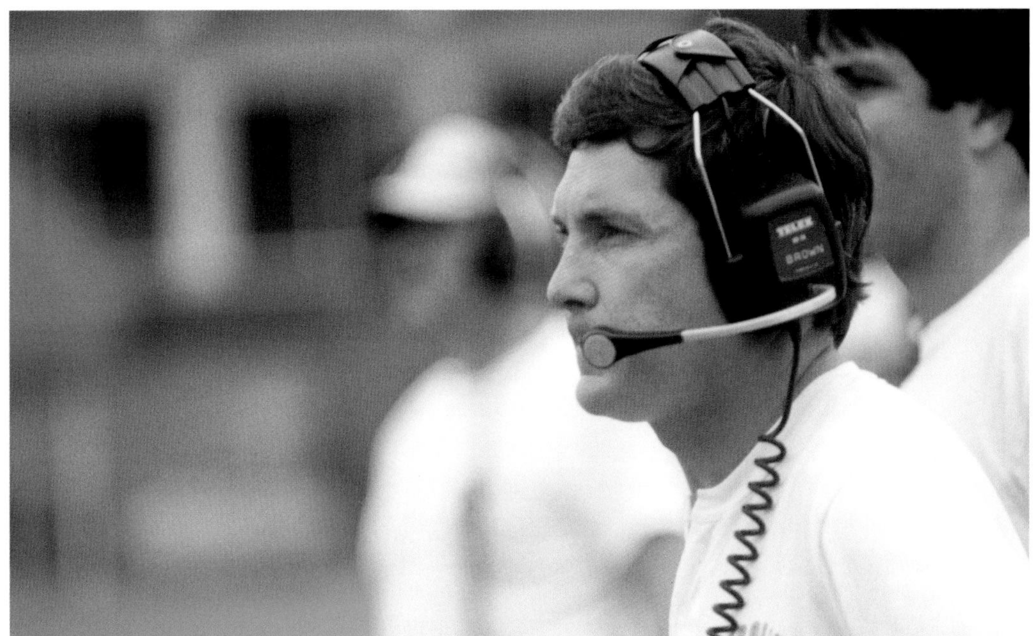

LEFT
Mack Brown rebuilt North Carolina's football program into a national power before leaving for Texas in 1997. His last two teams ranked in the top 10 and won back-to-back bowl games while going 21-3.

The Cavaliers, en route to a 7-4 season, were the only ACC squad with a winning record that didn't go to a bowl. Senior back Terry Kirby led the league in rushing with 141.3 yards per game, best since UNC's Don McCauley in 1970, and in all-purpose yardage (171.5), best in the ACC until 1998. Kirby was a special recruit at Virginia, having been ranked the top offensive prospect in the nation as a prep player in the state.

Second-place N.C. State (9-3-1) lost to Steve Spurrier's Florida Gators in the Gator Bowl. North Carolina was third, continuing its resurrection under Mack Brown, the former FSU running back. The Tar Heels' 9-3 season was capped by a 21-17 Peach Bowl victory over Mississippi State, the school's first bowl win in a decade. Wake made its second bowl appearance as an ACC member, first since 1979. Dooley, the 1992 coach of the year, directed the Deacons to a fourth-place finish and an 8-4 record that ended with a 39-35 win over Oregon in the Independence Bowl.

No one expected Pat Kennedy's basketball squad to match the prowess of Florida State football, but in 1991-92 it came close, finishing second in the ACC with essentially the same players who won the previous year's Metro Conference title. The effort earned Kennedy the '92 ACC coach of the year award.

In fact, FSU won its first official ACC game, at North Carolina no less, a stunning blow to ACC basketball conceit. The victory coincided with Ward's return to the basketball court. "Ward is unbelievable," UNC's Smith said. "I'll bet Bobby Bowden doesn't get him back. Is he something!"

Ward's take on the matter paralleled Smith's. "I kept telling people that I should have been on a basketball scholarship, but that didn't happen," the ACC's 1992 leader in steals said. "So I had to take the other route."

So important was the junior on that other route, Bowden delayed the start of spring football practice while Kennedy's squad played into the third round of the NCAAs. "It's a new rule," Bowden said, "the Charlie Ward Rule."

By Patrick O'Neill

ACC EXCELLENCE

N.C. STATE WOMEN RUN AWAY FROM PACK

Foot racing is sport stripped to its most basic elements.

A simple uniform, a light pair of shoes and "Runners, take your mark." Throw in a few hills, a mud puddle or two and you get cross country. In this realm, N.C. State's women have no equal in the Atlantic Coast Conference.

Heading into the 2002 season, the Wolfpack women were favored to win their 20th conference title out of the 25 years the event has been contested. The school's media guide says it best: "The complete and utter domination that N.C. State's women's program has enjoyed is quite astonishing."

Since that first ACC championship in 1978, the Wolfpack women also produced 16 individual conference champions. Sixteen of the ACC team championships have come under the leadership of Rollie Geiger, who also led the Wolfpack men to nine ACC titles in cross country. With 33 combined team titles in cross country and track and field, Geiger, 54, ranks second to North Carolina's Dennis Craddock (39) for total ACC team championships in any sport.

The program's success has not been limited to the ACC. The Wolfpack women sent a team to the national championship meet 23 times since 1977, a record among Division I schools. The 1979 and 1980 N.C. State teams won Association of Intercollegiate Athletics for Women (AIAW) national titles. Nine Wolfpack women's teams have finished fourth or higher in the national championship meet.

LEFT: N.C. State coach Rollie Geiger created a dynasty in women's cross country. His program has sent more teams to the national championships than any other school in the country. From 1987-2001, the Wolfpack won 13 of the 15 ACC titles.

RIGHT: Mary (left) and Julie Shea led N.C. State to a pair of national championships in cross country. Julie Shea was an All-American, and she was twice honored as the ACC athlete of the year.

"Our women's program has lined up at the national championship in women's cross country more times than any other school," Geiger said. "So we're the most consistent school in the country."

The Wolfpack women won 13 of 15 ACC team titles in cross country from 1987 to 2001. Only North Carolina, which won in 1994 and 1999, found a way to beat N.C. State. Craddock, whose women's program has won 25 combined ACC indoor and outdoor track championships, said there is no doubt Geiger's Wolfpack is the team to beat every fall.

"I think he's just done an outstanding job," Craddock said. "Not only in the ACC, but I think Rollie is recognized nationally as being one of the outstanding distance coaches in the country. People know about him, and they know about N.C. State. There's no question about that. He started a great tradition there, and he's kept it going."

Great runners have made such dominance possible. With 117 All-ACC honorees, N.C. State has produced some of the greatest distance runners in conference history. The heyday of the women's program began in the late 1970s with the emergence of Julie Shea and Joan Benoit, two superstars credited with helping women's distance running earn national recognition.

Benoit and Shea were N.C. State's first female All-Americans in cross country. As a post-collegiate runner, Benoit won two Boston Marathon titles before winning the 1984 Olympic marathon in Los Angeles. Shea was twice honored with the McKevlin Award as the ACC's outstanding athlete. She also won two individual national titles in cross country for the Wolfpack. Along with her younger sister, Mary, she led the Wolfpack to the AIAW team titles.

One of the top U.S. female distance runners in the late 1970s and early 1980s, Shea (now Julie Graw) never got her shot at Olympic glory because none of her events was offered in the 1980 Moscow Olympics (which the United States ultimately boycotted). By 1984, when women's distance events were contested in the Olympics for the first time, injury had cut short her career.

Graw, who has served three terms on the Raleigh City Council (1995-2001), was also nominated for the Sullivan Award (which goes to the nation's top amateur athlete) in 1980 after she won three NCAA outdoor distance races in 24 hours.

"That kind of caught

people's attention," Graw said. "Oh goodness, that really scrawny, emaciated-looking girl is respectable."

Graw treasures her memories of Benoit and their times at N.C. State.

"I really enjoyed training with Joan," Graw said. "She and I valued and respected each other. We usually roomed together and talked far into the night. They were special times. It was exciting, and we knew it was special. It was thrilling, and there was a little bit of magic in the air."

To keep the magic afloat, Geiger said he looks at two important factors in recruiting — athletes who like to compete, and those who appear to be running effortlessly.

"We have a very precise sport," said Geiger, who was a middle-distance runner for Kent State in the late 1960s. "It's measured; it's timed. I like a kid who likes to win."

Tom Jones, who coached at N.C. State from 1979 to 1984, said Benoit, the Shea sisters and two-time national champion Betty Springs (1981, '83) came along at "a growing time in athletics for women, and I think we were a little ahead of the curve."

Another major milestone came for the Wolfpack men's program when N.C. State strung together six consecutive ACC outdoor track titles (1983-1988).

The Wolfpack helped stop an amazing run by Maryland, which had a 24-year reign as ACC outdoor champions. The Terrapins also had a 25-year ACC indoor winning streak.

While track and field is recognized primarily as an individual sport, Geiger says cross country is first and foremost a team sport. Victories are determined by combining the finishing places of each team's top five runners and the low score wins.

"You can finish 1,2,3,4 in the ACC championship, and if your fifth runner is 60th, you're going to lose," Geiger said. "It's a team sport. You're only as good as your fifth runner."

Geiger emphasizes strength over speed in training. The program's top male runners can accumulate as many as 100 training miles per week, while the top women may log as many as 80. And training for distance runners is basically year-round.

"I don't think any other athlete at the college level has a training period as long as cross country and track," said Geiger, who tries to make all the work as much fun as possible.

"No one ever says, 'Let's go play running,'" Geiger said. "Most coaches use running as punishment. If you do something wrong, you're punished by running. Well, that's what we do. We can't use running as punishment.

"I always joke and say we shoot foul shots as punishment." ✦

FSU was not all Ward in posting a 22-10 record, 11-5 in the ACC. Doug Edwards and Rodney Dobard carried play inside. Besides Ward, the perimeter boasted Bob Sura, the 1992 ACC rookie of the year, and junior-college transfer Sam Cassell, noted for his scoring (a team-high 18.4 per game) and the observation that the fans at UNC's Smith Center were a laid-back "cheese and wine crowd."

The ACC's top two scorers came from losing teams for the first time since 1982 — Maryland's 6-8 Walt Williams (26.8) and N.C. State's Tom Gugliotta (22.5), a 6-9 forward. Both played for programs that endured NCAA probations, coaching changes and intense academic scrutiny. Within two years Maryland returned to the NCAA Tournament. The Terrapins started a run of nine straight appearances through 2002, an ongoing school record. N.C. State went to the NCAAs in 1991, led by the backcourt of Monroe and assist man Chris Corchiani. The Wolfpack would not make another NCAA Tournament appearance until 2002.

Virginia was left out of the 1992 NCAAs but won its second NIT title, defeating Notre Dame 81-76 in overtime in the final.

Ultimately, though, the 1992 basketball season belonged to Duke.

The Blue Devils started and ended the season ranked No. 1, an accomplishment unduplicated since. They led the ACC in scoring (88.0) and scoring margin (15.4), and in shooting accuracy from the field (.536) and foul line (.748). They were doing even better before playmaker Hurley broke a bone in his foot at UNC and missed three weeks.

The Devils lost twice in 36 outings, at North Carolina and later at Wake Forest without Hurley. They beat LSU with Shaquille O'Neal at Baton Rouge, UCLA at Pauley Pavilion and Michigan's "Fab Five" at Ann Arbor. They finished atop the ACC during the regular season, and in the first ACC Tournament to include a play-in game, defeated North Carolina by 20 to win the title. "That's the best Duke team I think I've seen," Smith said, "and I think I've seen most of them, haven't I?"

The Blue Devils reached their fifth straight Final Four and third straight NCAA title game. By now their presence in the game's premier event seemed almost foreordained. "Kids think Dr. Naismith created basketball, and then he created Duke," said ex-Georgia Tech assistant Perry Clark, then head coach at Tulane.

Duke achieved something far more enduring than fame in what Krzyzewski called his "most rewarding and best year in coaching." The Blue Devils of Hurley and Laettner, the '92 ACC player of the year, of Grant Hill and Thomas Hill, of Brian Davis and Tony Lang, repeated as national champions.

No ACC team before or since has managed that feat in basketball or football. Nationally, no other basketball program has won consecutive titles in 30 years, since UCLA in 1972 and 1973.

The Blue Devils were not just a team but a phenomenon, greeted by adoring young fans wherever they went. Hurley and Laettner, pouty but competitive, were especial heartthrobs. The crush of admirers was so great at Clemson, the team bus had to pull into Littlejohn Coliseum to pick up

1992

4.6.92
Duke finishes a wire-to-wire No. 1 season by beating Michigan 71-51 for NCAA men's basketball title

1993

4.5.93
UNC beats Michigan 77-71 for NCAA men's basketball title

11.20.93
Wake Forest back John Leach rushes for 329 yards against Maryland, an ACC single-game record

1994

1.1.94
FSU defeats Nebraska 18-16 in Orange Bowl for national football title

the team. "It felt like we were the Beatles, or something, coming to America, all the little girls squealing and stuff," Grant Hill said of a similarly tumultuous reception at a Winston-Salem hotel.

The accomplishments and adulation almost ended against Kentucky in the 1992 East Region final. Instead, the Blue Devils effected a 104-103 overtime escape, thanks to a remarkable 80-foot pass by Grant Hill and a statistically perfect performance by Laettner, capped by one of the greatest clutch shots in NCAA history.

"He's not afraid to fail," Krzyzewski said after Laettner caught Hill's pass, dribbled, wheeled and sank the winning jumper from beyond the foul line as the buzzer sounded. Laettner rose to the occasion in a game observers rank among the best ever played, going 10-of-10 from the floor and 10-of-10 from the line to pace all scorers with 31 points. The senior also outraged many by stepping on the chest of prostrate UK freshman Aminu Timberlake, smiling as he did. "It's so Laettner," said teammate Cherokee Parks, often the recipient of his teammate's barbs in practice.

The Final Four was far less dramatic. Duke opened by defeating Indiana, causing a rupture in the relationship between Krzyzewski and his mentor, the Hoosiers' Bob Knight, which lasted nearly a decade. The Blue Devils' second Big 10 opponent, Michigan, fell by 20 in the championship contest.

This royal-blue success inflamed an already-heated rivalry back in North Carolina. "By Duke being next door, you ride down the road, you see signs saying two straight national championships," George Lynch, UNC's senior captain and inspirational leader, said on the eve of the 1992-93 season. "You see T-shirts. You see those guys all the time. ... It gets under my skin a little. I'll be a liar if I tell you it didn't."

From such friction emerged the undisputed top rivalry in the nation, both in intensity and level of competition. Usually both UNC and Duke were ranked in the top 10 when they played; the last time neither was ranked at all upon meeting was 1955. Between 1986 and 2001, a span of 16 seasons, only twice did neither Duke nor North Carolina reach the Final Four. During the '90s the pair missed only in 1996, their combined Final Four appearances exceeding those of any league in the country.

The '93 season put an exclamation point to the rivalry — and to ACC basketball supremacy — as North Carolina won Smith's second national championship. That gave the league three straight titles involving two different teams, a feat unmatched to this day.

Six ACC teams received NCAA bids in 1993, compared to five the previous year. Clemson was the only league squad with a winning record left out of the NCAA field. The Tigers were on a two-year probation for recruiting violations. They went to the NIT.

The '93 Wolfpack endured a different sort of blemish by appearing in the ACC Tournament opener that, in an expanded league, matched the No. 8 and No. 9 seeds. The so-called play-in game was affectionately dubbed "The Les Robinson Invitational" after the genial but unsuccessful N.C. State coach whose teams qual-

4.3.94
UNC women beat Louisiana Tech 60-59 for NCAA women's basketball title

10.11.94
Former North Carolina and South Carolina head basketball coach Frank McGuire dies

1995

11.2.95
Virginia hands Florida State its first ACC football loss, 33-28 at Charlottesville

11.18.95
Wake quarterback Rusty LaRue passes for an ACC-record 545 yards versus N.C. State

Duke's Christian Laettner launches the game-winning shot as time expires in overtime against Kentucky in the 1992 East Region final in Philadelphia. Duke trailed 103-102 with 2.1 seconds remaining. The Blue Devils' Grant Hill threw an in-bounds pass three-quarters of the court to Laettner, who calmly dribbled, turned and fired. Laettner was a perfect 10-of-10 from the field and 10-of-10 from the free throw line that evening.

Left to right: Duke's Brian Davis, Christian Laettner and Thomas Hill won two straight national titles. The Blue Devils defeated Nevada-Las Vegas and Kansas in the 1991 Final Four for the school's first championship. In 1992, Duke was ranked No. 1 in the country from start to finish. The Blue Devils finished 34-2 after defeating Indiana and Michigan at the Final Four. Duke became the first school since UCLA (1967-73) and the only ACC program to repeat as champions. Three members of this group, Laettner, Bobby Hurley and Grant Hill made the ACC's 50th anniversary team.

ified four straight times from 1993 to 1996.

Robinson's close friend, Bobby Cremins, was the surprise winner of the 1993 conference championship, his third, after Georgia Tech beat UNC 77-75 in the ACC Tournament final. Forward James Forrest led the Jackets with 70 points in three games.

Rumors of Cremins' return to South Carolina, his alma mater, swirled around the Tech program for months. Sure enough, after the Yellow Jackets were bumped by Southern in their NCAA opener, Cremins accepted the Gamecock job. He reconsidered almost immediately and returned to Tech. "I made a mistake and this is the most embarrassing moment of my life," said the ever-honest Cremins.

North Carolina's march to the title resembled Duke's the previous year in that the Tar Heels barely survived the East Region final, defeating second-seed Cincinnati in overtime. The Final Four served up Kansas and Roy Williams, a former Smith assistant. The Heels won by 10, earning a rematch with Michigan, which beat them by a point in late December in the championship game of Hawaii's Rainbow Classic.

BELOW
North Carolina guard Donald Williams, the most outstanding player at the 1993 Final Four, stands at the free throw line at the end of the championship game against Michigan. The Tar Heels defeated the Wolverines 77-71 for the title. Williams went 8-of-12 and scored 25 points in the final game.

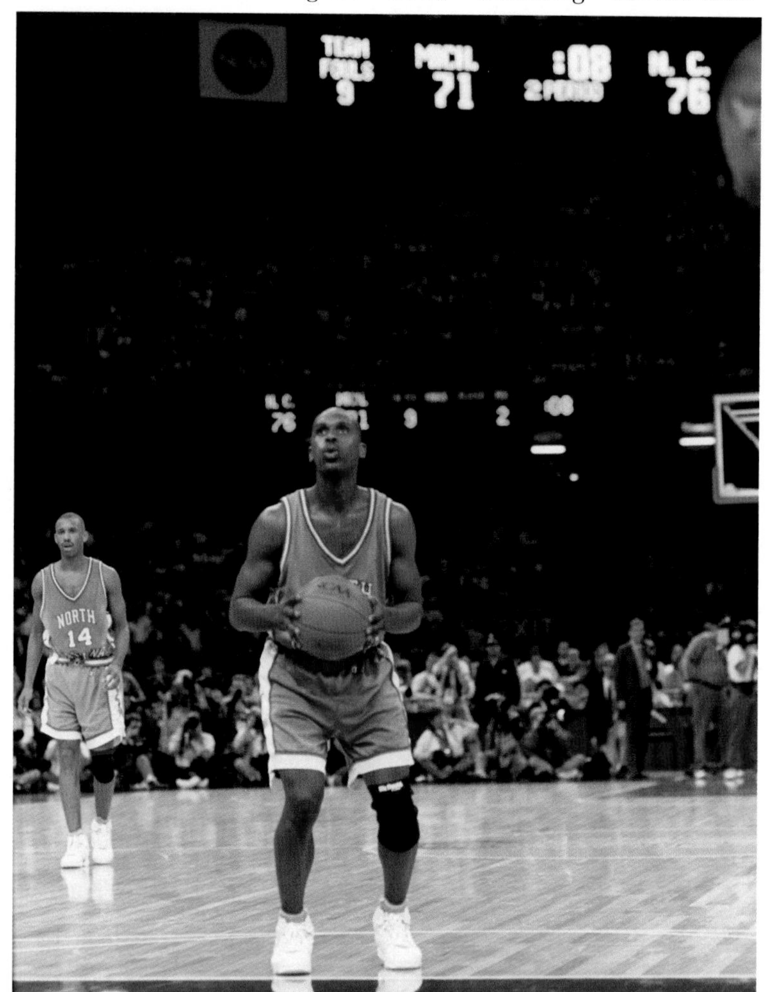

The Wolverines, making their second straight appearance in the NCAA title game, led by four points with less than four minutes remaining. But sophomore Donald Williams, most outstanding player of the Final Four, hit a 3-pointer, giving him eight straight points and pulling the Tar Heels within one.

The Fab Five, featuring Chris Webber, Jalen Rose and Juwan Howard, were an impressive crew. But so, too, was UNC's junior class of Eric Montross, Derrick Phelps, Brian Reese and Pat Sullivan. They did most of the scoring in the decisive moments as UNC took the lead, which it held at 73-71 with 20 seconds to go.

Michigan had used its allotted timeouts, but Webber, dogged by Lynch, raced into a Tar Heel trap along the sideline.

In an instant, Webber decided the game and secured a place in athletic infamy. Just as Roy Riegels' wrong-way run in the 1929 Rose Bowl clinched a national title for Georgia Tech, and Fred Brown's inadvertent pass to James Worthy placed the 1982 basketball crown firmly in UNC's possession, so Webber's mistake helped to decide the '93 NCAA title. "In the heat of the moment, strange things happen," said Steve Fisher, the Michigan coach.

Webber's fateful timeout incurred an automatic technical foul, two free throws and possession of the ball for UNC. Williams, who finished with 25 points, made four straight foul shots to seal the 77-71 win. "I've often said, you have to be lucky and good," noted Smith, the 1993

ACC coach of the year. As if completing a neighborhood ritual, the UNC coach accepted the championship trophy from Tom Butters, the Duke AD who chaired the NCAA Men's Basketball Committee.

The months following UNC's title run were not pleasant for ACC adherents.

Jim Valvano, graceful to the end, died of cancer in April at age 46.

N.C. State had staged a 10th-anniversary celebration of its 1983 national championship prior to a February game against Duke, using the occasion to honor its former coach. Valvano, stooped and slow, stood mid-court and told the overflow Reynolds Coliseum crowd the '83 team taught him many things, among them "the persistence, the idea of never, ever quitting. Don't ever give up! Don't ever stop fighting!"

Later Valvano added: "Today I fight a different battle. ... Cancer has taken away a lot of my physical abilities. I can't run over and yell at John Moreau, the referee, like I'd like to do right now. I can't do the back flips I like to do with our world-class cheerleaders. I can't do those things anymore. But what cancer can't touch is my mind, my heart and my soul. It can't touch those things."

In May, shortly after Valvano's death, Virginia was given a two-year NCAA probation with minimal penalties. The nine violations involved improper loans to student-athletes, many made between 1981-87 while Dick Schultz was athletics director. Denying knowledge of the matter, Schultz nevertheless resigned his position as the NCAA's executive director on May 11.

No ACC program has incurred a signifi-

BELOW
North Carolina coach Dean Smith and his Tar Heels hoist the national championship trophy as Duke director of athletics Tom Butters (right) watches. Butters was head of the NCAA Men's Basketball Committee that season.

cant NCAA probation in nearly a decade since Virginia was penalized.

Late in June, Dick Sheridan resigned as N.C. State's football coach, reportedly for health reasons. His seven-year record at the school was 52-29-3 with six bowl appearances. Hired in 1986 by Valvano, then the basketball coach and athletics director, Sheridan reportedly turned down jobs at Arizona, Georgia, South Carolina and Auburn to stay in Raleigh. Now, abruptly, he quit, the lesson of Valvano's physical hardships fresh in many minds.

Mike O'Cain, the quarterbacks coach, took over as Wolfpack head coach. The former Clemson quarterback brought in the 1993 team at 7-5 after a 42-7 loss to Michigan in the Hall of Fame Bowl.

Clemson and Virginia tied for third. Both earned bowl bids. Virginia was 7-5 after losing the Carquest Bowl to Boston College. The Tigers were 9-3 as, for the second time, a Clemson coach debuted by winning a bowl game. The first had been Danny Ford in 1978. This time it was Tommy West, who replaced unpopular Ken Hatfield and beat Kentucky 14-13 in the Peach Bowl.

North Carolina finished second, its six wins in the ACC and 10 overall highs to that point under Mack Brown. The Tar Heels burnished their reputation as "Tailback U" when Leon Johnson and Curtis Johnson each rushed for more than 1,000 yards, the fourth UNC pair to do so in the same season. Leon Johnson was voted 1993 ACC rookie of the year. No school in the nation surpassed the 23 1,000-yard rushers who had played at Chapel Hill, all since 1953, when the ACC began. The rest of the league combined to produce 35 1,000-yard rushers during that period.

The ACC's leading rusher in 1993 was not a Tar Heel, though. That honor went to Wake Forest senior John Leach. More striking than his 99.0-yard rushing average was Leach's performance in a loss at Maryland. He ran for three touchdowns and on 46 carries gained 329 yards, an ACC record.

(Wake itself set a record that '93 season. Jim Caldwell, who arrived in Winston-Salem after serving as a Joe Paterno assistant at Penn State, was the first African-American head football coach in conference history.)

Another player's superlative perform-

RIGHT
Jim Caldwell runs onto the field with his Wake Forest team. In 1993, Caldwell became the first African-American football coach in ACC history. He coached at the Winston-Salem school until 2000. His 1999 team won the Jeep Aloha Bowl to finish with a 7-5 record.

ance allowed the Terrapins to emerge with a 33-32 victory in the final-day battle with Wake to avoid last place. Maryland quarterback Scott Milanovich, the ACC leader in total offense (312.6), threw for five touchdowns including the game-winner on the final play to cap a 99-yard drive. The sophomore threw for 416 yards, one of five occasions in 1993 he surpassed 400. Milanovich's prime target, senior Marcus Badgett, paced the conference in receptions and receiving yardage.

Milanovich also led the ACC in punting (43.8), a rare modern double for a quarterback.

Milanovich was impressive, but the league's preeminent quarterback resided in Tallahassee. All the statistics compiled by Charlie Ward in '93 could be reduced to a single number, one, as in the premier player in the country after winning the Heisman Trophy, the first ACC performer so honored; and one, as in the leader of the top team, national champion Florida State.

There are, by definition, no one-man teams, especially championship teams. Florida State had a great defense in 1993, with five All-ACC performers. Derrick Brooks, an outside linebacker, and cornerback Corey Sawyer were consensus All-Americans. The defense shut out four opponents, held seven to a touchdown or less and surrendered four rushing touchdowns in 13 games. Brooks single-handedly outscored FSU's first three opponents by scoring three touchdowns.

Yet it was Ward who made Florida State go, directing the "Fast Break Offense" to 38.1 points per game in 1993, best in the ACC. FSU was a juggernaut, defeating its eight ACC opponents by an average score of 49-6, with 26 its smallest margin of victory. "He could run the football," Bowden said of Ward. "If you covered all the receivers when Charlie was in there, or if you rushed hard

RUSH JOBS

Most 1,000-Yard Rushing Seasons
By Player During ACC Career

No.	Player, School	Seasons Achieved
4	Amos Lawrence, NC	1977, 1978, 1979, 1980
3	Mike Voight, NC	1974, 1975, 1976
3	Ted Brown, NCS	1976, 1977, 1978
3	Kelvin Bryant, NC	1980, 1981, 1982
3	Warrick Dunn, FSU	1994, 1995, 1996

RUSHIN' ARMY

1,000-Yard Rushers By School
As ACC Member (Through 2001 Season)

School	Number	Most Recent, Season
Clemson	10	Woodrow Dantzler, 2001
Duke	4	Robert Baldwin, 1994
Florida State	3	Warrick Dunn, 1996
Georgia Tech	5	Joe Burns, 2001
Maryland	6	Bruce Perry, 2001
No. Carolina	24	Jonathan Linton, 1997
N.C. State	9	Tremayne Stephens, 1997
Virginia	11	Antwoine Womack, 2000
Wake Forest	8	Tarence Williams, 2001

CARRY NATION

First 1,000-Yard Rusher While ACC Member

School	Player	Year	Yards	Yds./Carry
Clemson	Buddy Gore*	1967	1,045	4.5
Duke	Steve Jones	1972	1,236	4.3
FSU	Warrick Dunn	1994	1,026	6.8
Ga. Tech	Robert Lavette	1982	1,208	4.3
Maryland	Steve Atkins	1978	1,261	4.5
UNC	Don McCauley*	1969	1,092	5.4
N.C. State	Willie Burden*	1973	1,014	6.8
South Carolina		None		
Virginia	Frank Quayle	1968	1,213	6.9
Wake Forest	Bill Barnes*	1956	1,010	6.0

*ACC player of year during season

BOTH PAGES: Charlie Ward, a quiet, unassuming young man from Thomasville, Ga., became one of the finest athletes in ACC history during his tenure at Florida State. Ward, a quarterback, led FSU to coach Bobby Bowden's first national championship in 1993. A two-time ACC player of the year in football, Ward received the Heisman Trophy as the nation's top player that same season. He set 19 school and seven ACC records and captured more than 30 individual awards during his career. Ward also played point guard for the Florida State basketball team, and he led FSU to second-place finishes during the school's first two seasons of ACC play in 1992 and '93. After he graduated, Ward moved on to play in the National Basketball Association.

and got out of your lane, he could run for a first down. He would do that. He would run for a touchdown, so you had to be careful how you rushed him."

Bowden's bunch easily handled bullyboy Miami for the first time since 1989, rolling up 450 yards and four touchdowns in a 28-10 win. The offense was supplied by the running of tailbacks Sean Jackson and Warrick Dunn, seven catches by Tamarick Vanover and the passing and scrambling of Ward. Later they snapped Florida's 23-game home winning streak, coming away with a 33-21 triumph on a day Ward had 475 yards of total offense.

The only blemish on FSU's record was a 31-24 loss at Notre Dame. The second-ranked Irish knocked down a final Ward pass at the goal line as time expired. The defeat dropped Florida State from first to second in the polls, but only for a week. Boston College upset Notre Dame in the next game, and FSU returned to No. 1 again.

The season came down to a meeting with Nebraska in the Orange Bowl. Just as Clemson won its 1981 national championship by beating the Cornhuskers and Georgia Tech won its 1990 title by beating them, so FSU topped Nebraska 18-16 to capture the national championship.

The outcome was in doubt quite literally until the final second. Field goals spelled the difference, as often happened to Bowden's teams.

Ward was his usual self, running the offense with aplomb. The game's MVP hit 28 of 43 passes for 286 yards and repeatedly scrambled to safety when necessary. Fullback William Floyd led the team in rushing, and Scott Bentley kicked four field goals. The defense intercepted two passes, the second stopping a drive deep in Florida State territory.

Nebraska trailed most of the second half but went ahead 16-15 on a field goal with 1:16 remaining. Undaunted, Ward led FSU to the Cornhuskers' 5-yard line in less than a minute, allowing Bentley to kick what proved the winning 22-yard

field goal with 21 seconds left.

Nebraska mounted a final drive, only to have time apparently expire. Florida State celebrated, but prematurely. Officials said the Huskers had called timeout with a second to go. "It was unbelievable," Bowden said. "Again, you've got to picture this: I had never won a national championship. We had just kicked the field goal that put us ahead..."

So Nebraska's Bryon Bennett came in and attempted a field goal, which sailed wide left, and Bowden had his 11th consecutive bowl victory, first 12-win season and first national championship.

"People ask me what [winning] the national championship was like," Bowden said. "It was like a relief, to be honest with you. It wasn't like something we accomplished. It was like: 'Y'all get off my back. Y'all get off my back. We finally got one.' Really, that's the way it was."

Another major national title came the ACC's way in 1993-94, this time in women's basketball.

Sylvia Hatchell took over women's basketball at North Carolina in 1987, replacing Jennifer Alley, a winner in each of nine seasons at Chapel Hill. Alley's Tar Heels made it to three straight ACC Tournament championship games from 1984-86, winning in '84. Hatchell's first squad made the NCAA Tournament, but her next four teams posted losing records. Then came consecutive 20-win seasons, and in 1994 a breakout year.

The Tar Heels returned every starter in '94 and added a multi-sport athlete in Californian Marion Jones, a playmaker whose true gifts lay in track and field. By the season's fourth game, Jones started alongside seniors Sylvia Crawley and Tonya Sampson and juniors Charlotte Smith and Stephanie Lawrence. Jones later emerged as one of the greatest performers in modern women's track, winning three gold medals and two bronze in the 2000 Olympics. She has since remained the fastest runner in women's track.

UNC opened with 11 straight wins in

BELOW
North Carolina's Charlotte Smith fires the game-winning three-point shot in the 1994 women's national championship contest against Louisiana Tech. She received an in-bounds pass with seven-tenths of a second left in the game. Smith scored 25 points and grabbed a career-high 23 rebounds as UNC won its first women's title to date, 60-59.

LEFT
Marion Jones (20) played point guard for the 1994 North Carolina women's national championship team. Jones later became the most accomplished female track and field athlete in the world. She won five medals at the 2000 Olympics in Sydney, Australia, and is one of the fastest women ever in the 100-meter dash.

1994, rising to fourth in the national polls before being brought to earth by Virginia. Led by Wendy Palmer, the ACC player of the year in 1995 and 1996, the Cavaliers twice beat the Tar Heels to edge them for first place. North Carolina won a third meeting 77-60 in the ACC Tournament final to secure its first title since 1984. The champion's toughest test came in the semifinals, a 65-64 win over Clemson, which boasted forward Jessica Barr, the '94 ACC player of the year, and Jim Davis, the coach of the year.

"We gained a lot of confidence at the ACC Tournament, especially in tough, tight games," Hatchell said. "That really prepared us for the NCAA Tournament."

Short of prayer or wishful thinking, nothing could prepare North Carolina for the decisive play of the NCAA championship game against perennial power Louisiana Tech. The Tar Heels were behind much of the day and trailed by two when they inbounded the ball in the frontcourt with seven-tenths of a second remaining. That was just enough time for Charlotte Smith to catch Lawrence's pass and release a 3-pointer from the right wing.

"I didn't look at it," said Smith, who had 25 points and a career-high 23 rebounds in the title game. "And the mob got me before I knew it had gone in."

The mob of teammates and coaches had seen the jumper secure a 60-59 victory. In four years, Smith and her classmates had gone from last in the ACC to first in college basketball. "This is the way I've always dreamed about it," said Crawley, who returned as a UNC assistant coach.

Duke also had a dreamy season on the men's side, reaching its fourth NCAA title game in five years. The Blue Devils finished first in the ACC behind Hill, now a senior and the 1994 ACC player of the year, but were knocked from the ACC Tournament by Virginia. The Cavaliers were rising again under Jeff Jones, the former UVa playmaker who replaced Terry Holland as head coach in 1991. But they couldn't stop North Carolina, which won Smith's 12th league title, 73-66.

The Tar Heels, ranked No. 1 in preseason, returned the core of their national championship squad and added a pair of superb freshmen in Jerry Stackhouse and Rasheed Wallace. There was so much talent on UNC's bench, Smith apportioned playing time like a pharmacist formulating a delicate compound. Too delicate, apparently. Despite finishing atop the final AP poll, the Tar Heels lost in the second round of the NCAA Tournament, their earliest ouster since 1984. The defeat by Boston College snapped a record streak of 13 consecutive Sweet 16 appearances.

Four other ACC squads made the 1994 NCAA field, although not Georgia Tech, excluded for the first time in a decade. Maryland was back in the NCAA Tournament and reached the Sweet 16, its best showing since 1984. The success was due in large part to Joe Smith. The freshman led the Terrapins in scoring and was the '94 ACC rookie of the year and a first-team All-ACC selection.

ABOVE
Virginia's Jeff Jones (left), Terry Holland and Craig Littlepage (right) watch the Cavalier men's basketball team from the sideline. Jones played for Holland at Virginia, served as an assistant coach under Holland and then succeeded Holland as head coach in 1990. Holland coached the Cavaliers from 1975-90. His teams won Virginia's first ACC championship in basketball in 1976 and earned the school's first Final Four bid in 1981. Holland eventually became the school's director of athletics. Littlepage served as an assistant basketball coach before moving into athletic administration. He became the ACC's first African-American director of athletics when he succeeded Holland as AD in 2001.

Duke made the NCAAs for the 11th straight year and as usual advanced the farthest of the ACC contingent, reaching its sixth Final Four in seven years. The Blue Devils finished 28-6, their 11th consecutive 20-win season. Since 1986, when they began making regular appearances in the Final Four, the Devils had more wins than any other Division I program.

A nucleus of Hill, Lang and Parks and an underclass backcourt of Chris Collins and Jeff Capel played a more conservative style than normal, relying heavily on Hill to do some of everything. The senior led the Blue Devils in scoring (17.4) and steals (64) as he enjoyed the freedom and capacity to run the offense or spearhead the defense.

"He's the best defensive player we've ever had," Krzyzewski said. "He's the best defensive player I've ever seen in college. It's not even close." Duke previously had national defensive players of the year in Tommy Amaker (1987) and Billy King (1988). Hill was similarly honored in 1993.

The coach's only complaint was that Hill, who had deferred to elders throughout his career, wasn't sufficiently assertive on offense. "Grant is almost too unselfish," Krzyzewski said.

Hill was far from shy in the 1994 NCAA Tournament, outplaying Purdue's Glenn Robinson, the national player of the year, as Duke took the Southeast Region final.

The '94 Final Four came to the Charlotte Coliseum, which had hosted the ACC Tournament. Duke opened by downing Florida as Hill had 25 points.

The title game against Arkansas was tied at 70-all with 51 seconds remaining, but while Collins misfired down the stretch guard Scotty Thurman hit a 22-footer to clinch a 76-72 win for the Razorbacks.

North Carolina captured the first Sears Directors' Cup for the 1993-94 season. The cup goes annually to the athletic department ranked tops in the country based on a point system for all men's and women's NCAA championships.

The big news between school years was Maryland's hiring of Debbie Yow as athletics director. Yow played basketball at Elon College for her sister, Kay, and later coached for eight seasons at Kentucky, Oral Roberts and Florida. The first female AD in the ACC and one of just four in Division I-A when hired, she inherited a program $6.7 million in debt and struggling in football under coach Mark Duffner. "We found that we're number nine in the conference in terms of private gifts and we're number nine in a nine-school conference based on ACC championships," Yow said. "We have to reach a level of achievement in the conference again."

The 1994 football season saw no

BELOW

Grant Hill walks off the court at Cameron Indoor Stadium after his final home game in 1994. Hill enjoyed a spectacular career at Duke and was known as much for his grace and unselfishness as for his offensive accomplishments. He played on two national title teams (1991 and '92) and led the Blue Devils to the NCAA championship game in 1994. In 1993, he was named the national defensive player of the year. He was named the national player of the year, the ACC player of the year and the most outstanding player in the NCAA Tournament Southeast Region in '94.

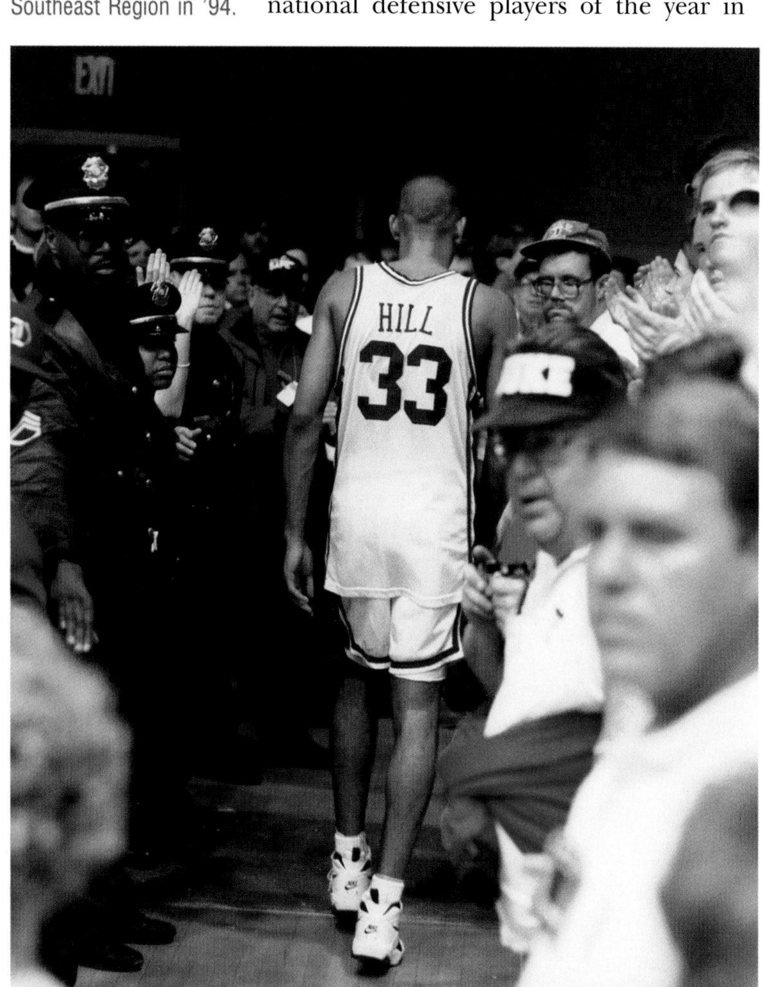

improvement for Maryland, which posted its fourth straight losing effort. Georgia Tech finished in the basement and 1-10 in its third year under Bill Lewis, who was replaced by George O'Leary.

Florida State was at the other end of the spectrum, again going through the league like a scythe in finishing 10-1-1 overall. Six FSU players made the All-ACC offensive unit, including 1,000-yard rusher Warrick Dunn, quarterback Danny Kanell, the ACC leader in total offense, and center Clay Shiver. On defense Brooks and corner Clifton Abraham were consensus All-Americans for the nation's No. 4 team.

FSU led the league in total offense and defense, and in scoring offense and defense. The only loss of the year came against Miami, as was the case in 1992, 1988 and 1987. The regular-season finale at Florida ended at 31-31 as Florida State tied an NCAA record by scoring 28 fourth-quarter points. Oddly, there was an immediate rematch in the Sugar Bowl, won by FSU, 23-17.

N.C. State finished second in the ACC and was 9-3 after beating Mississippi State 28-24 in the Peach Bowl. That would prove the high-water mark of Mike O'Cain's seven-year tenure. His teams never again won more than seven games or finished higher than tied for fourth in the ACC.

Virginia was likewise 9-3 and shared third with North Carolina and Duke. The trio all went bowling, but only Virginia won, beating Texas Christian 20-10 in the Independence Bowl. Duke lost to Wisconsin in the Hall of Fame Bowl, and Texas beat UNC in the Sun Bowl. The Blue Devils have not been to a bowl or posted a winning season since, the longest ongoing drought among ACC members.

The 1994 Cavaliers boasted a coach's son at the helm of the offense, gifted identical twins from Roanoke and a dangerous pass defense.

Quarterback Mike Groh paced the conference in passing efficiency in '94. (Today the younger Groh coaches Virginia's wide receivers, while his father, a UVa alumnus, returned as head coach in 2001.) The 5-10 Barber twins made an impact on both sides of the ball. Redshirt freshman Ronde Barber had eight interceptions, best in the conference. He was voted 1994 ACC rookie of the year and All-ACC. UVa had 27 interceptions on the year, tops in the nation and an ACC record. Sophomore Tiki Barber was second on the squad in rushing. The following two seasons he posted consecutive 1,000-yard efforts, a Cavalier first, and was the ACC's leading rusher his senior year.

By now such success was expected in Charlottesville. The surprise team was Duke, which opened with seven straight wins and finished 8-4 overall under newcomer Fred Goldsmith, the ACC coach of the year.

Duke's five league victories were more than Goldsmith's predecessor, Barry Wilson, managed during a four-year tenure. Duke also boasted the 1994 player of the year in Robert Baldwin, who led the league with 1,187 yards rushing, 107.9 per game. The 6-foot senior from Florida was the 10th Blue Devil named the league's top

BELOW
Twins Tiki and Ronde Barber played a big role as Virginia handed the Florida State football team its first loss in ACC play, which came in a nationally televised game in 1995. The Cavaliers earned a share of the ACC championship that season. Ronde, a defensive back, was the conference rookie of the year in 1994. Tiki (21), a running back, was the 1996 ACC player of the year and is a member of the league's 50th anniversary team. Tiki was also a two-time academic All-American. The brothers advanced to successful careers in the National Football League.

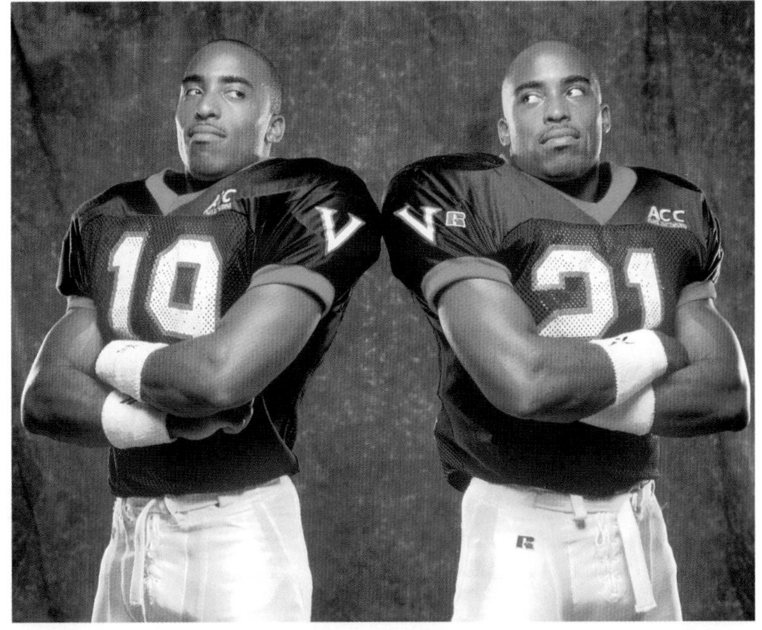

football player, still more than any other school.

Basketball excellence was as routine at Duke as football success had become unfamiliar. But, as North Carolina discovered to its dismay in 2002, the distance between superiority and struggle can be small indeed.

Injuries and academic problems plagued Duke basketball early in 1994-95. Yet the Blue Devils were 9-2 and ranked 11th when Clemson and new coach Rick Barnes came to Durham on Jan. 4 to open the ACC season. More devastating by far than the 75-70 defeat, the Tigers' first win at Cameron since 1984, was what followed.

Krzyzewski announced he was taking time off, ultimately the entire season, due to back problems and related exhaustion caused by inadequate rest following disk surgery in October. "He just found out he doesn't change his clothes in a phone booth," said Dr. Mel Berlin, Duke's team physician, in a reference to Superman.

A parade of close losses commenced. Perhaps the most painfully unsettling for a squad heavy with underclassmen was a home defeat after leading Virginia by 23 points in the second half. The Blue Devils set a school record by opening the ACC season with nine losses. A victory over Georgia Tech that ended the skid caused students to storm the Cameron court. Surveying the spectacle, sophomore Trajan Langdon, one of the team's few bright spots, said, "To tell you the truth, it's kind of embarrassing."

Duke finished 13-18, its first losing season since 1983, Krzyzewsk's third year. That brought an end to 11-year streaks of 20-win seasons and NCAA bids. The Devils failed to win an ACC road game, a first since 1975. They lost six straight games, worst at the school since 1939. They lost 18 games overall, a total unsurpassed in Duke history.

"My main regret is not being a part of the losing," Krzyzewski said. (The losses in his absence were charged to assistant Pete Gaudet, forced out at season's end. In similar circumstances Kansas had once likewise successfully petitioned the NCAA not to charge losses to Phog Allen, its Hall of Fame head coach.) "The fact that we lost was very, very difficult," Krzyzewski said. "But that's the way it is, so let's move on."

The 1995 men's season was remarkable in several respects, not only because of Duke's plummet from penthouse to basement.

Four teams tied for first for the only time in ACC history — Maryland, North Carolina, Virginia and Wake Forest. All were 12-4. All ranked among the top 13 in the nation. All got invited to the NCAA Tournament. All advanced to the Sweet 16 or beyond, the seventh time in 11 years at least four ACC squads got that far. No other conference approached that streak. Every ACC school sent at least one squad to the Sweet 16 between 1989 and 1995, also

BELOW
Center Tim Duncan and coach Dave Odom lifted Wake Forest basketball to its greatest heights in 30 years. The Demon Deacons won consecutive ACC championships in 1995 and '96. Odom, who coached at Wake Forest from 1990-2001, was named ACC coach of the year three times.

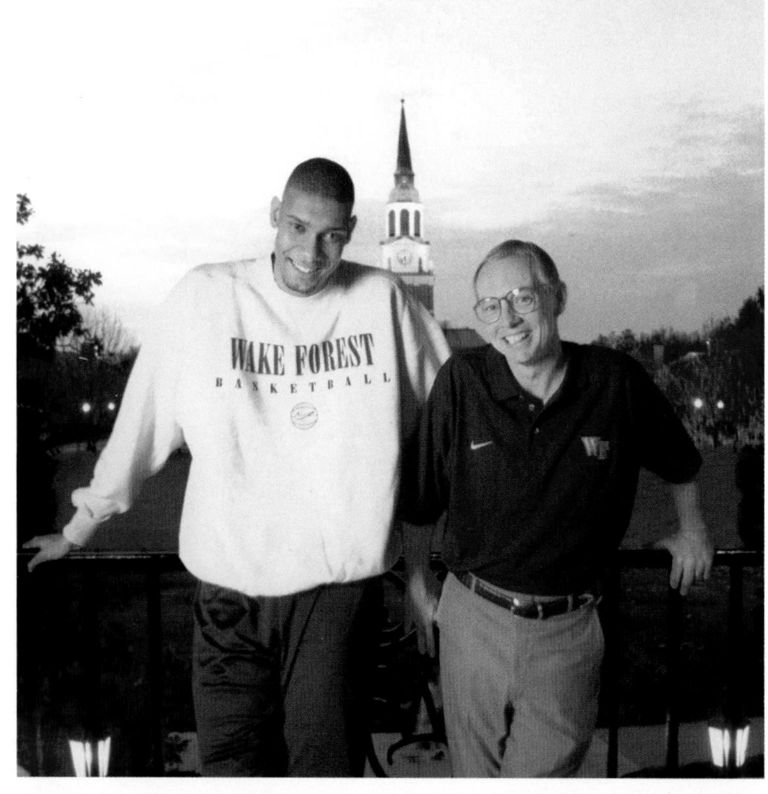

unrivaled excellence.

But four entrants was the league's smallest NCAA representation since 1983. The glaring omission was Georgia Tech, 8-8 in the ACC and 18-12 overall.

Maryland's Sweet 16 trip was its second straight, affirming the program's resurrection under Gary Williams. The Terps' 26-8 record was best at the school since 1972. A record four sophomores made first-team All-ACC in '95. Three left early for the pros, including Maryland's Joe Smith, the league's top scorer (20.8) and the ACC player of the year. Smith was the first pick in the National Basketball Association draft. UNC's Jerry Stackhouse and Rasheed Wallace went in the top four.

The three were among eight ACC players selected in the first round, a record for any conference.

Virginia reached the Midwest Regional final, its deepest advance in 11 years. Guards Harold Deane and Curtis Staples and forward Thomas "Junior" Burrough led the Cavaliers, who ousted top-seed Kansas in Kansas City, Mo., before being eliminated by Arkansas, the defending champs.

Wake got to the Sweet 16 for the second time in three years and finished 26-6. That was the most wins ever at the school and a total the Demon Deacons duplicated in 1996. The Deacons held opponents to 38.8 shooting from the floor, the stingiest defense by an ACC club since South Carolina in 1970. They finished third in the polls, their highest ranking ever.

Odom's club was built around the duo of All-ACC center Tim Duncan, the national defensive player of the year and the ACC leader in rebounds (12.5) and blocked shots (135), and senior guard Randolph Childress, the most valuable player in the 1995 ACC Tournament.

Childress was the only non-sophomore on the All-ACC squad. A cocky multi-purpose player, he led the league in minutes played, was third in scoring with 20.1 points and fourth in assists with 167. Good as Childress was during the regular season, he was downright sensational in the ACC Tournament, scoring a record 107 points in three games — 40 against Duke, 30 against Virginia and 37 against UNC in the championship contest. Childress' floating jumper from eight feet with four seconds to go gave Wake an 82-80 overtime victory to clinch the title, first at the school since 1962.

"There's never been a more fitting way to

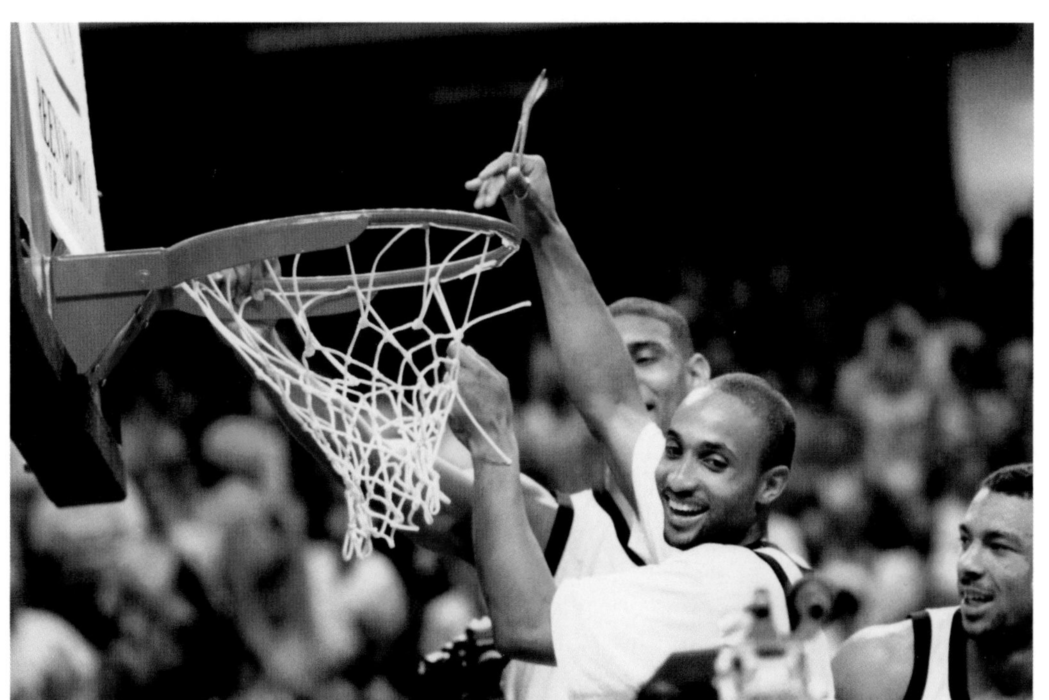

LEFT
Wake Forest's Randolph Childress celebrates after winning the 1995 ACC Tournament, the first championship in basketball for the Deacons since 1962. Childress, the tournament's MVP, scored a record 107 points in three games, including the game-winning shot in an 82-80 overtime victory against North Carolina in the final.

BELOW
Warrick Dunn, a running back from Louisiana, helped direct the way for Florida State football from 1993-96. A member of the 1993 national championship team, Dunn led FSU in rushing three consecutive seasons and finished as Florida State's career leader in rushing yards (3,959). His 1,242 yards in 1995 set a school single-season record. He also set the school career mark for touchdowns (41) and games of rushing for more than 100 yards (21).

end a career in the Atlantic Coast Conference Tournament," said Odom, who repeated as ACC coach of the year in 1995.

The ACC Tournament also saw a confrontation at the scorer's table between UNC's Smith and Clemson's Rick Barnes over roughness of play. Both coaches were fined $2,500, a first in the ACC. Told to give the money to charity, Smith said his gift would go "to fight beer advertising on televised ACC basketball games."

Barnes had replaced Cliff Ellis and took a modestly talented squad to a 15-13 record and the NIT. He admitted later purposely setting out "to change the image" of Clemson basketball. "We don't want to be anybody's whipping boy; we don't want to be anybody's highlight tape; we don't want to be anybody's poster boy," Barnes declared.

The 28-6 Tar Heels shook off the tournament contretemps and the last-gasp loss to Wake to reach the Final Four, Smith's 10th appearance in the event and third during the 1990s. The fourth-ranked Heels depended on Williams, a senior, and sophomores Stackhouse and Wallace, both first-team All-ACC choices. Like Virginia, UNC was bumped by Arkansas.

The mighty also fell in ACC football in 1995, although not far. Florida State still finished first, still ranked fourth in the final poll and still won a major bowl, beating Notre Dame 31-26 in the Orange Bowl.

FSU led the league in total offense for the third straight year and set a conference record with 550.7 yards per game. Six of its players made the All-ACC offensive unit, among them Warrick Dunn, who posted his second consecutive 1,000-yard season. Dunn's 7.48 yards per carry in '95 rank third in ACC history and tops among 1,000-yard rushers.

Yet it was a yard Dunn didn't gain that proved the difference as Virginia finally handed Florida State a loss in ACC competition, ending its winning streak at 29 games over four seasons. "Everyone thought they were invincible," said Virginia defensive tackle Todd White. "Well, we showed they're human. We showed they can bleed."

Close games were the norm for the Cavaliers in 1995. Four of their nine wins, including a Peach Bowl meeting with Georgia, and all four of their losses were decided by a touchdown or less. Virginia's record stood at 6-3 — its defeats at Michigan, UNC and Texas by a combined seven points — when Florida State came calling on Nov. 2. The visitors were top-ranked and undefeated, having scored 70 or more points in three of their seven games.

Playing at night on national television, FSU quarterback Danny Kanell, the 1995

ACC player of the year, passed 67 times for 454 yards and three touchdowns. UVa's Groh passed 37 times for 302 yards and three touchdowns. The offensive difference was at running back, where Tiki Barber gained 193 yards, a career high. He opened the scoring for Virginia with a 64-yard run and returned six punts for 73 yards.

The Cavaliers took a 33-21 lead midway through the fourth quarter, but Florida State closed the gap within 44 seconds on a touchdown run by Dunn. FSU's final drive began at its own 20 with 1:37 remaining. One Virginia penalty and five Kanell completions later, the ball was on the Cavalier 6 with four seconds left.

Seeking the element of surprise, FSU called on Dunn. "We ran a draw because they were dropping everybody back, they were just playing the pass, double-covering everybody," Bowden said. "So we were going to take a chance on Warrick running the draw, and we ran him and he was that short."

That short being inches from the goal line as defensive backs Anthony Poindexter and Adrian Burnim stopped Dunn for a 33-28 victory. "I'm sure they're celebrating all over the league now," said Clay Shiver, Florida State's All-America center.

Poindexter, a precocious freshman, finished his career in 1998 as a consensus All-American. Virginia went on to share the ACC title in 1995, matching FSU at 7-1. George Welsh was voted coach of the year.

The brief interruption in the status quo was remedied the following season, as Florida State again went undefeated in the league.

Consensus All-Americans Peter Boulware and Reinard Wilson, both defensive ends, helped FSU mount the ACC's best rushing defense in 1996, leadership it would continue through the 2000 season. Boulware

BELOW
Florida State running back Warrick Dunn is stopped within inches of a touchdown on the final play of Virginia's 33-28 victory over second-ranked FSU in 1995. Before that night, Florida State had won three conference titles and 29 consecutive conference games since starting ACC play in 1992. The victory, which was broadcast on national television on a Thursday night, enabled Virginia to tie FSU for the conference title.

FOREST
21
CLEMSON
15
21

set an ACC mark with 19 quarterback sacks. The '96 season also was the fourth straight in which Bowden's offense paced the ACC and the third straight in which Dunn rushed for at least 1,000 yards. Only five ACC players have three such seasons to their credit, none since Dunn.

Florida State started the 1996 season ranked third and finished third with an 11-1 record, becoming the first school in NCAA history to post 10 or more wins for 10 consecutive years. After defeating Florida 24-21 in the regular-season finale FSU topped the polls. But in a Sugar Bowl rematch for the national title, the Gators broke open a close game in the second half behind quarterback Danny Wuerffel and won going away, 52-20.

The '96 ACC football season was replete with other notable performances, beginning with North Carolina's 10-2 effort, climaxed by a 20-13 Gator Bowl victory over West Virginia. Freshman defensive back Dre' Bly, the ACC rookie of the year, set a league standard with 11 interceptions for the second-place Tar Heels. UNC led the country in several defensive categories, including scoring defense.

Tailback Leon Johnson finished his career with 5,828 all-purpose yards, an ACC career record. UNC was 10th in the final poll, giving the ACC a pair in the top 10 for the first time since 1990. Mack Brown was ACC coach of the year.

The four ACC squads with winning records received bowl bids, although Clemson and Virginia each lost to finish 7-5. The Cavaliers' Ronde and Tiki Barber made All-ACC, the third pair of twins to do so after N.C. State's Dave and Don Buckey (1975) and Maryland's Al and Keeta Covington (1985). Tiki Barber was 1996 player of the year.

A team also finished without a victory in ACC play for the fourth time in five years. Wake avoided that fate, which it suffered in 1995, on the strength of an unmatched passing performance by Rusty LaRue, a multiple-sport athlete who played guard in basketball and was a baseball pitcher.

The senior quarterback set ACC records with 55 completions and 78 pass attempts (for 478 yards) in a 17-16 victory over 0-11 Duke, two years removed from an eight-win season. The next week, in a loss at N.C. State, LaRue set an ACC mark for most passing yards gained (545). His 1,046 yards over two games are also best in league history.

LaRue started most Wake basketball games in 1995-96, supplying tough defense and timely 3-point shooting in a guard rotation with sophomores Tony Rutland and Jerry Braswell. But he and every other Deacon served as mere complements to Duncan, the 1996 and '97 ACC player of the year and the last repeat winner of the award, as of 2002.

Georgia Tech coach Bobby Cremins, who arrived in Atlanta in 1981-82, said: "Of all the years I've been coaching in this league, I think that Tim Duncan — I know there's Ralph Sampson and Brad Daugherty — but Tim Duncan is at least, at least, the best big man maybe ever to play in this conference. He's a great player, and he's a real winner."

The 6-10 product of St. Croix in the U.S. Virgin Islands ranks as the greatest find in recruiting history, virtually ignored in an era of scouting services and packs of recruiting experts eager to flush out new talent. Odom only heard of Duncan because Chris King, a former Deacon, saw the young big man during a playing tour of the Caribbean.

Duncan was an accomplished competitive swimmer until Hurricane Hugo

FACING PAGE
Tim Duncan (21) was a little-known recruit from St. Croix in the U.S. Virgin Islands. By the time he completed his career at Wake Forest, basketball fans across the country knew him well. The national player of the year in 1997, Duncan was a member of the ACC's all-freshmen team in 1994. He was a two-time ACC player of the year ('96 and '97), three-time first-team All-ACC and a two-time All-American. He set a modern ACC career record for blocked shots (481) and is among the career leaders in rebounds. Duncan was the first player taken in the 1997 National Basketball Association draft and was the 1998 NBA rookie of the year.

By Rob Daniels

ACC EXCELLENCE

VIRGINIA RULES COLLEGIATE MEN'S SOCCER

The early to mid-1990s were, in theory, an odd period for a dominant power to emerge in ACC men's soccer, particularly given the sport may be the least-predictable team game played.

But the Virginia Cavaliers didn't seem to mind what fate dictated, what people may have thought or what opponents did. The run of four consecutive NCAA championships they achieved during those years secured UVa's distinction as one of the great dynasties in the history of any ACC sport. A demanding coach, a mix of stars and former walk-ons, and an ability to win under almost any conditions brought the Cavaliers to exalted status.

"I wasn't going to coach soccer just to keep some fraternity boys happy," said Bruce Arena, architect of the excellence and now the most successful U.S. National Team coach ever. "I wanted to win."

When Arena came aboard in 1978, Clemson was king of ACC soccer, having taken the title from the dominant Maryland teams of the 1950s and '60s. His main job was assistant coach of the lacrosse team. Head man of soccer was essentially a part-time job, and it came with no pressure or expectations. The fraternity boys were more concerned with pursuits other than soccer.

Arena ultimately got what he wanted, though.

As the 1980s progressed, the Cavaliers gained a recruiting budget from the financial success of the Ralph Sampson basketball era. They produced gaudy regular-season records but developed the reputation as postseason failures. ACC brethren Clemson (1984, '87) and Duke (1986) claimed the conference's first solo NCAA championships, surpassing the Terrapins' split crown with Michigan State in 1968.

As the 1990s dawned, there was no sign any program would separate itself from the rest in the ACC. Of seven soccer-playing institutions, five planned major facility upgrades, while Duke had an NCAA title to its name, and N.C. State had developed a recruiting pipeline from New Jersey. Everybody had something to offer.

In the fall of 1990, Arena labeled his team "the worst I have ever been associated with." The supposedly inept Cavaliers went on to the national quarterfinals, losing at N.C. State in penalty kicks. For solace, their coach was quietly amassing what might be the best recruiting class in the history of college soccer.

A.J. Wood was the best forward in the prep ranks, Clint Peay the best defender.

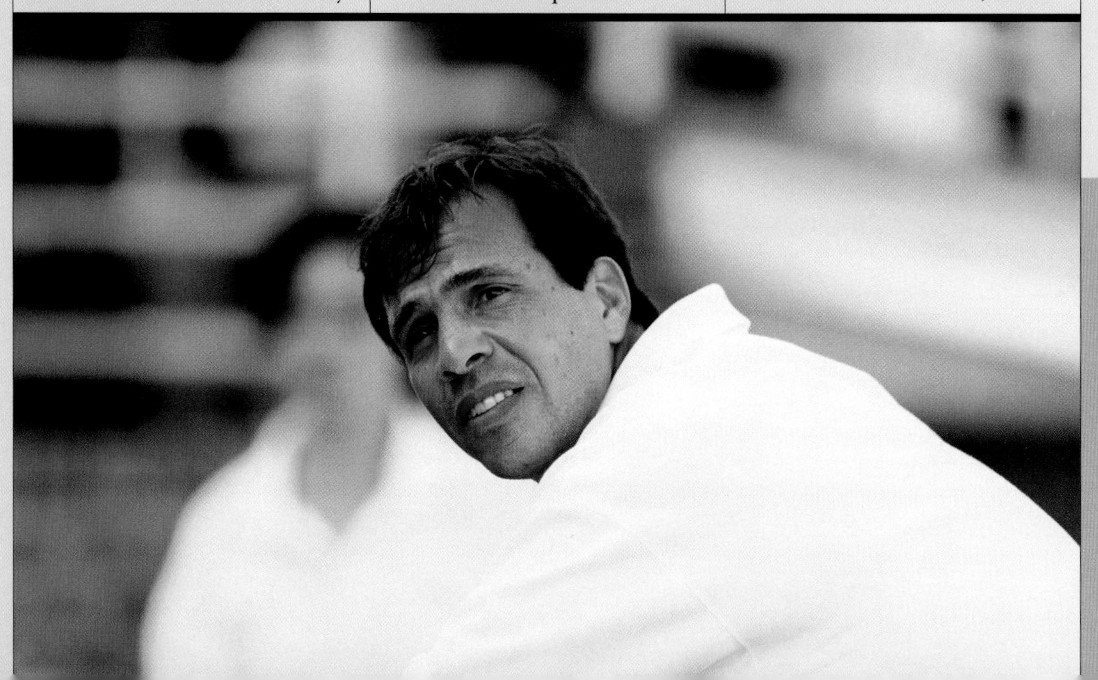

LEFT:
Coach Bruce Arena took college soccer by storm before leaving Virginia to coach the U.S. National team.

RIGHT:
The Cavaliers celebrate their fourth national championship in soccer.

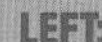

Midfielder Claudio Reyna was only "the future of American soccer," a title conferred on him during his junior year of high school. Reyna could see the whole field. He could insist on the ball in his team's defensive third and never give it up until the time was right. And he could bend shots around befuddled defenders and past goalkeepers.

Fans who had never seen soccer started coming to games. Even the clueless could identify the best player on the field by the 10th minute.

"I had to deal with the pressure, and it was there sometimes, especially at the beginning of the year," Reyna said. "People were wondering how good I was."

The newcomers gave Virginia nine prep All-Americans on the roster, an apparent embarrassment of riches in a game marked by parity at its highest level. The Cavaliers would need every one of their stars.

Of all the sports, soccer is the one in which domination is least likely to produce victory. One bad bounce on artificial turf — a beast more despised by purists in soccer than by those of any other game — and the superior team can go home with a 1-0 loss, despite outshooting the opponent 20-2.

Before the Virginia run, six teams had won consecutive NCAA tournaments and five had come back to make the title game in quest of three straight. Foreign players, teams with ineligible players and teams with ineligible foreign players did them in, however.

The Cavaliers defeated the odds by having enough weapons, enough of an aura, enough of whatever they needed to transcend soccer's inherent barriers.

In the 1991 NCAA semifinals in Tampa, Fla., the Cavaliers trailed Saint Louis 2-1 with 90 seconds left. Most teams with a late lead in soccer throw everybody back into the defensive third of the field, content with the score and desperate to keep it that way. For the trailing team, it's nice to have luck and even nicer to have skilled players.

A 30-yard cross from Mike Huwiler to the head of Ben Crawley tied the game. Less than two minutes into sudden-death overtime, Lyle Yorks chipped the same kind of ball, and Crawley headed it home.

Two days later, backup goalie Tom Henske, another high-school All-American and a guy who lost his starting job to a walk-on, made two saves in a penalty-kick shootout, and the Cavs had their first outright title.

The following year, the Cavaliers overcame a late-season slump and returned to the NCAA final. The Toreros of the University of San Diego thought they could play with the Cavs, and they could. They just couldn't do it long enough.

A former walk-on named Nate Friends scored with 20 minutes left, and the Toreros basically didn't see the ball again. Reyna would not have it and neither would the three starting defenders, all of whom had played with youth U.S. National teams.

"If they get one goal and pack it in, they might not be the better team, but they could foreseeably win," Peay said. "You can't allow anyone the chance to put you in that situation."

The elusive "Three-Peat," a phrase copyrighted by professional basketball coach Pat Riley, was next on the agenda. Loyola of Maryland led Virginia 1-0 in the second half of their 1993 second-round NCAA Tournament game. The superior team missed two headers inside of 10 yards, and the great Reyna smashed one off the crossbar in a 10-minute span.

Was this the end?

Were the 1971 Saint Louis Billikens — whose quest for a third straight championship ended against a Howard team with nine ineligible players — secretly smiling?

Wood scored with 21:45 to play. Shortly thereafter, Reyna drilled a 20-yard shot past the leap of a goalkeeper with a national-best 0.34 goals-against average.

Disaster averted, Virginia made history a week later with a 2-0 NCAA championship win over South Carolina. Friends, who had more interest from basketball coaches than soccer recruiters out of high school, scored both goals.

It takes all kinds, especially in soccer.

Even without Reyna, who had turned pro with one year of eligibility remaining, fortune favored Virginia in 1994 as the Cavaliers made it four consecutive titles. Their run ended with the dawn of Major League Soccer, the professional entity that began plucking great players from colleges and even high schools.

But the ACC kept going. North Carolina, playing with a largely intact senior class, captured the title in 2002 much as UVa often did. Only minutes from defeat in the national semifinals, the Tar Heels forced overtime and won. Their title seemed fated.

If you believe in such things, that is. ✳

destroyed the pool in which he trained. The tall teen-ager switched to basketball when the swim team began practicing at sea, learning the game from his brother-in-law on outdoor courts.

Wake coaches reveled in the big man's even temperament, unspoiled by recruiting attentions, and his stunningly polished game. "He just doesn't have any bad habits," Virginia coach Jeff Jones said.

From the first, Duncan proved composed, talented and skilled. On offense he possessed soft hands, a quick release, a smooth jumper and keen shot selection. On defense his timing was exquisite. He led the ACC in blocks each year and is the modern career leader with 481 in 128 games. He's also third in career rebounds, having paced the ACC from 1995-97. "Duncan is just fabulous," North Carolina's Smith said.

Duncan was only 17 when brought to Winston-Salem as the least acclaimed member of a class with Ricardo Peral and Makhtar Ndiaye, who was released from his scholarship because of recruiting irregularities. Before his 20th birthday, Duncan led Wake to consecutive ACC titles for only the second time in school history. (The other was 1961 and 1962.)

"He exudes so much confidence that it just automatically goes to the rest of the team," Duke forward Carmen Wallace said. "You know that if you get beat, he's going to be there to block shots, or you know if you shoot a shot, he's going to rebound it."

Duncan was a force in 1996, but the ACC was less potent than usual, failing to send a squad to the Final Four for the first time since 1987 and the last time through 2002.

Six teams had winning records. All received NCAA Tournament bids, a welcome change from the previous season. Duke, Maryland and Clemson, all finishers in the middle of the ACC pack, were eliminated in the first round. UNC made it to the second round. Best of the bunch were Georgia Tech, which got to the Sweet 16 for the first time in four years, and Wake, which advanced to the Midwest Regional final, losing 83-63 to Kentucky.

The 1996 season was a roller coaster for the Yellow Jackets. They started 6-7 but finished 24-12, their seventh 20-win season under Cremins. Tech finished alone in first for the only time as an ACC member after posting a 13-3 record during the ACC regular season. The Jackets also returned to the NCAAs after a two-year hiatus. Voted the league's coach of the year, Cremins admitted criticism of his coaching left him worrying. "Have I taken Georgia Tech as far as I can?" he wondered. "Is there something wrong?"

Key to the reemergence was freshman Stephon Marbury. The highly prized New York guard paced the squad in scoring (18.9) and was the '96 ACC rookie of the year. All-ACC forward Matt Harpring — an unsung prospect whom Cremins tried to steer to another school during the recruiting process — lent points (18.6), rebounds, smarts and toughness. Daring guard Drew Barry led the league in assists for the third straight season.

"The turnaround shocked me, and I hope we can build on that," Cremins said. Instead, stung when Marbury and later Dion Glover departed after a single season, Tech struggled anew and Cremins was

1996

1.26.96
Former Clemson football coach Frank Howard dies

1997

3.23.97
North Carolina defeats Louisville 97-74 for Dean Smith's 879th career victory, a major-college record

7.1.97
John Swofford replaces Gene Corrigan, who retired, as ACC commissioner

10.9.97
Bill Guthridge replaces retiring Dean Smith as North Carolina's head basketball coach

gone after the 2000 season.

Wake finished a game off the pace at 12-4 in 1996, splitting the season series with the Yellow Jackets. The rubber match came in the final of the ACC Tournament, which went down to the wire for the second straight year. Again the Deacons emerged victorious, this time because the opponent's shot missed. Marbury's contested baseline jumper with five seconds remaining hit the side of the backboard as Duncan came flying toward him.

"Duncan makes it tough to score for anybody inside," Maryland's Williams said. "He plays both ends of the court. And he's unselfish."

Duncan, the Case Award winner as MVP, had 27 points, six assists and four blocked shots in the championship contest. His 56 rebounds in three games set an ACC Tournament record, as did his 22 in the final.

Unfortunately the 75-74 victory proved crippling to Wake Forest's NCAA aspirations, because with about 14 minutes remaining Rutland injured his right knee. That allowed Tech to close with a rush after trailing by 18 points in the second half, and reduced the Deacons' ball-handling, defensive quickness and perimeter scoring strength.

Stopped short of an NCAA title but content with college life, Duncan announced he would return for his senior season. Consequently Wake became the favorite again in 1996-97. The predictions seemed apt as the Demon Deacons won their first 13 games, rising to second in the polls. They also beat Duke for the ninth straight time, fifth at Cameron, the most decisive dominance the Blue Devils suffered during Krzyzewski's career.

That was as good as it got. The Deacons were 11-7 the remainder of the season as others moved to the fore. The first blow was struck by Maryland, which came to Winston-Salem and upset the Deacons, 54-51. Wake followed with a visit to Clemson — 16-1 and second-ranked, best in school history — and emerged with a close 65-62 win.

Rick Barnes, product of a mill town in North Carolina, had quickly toughened and improved the Tigers. His first year he added 1995 ACC rookie of the year Greg Buckner, Clemson's only winner of the award to date, and took the Tigers to the NIT. In 1996 Clemson was in the NCAAs. The season highlight was Buckner's dunk at the buzzer to cap a rally to upset UNC 75-73 in the ACC Tournament. That remains Clemson's only win over the Tar Heels in the event.

In 1997 Buckner, big man Harold Jamison and 5-8 guard Terrell McIntyre lifted the Tigers to a fourth-place tie in ACC play. Clemson's 9-7 record was its first winning league mark since 1990. Ranked 14th, Clemson was one of six ACC teams in the NCAA Tournament. No. 9 Wake, which finished tied for second with North Carolina, went out in two rounds, ending Duncan's college career.

A Duke squad heavy with holdovers from its '95 collapse was the surprise first-place finisher under Krzyzewski, the 1997 coach of the year. The victory that supplied a one-game edge in the league race came at Charlottesville in February. Game officials mishandled a substitution in the final sec-

11.8.97
Florida State wins 20-3 at North Carolina in first match of top-5 ACC football teams

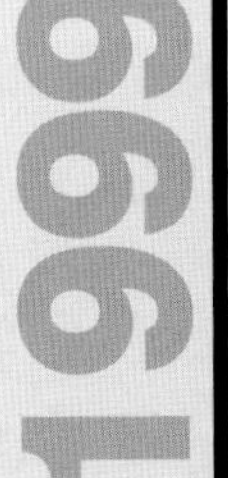

3.28.99
Duke women reach the NCAA basketball final, losing 62-45 to Purdue

10.23.99
Florida State and Bobby Bowden defeat Clemson and Tommy Bowden 17-14 in the first father/son coaching matchup in major-college history, known as Bowden Bowl I

11.19.99
N.C. State opens Raleigh's Entertainment and Sports Arena with a 67-63 win over Georgia

FACING PAGE
Dean Smith cuts down the nets at his final ACC Tournament. Smith retired in 1997 after 36 seasons as North Carolina's head coach. His teams won 13 ACC championships and two national titles. His 879 victories are more than any other Division I coach. Smith is a member of the Naismith Basketball Hall of Fame. He was voted the ACC coach of the year eight times. His last UNC team won the ACC title and earned a berth in Smith's 11th Final Four.

onds of a close contest, following a free throw by Virginia's Norman Nolan. Play continued while the scorekeeper vainly sounded the horn. Amidst the confusion, Steve Wojciechowski, later a Duke assistant coach, drove toward the Virginia basket and was fouled. The guard made two free throws and Duke had a 62-61 victory. The gaffe led the ACC to issue an unprecedented public censure of the officiating crew.

Duke's 1997 performance started an unequaled streak in which the Blue Devils finished with at least a part of first place every year through 2001. The '97 club didn't last long in the NCAA Tournament, however, falling in the second round to a Providence squad coached by Pete Gillen, hired as Virginia's head coach two years later.

The team that got deepest into the 1997 NCAA Tournament was North Carolina, which also won the ACC Tournament after surviving one of the great upset bids in league history.

N.C. State entered the tournament with a losing record and the eighth seed under new coach Herb Sendek. Four games later, the Wolfpack was in the final, the first No. 8 to advance that far. (Prior to Sendek's hiring, Wake coach Dave Odom was courted by N.C. State to replace Les Robinson. Odom was interested and called Gene Corrigan. The commissioner said he "probably" killed the idea of the coach moving from school to school within the league. "He said, 'What do you think?'" Corrigan recalled. "I said, 'Gee, I'd hate to see that happen.'")

The '97 Wolfpack employed an iron five, with point guard Justin Gainey playing 40 minutes in all four ACC Tournament games. No N.C. State starter was taller than 6-6. The team relied on tenacious man-to-man defense and an offense that spread the court and worked patiently for drives or 3-pointers. "I just think it's a group of guys who are very together, very focused," Sendek said.

The Wolfpack opened by dispatching No. 9 Georgia Tech, which like Clemson in 1991 and Duke in 1995 had plummeted in a year's time from first to last. Then came a 66-60 win over top-seed Duke as guard Clint "C.C." Harrison led all scorers with 28 points. Maryland fell next, giving N.C. State a chance to gain the league's automatic NCAA bid and strike a historic blow for underdogs.

Standing in the way was North Carolina and Smith, on the verge of his own place in the history books. The Heels had gotten off to an 0-3 start in ACC play. Now they punctuated their season-long comeback with a 64-54 victory over N.C. State behind guard Shammond Williams, the tournament MVP, and tough defense, including a

LEFT
N.C. State coach Herb Sendek took his first Wolfpack team to the ACC Tournament final, despite having no starter taller than 6 feet 6 and a limited roster. His 2002 team made it to the NCAA Tournament, breaking a school drought that dated to 1991.

1997 ACC
ATLANTIC COAST CONFERENCE
BASKETBALL
TOURNAMENT
CHAMPIONS
GREENSBORO

zone with 7-3 Serge Zwikker occasionally on the perimeter. The ACC title was Smith's 13th in 21 appearances in the final.

The Tar Heels defeated Colorado 73-56 in the NCAA East Region at Winston-Salem's Joel Coliseum two games later. Smith became the victory leader among major-college coaches, surpassing Kentucky's Adolph Rupp, another product of Phog Allen's Kansas program.

Williams, sophomores Antawn Jamison and Vince Carter, and playmaker Ed Cota, the ACC rookie of the year, propelled UNC to two more wins and a berth in the Final Four. That pushed North Carolina's winning streak to 16 and Smith's career total to 879 victories in 36 seasons. Finally Arizona, the eventual champion, stopped the Tar Heels 66-58 in what proved Smith's last game.

Smith abruptly announced his retirement on the eve of fall practice in early October 1997. Bill Guthridge, his 30-year assistant, replaced him. "I enjoy basketball," said Smith, whose teams won 77.5 percent of their games. "I enjoy coaching basketball. It's the out-of-season things I haven't been able to handle very well."

Just as North Carolina's place among ACC and national basketball powers was a given under a great coach, so it was in football for Florida State.

FSU was undefeated in 1997 league play, its fifth unblemished run in six years since joining the ACC. Bowden's club led the league in total offense for the fifth straight season. Senior quarterback Thad Busby was the ACC's total offense leader (330.1 yards per game) and running back Travis Minor was the '97 ACC rookie of the year. For the fourth time Florida State supplied the ACC player of the year, defensive end Andre Wadsworth. He was a consensus All-American along with linebacker Sam Cowart on a defense that led the ACC and the nation against the run, holding oppo-

IMMEDIATE RIGHT
North Carolina's Antawn Jamison exploded onto the scene as a proficient scorer and rebounder in all three of his ACC seasons. Jamison led his team to two Final Four appearances. He was a three-time first-team All-ACC selection. In 1998 Jamison led the league in scoring (22.2 points per game) and rebounding (10.5). He was also named the ACC player of the year, the ACC Tournament MVP, the national player of the year and won the McKevlin Award as the conference's athlete of the year.

FAR RIGHT
Joe Smith (1994-95) was not a highly acclaimed player before arriving at Maryland. But in 1995, his sophomore season, Smith was named a consensus All-American, the national player of the year, ACC player of the year and first-team All-ACC. He then declared for the National Basketball Association's draft and was selected No. 1 overall. He averaged 20.1 points and 10.7 rebounds in two years at Maryland.

nents to 51.9 yards per game.

Florida State rose as high as second in the polls and finished fourth after its 11th win, 31-14 over Ohio State in the Sugar Bowl. For the fifth time as an ACC member FSU suffered a single loss, dropping a 32-29 decision at Florida on the final weekend of the regular season. Bowden was voted ACC coach of the year.

There was another 11-1 squad in the conference in 1997. Bill Dooley in 1972 and Dick Crum in 1980 previously had taken North Carolina to those heights. Now Mack Brown gave the ACC its first and only pair of 11-victory teams as UNC concluded its sterling season with a 42-3 thrashing of Virginia Tech in the Gator Bowl.

Actually Brown left before the bowl game to coach at Texas. Carl Torbush, North Carolina's defensive coordinator, was promoted to head coach and completed the job.

North Carolina had more wins from 1992-97 than all but seven programs in Division I-A, Florida State among them. The '97 Tar Heels led the ACC in total defense for the third year in a row and were especially tough against the pass, holding opponents to 81.5 yards. Four Tar Heels made the ACC's all-defensive team, the third time for end Greg Ellis and Bly.

On offense, running back Jonathan Linton averaged 91.3 yards, second in the ACC to N.C. State's Tremayne Stephens, and became the school's 24th 1,000-yard rusher.

Good as North Carolina was, it couldn't beat Florida State, which visited Chapel Hill on Nov. 6 in the first battle of top five teams in ACC history.

FSU was ranked third, UNC fifth. A heated buildup attracted 500 media members to Kenan Stadium. A national TV audience saw the visitors emerge with a decisive 20-3 victory, their defense exerting what Brown called "total domination" in holding the Tar Heels to 73 yards, nine in the first half. Florida State notched nine sacks of quarterbacks Chris Keldorf and Oscar Davenport, who broke his ankle in the fourth quarter.

"They haven't had enough wide-rights yet," said Bowden, whose teams were toughened by several close losses when field goals sailed awry. The ACC's top offense handled the nation's No. 2 defense as Busby threw for two touchdowns, Minor rushed for 128 yards, and Sebastian Janikowski kicked a pair of field goals and a pair of extra points.

Four other ACC football teams had winning records that year as the league was victorious in 71 percent of its non-conference contests, third-best ever. The '97 Yellow Jackets got their first bowl bid under George O'Leary, in his fourth season, and beat West Virginia 35-30 in the Carquest Bowl. Clemson lost to Auburn 21-17 in the Peach Bowl. UVa stayed home for the first time since 1992.

Corrigan, a former UVa athletics director and coach, also decided it was time to stay home, becoming the first ACC commissioner to retire rather than die in office. On July 1, John Swofford became the league's fourth commissioner. The former North Carolina football player had

LEFT
Nomar Garciaparra is famous for being the shortstop for Major League Baseball's Boston Red Sox, but he got his start at Georgia Tech. He was a consensus first-team All-American in 1993 and '94. Twice first-team All-ACC, he also earned honors as a two-time academic All-American. He finished his Tech career batting .374 with 23 home runs and 66 stolen bases, and ranks among Tech's career leaders in batting average, doubles (58), triples (14) and stolen bases. Drafted in 1994, he won the American League rookie of the year award in 1998. He captured AL batting titles in 1999 and 2000.

been serving as athletics director at his alma mater.

Personable and gregarious, "full of Irish charm" as Wake President Thomas Hearn described it, Corrigan took with him a record of adding Florida State to the fold, improving the quality and stature of ACC football, bringing together university presidents and athletics directors to facilitate NCAA reform, widening exposure of ACC women's sports (particularly basketball) and boosting revenues. "This is prideful," Corrigan said, "but the league is where it is because it's had good commissioners. It's had commissioners who were respected and could get things done."

Among Corrigan's tasks late in his tenure was dampening several heated sideline encounters between Clemson's Barnes and UNC's Smith. With Smith gone, ACC basketball had a different timbre. The atmosphere changed again a year later when the combative Barnes followed Mack Brown to Texas.

North Carolina's excellence remained a constant. Guthridge, a bit of a hothead in his earlier days, coolly guided the veteran Tar Heels to 17 straight wins to open the 1997-98 season and a No.1 final ranking. UNC advanced to another Final Four, but lost 65-59 to Utah. The achievements earned the longtime sidekick 1998 ACC and national coach of the year recognition.

Jamison, a smooth 6-9 forward, became the first Tar Heel since Michael Jordan in 1984 to top the ACC in scoring (22.2). Jamison also led the league in rebounding (10.5), becoming the third player in two decades to achieve that double after Wake's Tim Duncan (1997) and Clemson's Horace Grant (1987). Voted the '98 ACC player of the year, the personable Jamison was joined on the All-ACC first team by classmate Carter. Cota was the ACC's top assist man, a status he maintained all four years of his career, surpassing any modern player.

Duke almost matched UNC step for step. Each finished in the nation's top three, received a No. 1 seed in the NCAA Tournament and had a 32-4 record, only the second time (after 1982) the ACC had two 30-win squads. The Blue Devils won 19 of their first 20 games and were first in the polls until they lost 97-73 at No. 2 North Carolina. Seven games later Duke evened the season series at Cameron to finish first in the league and third in the final AP poll. The Tar Heels then took the third meeting in the set 83-68 to win the ACC Tournament.

Duke, one of five ACC teams in the NCAA field, was stopped a game short of the Final Four. Kentucky, the eventual champion, rallied from 17 points down in the second half to win 86-84 in the Southeast Region final.

Maryland, the third-place ACC finisher, reached the Sweet 16 for the third time in five seasons, sparked by senior Rodney Elliott and a junior class of Laron Profit, Obinna Ekezie and Terrell Stokes. Clemson returned to the NCAA Tournament for a third straight year, a school record. New coach Steve Robinson took Florida State to the NCAAs in what would prove the only winning season of his five-year tenure.

ACC women similarly enjoyed a strong showing overall, with one team reaching the Final Four. Five women's squads got NCAA Tournament invitations, four had 20-win seasons and three finished in the top 10, a first for the conference.

No. 7 North Carolina, led by player of the year Tracy Reid and rookie of the year

Nikki Teasley, won its fourth ACC Tournament in five seasons. Reid led the league in scoring for the third year in a row and in rebounding for the second. Teasley was the assist leader, a feat she repeated the following two seasons. The Tar Heels got to the Midwest Region final and lost to Tennessee.

No. 8 Duke, emerging as a power under '98 coach of the year Gail Goestenkors, broke new ground by finishing first during the ACC regular season. Powered by guards Hilary Howard and Nicole Erickson, the Blue Devils reached the West Region final and lost to Arkansas.

No. 10 N.C. State tied Clemson for second during the regular season, a game behind Duke. After a quick exit in the ACC Tournament, the Wolfpack and All-ACC center Chasity Melvin advanced to the Final Four, a first for Yow's program. Louisiana Tech eliminated the Pack, 84-65.

N.C. State enjoyed a notable 1998 football season as well. The 7-5 record wasn't all that special, but there were other highlights. For the first time in four years, the Wolfpack got a postseason bid, losing to Miami in the Micron PC Bowl. For the first time in a quarter-century, the Wolfpack boasted the ACC player of the year, receiver and punt-return specialist Torry Holt. And, for the first time since the ACC added its ninth team, the Pack beat Florida State, 24-7.

"Nobody gave us a dog's chance of coming in here and having a chance to win this football game, not a prayer," O'Cain said.

FSU scored the first time it touched the ball at Raleigh and appeared it wouldn't have much difficulty extending a streak of 17 consecutive ACC victories. But things didn't go well for quarterback Chris Weinke after hitting receiver Peter Warrick with a 74-yard touchdown pass on Florida State's opening play from scrimmage. Late in the first quarter, with the ball on the Wolfpack 5, the 26-year-old Weinke threw the first of his school-record six interceptions.

N.C. State quarterback Jamie Barnette immediately initiated a 10-play, 99-yard drive to close the gap to 7-6. Two minutes

BELOW
Chris Weinke became the second ACC player to win the Heisman Trophy as the nation's top football player. And just as Charlie Ward before him, Weinke directed Florida State to a national championship. He led the nation with 4,167 passing yards as a senior in 2000. His 1999 team went 12-0 and stayed No. 1 in the polls from start to finish. He threw for more yards (9,839) than any player in ACC history.

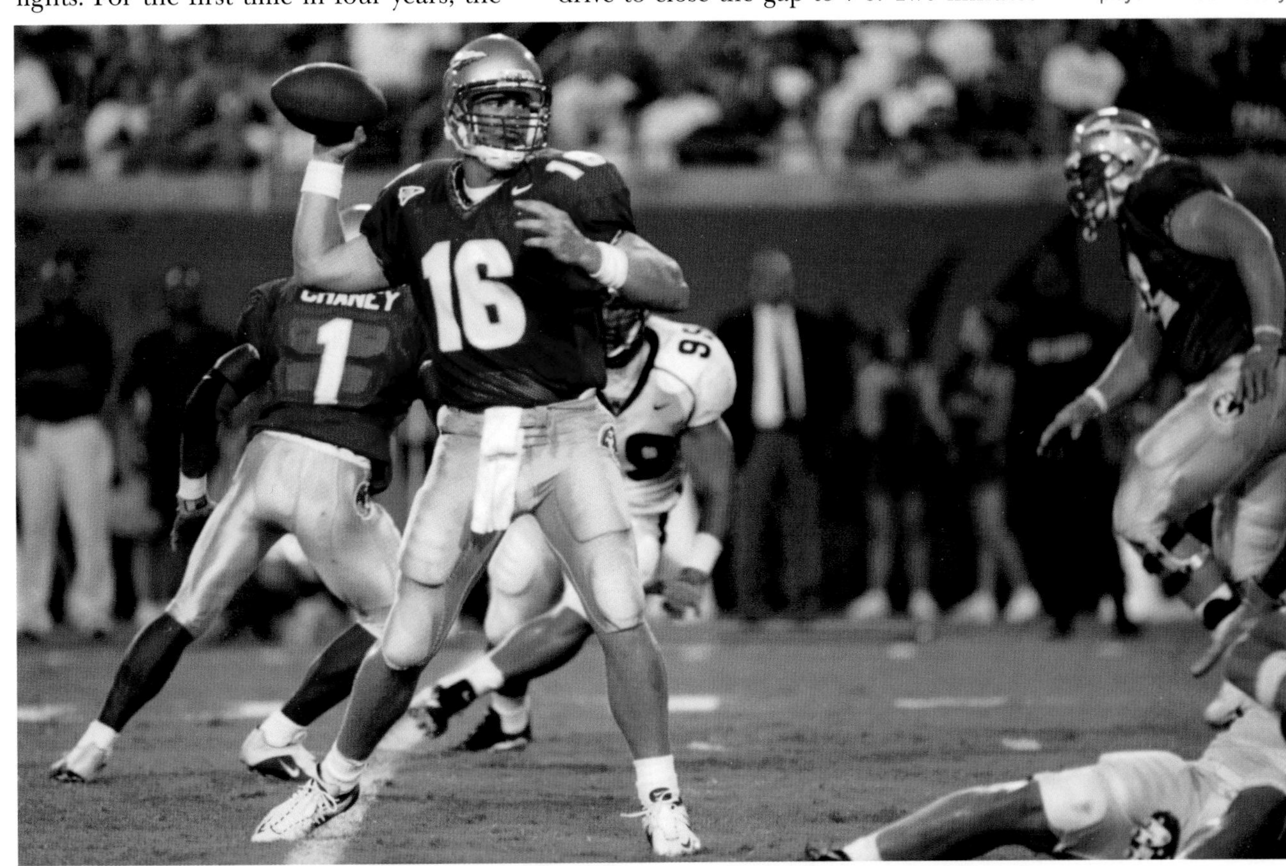

BELOW
N.C. State wide receiver Torry Holt (81) caught 31 touchdown passes in his career, five in one game against Florida State in 1997. He set ACC records for receiving yards and school records for receptions (191), touchdown receptions in a career (31) and in a season (16), and number of 100-yard receiving games in a career (14). A consensus All-American, Holt was the conference player of the year and the offensive player of the year in 1998.

later, Holt returned a punt 68 yards for a score. The Wolfpack wouldn't trail again. Holt later scored on a 63-yard pass from Barnette, who completed 17 of 32 passes for 287 yards and ended the year as the league's total offense leader (289.3 yards per game).

Holt led the league in receiving and receiving yardage in 1998. He also set single-season ACC records with eight receptions and 145.8 receiving yards per game, and with 88 catches and 1,604 receiving yards for the season. The consensus All-American's 179.9 all-purpose yards per game rank fourth in league history behind a trio of running backs. Holt's season overshadowed Wake Forest's Desmond Clark, a 6-3 wide receiver from Florida who finished his career with 216 receptions, tops in ACC history.

Weinke, who spent six years playing minor-league ball in the Toronto Blue Jays baseball organization before returning to college, was a different player following the loss at N.C. State. He didn't throw another interception in his next 218 pass attempts, a streak ended when he ruptured a disk and damaged ligaments in his neck in the 10th game of the '98 season, a 45-14 win over Virginia.

Florida State shared first in the ACC at 7-1 with Georgia Tech, which it beat 34-7 at Atlanta. Coach of the year O'Leary produced a 10-2 season, capped by a 35-28 win over Notre Dame in the Gator Bowl. Joe Hamilton, Tech's junior quarterback, led the ACC in passing efficiency, a feat he would repeat in 1999.

FSU, 11-2 and third in the polls, ended the year by dropping a 23-16 decision to top-ranked Tennessee in the Fiesta Bowl, the first Bowl Championship Series attempt to determine a national champion. FSU had beaten Florida in the final

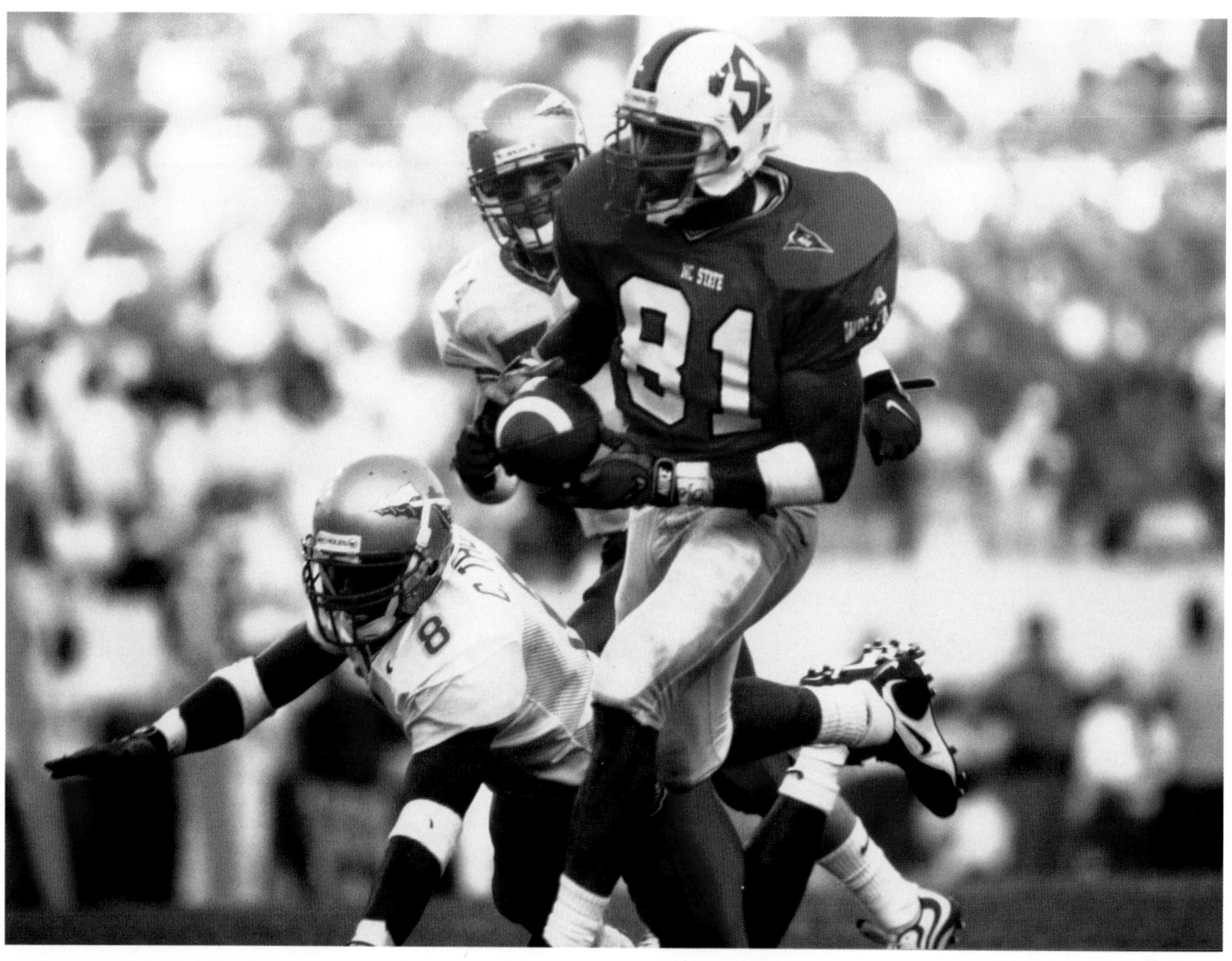

regular-season game to earn its way in with a third-string quarterback.

Tech finished ninth and Virginia 18th. UVa, a 35-33 loser to Georgia in the Peach Bowl, was 9-3. The Cavaliers' Thomas Jones led the ACC in rushing (118.5), a feat he duplicated in 1999.

The pendulum that swung so strongly in favor of Virginia football went the other way in basketball. In fact, the three schools with the top football teams in 1998 produced losing basketball squads in 1998-99. Georgia Tech almost avoided that fate with a breakeven record to end the regular season, but was 15-16 after dropping its NIT opener.

Clemson reached the NIT title game under new coach Larry Shyatt, but the Tigers lost 61-60 to California, ending the school's only shot at a men's basketball championship since the 1962 ACC Tournament. Four ACC teams played in the 1999 NIT, the first time since 1979 the league had more entrants in that event than in the NCAA Tournament.

Three ACC members — Duke, Maryland and North Carolina, which finished in that order for the second straight year — received NCAA Tournament bids, fewest since 1979.

The trio enjoyed the only winning records in ACC competition, in part because Duke won its 16 league outings and dominated in a manner not seen since UNC was undefeated in conference play in 1987. The Blue Devils beat league opponents by an average margin of 24.3 points, with only a game at Tech decided by fewer than 10. Duke defeated UNC 96-73 in the ACC Tournament championship game. That started an unprecedented run of four straight ACC titles by the Blue Devils, recovered as completely as Krzyzewski from the debacle of '95.

"They absolutely are dynamite offensively, which I think, more than their defense, gives them a chance to win the national championship," Wake's Odom said. "It is not likely that as many as three or four of them are going to be off on the same night. They've got eight players who can score."

Toughest to stop was 6-8, 265-pound Elton Brand, the ACC and national player of the year. Brand became the first Duke player to leave early for professional ball and was selected first overall in the 1999 draft.

Shane Battier, a complementary fellow sophomore, joined Brand in the frontcourt. The wing positions were filled by tough juniors Chris Carrawell and Nate

BELOW
Elton Brand played just two years at Duke, but he excelled. Brand led the ACC in field goal percentage (.620) in '99 while averaging 17.7 points and 9.8 rebounds on a team that went undefeated (16-0) in ACC play during the regular season, won the ACC Tournament and finished 37-2 overall. Brand was the 1999 ACC player of the year, the ACC Tournament MVP and the national player of the year.

BELOW
Coach Gail Goestenkors became head women's basketball coach at Duke in 1992 and has since turned the Blue Devils into a consistent national contender. She is a four-time ACC coach of the year. Her team played for the national championship in 1999, and her 2002 Blue Devils went undefeated in the conference (16-0), won the ACC Tournament and earned a trip to the Final Four.

James and explosive freshman Corey Maggette, and the guards were senior Trajan Langdon and sophomore William Avery.

Duke's talented collection soared to the top of the polls, a 32-game winning streak after a November loss to Cincinnati and a final 37-2 record. Carrawell would be ACC player of the year in 2000; Battier, ACC and national player of the year in 2001.

Maryland was almost as good, setting a new school standard with 28 wins. Junior-college transfer Steve Francis and sophomore Terence Morris were first-team All-ACC along with Brand, Langdon and UNC's Ademola Okulaja, the heart of a Tar Heel squad that finished 24-10. The Terps advanced to the Sweet 16 for the fourth time in six years. The Tar Heels were shocked in the first round by Weber State, 76-74.

Hailed as one of the best teams of modern times, Duke reached the NCAA title game, but Connecticut won, 77-74. Rather than etch their place in the pantheon of notable champions, the Blue Devils lost their fourth NCAA final under Krzyzewski and sixth overall, more than any program in history. "I've been fortunate to be in a bunch of terrific games," Krzyzewski said. "If anybody expects me to be down about this game, they don't understand me. I'm not going to be down about this game because it would take away from my experience with this group."

Just a day before Duke fell in St. Petersburg, across the country in San Jose, Calif., the school commenced a rare double by having its women's team also play for an NCAA basketball title. The feat remains unequaled in ACC history.

Five ACC women's squads reached the 1999 NCAA Tournament after a regular season in which Duke finished first, matching 1998. The Blue Devils ranked second nationally, highest by a league team since Virginia was top-rated seven years earlier. But the sailing wasn't always smooth. The Blue Devils, led by guards Nicole Erickson and Georgia Schweitzer and All-ACC center Michele VanGorp, got off to a 1-3 start before rallying to finish 29-7.

Duke was knocked out in the ACC Tournament semifinal by Clemson, which eventually reached the Sweet 16. The Tigers won their second league title in four years, defeating UNC, another eventual Sweet 16 contestant.

Coach Gail Goestenkors' squad prospered in the NCAA Tournament, advancing to the program's first Final Four after defeating Tennessee 69-63 in the East Region final. The Blue Devils beat Georgia to reach the championship contest but couldn't handle top-ranked Purdue in a 62-45 loss.

What Duke could not achieve in basketball in 1999, Florida State football handled with uncommon ease the following fall. A 12-0 record, capped by a 46-29 victory over Virginia Tech in the Sugar Bowl, secured Bobby Bowden's second national championship within a seven-year span. "Ninety-nine was something I always wanted, and I wish we could do again," Bowden said. "We were first in the nation on the first day of the season, and we were first in the nation every day, and that's the first time it's ever been done wire to wire."

Florida State, strong as it was, didn't run away from the rest of the ACC.

Georgia Tech, behind '99 ACC player of the year Joe Hamilton, battled down to the wire at Doak Campbell Stadium before falling, 41-35. Hamilton, who finished second in the Heisman balloting and started all but one game in his career, set new league standards for total offense in a season (344.9) and a career (10,640 yards). Directed by the mobile, 5-10 senior quarterback from South Carolina, Tech led the nation in total offense (509.0) in 1999, a first for an ACC club.

A trip to Clemson resulted in a 17-14 Florida State win, secured on a field goal with 5:26 left, in the first father-son matchup in major-college football history. That was the 300th career triumph for father Bobby Bowden. Son Tommy, in his first season with the Tigers, was the 1999 ACC coach of the year.

FSU later rallied from a 10-7 halftime deficit to win 35-10 at Virginia. The Cavaliers won seven games for a 13th straight season under George Welsh, their '99 offense powered by senior running back Thomas Jones. The 5-10 consensus All-American rushed for 1,798 yards, most in a season by an ACC back. UNC's Don

BELOW
Florida State flanker Peter Warrick was a two-time consensus All-American who scored a bowl-record 20 points with three touchdown receptions and a catch for a two-point conversion in the national championship game against Virginia Tech in the 2000 Sugar Bowl. He finished his career as the ACC's leader in receiving yardage (3,517).

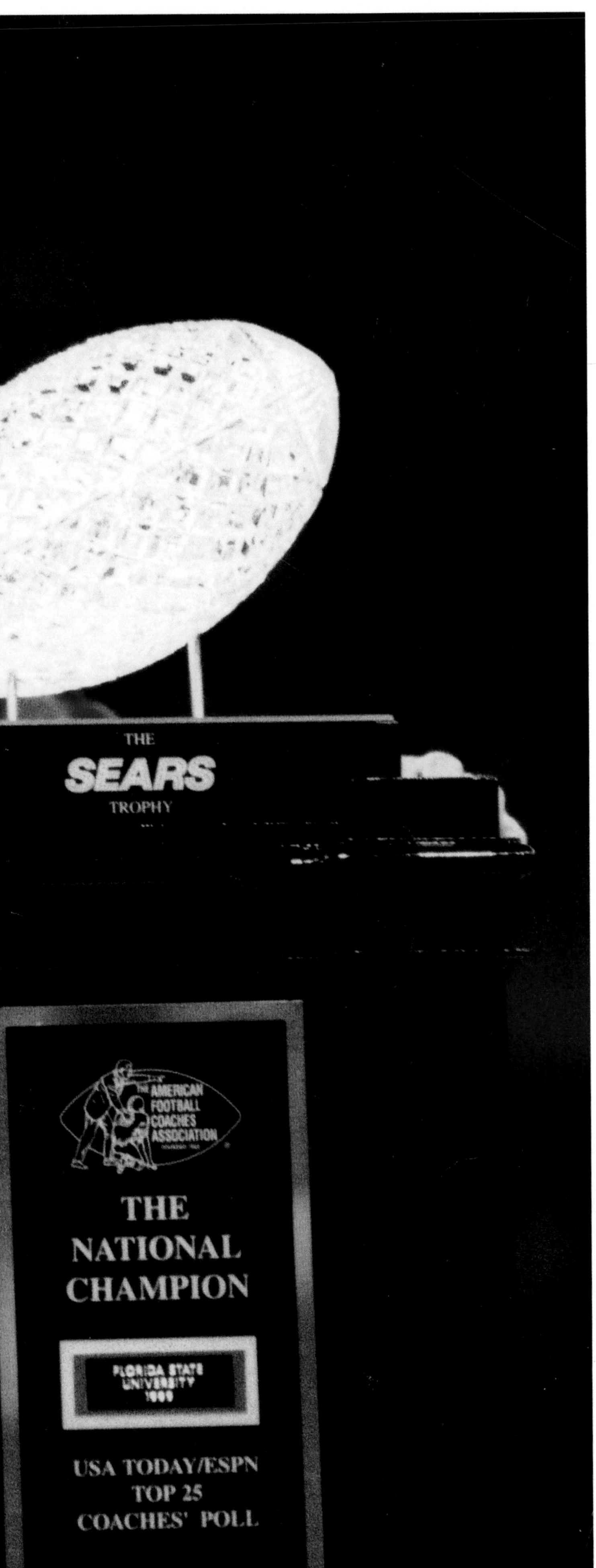

McCauley had set the record 29 years earlier.

Clemson, Tech and UVa all went to bowls, as did Wake Forest, a 23-3 victor over Arizona State in the Aloha Bowl. Only the ACC among Division I-A conferences had a team from every one of its schools invited to a bowl during the 1990s.

The team that went every year was Florida State, the first I-A school to win at least 10 games in each of 13 consecutive seasons. Powered as always by superior talent, much of it Florida-grown, FSU boasted four consensus All-Americans on its march to the national title: noseguard Corey Simon, offensive guard Jason Whitaker, Warrick and Janikowski. Warrick, an elusive senior, finished as the ACC career leader in receiving yardage (3,517).

Everything came down to the Sugar Bowl on Jan. 4, 2000, in the Louisiana Superdome, where UNC's Smith won both his basketball titles. Florida State jumped to a 28-14 halftime lead, fueled by the passing of Weinke and by Warrick, who set a Sugar Bowl record by scoring 20 points on two touchdown passes, a 59-yard punt return and a catch of a 2-point conversion pass.

The FSU lead grew to 21 points, but freshman Virginia Tech quarterback Michael Vick rallied his team to a 29-28 lead with 2:13 remaining in the third quarter. "He looked like Superman if I ever saw Superman on a football field," Bowden said of Vick. "We simply could not hem him up."

Weinke, unfazed by the pressure, threw a pair of scoring passes to Ron Dugans and Warrick. Sandwiched around a Janikowski field goal, the scores enabled Florida State to emerge with the fifth national football title by an ACC squad.

For Bowden, who had lost two title games in the previous three seasons, the second time was especially charming. "Ninety-three felt more like a relief," Bowden said. "Ninety-nine felt more like an accomplishment." ✯

FACING PAGE
Florida State football coach Bobby Bowden stands with the national championship trophy. Bowden's teams captured the title in 1993 and 1999. His teams played for the championship on two other occasions. Bowden began his career as a head coach at Samford in Alabama in 1959. Four years later he became the head coach at West Virginia, and in 1976 he took the job at Florida State. In all that time, Bowden has suffered just two losing seasons. In 2002, he passed Alabama's "Bear" Bryant as the second-winningest coach in NCAA Division I history. Bowden is the only coach in Division I history to win 10 games or more for 14 consecutive seasons. From 1990-99 his teams went 109-13-1, winning 89 percent of their games.

ARYLAND
TOL 3
00:0
2 TOL
NCAA
CHAMPIONS

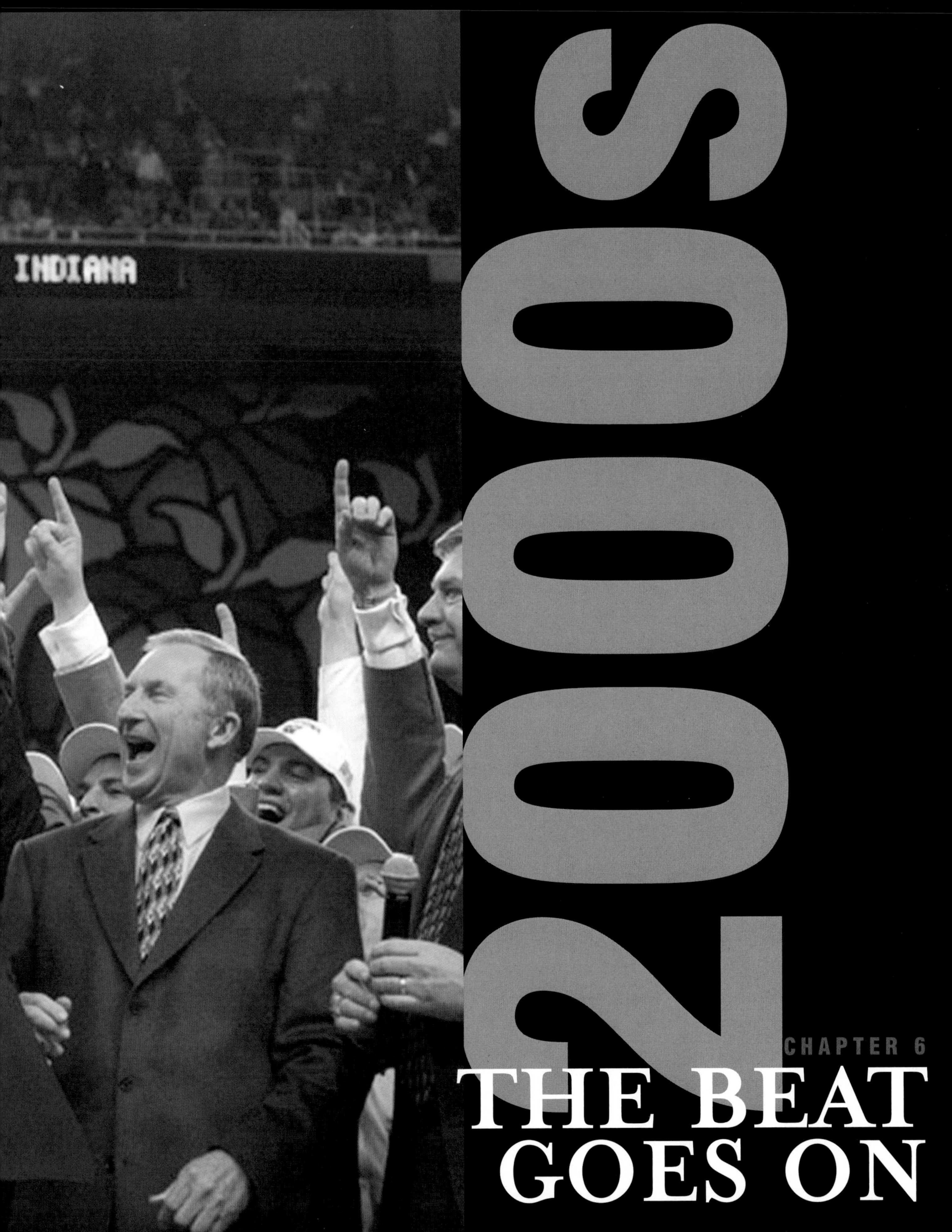

2000s

CHAPTER 6

THE BEAT GOES ON

BELOW
North Carolina defensive end Julius Peppers (49) won the Lombardi Trophy as the nation's top lineman and the Chuck Bednarik Award as the nation's top defensive player in 2001. Peppers then made himself eligible for the National Football League draft and was selected second overall in the first round by the Carolina Panthers. After leading the nation in quarterback sacks (15) his junior season, Peppers left UNC second on the career list in sacks (30.5) and tackles for loss (53). He also played two years of basketball for the Tar Heels and helped lead UNC to the 2000 Final Four.

Let individuals lament middle age, if they must, as their joints creak and their eyesight fails. Survival for five decades is cause for celebration, particularly within intercollegiate athletics, where alliances dissipate and recombine like clouds in a restless sky.

The Atlantic Coast Conference has done more than survive, remaining a force inside the councils and arenas, on the playing fields and airwaves of college sports. Along the way, the ACC developed a style and a culture that is distinctly its own.

"There is a much higher degree of cooperation and responsiveness and thoughtfulness, I think, in this conference than would be the norm in a lot of places in this country," said Wake Forest's Thomas Hearn, the ACC's senior administrator in terms of service. "It's something we're very proud of. As a matter of fact, when we talk about the conference and expansion and all of these things, these cultural pieces are critical to us. Namely, are these people going to be willing to work in this kind of collegial environment? Are they going to support the things the conference stands for?"

That enduring sense of common enterprise among like-minded institutions is as old as the league, handed down across generations.

"The thing I learned as a young coach in this league from Dean Smith, Terry Holland, Lefty Driesell, Bill Foster, all those guys, was that we're proud to be in the ACC," said Duke's Mike Krzyzewski, the league's senior coach. "What can we do to make the ACC be better?"

Over the years, the commitment to improvement spread throughout the ACC, spawning uncommon competitive balance. Sorely tested during a typical season, ACC teams routinely emerge among the nation's elite.

Certainly that was the story from the very outset of the current decade, beginning with a 1999-2000 men's basketball season

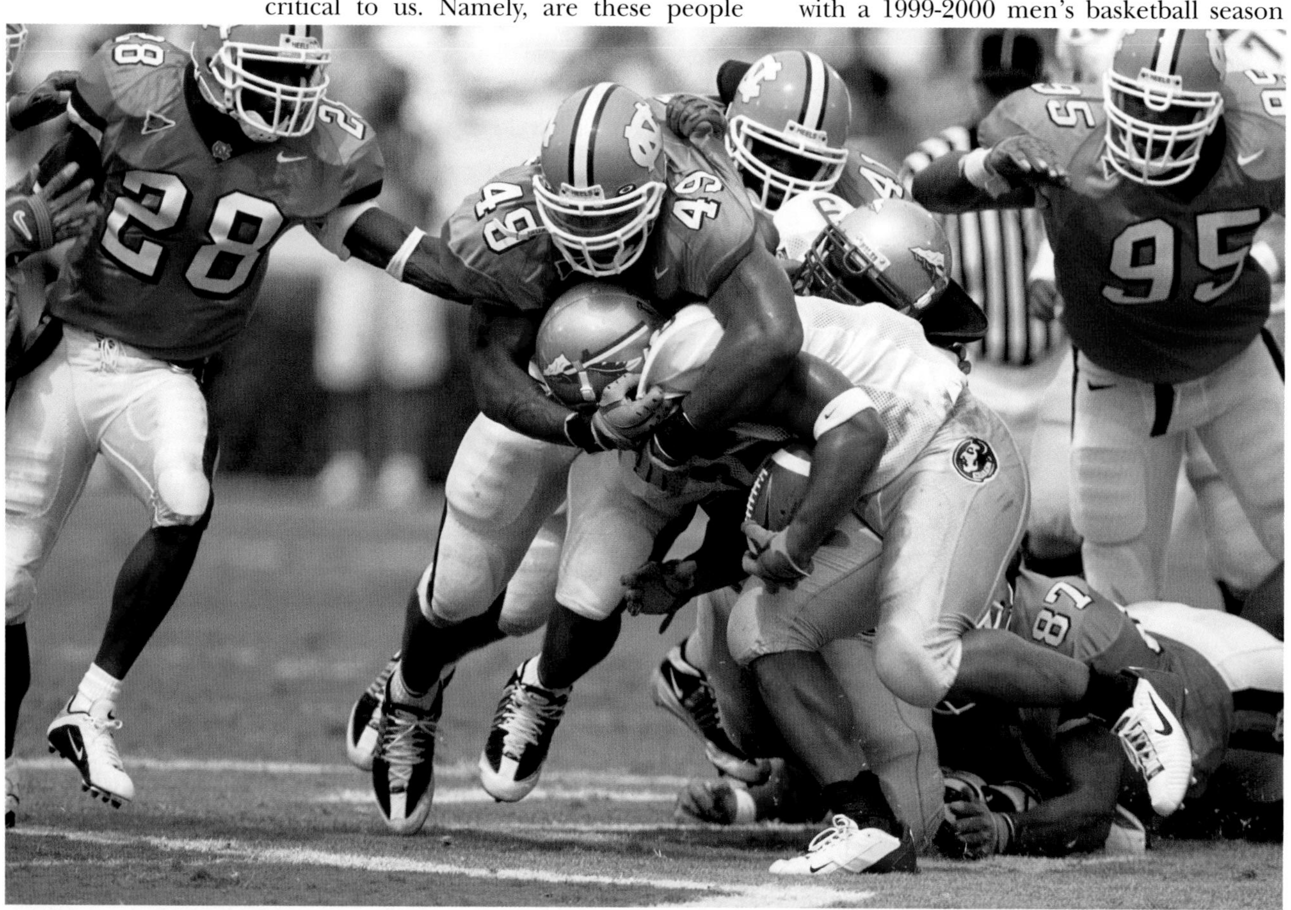

in which Duke finished atop the final regular-season poll, North Carolina reached the Final Four and Wake Forest won the NIT, the school's first national basketball championship.

Duke, the ACC's reigning basketball power, figured to suffer a drop-off in 2000 after Elton Brand, William Avery and Corey Maggette left for the National Basketball Association with eligibility remaining. Almost alone among the nation's elite, Krzyzewski's program had avoided such depredations. Yet when early departures finally hit, Duke took them in stride and prospered anyway.

The coach underwent hip replacement surgery following the '99 season and while recuperating at home was visited by holdovers Shane Battier, Chris Carrawell and Nate James. Months later — after Duke repeated as the college game's No. 1 team, repeated as the ACC's first-place finisher, repeated as the ACC Tournament champ — the visit was cited as pivotal to the team's fortunes.

Krzyzewski assured his upperclass leaders all would be well. "Coach, if you say so, I believe it," Carrawell said. The senior went on to earn recognition as the 2000 ACC player of the year. Krzyzewski was ACC coach of the year as his Blue Devils went 29-5 and reached the Sweet 16, where they were ousted by Florida.

A different challenge moved North Carolina, which got off to an 11-7 start, lost more home games (five) than in any season since World War II and finished tied for third. When the Tar Heels were booted by Wake in the ACC Tournament quarterfinals, the dissatisfaction with coach Bill Guthridge was palpable, the derision audible in the Charlotte Coliseum as opposing fans chanted: "NIT! NIT!"

Guthridge, an island of calm, proceeded to direct the Tar Heels on a surprise run to the Final Four, his second trip in three seasons since replacing the legendary Smith.

The Tar Heels relied inside on 7-foot center Brendon Haywood, flanked by sophomores Jason Capel and Kris Lang. Ed Cota, UNC's modern assist leader, was the senior playmaker. Football defensive lineman Julius Peppers added bulk and surprisingly deft basketball skills to the interior mix. Scoring leadership (16.7 points per game) came from a freshman, Joseph Forte, a first in Tar Heel history. The 6-4 guard was voted the 2000 ACC rookie of the year.

Eventually North Carolina emerged among the ACC's five 20-game winners. Virginia, which tied for third with UNC, was 19-11. But only three ACC squads received NCAA Tournament bids, marking a second straight season league advocates felt snubbed.

BELOW

Duke's Shane Battier (31) rises to block a shot by North Carolina's Joseph Forte in 2001. The pair shared the ACC player of the year award that season. The previous year, Forte captured the league's rookie of the year award and led the Tar Heels to the Final Four after being named the most outstanding player in the NCAA Tournament South Region.

Maryland, the second-place finisher and ACC Tournament runner-up with All-ACC sophomores Juan Dixon and Lonny Baxter, lasted two rounds, losing by 35 to UCLA. North Carolina went to the NCAAs as a No. 9 seed and upset Stanford, the top seed in the South, in the second round. "It is a little different to be an underdog," Guthridge said after assuring a 30th consecutive UNC season with at least 20 wins. "I don't want it to become a habit for us to be the underdog, but I don't mind it the rest of the year."

Three games later, the Tar Heels reached the Final Four for a record 15th time, only to lose 71-59 to Florida.

Virginia, Wake Forest and N.C. State were invited to the 2000 NIT. The Cavaliers, led by forward Chris Williams, the '99 ACC rookie of the year, went out in triple-overtime in their opener against Georgetown. N.C. State, which began the season by inaugurating a new arena, advanced to the NIT semifinals, where it was bumped 62-59 by Wake.

The Demon Deacons enjoyed one more victory in 2000. Led by tournament MVP Robert O'Kelley, the '98 ACC rookie of the year, they beat Notre Dame 71-61 for the NIT title. (Matt Doherty, a former UNC player and future North Carolina head coach, directed the Irish.) "This is just unbelievable," Wake point guard Ervin Murray said. "We've come so far this year. To finish the year off like this, with a national championship, is the greatest."

Some programs vie occasionally for championships. Others are national contenders every season. The perennial mix in contemporary football includes Florida State, which in 2000 again came close to a title. Ultimately the defending champs rode the Bowl Championship Series formula to a championship game against top-ranked Oklahoma, but came out on the short end of a 13-2 score in the Orange Bowl.

The 2000 season was the third in a row in which five ACC members went to bowls. Only N.C. State emerged victorious, dropping Minnesota 38-30 in the Micron PC Bowl. Junior Levar Fisher, an outside linebacker for the 8-4 Wolfpack, led the nation in tackles with 15.1 per game.

N.C. State had a demanding new coach, Chuck Amato, who reflected several hiring trends within the league. Amato was an N.C. State alumnus who had been a major cog in the vaunted "White Shoes Defense" of 1967. By 2001 alumni directed a majority of the ACC schools: Duke, Maryland, North Carolina, N.C. State and Virginia. Amato, like Clemson coach Tommy Bowden, also was a former assistant to FSU head coach Bobby Bowden.

Following in the elder Bowden's footsteps was certainly enticing after Florida State went undefeated in ACC action for the seventh time in its nine league seasons. FSU placed four players each on the All-ACC offensive and defensive squads, led by a trio of consensus All-Americans: defensive end Jamal Reynolds, cornerback Tay Cody and flanker Marvin Minnis.

Then there was Chris Weinke, the sec-

2000

1.4.00
FSU finishes a wire-to-wire No.1 season with a 46-29 Sugar Bowl win against Virginia Tech

2001

3.11.01
ACC Tournament sets NCAA attendance records at Atlanta's Georgia Dome

4.2.01
Duke beats Arizona 82-72 for NCAA men's basketball title

9.11.01
Terrorists attack World Trade Center and Pentagon

2002

4.1.02
Maryland beats Indiana 64-52 for NCAA men's basketball title

ond ACC player and second FSU quarterback awarded the Heisman Trophy as the nation's top football player. The first winner was Charlie Ward, who produced an NCAA title in 1993. Weinke did that his junior year, then improved as a senior while winning ACC player of the year honors.

Florida State led Division I-A in total offense in 2000 with 549 yards per outing. Weinke, big and strong with a quick release on his throws, paced the league in total offense (339.2 yards per game) and set a single-season passing standard with 4,167 yards in 13 games.

The combination of a potent attack and stifling defense enabled FSU to outscore ACC opponents by an average margin of 32.2 points. Only Georgia Tech among ACC members came close to the champs, falling 26-21 at Atlanta in September. The home team, a 22-point underdog, rallied to lead 15-12 early in the fourth quarter and had the ball with a chance to win on its final drive.

The Yellow Jackets eventually tied for second with Clemson, their other conference loss coming at N.C. State in overtime. Both the Jackets and Tigers finished 9-3 and ranked, with Clemson rising to fifth in the polls before suffering consecutive losses at Tech and FSU.

Virginia was fourth in the ACC but 6-6 overall after losing to Georgia in the Oahu Bowl. That ended the school's league-record streak of 13 consecutive seven-win seasons. Sadly for the Cavaliers, the loss ended coach George Welsh's career as well.

The 67-year-old announced he would retire after Virginia enjoyed its Hawaiian getaway, calling the 2000 season "physically and emotionally the toughest of my career." Welsh confided he had trouble sleeping, a first in his life. The coach with the most wins in ACC and Virginia history (134 in 19 years) said a primary regret was that "I don't think we ever finished in the top 10, which was a disappointment to me."

Welsh lamented the continued turnover among ACC colleagues, noting that "the guys who were winning got out, except for me."

That was true, anyway, for those "struggling to win, to catch up to Florida State," as Welsh put it. For Bobby Bowden, possessor of a legend's status, a talent-rich home state and a million-dollar annual contract, there was no need to go anywhere. His 25th FSU squad finished 11-2 and No. 3 in the 2000 polls, marking a 14th straight year in the top five.

Bowden wasn't the only ACC coach flirting with history every time he took the sidelines. Duke's Krzyzewski picked up the

BELOW
In 2000, Florida State quarterback Chris Weinke won the Heisman Trophy as the nation's top football player. He threw for a league-record 4,167 yards, and the defending champions returned to the national championship game but lost to Oklahoma in the Orange Bowl.

By Dan Collins

ACC EXCELLENCE

WAKE FOREST TEACHES ACC HOW TO PLAY GOLF

Human nature being what it is, the next best thing to winning is losing with a good excuse.

Richard Sykes, golf coach at N.C. State, can remember a time when teams unable to win the Atlantic Coast Conference golf championship could fall back on the best excuse around. They played in the same conference as Wake Forest, a perennial national power coached by the legendary Jesse Haddock.

"I can remember a moment back in 1973," Sykes said. "Wake Forest was going to kill everybody, and they had been killing everybody. And I remember being at the Atlantic Coast Conference championship, and it was just a battle for second place. Nobody talked about it. Nobody wanted to say it was a battle for second place.

"But I can remember one of my players running up the hill at Foxfire — it was a great big old hill from the 18th green up to the putting green — when we found out we were going to beat North Carolina, which was the big goal at that time. He came running up the hill hollering, 'We won, we won.'

"Jesse could have taken that trophy and gone home a long time before. Nobody else was playing for that but him."

Any biography of Haddock would all but render a history of ACC golf redundant. A housemate of Arnold Palmer — the winner of the first ACC championship in 1954 — Haddock practically ran the program through the 1950s in his capacity of assistant to the director of athletics. He was officially named head coach in 1960.

His game was far from polished, as one might expect from a man who didn't take up golf seriously until later in life. But his understanding of athletes and what allows one to finish ahead of another had been formed, fired and burnished during his days as an undergraduate on the old Wake Forest campus. One of his many duties was to drive coaches and notable officials on their appointed rounds.

The most influential people proved to be athletics director Jim Weaver, football coach D.C. "Peahead" Walker and basketball coach Murray Greason.

"I would say the base of my philosophy, particularly in athletics, was formed by those three men," Haddock said. "Of course, I had admiration for all three. I was a country boy [from Pitt County, N.C.], and they were big men. And that caused me to want to be associated with them, to learn from them."

The result was a coaching style that dealt far less with the mechanical than the mental. As Jay Haas, one of nine first-team All-Americans to play for Haddock, once put it: "He didn't know much about the swing, but he knew what made people tick."

For the golfers who accepted Haddock's offer to play at Wake Forest, that was usually more than enough. No other ACC team has won a national championship. Haddock's Deacons won three (1974, 1975 and 1986). No other coach has led his team to more than six ACC men's golf titles. The Deacons, under Haddock, won 15 — including 13 out of

RIGHT:
The 1975 Wake Forest golf team celebrates another national championship. The Demon Deacons have won three titles and are the only ACC club to capture the coveted crown.

LEFT:
Arnold Palmer, who went on to become one of the world's greatest professional golfers, played for Wake Forest in college and won the first ACC men's golf tournament in 1954.

14 from 1967 through 1980.

The list of Deacons who went on to make a nice living in the professional ranks would cover a loving cup stem to rim. Palmer was one of the greatest golfers to ever tee up a ball, but the likes of Haas, Curtis Strange, Lanny Wadkins, Scott Hoch, Leonard Thompson, Gary Hallberg, Jay Sigel, Joe Inman, Billy Andrade and Len Mattiace holed their share of winning shots.

Of the 20 golfers who followed Haddock's advice right into the professional ranks, 10 have pocketed at least $1 million in prize money.

Haddock, who retired in 1991, is a member of the Golf Coaches Association Hall of Fame. He described his approach to coaching as literally hands-on. "You pat them on the back," Haddock said. "What you're really doing is feeling if there's tenseness there. You will see pictures with my hands on their backs. I want to know if it's feeling soft and not rigid. Because once you tighten up, you can't swing in balance."

No college golf team has ever been more in the swing of things than the Deacons were in 1975. Coming off the school's first national title in 1974, Wake Forest — fielding a team that featured Strange, Haas, Bob Byman and David Thore — routed the field at Ohio State's Scarlet Course to finish 33 strokes ahead of runner-up Oklahoma State.

The next widest winning margin in NCAA Golf Championship history is 14 strokes.

Strange, who made an eagle on the final hole the year before to win the individual national championship, shot a closing tournament-best 67. Haas, with a final round of 70, won the individual national title in 1975. In 2001, *GolfWorld* magazine named the 1975 Demon Deacons as the greatest team in the history of college golf.

By the time Andrade, Mattiace, Barry Fabyan and Chris Kite led the Deacons to their third title in 1986, the rest of the ACC had, at long last, caught up. Since 1980, Wake Forest has won the conference title just once, in 1989. In the first 49 years of the ACC, North Carolina won 10 team titles. Georgia Tech won seven. Clemson won six outright and tied with N.C. State for the championship in 1990.

But to at least one interested observer, ACC golf will always remain synonymous with a single school and coach who showed the way and helped to pave the road for other programs.

"He did a great job, and he actually made jobs for the rest of us," said N.C. State's Sykes. "It was a job where you had about six other jobs at the university when you coached golf.

"Jesse, he changed the face of it — especially in this part of the world." ✶

torch every basketball season, with triumphal effect in 2001.

Forward Shane Battier was the latest floor leader in the Blue Devils' march to yet another first-place ACC finish, yet another top rank in the polls, yet another ACC Tournament championship and yet another NCAA title. "When you see Shane, you see Duke," teammate Jason (later Jay) Williams said of the near-consensus choice as 2001 national player of the year.

Battier was poised, versatile and cunning. He shot with range and accuracy. He was an adept rebounder and passer. His defense inside and out earned national defensive player of the year honors from 1999 through 2001. Wake's Tim Duncan and UNLV's Stacey Augmon are the only other three-time winners.

"It's all angles, that's all basketball is," Battier said. "It's all about playing angles right, and chess moves." No wonder ex-Duke assistant coach Quin Snyder called the articulate Battier "Bill Bradley for the new millennium," referring to the former Princeton All-American, Rhodes scholar and U.S. senator.

Battier was voted 2001 ACC player of the year but shared the honors with UNC's Joseph Forte, just as Duke shared first place with North Carolina, which resembled the powerhouses of old for much of the '01 season.

Program leadership was distinctly different at Chapel Hill, however, following a protracted and painful public search.

Roy Williams, the Kansas coach, former Tar Heel assistant and UNC alumnus, seemed destined for the job when Guthridge abruptly retired on the eve of the 2000 summer recruiting period. "I'm not sure what my plans are except for going to the beach," said Guthridge, whose 80 wins (against 28 losses) matched Everett Case, the late N.C. State coach, for the best three-year start in major-college competition.

Williams agonized publicly, then stunned UNC by turning down the chance to extend Smith's legacy. "Somebody asked me, 'Can you say no to Dean Smith?'" Williams said. "It would be hard. But it would be harder to say no to my players."

So the job went to Matt Doherty, a former Tar Heel (1981-84) who had assisted Williams and Davidson's Bob McKillop and had a year of head coaching experience at Notre Dame. "He has a passion; he has an intensity," Williams said of Doherty. "He is a perfectionist and very driven, and I think those qualities are more prevalent in his personality than anything else. He laughs; he loves his family, but he wants to win."

Doherty took essentially the same club that reached the 2000 Final Four, minus Cota, and got off to a 22-1 start, rising to No. 1 in the polls. An 18-game winning streak included victories on the home courts of four ACC teams that eventually made the NCAA Tournament: Georgia Tech, Maryland, Wake Forest and Duke.

Tech had the league's other new coach, Paul Hewitt. Hired from Siena to replace Bobby Cremins, the New Yorker was voted 2001 ACC coach of the year after directing the Jackets to a 17-13 record — their first winning season in three years and most ACC wins and first NCAA Tournament appearance since 1996.

Virginia was the ACC's other NCAA entrant, giving the league six, as many as in the previous two seasons combined. The Cavaliers won their first 10 games of the '01 season, rising to eighth in the polls.

FACING PAGE
In an era when many of the game's best players left college early, Duke's Shane Battier (31) stayed for four years. He proved to be every bit as good a leader as he was an individual player, too. He was named national defensive player of the year three times. In 2001 he was named the national player of the year and carried the Blue Devils to coach Mike Krzyzewski's third national championship. He was a consensus All-American, the most outstanding player at the Final Four and an academic All-American.

DUKE
31

They also broke Duke's record 24-game road winning streak in the ACC, finishing 20-9 and 16th according to the Associated Press.

Wake received its first NCAA bid since '97, but in coach Dave Odom's last season devolved down the stretch and unraveled entirely against Butler in its NCAA opener. North Carolina, too, faltered in the late going. The end came with a decisive 79-53 loss to Duke in the ACC Tournament final and a second-round NCAA defeat by Penn State.

The Tar Heels still finished 26-7 and sixth-ranked, extending college basketball's most remarkable streaks — top three in the ACC every year since 1965, 21 or more wins every year since 1971, participant in the NCAA Tournament every year since 1975, when multiple entrants from the same league were first allowed.

One subtle shift in North Carolina's standing already had taken place. The ACC's best and most intense rivalry now clearly involved Maryland and Duke, as evidenced by four electrifying encounters in 2001.

Duke arrived at College Park for the first meeting with a single loss in 19 games and a No. 2 ranking. The Blue Devils left with a 98-96 overtime victory that haunted the Terrapins. Eighth-ranked Maryland led by 10 points with a minute left, but Duke's Williams scored an astounding eight points in 14 seconds to spearhead a successful rally. Maryland returned the favor at Durham, winning 91-80. Adding injury to insult, Duke big man Carlos Boozer fractured his right foot.

An interior tag team of reserves took Boozer's place in the third meeting, a ferociously fought ACC Tournament semifinal decided in the final seconds when Nate James tapped in a miss by Williams to secure an 84-82 victory. The 2001 tournament, held in Atlanta's Georgia Dome, set NCAA attendance records for the entire event (182,525), per session (36,505) and for a single session (40,083) at a conference basketball tournament.

The fourth collision came in the Final Four, Maryland's first visit and Duke's 13th, ninth under Krzyzewski. Such a clash between ACC clubs had occurred only once previously, in 1981 between North Carolina and Virginia.

BELOW
Lonny Baxter (35), Steve Blake (center) and Chris Wilcox (54) were three parts of a very special Maryland team in 2001 and '02. The Terrapins earned back-to-back Final Four berths, won the ACC regular-season title in 2002 and finished the run with a national championship.

The Terrapins of Juan Dixon, big men Lonny Baxter and Terence Morris, and point guard Steve Blake jumped to a 22-point first-half lead against Duke, hitting 55 percent from the floor. But again Duke rallied. Battier had 25 points and eight rebounds, Williams 23 points and Boozer 19 in his third game back as the Blue Devils won, 95-84. Maryland finished 25-11.

Two nights later top-rated Duke beat Arizona 82-72, fueled down the stretch by Battier and sophomore Mike Dunleavy, who had 18 of his 21 points in the second half. The title was the third for Krzyzewski in an 11-year span and tied him with Bob Knight, his former coach, for third all-time in NCAA championships. Only UCLA's John Wooden (10) and Kentucky's Adolph Rupp (4) won more titles than the Duke coach, who was inducted into the Naismith Basketball Hall of Fame prior to the '02 season.

ACC athletic form was disrupted on several fronts during the 2001-02 academic year as Florida State in football and North Carolina in basketball won only eight games each. That was the fewest victories at FSU since 1986 and led to a team other than Florida State capturing the ACC title for the first time in a decade. UNC's eight victories were its fewest in basketball since 1962, Dean Smith's first year as head coach. With an 8-20 record the Tar Heels saw all their notable streaks vanish like morning mist, and finished tied for last with Clemson and FSU.

There were several other breaks with form that academic year. One occurred in late August 2001, as Virginia made administrative history with the hiring of Craig Littlepage, the ACC's first African-American director of athletics.

The other depatures were long-anticipated competitive breakthroughs at College Park.

First the football Terrapins, under newly returned alumnus Ralph Friedgen, came from nowhere to win the league football title, earning the right to represent the ACC in the Bowl Championship Series.

"Maryland coach Ralph Friedgen may be an offensive whiz," the *Washington Times* said of the 2001 ACC coach of the year, "a meticulous organizer and a tireless workaholic. But for all those attributes, his mastery of motivation has been the most critical factor in transforming a losing team full of self-doubt into a confident ACC champion headed to the Orange Bowl."

Then the basketball Terrapins, under alumnus Gary Williams, the 2002 ACC coach of the year, finished first during the regular season and took Maryland to the NCAA title.

"It's been a great year to be a Terrapin," Friedgen said.

BELOW
Mike Dunleavy proved to be a versatile player during his three years at Duke. At 6 feet 9, the son of a coach could play inside, handle the ball with the skills of a point guard and shoot jump shots with ease. He played a key role in Duke's 2001 national championship, making 8 of 17 shots from the floor, 5 of 9 3-pointers and scoring a team-high 21 points. He left Duke after his junior season and was selected in the first round of the National Basketball Association draft.

ACC
25
DUKE
22

FACING PAGE: The Duke-Maryland rivalry reached a new level during the 2001 and '02 seasons, with the schools meeting in the semifinals of the 2001 Final Four. As a testament to the teams' greatness, the two brought back-to-back national titles to the ACC in those years, with Duke claiming the crown in 2001 and Maryland in 2002. Clockwise from top left: Duke's Jason Williams was named the 2002 national player of the year, while Maryland's Juan Dixon was named the ACC player of the year and the most outstanding player at the Final Four. Coach Gary Williams directed his alma mater to new heights. Steve Blake (25) and Williams were two of the finest point guards in America at the turn of the century. And Duke coach Mike Krzyzewski continues to excel at a level few coaches ever reach. **ABOVE:** Krzyzewski wipes away a tear while point guard Jason Williams holds the national championship trophy following the Blue Devils' triumph in 2001. As Krzyzewski prepared to enter his 22nd season at Duke in the fall of 2002, his credentials stood alone among active collegiate coaches: nine Final Four appearances, six ACC championships, six national players of the year and three national titles.

BELOW
First-year Maryland football coach Ralph Friedgen (left) and his Terrapins stunned the country by winning the 2001 ACC championship in football and earning a trip to the Orange Bowl. The Terps dislodged Florida State, which had shared or won outright every ACC championship since FSU began playing a league schedule in 1992. Friedgen is a Maryland graduate who served as offensive coordinator at Georgia Tech before returning to his alma mater, which went 10-2 in his debut. Friedgen was named the national coach of the year.

The '01 football season took an unusual turn early, as sixth-ranked FSU journeyed to Chapel Hill and lost, 41-9. North Carolina scored 34 unanswered points after trailing at halftime. The ACC's top defense held Florida State to 34 yards in the second half, led by Peppers at defensive end. The 6-6, 270-pound junior won the Vince Lombardi Award as the nation's top lineman and the Chuck Bednarik Award as the nation's best defender, a first for an ACC player.

The Tar Heels, coached by alumnus John Bunting, ultimately finished third in the ACC. They were 8-5 overall after beating Auburn 16-10 in the Peach Bowl.

Meanwhile Friedgen, a 32-year assistant and Georgia Tech's longtime offensive coordinator, was the consensus 2001 national coach of the year. The heavyset former offensive lineman nicknamed "Fridge" took a program with a single winning season in the previous decade and jumped to a 7-0 start and a No. 10 rank in the polls.

Maryland was led on offense by sophomore tailback Bruce Perry, the first Terrapin since Charlie Wysocki in 1980 to pace the ACC in rushing (1,242 yards). The defense depended heavily on middle linebacker E.J. Henderson, a 6-2 local product voted '01 ACC player of the year and a consensus All-American.

The Terrapins dropped a 52-31 decision at Tallahassee, then didn't lose again until falling to Florida 56-23 in the Orange Bowl. They finished 10-2, 7-1 in the ACC, their first conference title since 1985. "Coach Friedgen made us believe stuff we never thought was possible," Henderson said. "He made dreams become reality."

Maryland was among a record six ACC squads that went to bowls, representation assured by contract starting in 2002. Florida State was in a bowl for the 22nd straight season, led by quarterback Chris Rix, the 2001 ACC rookie of the year. The 6-4 Californian recovered from a slow start to rank as the league's passing leader with 2,734 yards, best among the nation's freshmen. FSU finished 8-4 after topping Virginia Tech 30-17 in the Gator Bowl.

Georgia Tech went to its fifth consecutive bowl under coach George O'Leary and was

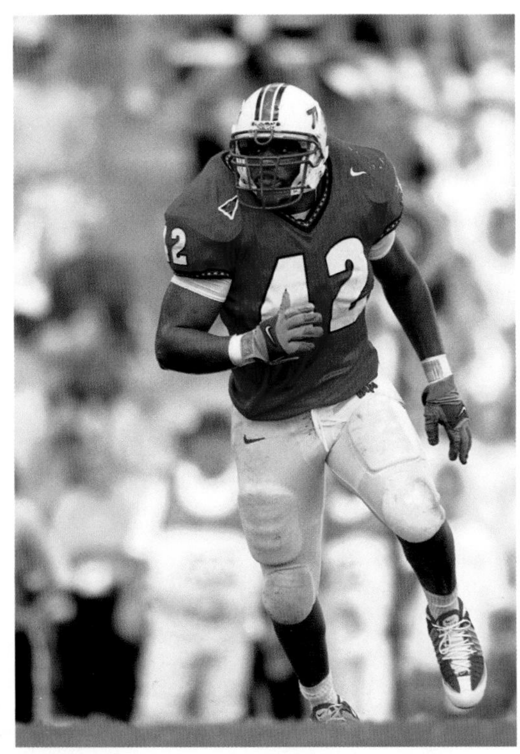

LEFT
Maryland linebacker E.J. Henderson was the 2001 ACC player of the year, the ACC defensive player of the year and a consensus All-American. He led the league in tackles for loss with 28, which were the most in school history.

8-5 after beating No. 11 Stanford 24-14 in the Seattle Bowl. O'Leary later resigned to briefly take the head job at Notre Dame. He was replaced as Yellow Jackets coach by Chan Gailey, who with UNC's Bunting and Virginia's Al Groh, were hired from the ranks of professional football.

Clemson went to its third bowl in three years under Tommy Bowden and beat Louisiana Tech 49-24 in the Humanitarian Bowl. The Tigers' elusive Woodrow "Woody" Dantzler, the All-ACC quarterback, became the first NCAA player to pass for at least 2,000 yards and rush for at least 1,000 in the same season. N.C. State also went bowling, matching Clemson at 7-5. Wake Forest was bowl-eligible as well, the first time the ACC had seven qualifiers.

The ACC's 49th basketball season saw Maryland, as Bowden, achieve a bit of athletic immortality. The Terrapins' 32-4 record, best in school history, culminated in a 64-52 victory over Indiana in the 2002 NCAA championship game.

The win put Maryland in select company as one of the few programs to own national titles in both football (1953) and basketball. The NCAA crown was the ninth for an ACC club but the first for a school outside North Carolina, a fact not lost on Terrapin coach Gary Williams.

"I always thought one of the toughest things in the league — I still do — is the fact that Duke and Carolina, you ask people to name two of the top five programs the last 50 years, they'd be on everybody's list," Williams said. "So you could be really good, but in people's minds you weren't as good as Duke and North Carolina. That's true with Maryland fans. You always had that, 'Well, you're good, but Duke or Carolina is this.'

"I think that's one of the things that's driven me these years, was to make Maryland people understood that we could be as good as anybody else. To me, that's what winning a national championship does. It shows you reached the ultimate, just like those schools have done. That was important to me personally, without having to say anything, to make that statement."

Consider the statement made.

Maryland was a team of many parts in 2002, enabling it to improve a year after losing two of its top six players from the '01 Final Four squad. The Terrapins led the ACC in rebounding margin thanks to frontline starters Lonny Baxter, Byron Mouton and explosive sophomore Chris Wilcox, supported by Tahj Holden and Ryan Randle. Drew Nicholas provided depth at both guard positions. Steve Blake, a high-voltage playmaker, led the ACC with 7.94 assists per game and hit the decisive shot in a 90-82 NCAA East Region final victory over Connecticut.

"[Blake] said, 'They're going to lay off me,' and he said, 'If they do, I'm going to shoot,'" Williams recalled of a preparatory team huddle. "I said, 'Well, go ahead,' because he was going to shoot anyway if I told him not to."

Maryland's win over the Huskies gave the ACC at least one participant in the Final Four for six straight seasons and in 14 of 15 since 1988. The conference is an unrivaled fixture on the game's greatest stage: From 1977 through 2002, a span of 26 seasons, the ACC sent 25 teams to the Final Four. Fourteen of the 25 reached the title game. Maryland became the seventh in that span to emerge victorious.

Setting the tone throughout the championship drive was the steady and relentlessly competitive Dixon. The Baltimore product overcame the deaths of both parents because of AIDS, a low recruiting profile, a late start in college and a slender 6-3 physique to become a three-time All-ACC pick and the 2002 ACC player of the year.

Dixon, second to Duke's Williams in scoring in 2002, led the ACC in free-throw accuracy, his 89.8 percent conversion rate third-best in league history after UNC's Shammond Williams (.911 in 1998) and Maryland's Greg Manning (.908 in 1980). Tricky Dixon led the ACC in steals for the second year in a row, his career total of 333 second to the Terrapins' Johnny Rhodes (344) in modern ACC history.

The '02 season began with Duke ranked No. 1 and Maryland No. 2. Neither dropped from the top 10 all season. Unlike 2001, they met only twice, with each holding service on its home court. But after opening the season with 12 wins in a row, Duke was upset at Florida State. That single additional defeat essentially assured first place for the 15-1 Terrapins, a feat Maryland last duplicated in 1980.

Duke also lost at Virginia to finish 13-3 in the league, but rallied to win an unprecedented fourth consecutive ACC Tournament, capped by a 91-61 victory over N.C. State. Both Duke and Maryland ended the season ranked No. 1, Duke by AP for a record fourth straight year and Maryland by *USA Today*/ESPN, a first for the school in any poll.

The ACC was laden with experienced players in 2002, an uncommon occurrence in an era rife with early moves to the professional ranks. Three of the most seasoned units got NCAA bids. "We were unusual from the standpoint that we had three seniors this year that had played a lot," Williams said. "That really helped us."

A veteran Duke squad finished 31-4, dissipating a large second-half lead in a 74-73 loss to Indiana in the South Region semifinal. After the '02 season the Blue Devils' entire junior class — first-team All-ACC performers Carlos Boozer, Mike Dunleavy and Jay Williams — went to the NBA.

Duke's women fared better. The eight-member squad reached the 2002 Final Four behind ACC Player of the Year Alana Beard, who led the league in scoring and steals, and ACC Tournament MVP Monique Currie. The Devils finished 31-4, won their third straight ACC Tournament and went undefeated during the ACC regular season. Gail Goestenkors became the third ACC women's coach, after Virginia's Debbie Ryan and Maryland's Chris Weller, to take more than one team to a Final Four. (Her Devils reached the title game in 1999.) Duke advanced to the semifinals before losing 86-71 to Oklahoma.

Back on the men's side, Wake Forest finished 21-13 in its first year under George Edward "Skip" Prosser, losing a 92-87 shootout with Oregon in the second round of the NCAA Tournament. Prosser replaced Odom, who went to South Carolina. He was the third coach with ties to Xavier to come to the ACC after Wake's Bob Staak in the mid-'80s and Virginia's Pete Gillen.

N.C. State was the league's only NCAA entrant that heavily accented youth. The 23-11 Wolfpack also featured a revamped offense. But on-court leadership was provided by a seasoned senior backcourt, particularly Anthony Grundy, a first-team All-ACC selection. The NCAA Tournament appearance was the Wolfpack's first since 1991, ending the longest drought in the league. UConn eliminated the Pack 77-74 in the second round.

Duke similarly opened the 2002 football season, the ACC's 50th, by happily escaping an unwelcome rut. The Blue Devils defeated East Carolina 23-16, ending a 23-game losing streak, the nation's longest.

Florida State opened with a 38-31 win over Iowa State, moving Bobby Bowden into second place in major-college victories.

The FSU coach entered the season tied at 323 wins with Alabama's Bear Bryant, whom he called "my idol" growing up in Birmingham, Ala. (Penn State's Joe Paterno had 327 victories as the '02 season dawned.) Bowden, whose .740 winning percentage in bowl competition (18-6-1) is best in NCAA history, said of his historical stature, "To be honest, it doesn't really feel like I should be there."

Pleasant dislocation also marked the start of the 2002-03 basketball season at Maryland. The Terrapins coincidentally celebrated their NCAA title by moving from Cole Field House to the 17,950-seat Comcast Center, a $125 million on-campus arena.

The new building reflected a trend. As the new millennium dawned, facilities for football, basketball, weight training, tutoring and other pursuits related to athletics were upgraded or replaced throughout the league. The enhancements solidified the conference's competitive standing nationally — to a point.

"It still doesn't matter. If you don't have a good coach, you're not going to win," said Gene Corrigan, the retired ACC commissioner.

Others found the building boom more ominous and sounded an alarm that echoed across the decades. Wake's Hearn cited a former NCAA executive director as he warned, "What Cedric Dempsey calls the athletic arms race, if we don't stop this, this cost structure is not sustainable." Hearn, a Knight Commission member, called the perpetual pressure to spend to remain competitive "a form of collective madness."

Confronting such challenges is part of ACC tradition, along with the constant effort to balance the sometimes-competing priorities of a university's academic and athletic missions. ACC commissioner John Swofford insisted "nationally competitive athletic programs run with integrity, in a nutshell to me that says what the first 50

BELOW
Byron Mouton was one of the emotional leaders for Maryland's national championship team in 2002. The title was the first for the Terrapins and ninth in men's basketball for the ACC.

years of the Atlantic Coast Conference have been all about and that's what the value system has been all about."

League representatives remain in the thick of debates nationally about admissions standards, eligibility requirements, graduation rates and benefits for student-athletes, topics at the forefront when the Atlantic Coast Conference came into being. Meanwhile, the ACC's stature assures that it will attract top athletes and coaches, producing high-quality competition and the tournament and bowl berths that go with them. That, in turn, generates more revenue per school for ACC members than any other conference in the country.

Swofford, only a few years older than the league he supervises, remained confident the ACC can handle the changing landscape, pointing to a record of principled, well-balanced and often trend-setting choices. "I think it's a mix of vision, of having the courage and commitment to try new things and be on the cutting edge, but not losing sight of our history," he said. "When all's said and done, this league has had a tremendous capacity to operate for the benefit of the whole and to have a sense of family and a sense of trust in how we work together and how we do our business."

Fans would want nothing less from those welcomed so readily into their homes, their hearts and their lives. ✶

RIGHT

Coach Gary Williams and his team celebrate their national championship. Maryland had a proud history in basketball, but Williams elevated the Terrapins to greater heights since returning to his alma mater in 1989-90. No Maryland team had played in a Final Four until Williams directed his clubs to back-to-back appearances in 2001 and '02. He has recruited and developed some of the nation's finest players along the way. Walt Williams, Joe Smith, Steve Francis and Juan Dixon all excelled under Williams' guidance.

By David Teel

ACC EXCELLENCE

WIRTZ MAKES NAME TO REMEMBER IN ACC

Lenny Wirtz just knew the call was a hoax.

The man identified himself as Dave Reese, commissioner of the Mid-American Conference. He claimed to need a replacement referee for that evening's college basketball game between Kent State and Toledo.

Dave Reese? Wirtz didn't know him. Officiate a college game? Wirtz, a humble high-school ref in suburban Cincinnati, had no such experience. But Wirtz played along with the hoax. He agreed to skip his high-school game and drive the 200 miles to Toledo. As is turned out, this wasn't a hoax. Reese was the caller, and Wirtz officiated his first collegiate assignment.

The year was 1954. Wirtz's age? He won't say, but he said plenty about a 40-year officiating career that led him to Tobacco Road and encounters with ACC icons from Everett Case to Dean Smith to Mike Krzyzewski.

"Dean once said that after 25 years of marriage it was time for him and I to get a divorce," Wirtz said. "I told him: 'Then I want the house. I want the Dean Dome.'"

As the ACC marks its 50th anniversary, the marquee is rightfully reserved for its unrivaled players and coaches. But the conference's game officials, especially in basketball, have served well as supporting actors — some comic, some dramatic, many colorful.

Charley Eckman, legend has it, once pulled up a chair during a North Carolina stall. Lou Bello entertained. Dick Paparo showboated. Joe Forte, Jess Kersey and numerous others graduated to the National Basketball Association, while Hank Nichols became NCAA supervisor of officials.

Wirtz, 5 feet 4 and sporting a perpetual glow long before tanning beds became chic, outlasted them all. He worked six Final Fours, stretching from 1961-1986, and three championship games — including the 1979 classic between Larry Bird and Indiana State and Magic Johnson and Michigan State. He officiated games in Europe, Asia, South America and Africa, and spent five seasons in the NBA.

But he made his reputation in the ACC, in which he worked a record 13 conference tournament championship games and where his first name became part of the basketball jargon.

There was Michael and Ralph, Dean and Lefty. And there was Lenny. Any serious follower of ACC basketball knew Lenny.

"I loved the ACC," Wirtz said.

He loved everything about it: the rivalries and arenas, coaches and players, fans and media. But mostly, he loved the caliber of competition.

Wirtz, you see, has this theory: The best players should follow the rules most closely. None of this swallow-your-whistle-the-fans-came-to-see-them-play stuff. If Christian Laettner pushed off a defender, call it. If Phil Ford carried the ball, call it.

"I considered it a competition with the players to have a game played by the rules," said Wirtz, who summers in Ohio, winters in

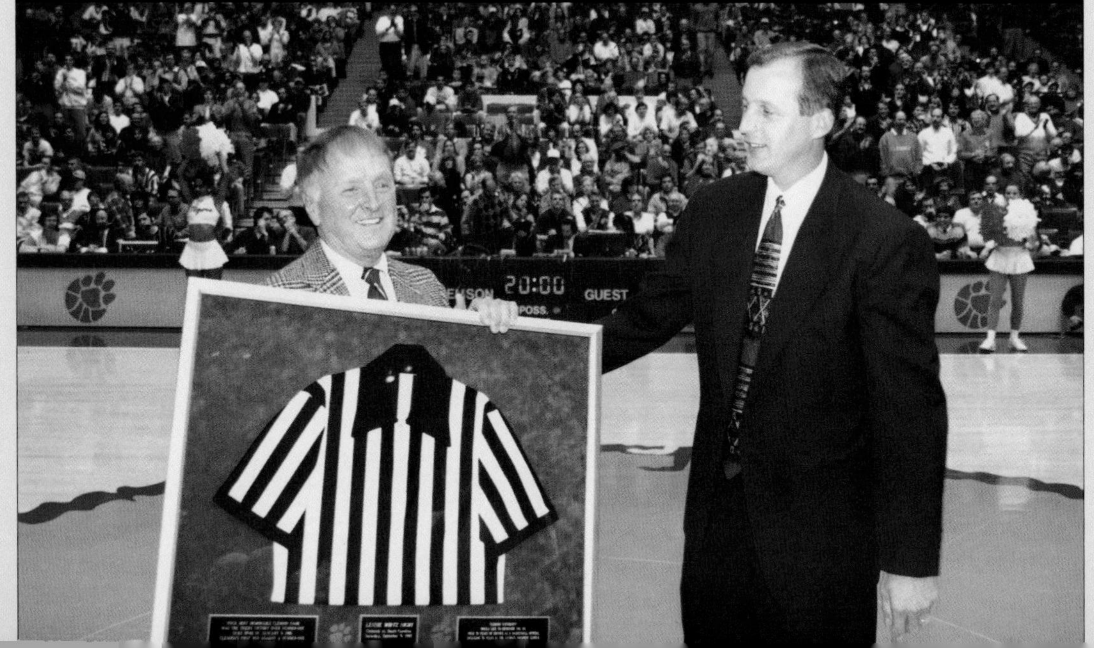

Florida and dotes on his wife of 50 years. "A foul in the first three minutes was a foul in the last three minutes, and a foul at home was a foul on the road. I preached those things to young officials."

Did he say young? Perfect. Another opening to pester Wirtz about his age. But Wirtz isn't playing. He guards the secret as Clemson's Tree Rollins did the basket.

"Supposedly Lenny's birth certificate went to the grave with [Southern Conference commissioner] Dallas Shirley," former Virginia coach Terry Holland said.

"I celebrated my 50th so long ago I can't remember," Wirtz said, laughing.

His first trip to the ACC also escapes him. He figures it transpired in the late 1950s, when he accompanied a Big Ten team to an ACC venue.

Among Wirtz's early Atlantic Coast Conference memories: the imposing size of Reynolds Coliseum and the imposing presence of Everett Case; the generosity of Footsie Knight and Bunn Hackney, the supervisors of officials in the ACC and the Southern Conference, respectively; the encouragement of his colleague, friend and idol, Red Mihalik; the good-natured exchanges with coaches such as Frank McGuire and Bud Millikan.

During an ACC Tournament game timeout, McGuire sent South Carolina player Jimmy Fox to speak with Wirtz.

"Mr. McGuire told me to tell you you're a thief."

"Jimmy, you go back and tell coach McGuire to look my way."

"When he looked at me, I hit him with a 'T,'" Wirtz said. "He burst out laughing."

Years later, as McGuire lay dying, Wirtz was among his bedside visitors.

But the ACC's camaraderie could not match the NBA's salary and benefits, and after officiating the 1970 national title game between UCLA and Jacksonville, Wirtz signed a pro deal.

Smith wrote him a congratulatory letter and said he would be missed. Not for long, as it turned out. Remember Wirtz's philosophy about the best players adhering to the rules?

"They hated me, and I didn't particularly like them," Wirtz said of the professionals. "I called too much for their taste."

Norvell Neve, then the ACC's supervisor of officials, welcomed Wirtz back to the college game in 1975 and made him an ACC regular. He remained a fixture until he retired 20 years later.

"You always wanted Lenny on the road since he refused to be intimidated by the home crowd," Holland said. "Or maybe he just loved being booed. At any rate, you felt you had a chance when you saw him on the road. But no one that I know wanted him at home, as you never knew what would set him off.

"I really gained great respect for him when I was on [the NCAA] basketball committee and got to see him prepare, particularly since he was definitely in his mid- to late-60s. All I know is that Lenny was an established official when I played [at Davidson in 1964] and was still going strong when I had been out of coaching for five or six years."

Wirtz witnessed the evolution of officiating. Two-man crews became three-man crews. A hobby became a job. Wirtz has mixed feelings about the changes.

Adding a third official, he figures, extended his career by 10 years. But the addition allowed some officials "to just stand there and watch the game while the others make all the calls." Wirtz never hid, and he certainly didn't run when the ACC increased top officials' pay and assigned them more and more games.

"But then it became too much of a business," he said. "Guys were just working for the check."

FACING PAGE: Then-Clemson coach Rick Barnes presents Lenny Wirtz with an award after he retired from officiating college basketball. Wirtz was a big part of ACC basketball for many years. He believed the best players should adhere to the rules.

Wirtz worked for the check, the game and the people.

A final story: During a timeout at Maryland one night, Wirtz saw a man hobbling toward him on crutches. He soon recognized his biggest coaching nemesis from the NBA, Dick Motta.

"Just wanted to say hello," Motta said. "We miss you."

Wirtz laughed.

"You miss me," he said, "as much as you'll miss those crutches." ✶

ACC 50TH ANNIVERSARY TEAMS

BASEBALL

Name	School	Years
Rusty Adkins	Clemson	1965-1967
Jake Austin	Wake Forest	1989-1992
Jeff Baker	Clemson	2000-2001
Scott Bankhead	North Carolina	1982-1984
Brian Bark	NC State	1987-1990
Brian Barnes	Clemson	1986-1989
Kris Benson	Clemson	1994-1996
Scott Bradley	North Carolina	1979-1981
Tom Bradley	Maryland	1967-1968
Kevin Brown	Georgia Tech	1984-1986
Brian Buchanan	Virginia	1992-1994
Mike Caldwell	NC State	1968-1971
J.D. Drew	Florida State	1995-1997
Nomar Garciaparra	Georgia Tech	1992-1994
Rusty Gerhardt	Clemson	1969-1972
Khalil Greene	Clemson	1999-2001
Tommy Gregg	Wake Forest	1982-1985
Seth Greisinger	Virginia	1994-1996
John-Ford Griffin	Florida State	1999-2001
Ty Griffin	Georgia Tech	1986-1988
Terry Harvey	NC State	1992-1995
Bert Heffernan	Clemson	1985-1988
Riccardo Ingram	Georgia Tech	1986-1987
Ryan Jackson	Duke	1991-1994
Jonathan Johnson	Florida State	1993-1995
Jimmy Key	Clemson	1980-1982
Billy Koch	Clemson	1994-1996
Matthew LeCroy	Clemson	1995-1997
Mike MacDougal	Wake Forest	1997-1999
Quinton McCracken	Duke	1989-1992
Marshall McDougall	Florida State	1999-2000
Billy Merrifield	Wake Forest	1980-1983
Shane Monahan	Clemson	1993-1995
Jeremy Morris	Florida State	1994-1997
Jim Norris	Maryland	1968-1970
Jon Palmieri	Wake Forest	1996-1999
Jay Payton	Georgia Tech	1992-1994
Jim Poole	Georgia Tech	1986-1988
Brad Rigby	Georgia Tech	1992-1994
Scott Schoeneweis	Duke	1993-1996
Billy Scripture	Wake Forest	1962-1964
Tom Sergio	NC State	1994-1997
Brick Smith	Wake Forest	1978-1981
Billy Spiers	Clemson	1985-1987
B.J. Surhoff	North Carolina	1983-1985
Mark Teixeira	Georgia Tech	1999-2001
Jason Varitek	Georgia Tech	1991-1994
Jake Weber	NC State	1995-1998
Walt Weiss	North Carolina	1983-1985
Paul Wilson	Florida State	1992-1994
Tracy Woodson	NC State	1982-1984
Turtle Zaun	NC State	1985-1988

MEN'S BASKETBALL

Name	School	Years
Kenny Anderson	Georgia Tech	1990-1993
Shane Battier	Duke	1998-2001
Len Bias	Maryland	1983-1986
Elton Brand	Duke	1998-1999
Tom Burleson	NC State	1971-1974
Len Chappell	Wake Forest	1960-1962
Randolph Childress	Wake Forest	1991,93-95
Billy Cunningham	North Carolina	1963-1965
Brad Daugherty	North Carolina	1983-1986
Charlie Davis	Wake Forest	1969-1971
Walter Davis	North Carolina	1974-1977
Johnny Dawkins	Duke	1983-1986
Juan Dixon	Maryland	1999-2002
Tim Duncan	Wake Forest	1994-1997
Len Elmore	Maryland	1972-1974
Danny Ferry	Duke	1986-1989
Phil Ford	North Carolina	1975-1978
Mike Gminski	Duke	1977-1980
Horace Grant	Clemson	1984-1987
Matt Harpring	Georgia Tech	1995-1998
Dickie Hemric	Wake Forest	1952-1955
Art Heyman	Duke	1961-1963
Grant Hill	Duke	1991-1994
Bobby Hurley	Duke	1990-1993
Antawn Jamison	North Carolina	1996-1998
Bobby Jones	North Carolina	1972-1974
Michael Jordan	North Carolina	1982-1984
Albert King	Maryland	1978-1981
Christian Laettner	Duke	1989-1992
Jeff Lamp	Virginia	1978-1981
John Lucas	Maryland	1973-1976
Tom McMillen	Maryland	1972-1974
Larry Miller	North Carolina	1966-1968
Rodney Monroe	NC State	1988-1991
Jeff Mullins	Duke	1962-1964
Barry Parkhill	Virginia	1971-1973
Sam Perkins	North Carolina	1981-1984
Mark Price	Georgia Tech	1983-1986
John Roche	South Carolina	1969-1971
Wayne "Tree" Rollins	Clemson	1974-1977
Lennie Rosenbluth	North Carolina	1954-1957
Ralph Sampson	Virginia	1980-1983
Charles Scott	North Carolina	1968-1970
Dennis Scott	Georgia Tech	1988-1990
Ron Shavlik	NC State	1954-1956
Joe Smith	Maryland	1994-1995
David Thompson	NC State	1973-1975
Buck Williams	Maryland	1979-1981
Jason Williams	Duke	2000-2002
James Worthy	North Carolina	1980-1982

WOMEN'S BASKETBALL

Name	School	Years
Val Ackerman	Virginia	1978-1981
LaQuanda Barksdale	North Carolina	1998-200
Jessica Barr	Clemson	1992-1994
Alana Beard	Duke	2000-2002
Genia Beasley	NC State	1977-1980
Tresa Brown	North Carolina	1981-1984
Vicky Bullett	Maryland	1986-1989
Heather Burge	Virginia	1990-1993
Tonya Cardoza	Virginia	87-89, 91
Tracy Connor	Wake Forest	93, 95-97
Sylvia Crawley	North Carolina	1991-1994
Summer Erb	NC State	1998-2000
Dena Evans	Virginia	1990-1993
Chrissy Floyd	Clemson	1999-2002
Kisha Ford	Georgia Tech	1994-1997
Tara Heiss	Maryland	1975-1978
Jessie Hicks	Maryland	1990-1993
Donna Holt	Virginia	1985-1988
Marion Jones	North Carolina	94-95,97
Barbara Kennedy	Clemson	1979-1982
Kris Kirchner	Maryland	1977-1980
Trudi Lacey	NC State	1978-1981
Pam Leake	North Carolina	1983-1986
Marsha Mann	North Carolina	1975
Rhonda Mapp	NC State	1989-1992
Bernadette McGlade	North Carolina	1977-1980
Katie Meier	Duke	86-88, 90
Chasity Melvin	NC State	1995-1998
Jenny Mitchell	Wake Forest	1988-1991
Chris Moreland	Duke	1985-1988
Linda Page	NC State	1982-1985
Wendy Palmer	Virginia	1993-1996
Tia Paschal	Florida State	1990-1993
Jasmina Perazic	Maryland	1980-1983
Joyce Pierce	Georgia Tech	1991-1993
Tracy Reid	North Carolina	1995-1998
Tammi Reiss	Virginia	1989-1992
Marcia Richardson	Maryland	1981-1984
Tonya Sampson	North Carolina	1991-1994
Georgia Schweitzer	Duke	1998-2001
Charlotte Smith	North Carolina	1992-1995
Dawn Staley	Virginia	1989-1992
Andrea Stinson	NC State	1989-1991
Deanna Tate	Maryland	86,88-89
Nikki Teasley	North Carolina	98-2000,02
Trena Trice	NC State	1984-1987
Itoro Umoh	Clemson	1996-1999
Michele VanGorp	Duke	1997-1999
Christy Winters	Maryland	1987-1990
Brooke Wyckoff	Florida State	1998-2001
Susan Yow	NC State	1975-1976

MEN'S CROSS COUNTRY

Name	School	Years
Abdul Alzindani	NC State	1996-1999
Roger Beardmore	Duke	1969-1971
Jim Beatty	North Carolina	1954-1956
Wayne Bishop	North Carolina	1958
Terry Brennan	Duke	1998-2000
Stuart Burnham	Wake Forest	1990-1993
Larry Clark	Clemson	1986-1990
John Cline	North Carolina	1994-1997
Mark Coogan	Maryland	1986-1987
Jim Cooper	North Carolina	1979-80,82
Mike Cotton	Virginia	1978-1981
Chris Dugan	NC State	1997-2001
Scott Eden	Duke	1972-1974
Jim Farmer	North Carolina	1984-1987
Cormac Finnerty	Clemson	1989-1992
Martin Flynn	Clemson	1983-1986
Steve Francis	NC State	1977-1980
Kevin Graham	Georgia Tech	1991-1994
Scott Haak	Clemson	1977-1979
Jim Haughey	Clemson	1979-1982
Bob Henes	NC State	1986-1990
Larry Henry	North Carolina	1958-1961
Gary Hofstetter	North Carolina	1977-1980
Kevin Hogan	Clemson	1991-1994
Dave Honea	NC State	1987-1991
Jon Hume	Wake Forest	1986-1989
Patrick Joyce	NC State	1994-1998
Sean Kelly	Duke	1999-2001
Ralph King	North Carolina	1975-1978
Hans Koeleman	Clemson	1980-1983
Dov Kremer	Clemson	1987-1990
Art Maillet	North Carolina	1963-1964
Jim Moorhead	Clemson	1959-1961
George Nicholas	North Carolina	1983-1986
Julius Ogaro	Clemson	1980-1982
Robbie Perkins	Duke	1974-1976
Pat Piper	NC State	1984-1987
Chan Pons	NC State	1995-1999
Corby Pons	NC State	1995-1999
Ron Rick	Wake Forest	1982-1985
Tony Riley	NC State	1992-1995
Dan Rincon	Maryland	1971-1975
Brendan Rodgers	NC State	1995-1999
Jon Russell	Wake Forest	1993-1996
Ben Schoonover	Wake Forest	1987-1990
Charlie Schrader	Maryland	1968-1970
Nathan Sisco	Wake Forest	1999-2001
Anderson Smith	NC State	2000-2001
Nolan Swanson	Wake Forest	1994-1997
Bobby Thiele	Virginia	1997-2000
Tony Waldrop	North Carolina	1971-1974
Bob Wheeler	Duke	1969-1971
Jim Wilkins	NC State	1970-1973
Andre Williams	North Carolina	1994-1997

WOMEN'S CROSS COUNTRY

Name	School	Years
Sheela Agrawal	Duke	1999-2001
Seana Arnold	Wake Forest	1986-1989
Joan Benoit	NC State	1978
Amy Beykirch	NC State	1997-2000
Sande Cullinane	NC State	1979-1983
Cindy Duarte	Clemson	1981-1984
Karen Dunn	Wake Forest	1983-1986
Anne Evans	Clemson	1989-1992
Shalane Flanagan	North Carolina	2000-2001
Claire Forbes	Virginia	1990-1993
Karen Godlock	North Carolina	1994-1997
Laurie Gomez	NC State	1988-1991
Ellison Goodall	Duke	1977
Margaret Groos	Virginia	1977-1980
Kristen Hall	NC State	1993-1996
Renee Harbaugh	NC State	1984-1987
Jill Haworth	Virginia	1980-1983
Ute Jamrozy	Clemson	1985-1987
Janelle Kraus	Wake Forest	1996-1999
Tina Krebs	Clemson	1982-1985
Beth Mallory	Georgia Tech	1993-1996
Patty Matava	Virginia	1985-1988
Susanna Matsen	North Carolina	1994-1996
Renee Metivier	Georgia Tech	2000-2001
Holly Murray	North Carolina	1983-1986
Joan Nesbitt	North Carolina	1981-1984
Christy Nichols	NC State	1996-2001
Trish Nervo	North Carolina	1997-2000
Aileen O'Connor	Virginia	1979-1982
Jennifer Owens	Virginia	1998-2001
Katrina Price	NC State	1988-1991
Kristin Price	NC State	2001
Mareike Ressing	Clemson	91-93,95
Laura Rhoads	NC State	1996-1998
Jennifer Rioux	Wake Forest	1984-1987
Connie Jo Robinson	NC State	1982-1985
Kerry Robinson	Clemson	1981-1984
Katie Sabino	NC State	1998-2001
Marissa Schmidt	Virginia	1979-1982
Julie Shea	NC State	1977-1980
Mary Shea	NC State	1979-1983
Dana Slater	Virginia	1979-1982
Janet Smith	NC State	1984-1988
Betty Springs	NC State	1979-1983
Nicole Stevenson	Wake Forest	1992-1995
Rosalind Taylor	Maryland	1986-1989
Suzie Tuffey	NC State	1985-1989
Stephanie Weikert	Clemson	1981-1984
Lesley Welch	Virginia	1980-1982
Lisa Welch	Virginia	1980-1982

FENCING

Name	School	Years
Thurbert Baker	North Carolina	1974
Charles Brown	North Carolina	1975
Dave Brown	North Carolina	1972
Thomas Clark	Duke	1973

ACC 50TH ANNIVERSARY TEAMS

Robert Cromartie	North Carolina	1972
Mark Eisenhardt	Maryland	1979
Manuel Garcia	NC State	1971
Steve Hatten	Virginia	1971
Chad Hilton	North Carolina	1971
Larry Hurwitz	Maryland	1978
A.J. Keane	North Carolina	1976-1977
Alan Knight	North Carolina	1974-1976
Jim Krause	North Carolina	1973-7475
Howard Labow	Maryland	1977
Dave Lynn	North Carolina	1972
Vince Mascia	Virginia	1975
Mark Meudt	Maryland	1980
Ed Pettiss	Duke	1973
George Podgorski	Clemson	1977
Ken Poyd	Maryland	19761978
Steve Renshaw	Clemson	1980
Jack Simes	Maryland	19781979
Bradley Thomas	Maryland	1979
Jay Thomas	Clemson	1980

FIELD HOCKEY

Kate Barber	North Carolina	1994-1997
Lori Bruney	North Carolina	1984-1987
Bashi Buba	North Carolina	1975-1978
Lisa Buente	Maryland	1987-1990
Jemima Cameron	Wake Forest	1999-2001
Cindy Carzo	Virginia	1976-1979
Jennifer Clark	North Carolina	1988-1991
Jessica Coleman	Virginia	1998-2001
Amy Cox	North Carolina	1989-1992
Kristen Daddona	Virginia	1991-1994
Christine DeBow	Maryland	1994-1997
Joy Driscoll	North Carolina	1994-1997
Jenny Everett	Wake Forest	1997-2000
Maryellen Falcone	North Carolina	1984-1987
Laura Gentile	Duke	1990-1993
Carrie Goodloe	Virginia	1998-2001
Barbara Hansen	North Carolina	1991-1994
Laurel Hershey	North Carolina	1987-1990
Louise Hines	North Carolina	1982-1985
Rachel Hiskins	Maryland	1998-2001
Christen Horsey	Wake Forest	1992-1995
Irene Horvat	Maryland	1991-1994
Judith Jonckheer	North Carolina	1984-1985
Kate Kauffman	Maryland	1993-1996
Carrie Lingo	North Carolina	1999-2001
Leslie Lyness	North Carolina	1986-1989
Amy Marchell	Wake Forest	199597-99
Lori Mastropietro	Virginia	1995-1998
Kristen McCann	North Carolina	1997-2000
Lynsey McVicker	Maryland	1995-1997
Meaghan Nitka	Wake Forest	1996-1999
Melissa Panasci	Duke	1994-1997
Nancy Pelligreen	North Carolina	1995-1998
Jen Pratt	Maryland	1995-1998
Sabrina Salam	Maryland	1990-1993
Amy Schubert	Maryland	1990-1993
Mary Sentementes	North Carolina	1981-1984
Keli Smith	Maryland	1997-2000
Courtney Sommer	Duke	1997-2000
Peggy Storrar	North Carolina	1990-1993
Carla Tagliente	Maryland	1997-2000
Jodie Taylor	Duke	1993-1995
Meridith Thorpe	Virginia	1995-1998
Jana Toepel	North Carolina	1997-2000
Kim Turner	Maryland	1985-1988
Boukje Vermeulen	Maryland	1990-1992
Michelle Vizzuso	Virginia	1995-1998
Caroline Walter	Maryland	1998-2001
Autumn Welsh	Maryland	1998-2001
Cindy Werley	North Carolina	93-94,96-97
Jessica Wilk	Maryland	1985-1988
Jana Withrow	North Carolina	1994-1997
Becky Worthington	Virginia	1997-2000

FOOTBALL

Bill Armstrong	Wake Forest	1973-1976
Tiki Barber	Virginia	1993-1996
Dre' Bly	North Carolina	1996-1998
Joe Bostic	Clemson	1975-1978
Peter Boulware	Florida State	1994-1996
Derrick Brooks	Florida State	1991-1994
Ted Brown	NC State	1975-1978
Kelvin Bryant	North Carolina	1979-1982
Jerry Butler	Clemson	1975-1978
Dennis Byrd	NC State	1965-1967
Dick Christy	NC State	1955-1957
Marco Coleman	Georgia Tech	1989-1991
Bennie Cunningham	Clemson	1973-1975
Jeff Davis	Clemson	1978-1981
Jim Dombrowski	Virginia	1982-1985
Warrick Dunn	Florida State	1993-1996
Boomer Esiason	Maryland	1981-1983
Steve Fuller	Clemson	1975-1978
William Fuller	North Carolina	1980-1983
Roman Gabriel	NC State	1959-1961
Joe Hamilton	Georgia Tech	1996-1999
Alex Hawkins	South Carolina	1956-1958
Clarkston Hines	Duke	1986-1989
Torry Holt	NC State	1995-1998
Sebastian Janikowski	Florida State	1997-1999
Marvin Jones	Florida State	1990-1992
Stan Jones	Maryland	1951-1953
Terry Kinard	Clemson	1978-1982
Amos Lawrence	North Carolina	1977-1980
Bob Matheson	Duke	1964-1966
Don McCauley	North Carolina	1968-1970
Mike McGee	Duke	1957-1959
Herman Moore	Virginia	1988-1990
Bob Pellegrini	Maryland	1953-1955
Julius Peppers	North Carolina	1999-2001
Michael Dean Perry	Clemson	1984-1987
William Perry	Clemson	1981-1984
Brian Piccolo	Wake Forest	1962-1964
Frank Quayle	Virginia	1966-1968
Jim Ritcher	NC State	1976-1979
Anthony Simmons	Clemson	1995-1997
Chris Slade	Virginia	1988-1992
Norm Snead	Wake Forest	1958-1960
Ken Swilling	Georgia Tech	1988-1991
Lawrence Taylor	North Carolina	1977-1980
Mike Voight	North Carolina	1973-1976
Charlie Ward	Florida State	1990-1993
Peter Warrick	Florida State	1996-1999
Chris Weinke	Florida State	1997-2000
Randy White	Maryland	1972-1974

WOMEN'S GOLF

Alicia Allison	Duke	1994-1998
Kalen Anderson	Duke	1997-2001
Donna Andrews	North Carolina	1986-1989
Alexandra Armas	Wake Forest	1994-1998
Jean Bartholomew	Duke	1985-1989
Beth Bauer	Duke	1998-2000
Tonya Blosser	Duke	1990-1994
Amy Bond	Florida State	1996-1999
Lisa Brandetsas	Duke	1988-1992
Jamie Bronson	NC State	1982-1985
Leslie Brown	NC State	1983-1986
Kimberly Byham	North Carolina	1990-1993
Kim Cayce	Duke	1990-1993
Jenny Chuasiriporn	Duke	1995-1999
Brenda Corrie Kuehn	Wake Forest	1982-1986
Laura D'Alessandro	Wake Forest	1986-1990
Debbie Doniger	North Carolina	1989-1992
Kristina Engstrom	Duke	1999-2000
Maria Garcia-Estrada	Duke	1998-2001
Charlotte Grant	Wake Forest	1977-1981
Candy Hannemann	Duke	1998-2001
Filippa Hansson	Duke	1995-1999
Leigh Anne Hardin	Duke	2000-2001
Patty Jordan	Wake Forest	1978-1982
Kandi Kessler	North Carolina	1984-1986
Stephanie Kornegay	North Carolina	1977-1980
Sarah LeBrun	Duke	1984-1988
Amie Lehman	Duke	1996-2000
Jodi Logan	Duke	1982-1986
Page Marsh	North Carolina	1982-1985
Kelly McCall	North Carolina	1994-1997
Linda Mescan	North Carolina	1980,82-84
Michele Miller	Duke	1982-1986
Megan Morgan	North Carolina	1995-1998
Stephanie Neill Harner	Wake Forest	1991-1995
Marcy Newton	North Carolina	1997-2000
Virada Nirapathpongporn	Duke	2000-2001
Karen Noble	Wake Forest	1985-1989
Evelyn Orley	Duke	1984-1988
Katie Peterson	North Carolina	1986-1989
Laura Philo Diaz	Wake Forest	1993-1997
Kathi Poppmeier	Duke	1992-1996
Marta Prieto	Wake Forest	1997-2001
Stephanie Sparks	Duke	1991,94-96
Karen Stupples	Florida State	1992-1995
Kelly Tilghman	Duke	1987-1991
Helen Wadsworth	Wake Forest	1984-1987
Mary Anne Widman	Duke	1980-1984
Jessica Wood	North Carolina	1990-1993
Louise Wright	Florida State	1998-2001

MEN'S GOLF

Billy Andrade	Wake Forest	1983-1987
Deane Beman	Maryland	1958-1961
Tee Burton	North Carolina	1988-1991
Jonathan Byrd	Clemson	1996-2000
Bill Calfee	Maryland	1968-1971
Lewis Chitengwa	Virginia	1995-1998
Stewart Cink	Georgia Tech	1992-1995
Tim Clark	NC State	1996-1998
Simon Cooke	Virginia	1993-1996
Richard Coughlan	Clemson	1993-1997
James Driscoll	Virginia	1997-2000
David Duval	Georgia Tech	1990-1993
Danny Ellis	Clemson	1989-1993
John Engler	Clemson	1997-2001
Frank Fuhrer	North Carolina	1978-1981
Fred Funk	Maryland	1977-1980
Lucas Glover	Clemson	1997-2001
Nicky Goetze	Clemson	1989-1993
Jay Haas	Wake Forest	1973-1976
Gary Hallberg	Wake Forest	1977-1980
Max Harris	North Carolina	1997-2000
Vance Heafner	NC State	1973-1976
Scott Hoch	Wake Forest	1974-1978
Joe Inman	Wake Forest	1966-1969
John Inman	North Carolina	1981-1984
Kevin Johnson	Clemson	1985-1989
Matt Kuchar	Georgia Tech	1997-2000
Jack Lewis	Wake Forest	1966-1969
Davis Love III	North Carolina	1983-1985
Bill Mallon	Duke	1970-1973
Len Mattiace	Wake Forest	1986-1989
Nolan Mills	NC State	1980-1983
Kelly Mitchum	NC State	1990-1993
Bryce Molder	Georgia Tech	1998-2001
Mike Muehr	Duke	1990-1994
Joe Ogilvie	Duke	1993-1996
Arnold Palmer	Wake Forest	48-50,53-54
Chris Patton	Clemson	1986-1990
Carl Pettersson	NC State	1999-2000
Dillard Pruitt	Clemson	1980-1984
Clarence Rose	Clemson	1978-1980
Tom Scherrer	North Carolina	1990-1992
Dick Siderowf	Duke	1956-1959
Jay Sigel	Wake Forest	1964-1967
Mark Slawter	NC State	1993-1996
Curtis Strange	Wake Forest	1973-1975
Leonard Thompson	Wake Forest	1966-1969
D.J. Trahan	Clemson	1999-2001
Lanny Wadkins	Wake Forest	1969-1972
Charles Warren	Clemson	1994-1998
Jason Widener	Duke	1990-1993

GYMNASTICS

Vicki Kreider	NC State	1981-1984
Angela Reagan	NC State	1983-1984
Michele Ritenhour	Maryland	1983-1984
Robin Swick	Maryland	1984-1987

MEN'S INDOOR TRACK & FIELD

Derrick Adkins	Georgia Tech	89-90,92-93
Mike Armour	Georgia Tech	198183-85
Jim Beatty	North Carolina	1954-1957
Eric Bishop	North Carolina	1995-1998
Andy Bloom	Wake Forest	1992-9496
Jeff Bray	Florida State	1990-1993
Ray Brown	Virginia	1981-1984
Bob Calhoun	Maryland	1978-1979
Milton Campbell	North Carolina	1995-1998
Greg Canty	Virginia	1977-1980
Mike Cole	Maryland	1963-1965
Frank Costello	Maryland	1965-1968
Shawn Crawford	Clemson	1997-2000
John Davenport	Maryland	1975-1977
Paul Ereng	Virginia	1988-1989
Cormac Finnerty	Clemson	1989-1992
Michael Green	Clemson	1990-1993
Philip Greyling	Clemson	1989-1991
Terrance Herrington	Clemson	1985-1989
Jeff Howser	Duke	1968-1971
Dennis Ivory	Maryland	1977-1979
Allen Johnson	North Carolina	1990-1993
Ralph King	North Carolina	1975-1978
Hans Koeleman	Clemson	1980-1983
David Krummenacker	Georgia Tech	1994,96-98
Reggie McAfee	North Carolina	1970-1973
Tony McCall	North Carolina	1994-1997
Antonio McKay	Georgia Tech	1984-1985
Derek Mills	Georgia Tech	1991-1994
Kendrick Morgan	North Carolina	1993-1996
Renaldo Nehemiah	Maryland	1978-1980
Conrad Nichols	Georgia Tech	1992-1995

ACC 50TH ANNIVERSARY TEAMS

Michael Patton	NC State	1986-1989
Robbie Perkins	Duke	1974-1976
Chan Pons	NC State	1997-2000
James Purvis	Georgia Tech	1985-1988
Phillip Riley	Florida State	1993-1996
Duane Ross	Clemson	1992-1995
Wesley Russell	Clemson	1992-1993
Joel Shankle	Duke	1954-1956
Dave Sime	Duke	1954-1957
William Skinner	Maryland	1986-1987
Angelo Taylor	Georgia Tech	1997-1998
Octavius Terry	Georgia Tech	1992-1995
James Trapp	Clemson	1990-1992
Sultan Tucker	Clemson	1997-2001
Tony Waldrop	North Carolina	1971-1974
Bob Wheeler	Duke	1970-1973
Alvis Whitted	NC State	1994-1997
Keith Witherspoon	Virginia	1973-1976

WOMEN'S INDOOR TRACK & FIELD

Natasha Alleyne	Georgia Tech	88-90, 92
Ayo Atterberry	North Carolina	1991-1994
Kim Austin	North Carolina	1987-1990
Ann Bair	Virginia	1980-1983
Penny Blackwell	North Carolina	1989-1992
Dana Boone	Virginia	1988-1991
Nikkie Bouyer	Clemson	96,98-99
Kerrie Bowes	Maryland	1996-1997
Gail Bryant	Virginia	1982-1985
Tonya Carter	Florida State	1997-2000
LaShonda Christopher	North Carolina	1996-1999
LaTasha Colander	North Carolina	1995-1998
Sharon Couch	North Carolina	1988-1991
Sheryl Covington	Florida State	1991-1994
DeAnne Davis	North Carolina	1997-2000
Sara Day	Wake Forest	2000-2001
Lisa Dillard	Clemson	1989-1991
Michelle Faherty	North Carolina	1988-1991
Shalane Flanagan	North Carolina	2001,2002
Claire Forbes	Virginia	1990-1993
Sonja Fridy	Virginia	1984-1987
Nicole Gamble	North Carolina	1996-1999
Joy Ganes	North Carolina	1998-2001
Samantha George	Florida State	1997-2000
Laura Gerber	Florida State	1999-2001
Laurie Gomez	NC State	1989-1992
Sherry Gould	Virginia	1991-1994
Kim Graham	Clemson	1991-1993
Kathy Harrison	Georgia Tech	1986-1987
Karen Hartmann	Clemson	1992-1995
Monyetta Haynesworth	Clemson	1992-1993
Monique Hennagan	North Carolina	1995-1998
Janeen Jones	Georgia Tech	1991-1994
Andria King	Georgia Tech	1996-1999
Janelle Kraus	Wake Forest	1997-2000
Tina Krebs	Clemson	83,85-87
Kendra Mackey	North Carolina	1988-1991
Cydonie Mothersill	Clemson	2000-2001
Jamine Moton	Clemson	1998-2001
Joan Nesbit	North Carolina	1981-1984
Shellie O'Neal	Georgia Tech	1989-1992
Nelrae Pasha	Georgia Tech	89-90,92-93
Marchelle Payne	Maryland	1990-1993
Michele Rowen	Virginia	1983-1986
Jillian Schwartz	Duke	1998-2001
Erica Shepard	Florida State	1994-1997
Janet Smith	NC State	1986-1989
Jill Snyder	Wake Forest	1998-2001
Rosalind Taylor	Maryland	1987-1989
Tisha Waller	North Carolina	1989-1992
Shekera Weston	Clemson	97-99,2001

MEN'S LACROSSE

Clayton Beardmore	Maryland	1960-1962
Bob Boniello	Maryland	1977-1980
Joe Breschi	North Carolina	1987-1990
Jim Buczek	North Carolina	1989-1992
Michael Burnett	North Carolina	1981-1984
Steve Byrne	Virginia	1980-1983
Steve Card	Duke	1997-2000
Kevin Cassese	Duke	2000-2001
Stan Cockerton	NC State	1977-1980
Jay Connor	Virginia	1969-1972
Doug Cooper	Virginia	1971-1974
Randy Cox	North Carolina	1981-1984
Ryan Curtis	Virginia	1997-2000
Brian Doughtery	Maryland	1993-1996
Mark Douglas	Maryland	1988-1991
Tom Duquette	Virginia	1970-1973
Peter Eldredge	Virginia	1969-1972
Mike Farrell	Maryland	1973-1976
Mac Ford	North Carolina	1982-1985
Conor Gill	Virginia	1999-2001
Dennis Goldstein	North Carolina	1987-1991
Jim Gonnella	Duke	1994-1997
Kevin Griswold	North Carolina	1979-1982
Graham Harden	North Carolina	1988-1991
Tyler Hardy	Duke	1994-1997
Tom Haus	North Carolina	1983-1987
Jack Heim	Maryland	1965-1967
Jay Jalbert	Virginia	1997-2000
James Kappler	Maryland	1955-1957
John Kastner	Maryland	1969-1972
Doug Knight	Virginia	1994-1997
Andy Kraus	Virginia	1987-1991
Alan Lowe	Maryland	1965-1967
Roddy Marino	Virginia	1983-1986
Ed Mullen	Maryland	1973-1976
Matt Ogelsby	Duke	1992-1995
Kevin O'Shea	Virginia	1977-1980
Kevin Pehlke	Virginia	1990-1993
Harper Peterson	North Carolina	1968-1970
Douglas Radebaugh	Maryland	1973-1976
Tucker Radebaugh	Virginia	1996-1999
Rodney Rullman	Virginia	1972-1975
Douglas Schreiber	Maryland	1972-1973
Tom Sears	North Carolina	1980-1983
Joey Seivold	North Carolina	1983-1987
John Simmons	Maryland	1954-1956
Mike Thearle	Maryland	1972-1973
Roger Tuck	Maryland	1973-1976
Frank Urso	Maryland	1973-1976
Peter Voelkel	North Carolina	1980-1983
Jason Wade	North Carolina	1991-1994
Ryan Wade	North Carolina	1993-1996
Michael Watson	Virginia	1994-1997
Tim Whiteley	Virginia	1993-1996
Charles Wicker	Maryland	1953-1956
Pete Worstell	Maryland	1977-1981
Tom Worstell	Maryland	1985-1988

WOMEN'S LACROSSE

Jen Adams	Maryland	1998-2001
Kelly Amonte-Hiller	Maryland	1993-1996
Kara Ariza	Virginia	1995-1998
Lauren Aumiller	Virginia	2000-2001
Peggy Boutilier	Virginia	1995-1998
Amy Breen	Virginia	1990-1993
Jamie Brodsky	Maryland	92,94-96
Erin Brown	Maryland	1989-1990
Quinn Carney	Maryland	1998-2001
Alison Comito	Maryland	1998-2001
Michelle Cusimano	Virginia	1993-1996
Heather Dow	Virginia	1980-1982
Liz Downing	Maryland	1993-1996
Debbie Easter	Virginia	1980-1983
Betsy Elder	Maryland	1991-1994
Anysia Fedec	Maryland	1984-1987
Sarah Forbes	Maryland	1994-1997
Leigh Frendburg	Maryland	1990-1992
Amy Fromal	Virginia	1997-2000
Cherie Greer	Virginia	1991-1994
Laura Harmon Schumann	Maryland	1992-1995
Mandy Hudson Stevenson	Maryland	89,91-93
Christie Jenkins	Maryland	1997-2000
Alex Kahoe	Maryland	1997-2000
Kate Kaiser	Duke	1999-2001
Mary Kordner	Maryland	1987-1990
Sandy Lanahan	Maryland	1979-1981
Karen MacCrate	Maryland	1993-1996
Elaine Maddox	Virginia	1984-1987
Kerstin Manning Kimel	Maryland	1990-1993
Tricia Martin	Duke	1997-2000
Cynthia Mathes	Virginia	1988-1991
Maggie McInnes	Virginia	1977-1980
Mary Lynn Morgan	Maryland	1981-1984
Cathy Nelson	Maryland	1995-1998
Tracy Nelson	Virginia	1986-1989
Sascha Newmarch	Maryland	1995-1998
Robyn Nye	Virginia	1988-1991
Mary Ann Oelgoetz Meltzer	Maryland	1987-1990
Carin Peterson	Maryland	1986-1988
Tonia Porras	Maryland	1997-2001
Bonnie Rosen	Virginia	1989-1992
Kay Ruffino	Maryland	1982-1998
Maureen Scott	Maryland	1991-1994
Lindsay Sheehan	Virginia	1984-1986
Jenny Slingluff	Virginia	1989-1992
Kristin Sommar	Maryland	1997-2000
Tracy Stumpf	Maryland	1984 1986
Karen Trudel	Maryland	1983-1985
Michele Uhlfelder	Maryland	1988-1991
Jennifer Ulehla	Maryland	1990-1991
Jess Wilk	Maryland	1989-1990
Julie Williams	Virginia	1983-1986
Dawn Wisniewski	Virginia	1984-1987
Anna Yates	Virginia	1992-1995

MEN'S OUTDOOR TRACK & FIELD

Derrick Adkins	Georgia Tech	1989-1992
Joe Allen	Florida State	2000-2001
Nick Basciano	Maryland	1974-1976
Jim Beatty	North Carolina	1954-1957
Eric Bishop	North Carolina	1996-1998
Andy Bloom	Wake Forest	199294-96
Kevin Braunskill	NC State	1988-1991
Ray Brown	Virginia	1981-1984
Steve Brown	Wake Forest	1987-1990
Milton Campbell	North Carolina	1995-1998
Jonathan Carter	Florida State	1993-1996
Mike Cole	Maryland	1964-1965
Roger Collins	Clemson	1967-1970
Mike Columbus	Clemson	1975-1978
Frank Costello	Maryland	1965-1968
Mike Cotton	Virginia	1978-1981
Shawn Crawford	Clemson	1997-2000
Paul Ereng	Virginia	1988-1989
Michael Green	Clemson	1990-1993
Ken Harnden	North Carolina	1994-1995
Terrance Herrington	Clemson	1985-1989
John Hinton	Virginia	1981-1984
Dennis Ivory	Maryland	1976-1979
Allen Johnson	North Carolina	1990-1993
Hans Koeleman	Clemson	1980-1983
David Krummenacker	Georgia Tech	1994,96-98
Reggie McAfee	North Carolina	1970-1973
Kevin McGorty	North Carolina	1986-1989
Antonio McKay	Georgia Tech	1984-1985
Harvey McSwain	NC State	1983-1986
Derek Mills	Georgia Tech	1991-1994
Renaldo Nehemiah	Maryland	1978-1980
Conrad Nichols	Georgia Tech	1992-1995
Danny Peebles	NC State	1985-1988
Robbie Perkins	Duke	1974-1976
Chris Person	Maryland	1979-1982
James Purvis	Georgia Tech	1985-1988
Phillip Riley	Florida State	1993-1996
Greg Robertson	Maryland	1976-1979
Duane Ross	Clemson	1992-1995
Joel Shankle	Duke	1954-1956
Dave Sime	Duke	1954-1956
William Skinner	Maryland	1986-1987
Nolan Swanson	Wake Forest	1996-1999
Tyrell Taitt	NC State	1990-1994
Angelo Taylor	Georgia Tech	1997-1998
Octavius Terry	Georgia Tech	1992,94-96
James Trapp	Clemson	1990-1992
Tony Waldrop	North Carolina	1971-1974
Cary Weisiger	Duke	1957-1960
Bob Wheeler	Duke	1970-1973
Tony Wheeler	Clemson	1994-1997

WOMEN'S OUTDOOR TRACK & FIELD

Natasha Alleyne	Georgia Tech	1988-1991
Catrina Bindel	Wake Forest	1993-1996
Dana Boone	Virginia	1988-1991
Gail Bryant	Virginia	1982-1985
Tonya Carter	Florida State	1997-2000
LaShonda Christopher	North Carolina	1996-1999
LaTasha Colander	North Carolina	1995-1998
Sharon Couch	North Carolina	1988-1991
Ann Crouse	Virginia	1995-9799
Sophia Danvers	Florida State	1994-1997
Sara Day	Wake Forest	2000-2001
Lisa Dillard	Clemson	1989-1991
Angela Dolby	Clemson	1989-1992
Shalane Flanagan	North Carolina	2001,2002
Angel Fleetwood	Clemson	1989-1992
Claire Forbes	Virginia	1990-1993
Sonja Fridy	Virginia	1984-1987
Nicole Gamble	North Carolina	1996-1999
Joy Ganes	North Carolina	1998-2001
Samantha George	Florida State	1997-2000
Paula Girven	Maryland	1978-1980
Laurie Gomez	NC State	1989-1992
Kim Graham	Clemson	1991-1993
Kathy Harrison	Georgia Tech	1986-1987
Karen Hartmann	Clemson	1992-1995
Monique Hennagan	North Carolina	1995-1998
Trinette Johnson	Florida State	1990-1993
Janeen Jones	Georgia Tech	1991-1994
Marion Jones	North Carolina	1994-1995

ACC 50TH ANNIVERSARY TEAMS

Andria King	Georgia Tech	1996-1999
Janelle Kraus	Wake Forest	1997-2000
Tina Krebs	Clemson	198385-87
Angela Lee	Virginia	1996-1999
Lynda Lipson	North Carolina	1990-1993
Kendra Mackey	North Carolina	1988-1991
Cydonie Mothersill	Clemson	2001
Jamine Moton	Clemson	98-99,2001
Joan Nesbit	North Carolina	1981-1984
Nelrae Pasha	Georgia Tech	89,91-93
Marchelle Payne	Maryland	1990-1993
Mareike Ressing	Clemson	91,93-95
Ellen Reynolds	Duke	1993-1996
Rebecca Russell	North Carolina	1989-1992
Julie Shea	NC State	1978-1981
Janet Smith	NC State	1985-1988
Julia Solo	Virginia	1986-1989
Betty Springs	NC State	1980-1983
Rosalind Taylor	Maryland	1986-1989
Tisha Waller	North Carolina	1989-1992
Marita Walton	Maryland	1980-1983
Shekera Weston	Clemson	97-99,2001

ROWING

Maren Betts-Sonstegard	Duke	1998-2001
Sarah Brennan	Virginia	1999-2001
Amy Burns	Virginia	1995-1998
Lucy Doolittle	Clemson	1999-2001
Emily Egge	Virginia	1997-2000
Aimee Fox	Clemson	1999-2001
Sara Garrett	Virginia	1997-2000
Michelle Giller	Virginia	1997-2000
Sarah Harrick	Virginia	1996-1999
Jennifer Herberger	Virginia	1998-2001
Marie "Sam" Hermitte	North Carolina	1998-1999
Christina Hillson	Virginia	1997-2000
Joanna Hingle	Duke	2000-2001
Claire Hozier	North Carolina	1998-1999
Risa Mandzuk	Virginia	2000-2001
Ang McCallum	Virginia	1996-1999
Brooke McFadden	Virginia	1996-1998
Kara McPhillips	Virginia	1998-1999
Erin Neppel	North Carolina	1998-2001
Margot Noordzij	Virginia	1998-2001
Lucienne Papon	North Carolina	1998-1999
Dana Peirce	North Carolina	1998-2001
Ellen Perry	Virginia	1996-1999
Charlotte Quesada	Virginia	1996-1999
Jennifer Reck	Virginia	2001
Andrea Saathoff	Virginia	1996-1999

MEN'S SOCCER

Jeff Agoos	Virginia	1986-1990
Desmond Armstrong	Maryland	1982-1985
Keith Beach	Maryland	1995-1998
Gregg Berhalter	North Carolina	1991-1993
Dario Brose	NC State	1988-1991
Clyde Browne	Clemson	1972-1975
Danny Califf	Maryland	1998-1999
Chris Carrieri	North Carolina	1998-2000
Neil Covone	Wake Forest	1987-1990
Leo Cullen	Maryland	1995-1997
Ali Curtis	Duke	1997-2000
Serge Daniv	Wake Forest	1995-9698
Mark Dodd	Duke	1986-1987
Anson Dorrance	North Carolina	1971-1973
Eric Eichman	Clemson	1983-1986
Mike Fisher	Virginia	1993-1996
Jeff Gaffney	Virginia	1982-1985
George Gelnovatch	Virginia	1983-1986
Jimmy Glenn	Clemson	1990-1993
Henry Gutierrez	NC State	1988-1991
John Harkes	Virginia	1985-1987
Wolde Harris	Clemson	1993-1995
Jay Heaps	Duke	1995-1998
Mike Jeffries	Duke	1980-1983
Matt Jordan	Clemson	1994-1997
Miles Joseph	Clemson	1992-1994
Tom Kain	Duke	1982-1985
John Kerr	Duke	1983-1986
Wojtek Kiakowiak	Clemson	1997-1998
Jason Kreis	Duke	1991-1994
Roy Lassiter	NC State	1990-1991
Mark Lisi	Clemson	1997-2000
Ken Lolla	Duke	1980-1983
Kyle Martino	Virginia	1999-2001
Pablo Mastroeni	NC State	1994-1997
Tony Meola	Virginia	1988-1989
Bruce Murray	Clemson	1984-1987
Nnamdi Nwokocha	Clemson	1979-1981
Chris Ogu	NC State	1980-1983
Sam Okpodu	NC State	1981-1984
Ben Olsen	Virginia	1995-1997
Oguchi Onyewu	Clemson	2000-2001
Abudarie Otorubio	Clemson	1981-1984
Eddie Pope	North Carolina	1992-1995
Tab Ramos	NC State	1984-1987
Claudio Reyna	Virginia	1991-1993
Robert Russell	Duke	1997-2000
Scott Schweitzer	NC State	1989-1992
David Smyth	North Carolina	1984-1987
Chris Szanto	NC State	1985-1989
Carey Talley	North Carolina	1994-1997
Taylor Twellman	Maryland	1988-1989
Joe Ulrich	Duke	1981-1982
Clyde Watson	Clemson	1973-1976
A.J. Wood	Virginia	1991-1994

WOMEN'S SOCCER

Julie Augustyniak	Clemson	1997-2000
Nancy Augustyniak	Clemson	1997-2000
Tracey Bates	North Carolina	1985-1989
Danielle Borgman	North Carolina	1998-2001
Sara Burkett	Clemson	1995-1998
Robin Confer	North Carolina	1994-1997
Amanda Cromwell	Virginia	1988-1991
Michelle Demko	Maryland	1993 1995
Lorrie Fair	North Carolina	1996-1999
Nel Fettig	North Carolina	1994-1997
Meredith Florance	North Carolina	1997-2000
Fabienne Gareau	NC State	1987-1991
Wendy Gebauer	North Carolina	1985-1988
Mia Hamm	North Carolina	89-90,92-93
Emmy Harbo	Maryland	1995-1998
April Heinrichs	North Carolina	1983-1986
Thora Helgadottir	Duke	2000-2001
Lori Henry	North Carolina	1986-1988
Shannon Higgins	North Carolina	1986-1989
Seattle Wash.		
Charmaine Hooper	NC State	1987-1990
Angela Hucles	Virginia	1996-1999
Emily Janss	Maryland	1996-1999
Beth Keller	Clemson	1996-1999
Debbie Keller	North Carolina	1993-1996
Angela Kelly	North Carolina	1991-1994
Laura Kerrigan	NC State	1985-1988
Sherrill Kester	Duke	1996-1999
Jena Kluegel	North Carolina	1998-2001
Kristine Lilly	North Carolina	1989-1992
Lori Lindsey	Virginia	1998-2001
Marcia McDermott	North Carolina	1983-1986
Andi Melde	Duke	1994-1997
Siri Mullinix	North Carolina	1995-1998
Carla Overbeck	North Carolina	1986-1989
Cindy Parlow	North Carolina	1995-1998
Tiffany Roberts	North Carolina	1995-1998
Stacy Roeck	Wake Forest	1998-2001
Andrea Rubio	Virginia	1989-1992
Jill Rutten	NC State	1986-1988
Keri Sanchez	North Carolina	1991-1994
Keri Sarver	Maryland	1995-1997
Thori Staples	NC State	1992-1995
Emily Taggart	Wake Forest	1998-2001
Erin Taylor	Maryland	1993-1996
Tisha Venturini	North Carolina	1991-1994
Kelly Walbert	Duke	1992-1995
Kristy Whelchel	Duke	1995-1998
Staci Wilson	North Carolina	1994-1997
Kim Yankowski	NC State	1990-1993
Catherine Zaborowski	NC State	1992-1995

SOFTBALL

Rebecca Aase	Florida State	1991-1994
Natalie Anter	North Carolina	1999-2001
Brandy Arthur	North Carolina	1995-1998
Virginia Augusta	North Carolina	1984-1987
Dana Bailey	Florida State	1996-1999
Leslie Barton	Florida State	1990-1993
Amanda Bettker	Maryland	1999-2001
Sonya Bright	North Carolina	1990-1993
Serita Brooks	Florida State	2000-2001
Michelle Burrell	Maryland	1998-2001
Susan Buttery	Florida State	1990-1993
Elysa Calderone	Virginia	1993-1996
Myssi Calkins	Florida State	1994-1997
Kimmy Carter	Florida State	1999-2001
Michelle Collins	Virginia	91,93-95
Danielle Cox	Florida State	1998-1999
Lisa Davidson	Florida State	1991-1994
Kristen Dennis	Virginia	1999-2001
Renee Espinoza	Florida State	1995-1996
Kristy Fuentes	Florida State	1994-1997
Toni Gutierrez	Florida State	1990-1993
Jamie Hahn	Virginia	1993-1996
Crystal Henderson	North Carolina	1997-2000
Vicki Huff	North Carolina	1991-1994
Kristy Hull	Florida State	1995-1998
Anne Knobbe	Georgia Tech	1997-2000
Christine Kubin	North Carolina	1993-1996
Cindy Lawton	Florida State	1994-1995
Marla Looper	Florida State	1993-1994
Cortney Madea	Maryland	1997-2000
Leslie Malerich	Florida State	1999-2001
Radara McHugh	North Carolina	1998-2001
Shannon Mitchem	Florida State	1989-1992
Misty Molin	Florida State	1995-1998
Lisa Palmer	Virginia	1986-1989
Jennifer Potzman	Maryland	1998-2001
Lori Reese	Virginia	1996-1999
Ruby Rojas	Virginia	2000-2001
Eileen Schmidt	Virginia	1991-1994
Michelle Semmes	North Carolina	1998-2001
Kelly Shipman	Maryland	1996-1999
Penny Siqueiros	Florida State	1989-1992
Beverly Smith	North Carolina	1991-1994
Brandi Stuart	Florida State	2000-2001
Jessica van der Linden	Florida State	2001
Stacy Venable	Florida State	1997-1999
Stephanie Weitman	Georgia Tech	1992-1995
Jen White-Stokes	Florida State	1998-2001
Laura Williams	Georgia Tech	1994-1997
Shamalene Wilson	Florida State	1993-1995
Meaghan Young	Virginia	1998-2001
Stacey Zagol	Virginia	1997-2000

MEN'S SWIMMING & DIVING

Luke Anderson	Virginia	2001-2002
Rick Aronberg	Clemson	1985-1988
Shilo Ayalon	Georgia Tech	1999-2001
Rob Braknis	Florida State	1994-1998
Neil Brophy	Clemson	1979-1982
Coy Cobb	Clemson	1981-1984
Tony Corliss	NC State	1972-1975
John Davis	North Carolina	1988-1991
Yann de Fabrique	North Carolina	1992-1995
Brendon Dedekind	Florida State	1996-1999
Phil Drake	North Carolina	1953-1955
Eric Ericson	North Carolina	1981-1984
Dick Fagden	NC State	1954-1958
Doak Finch	Virginia	1997-2000
Peter Fogarassey	NC State	1961-1964
David Fox	NC State	1990-1993
Duncan Goodhew	NC State	1976-1979
Steve Gregg	NC State	1974-1977
Jamie Grimes	Virginia	1998-2001
Dan Harrigan	NC State	1975-1978
Braden Holloway	NC State	1998-2001
Eddie Houchin	NC State	1975-1978
Glenn Houck	Virginia	1986-1989
Greg Indrisano	Virginia	1989-1992
Kenny Ireland	North Carolina	1977-1980
Jack Jackson	Virginia	1987-1990
Charlie Krepp	North Carolina	1955-1957
Mike Lambert	Maryland	1986-1989
Thompson Mann	North Carolina	1962-1964
Gary Marshall	Virginia	2001-2002
Harrison Merrill	North Carolina	1963-1965
David Monasterio	North Carolina	1990-1993
Ed Moses	Virginia	1998-2000
Mike Noonan	Maryland	1990-1992
Stephen Parry	Florida State	1996-1999
Brett Peterson	Florida State	1997-2000
Shamek Pietucha	Virginia	1996-1999
Ian Prichard	Virginia	2001-2002
Austin Ramirez	Virginia	1997-2000
Steve Rerych	NC State	1965-1968
Phil Riker	North Carolina	1965-1967
Trevor Runberg	North Carolina	1995-1998
Kirk Sanocki	Maryland	1980-1983
Julio Santos	Florida State	1997-1999
Bill Smyth	Virginia	90-91,93-94
Ed Spencer	NC State	1961-1963
Eric Steinhouse	Duke	1979-1980
Jim Umbdenstock	NC State	1976-1979
Luke Wagner	Virginia	2001-2002
Andy Wren	Virginia	1980-1983
Peter Wright	Virginia	1992-1995

WOMEN'S SWIMMING & DIVING TEAM

Erika Acuff	North Carolina	1997-2001
Jill Bakehorn	Clemson	1987-1990
Cami Berizzi	North Carolina	1981-1984

ACC 50TH ANNIVERSARY TEAMS

Mirjana Bosevska	Virginia	2000-2002
Bonny Brown	North Carolina	1977-1980
Melanie Buddemeyer	North Carolina	1985-1989
Karen Burgess	Virginia	1990-1993
Courtenay Carr	Maryland	1985-1988
Christy Cech	Florida State	2000-2002
Rebecca Cronk	Virginia	1997-2000
Dorothy Dilts	Virginia	1975-1978
Melissa Douse	North Carolina	1989-1992
Lauren Dupree	North Carolina	1978-1980
Beth Emery	NC State	1980-1983
Richelle Fox	North Carolina	1997-1998
Agnes Gerlach	NC State	1992-1995
Ruth Grodsky	Clemson	1986-1989
Kari Haag	North Carolina	1993-1996
Janis Hape	North Carolina	1977-1980
Beth Harrell Learn	NC State	1978-1981
Barb Harris	North Carolina	1979-1982
Katie Hathaway	North Carolina	1999-2002
Pam Hayden	Clemson	1985-1988
Gayle Hegel	North Carolina	1980-1983
Nancy Hogshead	Duke	1981
Jane Holliday	NC State	1976-1979
Jan Kemmerling	Clemson	1985-1988
Mitzi Kremer	Clemson	1987-1989
Cara Lane	Virginia	2000-2002
Amy Lepping	NC State	1979-1982
Ann Marshall	North Carolina	1976-1979
Jennifer Mihalik	Clemson	1997-1999
Chrissy Miller	North Carolina	1995-1998
Sudi Miller	Virginia	1985-1988
Susan O'Brien	North Carolina	1985-1988
Beth O'Connor	Virginia	1980-1983
Betsy O'Donnell	Virginia	1986-1989
Sarah Perroni	North Carolina	1990-1993
Jessi Perruquet	North Carolina	2001
Amy Pless	North Carolina	1981-1984
Leslie Ramsey	North Carolina	1992-1995
Allyson Reid	NC State	1979-1980
Michelle Richardson	Clemson	1989-1992
Paulette Russell	Clemson	1990-1993
Melanie Valerio	Virginia	1988-1991
Laurie Wagner	Virginia	1993-1996
Sue Walsh	North Carolina	1981-1984
Christy Watkins	North Carolina	2000-2002
Lori Werth	Virginia	1990-1993
Samantha White	Florida State	1996-1999
Hope Williams	NC State	1982-1985
Polly Winde	North Carolina	1983-1986

MEN'S TENNIS

Gilles Ameline	Wake Forest	1989-1990
Andy Andrews	NC State	1978-1981
Chiam Arlosorov	Duke	1982-1984
Peter Ayers	Duke	1993-1996
Jay Berger	Clemson	1985-1986
Roberto Bracone	NC State	1996-1999
Billy Brock	North Carolina	1973-1976
David Caldwell	North Carolina	1993-1996
Owen Casey	Clemson	1989-1990
Marko Cerenko	Duke	1998-2001
Jeff Chambers	North Carolina	1984-1987
Rob Chess	Duke	1993-1996
Jean Desdunes	Clemson	1980-1983
Mark Dickson	Clemson	1979-1982
Lawson Duncan	Clemson	1984
Marc Flur	Duke	1980-1983
Mike Gandolfo	Clemson	1977-1980
Geoff Grant	Duke	1989-1992
Mark Greenan	Wake Forest	1984-1988
Bobby Heald	South Carolina	1966-1968
Jeff Hersh	Duke	1985-1988
Don Johnson	North Carolina	1987-1990
Bryan Jones	North Carolina	1989-1992
Kent Kinnear	Clemson	1985-1988
John Lucas	Maryland	1973-1976
Richard Matuszewski	Clemson	1983-1986
Matt McDonald	NC State	1977-1980
Richie McKee	North Carolina	1971-1974
Freddie McNair	North Carolina	1970-1973
Huntley Montgomery	Virginia	1997-2000
Pender Murphy	Clemson	1978-1981
Miguel Nido	Clemson	1982-1985
O.H. Parrish	North Carolina	1963-1965
Andres Pedroso	Duke	1998-2001
Tripp Phillips	North Carolina	1996-2000
Chris Pressley	Duke	1992-1995
Doug Root	Duke	1997-2000
Rick Rudeen	Clemson	1981-1984
John Sadri	NC State	1975-1978
Bryan Shelton	Georgia Tech	1985-1988
Jens Skjoedt	Georgia Tech	1987-1990
Ramsey Smith	Duke	1998-2001
George Sokol	North Carolina	1962-1964
Mitch Sprengelmeyer	Clemson	1994-1997
John Sullivan	Clemson	1986-1989
Kenny Thorne	Georgia Tech	1985-1988
Roland Thornqvist	North Carolina	1991-1993
Brian Vahaly	Virginia	1997-2000
Vince VanGelderen	Clemson	1986-1989
Brandon Walters	Clemson	1984-1988
John Zahurak	Maryland	1986-1988

WOMEN'S TENNIS

Jennifer Balent	North Carolina	1978-1981
Liz Barker	Wake Forest	1991-1994
Kathy Barton	North Carolina	1981-1984
Janet Bergman	Wake Forest	1999-2001
Angela Bernal	North Carolina	1992
Bea Bielik	Wake Forest	2000-2001
Claudia Borgiani	Maryland	1984-1988
Margie Brown	North Carolina	1979-1982
Jen Callen	Virginia	1991-1994
Cristina Caparis	Wake Forest	1994-1997
Ansley Cargill	Duke	2000-2001
Alison Cohen	Virginia	1993-1996
Ingellse Driehuis	Clemson	1986-1987
Laura DuPont	North Carolina	1967-1970
Dana Evans	Wake Forest	1992-1995
Julie Exum	Duke	1989-1993
Gigi Fernandez	Clemson	1983
Jane Forman	Clemson	1981-1984
Alida Gallovits	Florida State	1998-2001
Carmina Giraldo	Clemson	1999-2000
Gina Goblirsch	North Carolina	1987-1990
Katrina Greenman	Duke	1987-1991
Meg Griffin	Maryland	1996-1999
Cinda Gurney	North Carolina	1990-1993
Bobbi Guthrie	Georgia Tech	1997-2001
Maggie Harris	Wake Forest	1994-1997
Maren Haus	Wake Forest	1999-2001
Susan Hill	Clemson	1977-1980
Cathy Hofer	Clemson	1986-1989
Kylie Hunt	NC State	1994-1995
Jeri Ingram	Maryland	1989
Kristy Kottich	Georgia Tech	1988-1991
Monica Kowalewski	Wake Forest	1985-1988
Wendy Lyons	Duke	1991-1995
Marlene Mejia	North Carolina	2000-2001
Karin Miller	Duke	1996-1997
Monica Mraz	Duke	1991-1995
Christine Neuman	Duke	1990-1994
Patti O'Reilly	Duke	1986-1990
Alisha Portnoy	North Carolina	1990-1993
Leigh Roberts	Georgia Tech	1987-1990
Susan Sabo	Duke	1988-1991
Melissa Seigler	Clemson	1982-1985
Jenny Sell	NC State	1989-1992
Kathy Sell	Duke	1997-2001
Susan Sommerville	Duke	1989-1993
Lori Sowell	Florida State	1993-1996
Nicole Stafford	Clemson	1985-1988
Vanessa Webb	Duke	1995-1999
Jaime Wong	Georgia Tech	1999-2001
Sophie Woorons	Clemson	1996
Terry Ann Zawacki	Wake Forest	1993-1996

VOLLEYBALL

Kerry Annel	Georgia Tech	1992-1995
Erin Berg	North Carolina	1995-1998
Liz Berg	North Carolina	1987-1990
Jill Berkebile	North Carolina	1983-1986
Fiona Bolten	Florida State	1997-1998
Beth Brockell	Virginia	1986-1989
Diane Brown	Duke	1982-1985
Kristin Campbell	Duke	1994-1997
Norisha Campbell	Florida State	1998-2001
Alison Coday	Clemson	1996-1999
Melinda Dudley	NC State	1985-1988
Elizabeth Efron	Maryland	1996-1998
Carla Gartner	Georgia Tech	1995-1998
Sharon German	North Carolina	1986-1989
Karen Greiner	Duke	1988-1991
Anne Marie Hammers	Virginia	1988-1991
Tricia Hopkins	Duke	1987-1990
Colleen Hurley	Maryland	1989-1991
Heather Kahl	Clemson	1991-1994
Robin Kibben	Clemson	1991-1994
Laura Kimbrell	NC State	1995-1998
Daune Koester	Maryland	1993-1996
Rochelle Komula	Georgia Tech	1994-1997
Linda Kraft	Duke	1983-1986
Eden Kroeger	Maryland	1994-1999
Patty Lake	NC State	1984-1988
Nicole Lantagne	Maryland	1990-1993
Trina Maso de Moya	Wake Forest	1998-2001
Donna Meier	North Carolina	1981-1983
Andrea Nachtrieb	Georgia Tech	1993-1996
Adrian Nicol	Duke	1991-1994
Cris Omiecinski	Georgia Tech	1992-1995
Maja Pachale	Georgia Tech	1998-2001
Amy Peistrup	North Carolina	1989-1992
Pam Pounds	Wake Forest	1980-1983
Luiza Ramos	Florida State	1991-1994
Julie Rodriguez	Clemson	1993-1996
Jen Rohrig	Duke	1990-1993
Stacey Schaeffer	NC State	1978-1981
Susan Schafer	NC State	1978-1981
Holly Schneider	Florida State	1995-1998
Mary Frances Scott	Virginia	1996-1999
Tori Seibert	North Carolina	1996-1999
Sherry Smith	Maryland	1992-1995
Jodi Steffes	Clemson	1998-2001
Cindy Stern	Clemson	1996-1999
Michelle Thieke	Clemson	1994-1997
Aisha Thornton	Florida State	1996-1999
Volire Tisdale	NC State	1984-1988
Amy Verhoeven	Duke	1989-1992
Ashley Wacholder	Duke	1991-1994
Susan Wilson	Duke	1984-1986
Deanna Zwarich	Virginia	1997-2000

WRESTLING

Stan Banks	North Carolina	1992-1995
Lenny Bernstein	North Carolina	1985-1988
Shane Camera	North Carolina	1990-1994
Derek Capanna	Virginia	1985-1989
Frank Castrignano	NC State	1979-1982
Enzo Catullo	North Carolina	1987-1990
Dave Cooke	North Carolina	1978-1982
Marshal Dauberman	Maryland	1962-1964
Steve Garland	Virginia	1996-2000
Tim Geiger	Maryland	1963-1965
Jim Guzzio	Maryland	1995-1997
Jim Harshaw	Virginia	1994-1999
Justin Harty	North Carolina	1993-1997
Donnie Heckel	Clemson	1987-1991
Sam Henson	Clemson	1993-1994
Brian Jackson	NC State	1989
T.J. Jaworsky	North Carolina	1993-1995
Henry Jordan	Virginia	1953-1957
Gobel Kline	Maryland	1967-1969
Rob Koll	North Carolina	1985-1988
Mike Koob	NC State	1977-1980
Bob Kopnisky	Maryland	1963-1965
Mike Krafchick	Virginia	1990-1995
Chris Kwortnik	NC State	1991-1994
David Land	Maryland	1995-1997
Joe Lidowski	NC State	1977-1980
Noel Loban	Clemson	1977-1980
John Matyiko	Virginia	1986-1991
Jan Michaels	North Carolina	1981-1984
Mike Miller	NC State	92-93,95-96
Tom Miller	Maryland	1995-1997
C.D. Mock	North Carolina	1978-1982
Bob Monaghan	North Carolina	1979-1982
Chris Mondragon	NC State	1981-1984
Al Palacio	North Carolina	1982-1987
Steve Peperak	Maryland	1985-1987
Tom Reese	Maryland	1986-1988
Matt Reiss	NC State	1980-1982
Matt Roth	Virginia	1994-1999
Mike Sandusky	Maryland	1955-1957
Bob Shriner	North Carolina	1983-1986
Marc Sodano	NC State	1986-1987
Jody Staylor	North Carolina	1991-1992
Michael Stokes	NC State	1986-1989
Sylvester Terkay	NC State	1990-1993
Tab Thacker	NC State	1981-1984
Scott Turner	NC State	1984-1988
Steve Williams	NC State	1989-1992
Doug Wyland	North Carolina	1988-1990
Jim Zenz	NC State	1977-1980

INDEX of NAMES

INDEX of NAMES

PHOTO CREDITS

Eddy Gary Alter: 174

John Atkins: 94, 136

Michael Bailey: 237

Burnie Batchlor: 195

Scott Berg: 144 & 145

Jim Bounds: 269, 272 top left, 272 bottom right

Jeffrey A. Camarati: 190

Jim Carpenter: 169

Pete Casabonne: 181 right, center, 214

Clemson Sports Information: 34, 35, 63, 88, 89, 100 & 101, 108, 142, 143, 146 left, 170 top, 171, 187, 196, 197 left & right, 209, 280

Phil Coale: 241 left

Corbis: 48, 176 & 177

Robert Crawford: 161, 236, 242, 248, 255, 263, 271, 272 bottom left, 272 top right

Scott Cunningham: 216

Phil Davis: 217

Bob Donnan: 178 left and right, 186, 262, 270 left, center, right, 281 top and bottom

Keith Donnelly: 241 right

Duke Sports Information: 64, 65, 66, 86, 115, 144 & 145, 147 left & right, 179 left & right, 198, 200 left & right, 204 & 205, 218 left & right, 256, 273

Duke University Archives: 67, 68 & 69

The Durham Herald-Sun: 226

Florida State Sports Information: 80, 81 top & bottom, 220, 232, 233 left, 233 right, 253, 257, 258 & 259, 265

Georgia Tech Sports Information: 121 top left, 159, 202, 211

Getty Photos: 234 left

Jon Golden: 185, 201

David Greene: 210, 244

Simon Griffiths: 156 & 157, 182, 183, 219, 222

Dan Grogan: 136, 184, 189, 206 & 207, 235

Grant Halverson: 191, 221, 227, 234 right

Todd Huvard: 150

Caroline Joe: 120

Meade R. Jorgensen: 146

Stanley Leary: 121 bottom right

Ryals Lee: 240

Maryland: 21, 25 left, center, & right, 26, 107, 117 right, 126, 129, 141, 250 right, 260 & 261, 274 left & right, 277 left & right, 278 & 279

Hugh Morton: 20, 43, 61, 71, 76 right, 77, 84 & 85, 91, 98 & 99, 102 &103, 109, 114, 117 left, 132, 133, 137, 149, 162, 165, 166, 167, 168, 172, 193, 194, 199, 225, 228, 229, 239, 246, 249, 250 left, 266

North Carolina Sports Information: 17, 46, 58 right, 95, 134, 164

N.C. State Sports Information: 27, 30 & 31, 42, 51, 58 left, 70, 90, 116, 123, 124, 125, 128, 130, 131, 135, 152, 153, 203, 223, 254

Rip Payne: 112

Raleigh's *The News & Observer*: 29, 41, 52 & 53

Jack Reimer: 181 left, 192, 251

Ed Rosenberry: 151

South Carolina Sports Information: 47, 50, 87, 97, 105

David Allen Steele: 215

Virginia Sports Information: 39, 160, 169

Wake Forest Sports Information: 18, 36, 38, 55, 58 left, 74 & 75, 82 & 83, 92 & 93, 122, 127, 138, 230, 238, 267

Wake Forest University Archives: 38, 76 left, 155

Mark Wagoner: Cover, Table of Contents, Golf Ball (266), Statues (

Bob Waldrop: 170 bottom

J. Brett Whitesell: 245